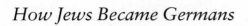

How Jews Became Germans

DEBORAH HERTZ

How Jews Became Germans

THE HISTORY OF CONVERSION AND ASSIMILATION IN BERLIN

Yale University Press
New Haven &
London

Published with assistance from the Louis Stern Memorial Fund.

Set in Sabon Roman by Keystone Typesetting, Inc., Orwigsburg, Pennsylvania. Printed in the United States of America by Thomson-Shore, Inc., Dexter, Michigan.

Library of Congress Cataloging-in-Publication Data

Hertz, Deborah Sadie.
How Jews became Germans : the history of conversion and assimilation in Berlin / Deborah Hertz.
p. cm.
Includes bibliographical references and index.
ISBN 978-0-300-11094-4 (cloth : alk. paper)
1. Jews — Germany — Berlin — History. 2. Jews — Conversion to Christianity — Germany — Berlin — History. 3. Berlin (Germany) — Ethnic relations. 4. Jews — Germany — Berlin — Identity. I. Title.
DS134.3.H47 2007
305.892'4043155 — dc22
2007013495

A catalogue record for this book is available from the British Library.

The paper in this book meets the guidelines for permanence and durability of the Committee on Production Guidelines for Book Longevity of the Council on Library Resources.

10 9 8 7 6 5 4 3 2 1

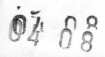

This book is dedicated to the activists in the Israeli peace movement

Contents

Acknowledgments

I have written this book because I cannot decide whether a passionate ethnic identity is necessary for personal happiness. Many family and individual experiences have contributed to my obsession with this vexing question. When I was growing up in Saint Paul, Minnesota, in the 1950s, my parents would not allow us to celebrate Christmas with my first cousins, whose father had converted to become a Catholic. The message was that he and his kin were to be exiled from our warm extended family. I often wondered whether these relatives suffered from their exclusion. Later, as a young adult in the late sixties, I was the one who sought to escape family bonds. I raged mightily against my family's attempts to control my life. To be 18 in 1968 was to live through a harsh war of the generations, a vivid, rowdy era, full of conflict at every turn.

Over the years I have wrestled with how to balance freedom with belonging. When and how can immersion in a cohesive culture bring satisfaction and pleasure, energy and creativity? When is such immersion a prison for the body, mind, and heart? I feel lucky to have found in the German Jewish past a historical landscape filled with individuals, movements, and institutions which help me work through this universal dilemma. History is at once an objective scholarly project and a huge therapeutic space. The past is buried in obscure books in libraries and yet ever present, ready to serve as a mirror to very personal quests.

When I first discovered the Berlin conversion records during my dissertation research, I knew that when my work on the Berlin salons was finished, I would write a book on conversion in the Berlin past. For years I joked that the book about those converting into Judaism was the thin book, whereas my book about conversion out of Judaism was the thick book. In the end the book is perhaps not so thick, but it has, alas, taken all too many years to complete.

Along this long road I have received much gracious help from many institutions. Dr. Fischer, Frau Scharf, and Dr. Wischnath of the Evangelische Zentralarchiv in Berlin were patient with my inquiries. Frau Cécile Lowenthal-Hensel suggested my first visit to that important archive. The German Academic Exchange Service and the State University of New York at Binghamton generously funded my research at the Zentralarchiv. Archivists at the Leo Baeck Institute in New York City, the Central Archive of the Jewish People in Jerusalem, the Hessisches Hauptarchiv Wiesbaden, the Bundesarchiv in Koblenz, and the Berlin municipal archives all graciously helped me find the right primary sources.

I truly embarked on this book in the summer of 1987, while teaching at the State University of New York at Binghamton. Over my sixteen years there, Warren Wagar, Norman Stillman, Thomas Dublin, Katherine Kish Sklar, Sarah Elbert, Maureen Turim, Linda Forcey, Josephine Gear, Leslie Levene, Jean Quataert, and the late Constance Coiner and the late Joan Smith were stimulating, resourceful colleagues. Krista O'Donnell was a treasured research assistant. During my Fulbright year at the Hebrew University in 1987–88, I explored many of the book's themes with Paul Mendes-Flohr, Steven Aschheim, Robert Wistrich, Gordon Fellman, Aaron Back, Beth Sandweiss, Rita Mendes-Flohr, Sharon Gillerman, Michael Graetz, Sassona and Yossi Yovell, Kathryn Hellerstein, and Vanessa Ochs. A year at the Harvard Divinity School in 1991–92 provided another opportunity for intensive work on the book. I am grateful to the late Catherine Prelinger and especially to Constance Buchanan for their help that year. Connie's sage advice to avoid the era of religious conversions and concentrate on the era of assimilation helped me decide on the ultimate shape of the book. Two years hence, in 1994–95, I taught at the University of Haifa while living with my family on Kibbutz Ramat Hashofet. The kibbutz provided a provocative perch for looking back at the Jewish past. I chuckled to myself reading about the Court Jews in a little kibbutz hut, wondering how we traveled from then to now. The late Eliezer Rabinovitz provided me with a fabulous work space in the kibbutz archive, and the baby nursery cared for our toddler beginning at seven in the morning! That year Kenneth Stow, Judith Tydor Baumel, Richard Cohen, Nancy and Zvi Rosenfeld, and Esther Carmel Hakim all helped me in matters practical and intellectual. I loved living in such a special destination of Jewish history.

When I moved to Sarah Lawrence College in 1996, I found another circle of special intellects who talked with me about this book, including Bella Brodzki, Roland Dollinger, Melvyn Bukiet, and Alice Olson. A semester's leave in the fall of 2001 provided necessary time to write. My year and a half at Tel Aviv University in 2002 and 2003 was made possible by Shulamith Volkov, Billie Melman, and Hannah Nave, and I am grateful for their warm hospitality. Shlomo Meyer at the Leo Baeck Institute Jerusalem provided a serene work environment and my favorite collection of dusty reference books. Rahel Livne-Freudenthal, Emily Bilski, Gabriel Motzkin, Deborah Harris, Elliot Horowitz, Michael and Ilana Silber, Margalit Shilo, Shmuel Feiner, Dafna and Amotz Golan, Tal Ilan, Rene Melamid, Dominique Bourel, and Moshe and Alice Shalvi all talked avidly with me about the themes of the book.

Our friends in Princeton, New Jersey, during our seventeen years on Wheatsheaf Lane, followed my progress with good humor and affectionate nagging, especially Esther Schor, Phyllis Mack, Ziva Gallili, Dorothy Sue Cobble, Michael Merrill, David and Sandy Abraham, Diane Krumrey, Eric Lubell, Hannah Fink, Martin Oppenheimer, Monica Lange, Hilary Brown, Diane Winston, Diane and Robert Hackett, and Barbara Mann. What fun we enjoyed on our protected little village street! I am especially grateful to the pack of wild kids who regularly trooped through our home and yard and provided a very welcome distraction from the tasks of the book. The atrium room on the C floor of the Firestone Library at Princeton University was a refuge for quiet work and a beloved space.

When I came to the University of California at San Diego in 2004 I found a marvelous combination of nature, culture, and community. Richard Elliot Friedman, William Propp, David Goodblatt, Tom Levy, David Noel Freedman, Rachel Klein, Robert Westman, Cynthia Walk, Frank Biess, and David Luft have welcomed me to this enchanted place with much graciousness. I am grateful to those who established the Herman Wouk Chair in Modern Jewish Studies and to Mr. Wouk himself for his acts of kindness. Susanne Hillman has become a valued research assistant.

Throughout my wanderings I have often relied upon a special circle of women historians who have been meeting monthly since 1977 on the Upper West Side of Manhattan to discuss our work. We have shared career crises, political debates, baby clothes, advice about teenagers, and a long stream of cakes, cookies, and coffee. Members of the German Women's History Study Group teased me about my obsessions, read my work in progress, and helped me become a better historian. I cannot imagine a career in the field without this magic entourage, a miniature utopia of authentic intellectual sharing, free from the pretentious posturing that academics typically generate and endure. I thank the founding participants in this circle: Renate Bridenthal, Marion Kaplan, Mary Nolan, Atina Grossmann, Jane Caplan, Claudia Koonz, Bonnie Anderson, and Amy Hackett, as well as those who have joined the group more recently.

In addition, several scholars in the field of German-Jewish history have become treasured lifetime colleagues, including Steven Lowenstein, Liliane Weissberg, Monika Richarz, Frank Mecklenburg, Benjamin Maria Baader, and Elisheva Carlebach. Todd Endelman, Paula Hyman, Natalie Zemon Davis, and Harriet Barlow have been generous with their time and practical aid.

My deep roots in Minnesota have always been a sustaining resource. Rabbi Bernhard Raskas introduced me to Jewish history when I was young, and Mischa Penn of the University of Minnesota helped me find my husband, Martin, at just the right moment. Professor Otto Pflanze channeled my restless mind and helped me become a professional. My parents Lorraine and Marcus Hertz have endured my rebellions and my prodigal returns with grace. My brothers, Frederick and Robert, have long been agile debate partners and loyal siblings. Fred was an indefatigable critic of earlier drafts of the manuscript.

Along the way Debra Ginsburg, Yung Seop Lee, Michael Broderick, Jeannette Ibarra, Elliott Kanter, Daniel Kurowski, and the editors and referees at Yale University Press, especially Jessie Hunnicutt and Kay Scheuer, have helped with intellectual and technical details.

My husband, Martin Bunzl, is a wonderfully combative intellect, always ready for another good chat about life, politics, history, and philosophy. Without his lively companionship I could never endure the lonely life of a scholar. I thank him for the gift of the title of this book. Our son Noah and our daughter Zola may well have felt neglected as I crammed my work into our harried schedules. Men so often apologize to their families for the time and isolation which book creation requires. I rather apologize to my book for the time which I lavished on our children. But Martin, Noah, and Zola bring me huge joy, and I thank them for their love.

I

The Black Notebooks

The Nazi Genealogy Bureaucracy

Quite a number of years ago I found the *Judenkartei* in a church archive in West Berlin. This book was born on that day, when I stumbled upon several bookcases crammed with short, rectangular black notebooks. I soon learned that these notebooks were the fruit of an enormous Nazi genealogical research project. The notebooks appeared to include every single Jew who became a Protestant in Berlin, over the three centuries spanning 1645 to 1933. Converts out of Judaism had to be identified as such, because they and their descendants were false Aryans with no place in a racially purified Germany.

From my first day in the archive, I planned a book using the notebooks to write Jewish history. At first I did not know how the notebooks had been used in the Third Reich. Nor was it clear what the lessons of the notebooks would be. But I found myself immediately committed to the project. I knew that I must redeem the records from the evil system that had created them.

I found myself in the church archive in the first place because of a central question that arose in my dissertation research: Were the frequent conversions among wealthy Jewish salon women in Berlin during the last decades of the eighteenth century isolated cases, or rather part of a trend? To answer this question, I needed very detailed sources. Did more women than men leave

Judaism then? These were, after all, dramatic decades, when traditional Judaism was under attack and a reformed Judaism had not yet been created.[1]

And so I traveled to Berlin, in search of conversion records. Luck smiled upon me, and I obtained a multiple-entry visa to the German Democratic Republic. Daily, I crossed the Friedrichstrasse border between the two Berlins to explore the archives in what was then called East Berlin. At the municipal city archive there I was shown several large leather volumes of baptisms, filled with irregularly sized pages of old paper, poorly bound together. On these pages were listed local parish birth records, which had been sent yearly to the Prussian government by the Catholic, Lutheran, and Calvinist clergy from across Prussia.[2]

After spending some hours studying the large leather volumes, I realized that they could help me discover the truth about conversion trends. But isolating the former Jews among the baptisms was not going to be easy. The problem was that two very different kinds of *Taufen,* or baptisms, were included in the local parish lists. Most of those who were baptized were infants, often only a few days old, who had been born to Christian parents. Few Jewish converts were that young. To create a list of formerly Jewish converts, one would have to use their names and ages to separate them out from the far more numerous baptisms of infants born into Christian families.

As I was contemplating whether I should take on this mammoth task, I kept up my search for more original conversion records. Perhaps I could discover a source in which the Jewish conversions were already separated out from the infant baptisms. And so I wrote to a number of historians and archivists in Berlin, asking for leads. It felt like only a few days after the letters left my desk when the phone rang in my *Wohngemeinschaft,* my communal apartment, on the Geneisenaustrasse in West Berlin. On the line was Frau Cécile Lowenthal-Hensel from the Mendelssohn Archive, and herself a descendant of Moses Mendelssohn, German Jewry's most important eighteenth-century intellectual. Frau Lowenthal-Hensel suggested that I visit the Evangelical Central Archive on the Jebenstrasse, across the street from the Zoological Garden train station, near the center of West Berlin.

The next morning I was there. In that quiet archive inside an austere, gray-carpeted building, I first saw the Judenkartei, about sixty narrow rectangular black volumes. Looking about me, I saw that the shelves with the black notebooks took up only a small section of the quite enormous archive. Otherwise, the walls of the entire large room were filled floor-to-ceiling with narrow wooden file drawers containing small index cards. What was all of this, I wondered?

The archive's director, a kindly gentleman named Dr. Fischer, sat with me and explained the story behind the notebooks and the file drawers. He recounted how Protestant pastors had been funded by the Nazi government to create precisely the detailed record of conversions for which I had been searching — a story that, after much further study, I came to understand in detail. Like so many sad tales from the twentieth century, this one had begun in 1933. Three months after taking power, in April, the Nazi government announced new laws which required that all citizens document their racial descent. The idea was that underneath religion one could find something more basic, which the Nazis called race. The plan was to replace the religious polarity of Christians and Jews with the racial polarity of Aryans and Jews.[3]

But it soon became obvious that replacing Christians with Aryans was not at all simple. The connections between religion and ethnicity were terribly tangled, complicated, and messy. Judaism, to be sure, is both a religion and an ethnicity. But Christianity is a trans-ethnic religion, at least in principle. For centuries Christianity has attracted believers born into very diverse ethnic groups. Entry into Judaism is by birth to a Jewish mother, whereas entry into Christianity is always by baptism or confirmation.[4] What was problematic for the Nazi plan was that thousands and thousands of Jews had been baptized over the centuries in Germany. The point is that if Christians were to be recast into Aryans, the Jewish converts and their descendants could no longer be considered legitimate Christians.

Thus overnight there was a huge demand for genealogical knowledge. Most individuals needed to document their family tree back to their four grandparents, because that was the initial limit placed on genealogical research. But those who aspired to enter the Nazi system at a high level had to document even more generations back into their pasts. And where could one find all the original records? Few Germans knew at which church they should search for all these documents. For already back in the eighteenth century, Berlin had more than fifty Protestant churches. Here was the impetus to create the file drawers, whose cards allowed descendants to find the right parish for each ancestor. Each card in the wooden drawers in the Jebenstrasse archive listed the name, birth date, and local parish of every infant born into a Protestant family and baptized in Berlin, going back to 1645.[5] Using the cards in the drawers, any descendant could know at which local parish they could find their original baptismal documentation.

This vast carding project was organized by Pastor Karl Themel of the Luisenstadt Church in Berlin. Using funds provided by the Ministry of the Interior, Themel assembled a crew of paid workers and volunteers, called the *Verkartungstruppen* or the "carding troops." Their task was to copy out the details from the original records. If the ancestor was an infant born into a

Protestant family, the individual's data was noted on the cards, which went into the wooden drawers. But if the ancestor had been born into another faith and then had entered the church by baptism, the information was copied onto a notebook page, and it was these pages which filled the Judenkartei. Pastor Themel's carding troops filled in 50,000 cards and notebook pages per week. By 1937, they had logged over a million baptisms and conversions.[6]

In Nazi Germany, having information about someone's genealogy became a crucial kind of power. Secret ancestries discovered in dusty files were used to make accusations, perhaps demand blackmail, in private and in public. Indeed the information Pastor Themel's carding troops were collecting became ever more sensitive over time, as the meaning of the new categories sharpened, and the fateful consequences of belonging to the Jewish category grew more and more clear. It became apparent to the government that such an important classification project could not be left to church officials, no matter how vigilant they might be. This was a job for the Nazi state to supervise.

And so what began as a project of the Nazi party was soon enough taken over by the state. The special office which coordinated Pastor Themel's carding project and the other genealogy efforts was originally called the Reichssippenamt, or the Kinship Research Office, which I abbreviate here as the RSA. Before the seizure of power in January 1933, the Kinship Research Office had been a section of the Nazi party, used to inspect the racial heritage of new party members. But once the party had attained state power, the RSA became a government genealogy office, housed in the Ministry of the Interior.[7]

Now because the Nazis were so obsessed with race, the RSA was not the only office in Nazi Germany collecting the details about people's backgrounds. As was entirely typical then and there, state offices and party offices often were charged with overlapping missions. Even after the RSA became a state office in 1933, the Nazi party still maintained its own genealogy division, and so did the SS. During the 1920s, the SS had been a small organization of bodyguards for Hitler. Eventually it would become a huge and diverse "state within a state" inside the Nazi system. The point for our story is that the SS needed the information in the black notebooks, because their applicants had to be especially pure racially. Then, too, researchers writing about Jews and race also needed the data collected by the RSA. For instance, the staff of the Research Division on the Jewish Question of the National Institute for the History of the New Germany set to work calculating historical statistics on conversion and intermarriage.[8]

The RSA staff coordinated the sudden need for genealogy research in a variety of ways. They organized the transfer of original local parish registers from towns across Germany to the RSA offices in Berlin for microfilming.

They justified this mammoth project by claiming that the original registers were deteriorating quickly, due to the explosion in genealogical research after the Aryan laws of 1933. The RSA staff also instructed local pastors how to fill in the myriad versions of the family trees required of descendants. The RSA printed up long and short versions of the so-called Aryan Pass, which summarized an individual's genealogical descent. RSA staff also coordinated the work of freelance genealogy researchers who were hired by individuals to track down all of the affidavits from the archives. And when the paper trail was ambiguous, the RSA staff turned to scholars from the Kaiser Wilhelm Institute for Anthropology in Berlin. The anthropologists working with the Institute were charged by the RSA with the task of investigating the racial status of individuals whose racial descent was disputed.[9] Noses, head shapes, hair color, and body size were measured in an attempt to sort individuals into the Aryan or the Jewish category. The idea, if not the reality, was that the borders around each group were sharp and clear.

By 1935, most of the German population had already completed their family trees. But the RSA staff was still busy locating the odd missing bits of information needed for a precise racial label. Once they had finished filling in the narrow pages in the Judenkartei notebooks, they planned to create additional card indexes using marriage and even death records. The RSA director estimated that with approximately 350,000 parish register volumes from 50,000 local communities across Germany, there would be as many as 800 million birth, marriage, and death entries to be carded, at a potential cost of 80 million marks.[10]

The collapse of religious differences into sharply enclosed racial divisions looks to us now to be a step that made genocide possible. But we must force ourselves to see genealogical research in its proper frame, as it must have appeared in the 1930s. This point is made shockingly clear when we learn the Nazis were not the only Germans who had a passion in these years for race and genealogy. An enthusiasm for roots investigations was not necessarily a step toward genocide before the Nazis seemed to make it so. If Jews could be obsessed about race and genealogy, then surely it was a trend of the times. For example, in 1934, Arthur Czellitzer, a Jewish physician, published a little book called *Mein Stammbaum,* "My Family Tree." In the introduction Czellitzer reminded his readers that the "new government strives to make us all conscious of the importance of the family's worth to the state, and the significance of race and an interest in one's ancestors." No wonder, he noted, that Jews too were interested in these themes.[11] Czellitzer's words show us that even after the Nazis had taken power, Jews could value genealogical research. This truth forces us to understand why the work of the RSA did not seem so disturbing and shocking to contemporaries, Jewish and Christian alike. Our own hindsight interferes with our ability to see the past clearly.

The RSA staff took a keen interest in the several hundred thousand individuals whose family trees were not completely Aryan. For this task Jewish birth and marriage records were indispensable. To coordinate the Jewish side of the project, the RSA staff turned to the Gesamtarchiv der deutsche Juden, or the Central Archive of the German Jews, which I abbreviate here as the GSA. The archive had been founded in 1906. Its offices were on the top floor of the community building that adjoined the Oranienburger Street synagogue, a famous synagogue in the heart of Berlin's old Jewish neighborhood. Before 1933, the GSA had been a rather obscure and modest institution. The elevator did not go up to its top floor offices, and its board of directors had not met once since 1923.[12] But beginning in 1933, it suddenly became a bustling center of research activity. Since 1920, the director of the archive had been Jacob Jacobson, a productive genealogy scholar with remarkably conservative and nationalist political views.[13] Jacobson faced difficult practical and political problems when the GSA was swept up in the genealogy mobilization in the spring of 1933.

The plot very much thickens when we learn that Jacobson had his own genealogical ambitions, including a plan to make the GSA into a truly national collection of community records. Here, oddly enough, the RSA concurred, for it too needed to centralize Jewish community records. The RSA sent Jacobson all across Germany, collecting birth, marriage, and death registers from local synagogues. Eventually, the GSA would house the records of some 400 Jewish communities. Jacobson also found card indexes a useful research tool. In 1935, he reported that his staff had begun work on an index of all Jewish births in Berlin during the eighteenth and nineteenth centuries.[14]

Jacobson lived in dark times, and he often found himself in painful circumstances. Reading his memoir can be unsettling indeed. At one juncture in the early 1940s several of Jacobson's relatives were being deported "to the east" from Hamburg, and RSA officials sent him on a research trip to Hamburg so that he could bid goodbye to his family. But at least in his memoirs, Jacobson never articulated a critique of the RSA's ambitions or functions. He later remembered that "the curious relationship between the RSA and me was conducted in an absolutely correct fashion. However things were going, the gentlemen from the RSA were helpful to me and they had the same attitude to all the employees of the Archive."[15]

One of the few ways that Jacobson could help partial Jews move out of the Jewish category was to find an Aryan paternal ancestor who might have had a real or fictitious adulterous affair with a Jewish woman. The "discovery" of an

Aryan father or grandfather would render the descendant less Jewish from the Nazis' point of view. Unlike traditional Jews, who measured descent through the mother, Nazi rules allowed paternal descent. In some lights Jacobson appears to have been a naïve collaborator. But other episodes illustrate that he definitely had his principles. He was furious with those who wanted to find records which would make them less Jewish so as to secure a better position in the Nazi system. One day a Jewish-looking army officer came to the GSA, sent by his superiors to inquire into whether or not he had been born into a Jewish family. Jacobson was not particularly eager to help the officer. But he found no Jewish ancestors, and he sent the man away happy. By chance, the very next day, Jacobson found that both the man's parents were buried in one of the local Jewish cemeteries. But his knowledge came too late to hurt the officer's career as a hidden partial Jew in the army.[16]

Beyond his own convictions, perhaps a more salient reason for Jacobson to be cautious was that he actually had very little freedom to alter the details in the GSA records. For the RSA had created two complete sets of the Judenkartei notebooks, one for the church archive and one for its own use. The "carding troops" had filled in two identical notebook pages for each convert included in the original parish registers. One page went into the black notebooks now housed at the Jebenstrasse archive. An identical page went into a duplicate set of notebooks in the RSA's own archive. Desperate partial Jews who came to Jacobson and begged him to destroy their ancestor's page in the notebooks could well be provocateurs, sent by the RSA staff to check up on his work.

Jacobson's life would become ever more difficult. He and his wife and son were planning to leave Germany in the fall of 1938, just after Crystal Night in November. All three had the necessary passports and visas. But hours before their departure, their passports were confiscated. After Jacobson petitioned the Gestapo, his wife's and son's papers were returned to them. Their son left immediately for England, and Frau Jacobson also left Germany just before the war began in September 1939. Jacobson himself, however, was forced to remain in Berlin to work for the RSA.

At the same time that the Jacobson family was facing such difficult decisions, institutions with far more power than the RSA decided to move the RSA offices into the Oranienburger Street Jewish community building.[17] During the terrible night of November 9, later called Crystal Night because of the broken glass from Jewish stores and synagogues which covered the streets, the Gestapo seized the community records housed in many synagogues. They wanted to consolidate all of the Jewish registers, so they moved the RSA into the community building where the GSA had its offices. At one level this was a practical decision, but the symbolism was and remains chilling. I will always remember the shock and anger I felt, sitting in the Bundesarchiv in Koblenz, when I came upon a piece of stationery with the letterhead Reichssippenamt, Oranienburgerstr. 28. It made me furious and sad to see that genealogy policing office publicly, graphically, identified with that Jewish space. The Nazi genealogy machine was no longer just exploiting Jacobson's labors; now they had taken over his archive. His always awkward position had become much, much worse.

The decision to keep Jacobson in Germany after 1938 shows that long after the entire German population had been placed into racial categories, the RSA was still filling drawers and notebooks with data about Jews and former Jews and partial Jews. After 1938 its domain was merely a paper empire. We know from the complaints of its director that the RSA was in fact given no role in setting Jewish policy. But the staff continued to collect genealogical records in their new quarters on Oranienburger Street.

In 1943, once Germany was declared empty of Jews, Jacobson himself was deported to the ghetto of Theresienstadt. And here too he pursued his genealogical researches, for he was allowed to take his research documents with him. He survived and later joined his family in England. Many years after the war ended, Jacobson would publish two large volumes of Berlin Jewish history, rich fruits of his long years of archival work. Indeed as I have written this book I have often turned the pages of Jacobson's wonderfully detailed volumes, searching out birth dates and correct spelling and family relationships. But it is impossible to use his books without pondering the complexities of the RSA exploitation of his focused dedication to Jewish genealogy.[18] It is no easy task to determine whether he was a pathetic victim, a self-interested collaborator, or a secret hero of Jewish scholarship.

Because they were organizing Christian as well as Jewish genealogical research, in principle the RSA staff should have been well informed about the *Mischlinge,* or partial Jews.[19] After all, there was considerable pressure to learn the details, since decisions about the status of the partial Jews were a subject of protracted debate among Nazi officials. Yet the supposedly hyper-efficient Nazi state had begun to murder Jews before it had finished identifying who belonged to the unlucky race. As late as the Wannsee Conference in January 1942, there was still debate about the status of the partial Jews.[20] In other words the question of *who was a Jew* was still continuing even after real genocide had already begun. As the policymakers sat in the villa on the shores of the Wannsee lake in Berlin, gas vans had already been used to murder over forty thousand Jews and gypsies in the extermination camp in Poland called Chelmno.[21]

What drove the so-called racial experts mad was that there were a number of ways that individuals could combine what the Nazis called race and what they called religion. First of all there were those who were of completely Jewish descent, but who were not tax-paying members of a local Jewish community. For beginning in 1876, Jews were able to resign from their local Jewish community, without becoming Christian by baptism. Quitting the community, sometimes because one was an Orthodox rather than a Liberal Jew, was called *Austritte*.[22] Of course in Nazi Germany any Jew who had left the community in this way, past or present, was still labeled a racial Jew.

Then too, an individual might have had four all-Jewish grandparents, but she or he might have converted. That would make the person a full Jew by descent, but Christian by religion. Sometimes several generations had elapsed since the conversion. People who thought of their ancestry as thoroughly Christian might discover that some or all of their apparently Christian grandparents or parents had been born Jewish. There were inevitably surprises when such a significant fact had been kept secret across the generations.[23]

But most of the Christians of Jewish descent were not 100 percent racially Jewish, but rather the descendants of mixed marriages. When we examine their status we see how difficult it was to halt degrees of Jewishness at any one generation. The logic of the Nazi project was the logic of infinite regress into the past, of never being clean of the Jewish stain. For instance, a debate emerged about whether converted grandparents should be classified by their race or by their religion. Some advocated going beyond the grandparent generation and introducing eighth and possibly sixteenth degrees of Jewish heritage. Indeed, it was precisely because some Germans needed extensive roots documentation that the Judenkartei began with the year 1645. Eventually, however, it was decided to limit most genealogical investigations to the four grandparents. This meant that if a grandparent had converted, a descendant's race was considered Aryan, rather than being retroactively re-classified as Jewish. But this stance completely contradicted the supposed aim of the entire genealogy project, which was to uncover race underneath religion. After all, the baptism of parents and the current generation was not allowed to make them into Aryans. Perhaps compromises such as this one gave the individuals forced to discover long-hidden family secrets a sense that the system had some flexibility after all.

Just how many Jewish ancestors made a descendant Jewish was a topic of intense debate during the Third Reich. Surprising as it might sound, in the beginning, in 1933, the definition of who was a non-Aryan was actually broader than it became in 1935. According to the first set of regulations issued in 1933, the non-Aryan category included quarter, half, three-quarter, and full

Jews. Later, after the Nuremberg Laws of September 1935, all of the quarter Jews and some of the half Jews were removed from the non-Aryan category and declared to be functionally Aryans. Or put in other words, these individuals thus became a kind of privileged partial Jews. Here was the rare occasion where Jewish policy became more lenient over time.

In April 1933 no one knew how many Germans of Jewish descent there were. In 1933, the size of the official Jewish community was just over half a million, most of them full Jews by descent. Eventually it became clear that there were almost as many non-Aryan Christians as there were affiliated Jews. The upshot was that close to a million Germans could be labeled with some degree of Jewishness.[24] The policy guidelines during the war years were to allow the quarter Jews to leave the Jewish category, and to temporarily protect the half Jews from deportation. But the reprieve for the latter was only temporary; ultimately they too were slated for deportation. Luckily, the war ended too soon for many of them to meet this fate.

Looking back at the Nazi regime's efforts to classify and count and then persecute the partial Jews, it is difficult not to see their labors as steps on the road to genocide. At the time, however, those caught up in the genealogy mobilization sometimes interpreted the discoveries of the RSA in a quite positive way. One non-Aryan Christian, Victor Klemperer, an academic who lived in Germany throughout the Nazi era, was actually proud of the high number of partial Jews. Klemperer was the son of a Reform rabbi, and he converted to become a Protestant and married a Christian by descent. Klemperer was proud to be a German and disdained his Jewish heritage, even equating Zionism with Nazism as a racialist regime. Obviously he agonized at the contrast between how he saw himself and how the Nazi state saw him. In a 1939 entry in his diary, Klemperer wrote that "until 1933, and for a good century before that, the German Jews were entirely German and nothing else. Proof: the thousands upon thousands of 'half' and 'quarter' Jews. Jews and Germans lived and worked together in all spheres of life."[25] But despite Klemperer's pride, the degree of success of intermarriage, assimilation, and integration is one of the burning questions of this book. We shall return again and again to Klemperer's conviction that the "German Jews were entirely German and nothing else."

In these pages we explore the lives of the grandparents and the great-grandparents of the partial Jews who suffered so horribly during the Nazi era. Once we enter their lives we uncover the color, detail, and nuance that Nazi genealogists necessarily obscured when they created their categories.[26] Here we learn the actual history of conversion by revisiting those many individual decisions which resulted in the hundreds of thousands of partial Jews and non-Aryan

Christians whose identities so vexed the Nazi policymakers. We learn that the converts in past time did not, fortunately, find themselves so rigidly defined by the harsh categories which determined the fates, the often very bitter fates, of many of their descendants.

Could Conversion Be Emancipation?

It has not been easy to concentrate on past centuries with the persistent background noise emanating from the Judenkartei notebooks. Not for a moment could I forget that the Judenkartei were used by an evil system that had robbed many descendants of the converts in the notebooks of their inner identities, their homes, and even their lives. More than most sources, the notebooks carry baggage it would be naïve to ignore. They are no ordinary source, and this was no ordinary past, for genealogy and place have been permanently severed. Perhaps if their Jewish stain was very faint and far-distant in the past, some descendants of the converts whose names were listed in the Judenkartei notebooks are today walking the streets of a town in Germany. But most descendants of those converts are more likely to make their homes in New York or Tel Aviv.

This jagged relationship between genealogical research and contemporary life is different from links between genealogy and historical research elsewhere. In England, for instance, genealogy buffs researching their families in local parish archives ultimately made it possible for the historian Peter Laslett to construct a huge population database at Cambridge University.[27] But, alas, there are no easy continuities for Jews in Germany, or for their historians.

My quandaries about the notebooks are illustrative of the larger challenges facing all those who contemplate the history of Jews in Germany. Just as the notebooks kept reminding me of why the Nazi state needed them, so too all who study the history of the Jews in Germany must face the difficult fact that in some ways this history ended with the Nazis. When I found the Judenkartei in the Protestant church archive during the 1970s, the history of Jewry in Germany seemed quite over. Now, as I finally finish this book, Jewish life has to a point revived there. But when I began the project most observers were sure that Jewish history had come to a decisive close when Josef Goebbels proclaimed Germany to be *Judenfrei* (free of Jews) on June 19, 1943.[28] How could the Holocaust not seem to be a teleology, an end destination? Indeed, after the war, some of German Jewry's finest minds saw this teleology as an aid to greater understanding. For instance Hannah Arendt argued in 1957 that "only now, after the history of the German Jews has come to an end," can we "investigate" the "unique phenomenon" of the "German-speaking Jews and their history."[29]

Those words inspired me, gave me confidence that the German-Jewish past needed me precisely because of my own place in history. I could do justice to the early nineteenth century because the entire narrative of Jews in Germany had achieved closure, at a terrible, awful price in human suffering.

Certainly not everyone would agree that the Holocaust provides a closure that aids our search for clarity. But few would deny that the Holocaust casts a giant shadow over the German-Jewish past. We who are haunted by this past return again and again to the same questions, sifting evidence as we debate how so much could go so wrong. Evaluating assimilation is at the heart of our troubles about the German-Jewish past. For German Jews were known far and wide, were loved or hated, for what seemed at the time to be their successful assimilation. Because conversion was one of the more radical acts of assimilation possible, we cannot enter the past without pondering the postwar debates about assimilation.[30] The more one reads the huge literature on Jewish assimilation in Germany, the clearer it becomes that historians seem to tilt toward one pole or the other, some valuing assimilation and others pointing to its high personal and ethnic costs.

Take first the pro-assimilation point of view. For generations, Jews in Germany saw themselves and were seen as the model of successful assimilation. Polish and Russian Jews looked to Germany for refuge and inspiration. Often they saw their own mother tongue, Yiddish, as a German language, a language that could serve as their bridge to German culture. Throughout the nineteenth century Jews to the east often watched the Jews of Germany with admiration, sometimes with envy. At home in Germany, Jews had much about which they could be proud. Leo Baeck, the leading rabbi during the Nazi era, believed that the Jews in modern Germany had created the "third golden age" in Jewish history.[31] At the time, the religious creativity, the economic success, and the cultural accomplishments of many Jews in the German lands were a notable phenomenon. Many of the leading personalities in this book have been seen from afar as exemplary cases of successful assimilation. Felix Mendelssohn, Rahel Levin Varnhagen, Eduard Gans, Fanny Lewald, Giacomo Meyerbeer, Ludwig Börne, and Heinrich Heine are among those we come to know here, and we try to get behind the myths to discover the sometimes painful realities of their lives.

Across the generations, throughout the nineteenth and early twentieth centuries, all the way up to Hitler's appointment as chancellor in 1933, Germany was still seen as a positive place for Jews to live. We understand this stance from listening to the character Henriette in Shmuel Agnon's novel *Shira*. The novel is set among the German refugee academics of Jerusalem during the 1930s, during the years when it was still possible to leave Germany. Henriette spends her days trying to obtain the necessary visas to allow her relatives to leave Germany and enter Palestine. As she proceeds with her very frustrating efforts, she ponders the troubling fate of German Jewry and comments to her husband how difficult it is to comprehend that this has all come to pass in Germany. As she says, "between yesterday and tomorrow, events occurred in Germany that transformed it into an inferno — the very country about which it was said: every Jew should bless God daily for the privilege of living there."[32] And Agnon's Henriette had good reason to express an accurate historical perspective, for Agnon himself lived in Germany from 1913 until 1924.

Many of those whose life stories are told in this book would have agreed with Henriette that living in Germany was a privilege. But praying in thanks to the Jewish God was not the only religious choice among those who felt lucky to live there. Thousands of Jews across the German lands in the nineteenth century chose not the Jewish God but life as a Protestant. Yet few observers, then and since, have been convinced that those who converted did so because of spiritual experiences.[33] The suspicion is that motives were either careerist, because prestigious jobs in Germany were generally open only to Christians, or romantic, because ethnic intermarriage was not legal until later in the nineteenth century. In this book we meet many converts whose motives do fit the stereotypes, those who sought prestigious careers or marriage with Christians by descent. But we also meet others whose motives for converting were cultural and national. Well-to-do, educated, sophisticated Jews who were writing significant books and poems and music often saw Protestant, especially Lutheran identity as an important avenue to becoming more German on the inside.

If we discover that a convert's motives were not truly religious, does that mean the decision to change faith was hypocritical? Over the years scholars have addressed this vexing problem by recasting the conversion problematic in post-religious terms. They have argued that in nineteenth-century Europe, many saw Christianity not so much as "a name for a religion" as "the only word expressing the character of today's international civilization." In the words of one historian, "a man felt he had to become a Christian in the nineteenth century in the same way he felt he had to learn English in the twentieth."[34] If one interprets modern Christianity as a culture rather than a religion, the frequent lack of authentic spiritual transformation becomes less disturbing.

Sparks can still fly when contemporaries now try to defend conversion as a legitimate way to become more German, as when the novelist Martin Walser spoke at the ceremony for the Scholl Sisters Prize for Civic Courage, awarded posthumously to Victor Klemperer in November 1995. Walser, an enthusiastic reader of Klemperer's wartime diaries, published to great acclaim in the late 1990s, declared that for Klemperer conversion had been an "act of emancipation."[35] The philosopher Jürgen Habermas, who was in the audience, walked out of the room when Walser uttered these words. Walser's defense of conversion as emancipation is the strongest possible statement of what is at issue in this book. For Walser has articulated a view that many converts described here surely would have agreed with, and indeed celebrated. Certainly more of them would have agreed with Walser than with Habermas. My aim is to tell the historical story so that each of us, myself included, can decide whether Walser was right, in any sense and in any way. Could conversion in nineteenth-century Germany be justly described as having been a *personal emancipation*?

If the converts themselves would tend to agree with Walser, some of their friends and relatives who remained Jewish might rather have seen matters from Habermas's perspective. In the early nineteenth century, as the assimilation trend was becoming more and more visible, most of the critics of conversion were loyal to traditional Judaism. A century later, Zionist critics would concentrate more on psychological or national problems with baptism. In the era of Freud, some medical observers were convinced that many converts were "manifestly diseased," that their conversion was the "primary symptom of their mental instability." One critic argued that converts bore the sign of a "baptismal hydrocephaly."[36]

Perhaps the most uncanny Zionist critic of assimilation was Felix Theilhaber. Theilhaber was a young physician in 1911, when he published *Der Untergang der deutschen Juden* ("The Disappearance of the German Jews"), arguing that the Jews of Germany had for several generations been involved in a kind of collective "racial suicide." Theilhaber's list of suicidal behaviors included conversion, intermarriage, late ages of marriage, low rates of marriage, and low birth rates. Looking at the patterns in place in 1911, Theilhaber predicted that by the close of the twentieth century German Jewry would have disappeared.[37] His forecast was discounted at the time, but he turned out to be more correct than he could ever have imagined, in the saddest way possible. He himself and his immediate family, luckily enough, emigrated to Palestine in 1935.

After the war, many Jews in Europe and beyond concluded that the tragic events of the Nazi era showed that assimilation had never actually been achieved at all, even when it seemed to be going so well. Whoever was not convinced by Theilhaber's argument in 1911, or even in 1935, may well have found his Zionist critique of assimilation quite convincing after 1945. In the years since 1945, voices lamenting assimilation in general and the assimilation of the Jews in Germany especially have only grown stronger. Moreover the tendency to judge assimilation harshly is very much in step with wider shifts in opinion. In spite of or because of all the deadly ethnic conflict in the world, in the United States at least ethnicity is now celebrated. A mosaic of intact and distinctive cultures has replaced the model of the melting pot in American public opinion. In addition to the giant shadow of distortion cast by the Holocaust, we may well find it difficult to empathize with the dead converts because in our time many assume that a positive ethnic identity is necessary for personal happiness.

Perhaps the harshest and most eloquent critic of the German assimilation pattern was Gershom Scholem, who left Germany in 1921 and settled in Palestine, where he became a renowned scholar of Jewish mysticism. Scholem argued that it was in the early nineteenth century, the era we explore in this book, that the leading Jews in Germany turned in the wrong direction. For Scholem, these years constituted a "false start" to the modern era.[38] He fumed at the traditional elites, who too easily gave up their religious autonomy as the price for civic emancipation. Scholem denied that there had ever been an authentic symbiosis of Jewish and German culture. He criticized precisely the achievements which had always evoked praise, pointing out that few Jews who wrote music or poetry or pursued scholarship brought Jewish ideas, values, or symbols into their work.[39]

Some critiques go beyond how assimilation was bad for the individual Jews themselves, and magnify the blame to include the tragedies of subsequent German history. Since Scholem's time a passionate retroactive pessimism about assimilation in Germany has become even more pervasive. Some compare the Jewish "love affair" with German culture and society to an "abusive marriage."[40] Then there are those who blame assimilation for helping make the Third Reich possible. A recent book on the theme argues that "the unrequited love affair of Germany's Jews with their native country *led* to the unspeakable horrors of the Holocaust."[41]

Daniel Goldhagen's controversial 1996 book, *Hitler's Willing Executioners,* has popularized this pessimistic stance toward assimilation. Overtly he blames Christian Germans for the tragedy of the Holocaust, but he is also blaming Jewish Germans. Goldhagen argues that the Nazi era evolved as it did because eliminationist antisemitism was uniquely strong in Germany, going all the way back to the era I focus on in this book.[42] The message is clear that the Jews above all should have known that it was an error to even attempt to assimilate into such a society. Goldhagen's deterministic pessimism about how hardwired antisemitism was in the German past has led to his being labeled *Zionist* by some of his critics.[43]

This repudiation of assimilation is also visible in contemporary Jewish life.

Although statistically Jews continue to disappear through skyrocketing rates of intermarriage, we also see a vibrant renewal of Jewish religious practice and high culture. A flood of films, books, songs, museums, study groups, and magazines make it clear that contemporary Jews no longer base their identity only on the state of Israel and the Holocaust. So much positive investment in Judaism is of course a dramatic reversal from the immediate past, when Jews were rounded up and murdered in the millions, and many were ashamed of their Jewish noses, their Jewish names, their Jewish hair. Those who celebrate ethnicity today might well disdain the dead converts in this book, and blame them for hypocrisy or even for self-hatred.[44] Such easy judgments are tempting. But here I aim to make pat judgments more difficult. In these pages we meet the converts and explore the external pressures they faced, as well as their own inner desires. Perhaps after doing so we can understand why they decided to leave Judaism.

None of us alive today can easily presume to know what Jews in nineteenth-century Germany should have done. Still, we wonder. And to wonder at a high level we crave details, details about individual experiences, about the climate of opinion, about institutional decisions. We cannot put ourselves in the place of people caught in a past difficulty unless we can imagine their temptations, their principles, their family relationships, their ambitions, and their fears. I have written this book to give myself those details, and to share them with my readers. Only then can we make up our own minds about assimilation in the German Jewish past, especially about why so many chose to become Christians. We ponder whether a conversion without spiritual motives could ever be an honorable way to achieve emancipation, felt to be honorable from the inside and seen by others as honorable on the outside. The aim here is to see the choices made in the early nineteenth century in the terms that contemporaries saw them.

Still, at the end of the day it would be naïve to pretend that we can easily leave the modern era behind and bury ourselves in the nineteenth century. Our vantage point is unavoidably that of over a half century after World War II ended. And for better or worse the entire experience of the Holocaust has led many to question assimilation, however successful that assimilation might have seemed to the participants at the time. Thus, however passionately the characters in this book recommend assimilating, the contemporary critics of assimilation will always be a chorus that we hear, sometimes loudly, and sometimes in the distance.

2

The Era of Religious Conversion, 1645–1770

Arriving with Their Chandeliers, 1671

We can justly surmise that the rationale for beginning the black note-books with the year 1645 was to bring the roots investigation of applicants for higher-level Nazi posts back that far into the past. The choice of that year shows that the genealogy officials were not attending to the landmark dates in the Jewish historical narrative, or they would have begun their records in 1671, not in 1645. In Jewish time, the key date was May 21, 1671, when the ruler of the ambitious state of Prussia invited two large Jewish clans threat-ened with expulsion from Vienna to move to his capital city, Berlin. On that momentous day, a policy of keeping Jews out of Berlin that had been in place for almost a century was reversed. In this chapter we return to the seven-teenth century, to illuminate the conflicts then faced by Jews, and we learn why a tiny trickle of mainly poor Jews converted to become Lutherans in that era.

To understand the significance of the 1671 invitation, we must look at the catastrophic episode of the Jews' earlier expulsion, which took place a century before. The sorry tale began with an accusation against Berlin's leading Court Jew, Yom Tov ben Yehuda Ha-Cohen, who was called Lippold by his Chris-tian contemporaries. "Court Jew" was the contemporary label for a Jewish trader who served a local ruler, sometimes minting coins, sometimes collecting taxes, sometimes buying horses, weapons, and food for soldiers. Lippold's prince was the Elector of Brandenburg, also called Joachim II. In the sixteenth century, Brandenburg was the most important province in the realm of the plucky and ambitious Hohenzollern dynasty. Ultimately the Hohenzollern rulers would create a large, prosperous, and well-armed state, Prussia, which would become the guiding force in German unification two hundred years into the future. Prussia's traditions matter greatly, because in so many ways those traditions became Germany's traditions in the modern era. But back in the time of Lippold's unhappy end, in 1572, there was no German state. The area we now call Germany was a maze of tiny units of government, with different currencies, trade regulations, and social policies.

It was precisely the large number of tin-pot rulers which created the need for so many Court Jews. In Berlin, Lippold made himself useful to Elector Joachim by funding his expensive alchemy experiments and arranging his trysts with his mistresses. Lippold's downfall began the morning after Elector Joachim II died, on January 3, 1571. It seems that Lippold, who regularly socialized in court circles, happened to serve the Elector his last cup of wine, and some of Lippold's more powerful enemies accused him of poisoning Joachim. Many Berliners believed the claim, and soon a mob began plundering Jewish homes and desecrating the synagogue. Local merchants and artisans had long resented Jewish competition. Even if the Jews had possessed any bargaining power in court circles, Lippold found few defenders in the local community, because he was vigorously disliked by his own people. He was arrested and tortured extensively until he confessed to the poisoning. Joachim's successor, the Elector Johann Georg, proceeded to order all the Jews in Brandenburg to leave immediately.[1] As for Lippold, his confession had been to no avail, and after two years in prison, he was burned to death in a public ceremony. His body was then cut into quarters on January 28, 1573, in the town square.[2]

The Electorate of Brandenburg would be without any Jewish families at all for several generations. Indeed the 1572 expulsion of the Jews from Brandenburg was typical for those times. In lands with strong central rulers, such as Spain, Portugal, France, and England, Jews were expelled during the fourteenth, fifteenth, and sixteenth centuries. But across the towns and small territories of central Europe, no single ruler had the power to expel the Jews. We still see expulsions, but on a smaller scale. Banished Jews moved from the larger to smaller towns, and many chose to migrate further eastward to Poland, then a welcoming place for them. Those who failed to gain official permission to settle anywhere wandered the roads with packs of household goods on their backs, selling to peasants and villagers, regularly appealing to the established communities for lodging, protection, and aid of all kinds.

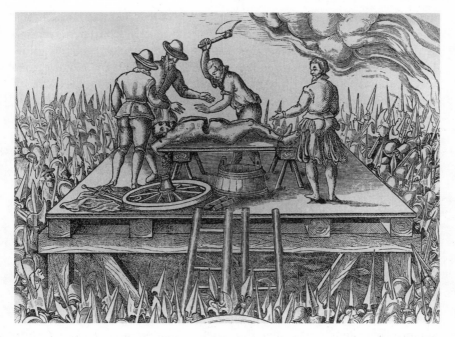

2.1. Death of the Court Jew Lippold in 1573. Detail from a late sixteenth-century broadsheet. Bildarchiv Preussischer Kulturbesitz/Art Resource, NY.

A half century after Lippold's death, war came to Brandenburg, and it was war which brought Jews back to Berlin. During the Thirty Years' War, between 1618 and 1648, Protestant and Catholic rulers sent their armies across the German and Hapsburg domains to fight out the consequences of the Reformation. The Treaty of Westphalia formally concluded the war in 1648, but in fact within Brandenburg, war continued for decades, because the Swedish army continued to occupy various areas of the Electorate. Jewish army contractors were needed to supply the Prussian army in their attempts to drive out the Swedish troops. The man who made the momentous decision to allow Jews to return to Brandenburg was the Elector Frederick William, the Hohenzollern who came to power in 1640. Frederick William, later called the Great Elector, contributed mightily to industry, culture, and social relations in his lands. Keeping his armies supplied with food, horses, uniforms, guns, and blankets was a mammoth project, since soldiers then traveled about with their entire families. In principle Frederick William was opposed to allowing Jews to return to Berlin. But in 1663, in his desperation for military provisions, he decided to allow the family of one Jewish man to settle in the city.

The lucky man was Israel Aaron. Actually, for years Aaron had been supplying the Prussian army, by organizing the services of Jewish traders in Mecklenburg and Pomerania. But Aaron himself was continually denied permission to settle his family in Berlin. Finally, in 1663, the Great Elector agreed to allow Israel Aaron, his wife Esther, and their children to move there. Not everyone was pleased with this decision. One city councilman known for his dislike of Jews complained that the home the Aaron clan was renting attracted "many Jews from elsewhere." He protested that the "Jews who bargain and swindle have again made a good beginning" in Berlin.[3] He could not have been happy eight years later, when the Great Elector decided to welcome to Berlin two extended families that the Habsburgs were threatening to expel from Vienna.

The two clans may have lost their homes in Vienna, but they were nevertheless very wealthy. On the day they arrived in Berlin, the locals watched with astonishment as the new arrivals unloaded their wagons. The local women cast furtive glances at their clothes, cut from expensive fabrics, and decided that their furniture, carpets, and chandeliers were far grander than those in the Elector's palace.[4] We can well understand why Berliners in 1671 would feel shabby in comparison to the new arrivals. Berlin in these years had still not recovered from the Thirty Years' War. More like "a dirty provincial village than a capital city," Berlin was a town of only 30,000. Its streets were sandy in summer and muddy in spring, and without lighting at night. Visiting foreigners mocked the locals for their "uncouth manners."[5]

That the Viennese exiles owned carpets and chandeliers which were grander than those in the Elector's palace is a telling detail for the first moment in the modern history of Berlin Jewry. Wealth was central to why Jews were invited into Berlin in 1671 and to how the community grew as the years passed. The rulers of Prussia favored the rich and then taxed them mightily. The wealth of the Berlin Jewish community was highly atypical for the time, since most Jews in Germany then were poor and lived in small villages. The Viennese families who arrived in 1671 were not the only foreigners whom Elector Frederick William welcomed into Prussia at this juncture. For him, tolerance was a practical matter. Indeed, his invitation to the Viennese Jews fit into the Elector's larger dreams. He realized that importing skilled foreigners into Brandenburg was a good way for his territory to recover from the devastation of the Thirty Years' War. His plans for Berlin were extensive. He aimed to revive agriculture and the crafts, repair the courtly palace, plant trees along the main boulevards, pave the sandy streets with cobblestones, install street lighting, build new suburbs, replace the old medieval wall around the city, and construct a canal with eleven locks to link the Oder and Elbe rivers.[6]

Before the Jews had come the Dutch, who arrived toward the close of the Thirty Years' War, during the 1640s. Frederick William's first wife had been

Dutch, a special reason for this invitation. Thousands arrived and planted the area's first potatoes and produced butter and cheese. Then came the Viennese Jews with their chandeliers, and fifteen years later an invitation was made to the Huguenots, Protestants expelled from Catholic France. By 1687 one in every five Berliners was a Huguenot, and contemporaries quipped that "Berlin seemed more like a French than a German town."[7] The industrious Huguenots founded printing presses, textile workshops, bakeries, and pharmacies, and sold soap, linseed oil, watches, and eyeglasses.[8] Berliners were especially fond of the new knick-knack stores, where they could buy fashionable buttons and braids and other inexpensive finery.[9] Thanks to the wide-ranging generosity of the Elector, by 1700 half of the Berlin population had been born abroad.[10]

Religious conflict as well as a sound economic policy motivated Prussia's magnanimous immigration policy. The Hohenzollern dynasty had become Calvinist, or Reformed as they were called in Berlin, back in 1613. Their conversion made ruling more difficult, since almost all of their subjects had remained Lutheran. For instance, one day soon after the first Calvinist preacher arrived in Berlin, "a Lutheran mob broke into his house, beat him up and stole everything but his green underwear — in which he was forced to preach the following Sunday."[11] The religious tolerance showed by the Hohenzollerns, however, diffused the intensity of their struggle as Calvinist rulers over their Lutheran subjects.

But let us return to the story of Israel Aaron and the new arrivals of 1671. Behind the scenes of the founding of the modern Berlin community, we see a cut-throat competition between wealthy Jews, rather than solidarity in the face of the regulations imposed by powerful rulers. Israel Aaron was openly furious about the Viennese refugees, because he preferred to be the sole merchant with privileged access to the Elector. He went so far as to try to convince his patron not to take in any of the Viennese families at all. Israel Aaron had a reputation as a "stern and cross-grained" man, and his behavior at the founding of the modern Jewish community of Berlin fits this image perfectly.[12] He wanted to be the only Court Jew in Berlin; it was the Elector who wanted to expand the circle of wealthy Jews in the little capital. Not surprisingly, as a Jewish community emerged, Aaron was passionately hated and seen as a "Judas" figure. A mock will distributed after his death in 1673 awarded his undershirt to a government official, his "patched stockings" to a local woman, and his "last bowel movement" to a rabbi in Vienna![13]

Soon after the Viennese families arrived with their chandeliers, an elaborate edict was drawn up to define the conditions under which they would live, conditions which were quite favorable for those years. Word spread quickly that Berlin was a good place for Jews if they had the resources to meet the steep

2.2. View from the Rosenthaler Gate. Watercolor by Leopold Ludwig Mueller. Bildarchiv Preussischer Kulturbesitz/Art Resource, NY.

requirements. But still, even admitting a few rich families forced the state to allow in those who would serve the rich as their domestic staff, rabbis, teachers, kosher butchers, clerks, and tutors.[14] The two gates of Berlin where Jews were allowed to enter were policed by gatekeepers provided by the community. The Judenherberge was a dormitory just inside the city gates where those seeking entrance could stay for a few days while their documents and assets were investigated.

As Israel Aaron's selfish behavior makes clear, politics inside Jewish communities then were really very nasty. Money and access to the ruler established the internal community hierarchy. Jewish power struggles were illustrated dramatically in decisions about where to attend religious services. Because the 1671 Edict forbade the construction of a public synagogue, the leading families sponsored synagogues in their homes. Observers were shocked to watch fistfights in the street on Saturday mornings, as rival factions tussled over who would pray where. Precisely because the setting for both commerce and prayer

2.3. Jost Liebmann, "Der Schutzjude" (Protected Jew). Portrait by Anthoni Schoonjans, 1702. Bildarchiv Preussischer Kulturbesitz/Art Resource, NY.

was domestic, it is not surprising that a powerful woman played a central role in these conflicts. She was Esther Liebmann, the clever and reportedly beautiful widow of Israel Aaron, who had moved with him to Berlin in 1663. They had enjoyed a decade of joint economic success before Aaron died in 1673. Esther was then appointed an official Court Jew in her own right, a unique privilege for a woman in those times. Three years after Aaron died, she married the up-and-coming jewel trader Jost Liebmann. For a quarter of a century Jost and Esther Liebmann were important financiers for the Great Elector and later for his son King Frederick. They in turn ruled the tiny Jewish community with absolute control, and it was this absolute control which was behind the fistfights on the street on Saturday mornings.

The Elector was a rather coarse and practical man with military ambitions for his territories, and his main project for Esther and Jost was army supply. But after he died, his son Frederick had very different uses for their loyal services. Frederick took ostentation very seriously indeed, and decorating his body and his palace became increasingly important after he became king in Prussia in 1701. His promotion to a kingship would seem impossible, for an empire could not contain a kingship within it. Yet because some areas of eastern Prussia lay outside the borders of the Holy Roman Empire, he achieved his goal, and during an elaborate town festival in 1701 in Königsberg, Elector Frederick literally crowned himself King Frederick. Throughout his reign, keeping his royal highness supplied with jewels and other expensive finery became Esther Liebmann's special task.

After a quarter century of prosperity and power, Jost died in 1702. As a second-time widow, Esther retained her tremendous influence over Jewish Berlin. Indeed, critics complained behind her back that the extent of her control made their community "a laughingstock" across Europe.[15] Resistance to her domination focused on where to pray, and the conflicts on Saturday mornings became more and more intense. Finally, state officials decided to allow a public synagogue to be built. Privileged as she was, this was a blow to Esther, who had adamantly opposed a public house of prayer. She did not, however, have to endure the insult of seeing it, for she died months before the new synagogue opened its doors in the fall of 1714.

The Berlin community had to pay steeply for the privilege of constructing their grand synagogue on the Heidereutergasse. But the expense and trouble were worthwhile indeed. The new synagogue was seen by many as the most handsome of its kind in central Europe, surpassed only by the Portuguese synagogue in Amsterdam. Imagine the pride local Jews felt when, on the Sabbath before Rosh Hashannah in 1714, Queen Sophie Dorothea arrived at the new synagogue to attend the opening service. In her retinue were twenty

צורת ותבנית הבית הכנסת אשר הוקם ונבנה פה בעיר לק עיר המלוכה בר שין
אדונינו המלך האדיר וחכי וחס מאר פ ר ד ר י ך. ויך לה ערם ותשלם המלאכה
בשנה ואה להם למקדש מעט לפק

Abriß der Priviligirten Jüden Synagoge
in der Königlichen Residenz Berlin
welche erbaut worden Anno 1714.

2.4. Interior of the Heidereutergasse synagogue. Engraving by A. B. Göblin from a drawing by
Anna Maria Werner, 1720. Bildarchiv Preussischer Kulturbesitz/Art Resource, NY.

carriages, and in them sat various prestigious government ministers.[16] With the opening of the Heidereutergasse synagogue, Berlin Jewry had acquired a most impressive external space to represent their religion. But all was not well inside the hearts and minds of the Jews in Berlin and beyond, and the traditional Judaism of the official synagogue would soon come under painful attack from a variety of directions.

Why the Rabbis Lost Their Influence

We may well wonder just what it was that the Berlin Jews were quarreling about on Sabbath mornings. No surviving testimonies suggest that the conflicts were about competing theologies or alternative rituals and prayers. Rather, the fistfights seem to have revolved mainly around local personalities and local power struggles. But far away from obscure Berlin, Judaism was seething with truly revolutionary conflicts which went to the heart of what it meant to be Jewish. From diverse corners of Europe and the Middle East, the authority of traditional Judaism was increasingly under attack. Strange combinations of religious ideas and practices complicated the spiritual landscape. Some, like the followers of Shabbatei Zevi and Jacob Frank, were leaving Judaism, claiming that they were actually taking it with them into a different faith. Others, like the descendants of the hidden Jews from Spain and Portugal, were returning to Judaism while claiming that they had never left it. Across Germany, pietist activists struggling against the Lutheran establishment became more interested in Hebrew and Judaism and more sympathetic to Jewish suffering.

These were hard times for even the richest and most educated Jews in the German lands. Because it was so difficult to settle in the towns of central Europe, stability was a privilege of the super-rich. Geographic dispersion made passionate intellectual life all but impossible, because no single community could attract charismatic teachers and students from near and far. Another problem was that local town councils rarely allowed Jews to own retail stores, which meant that women's commercial labor was difficult for husbands to exploit. Wives who ran small stores would have been useful for husbands who wanted to spend their days studying in the yeshiva. The ban on retail trade also forced many men into peddling, so that husbands were forced to leave home for days, weeks, and months at a time, selling their wares in small villages. We should thus not be surprised to learn that across the Germanic lands, religious practice was becoming more and more lax.[17]

The rabbis lamented that knowledge of Hebrew was waning by the year, and thus prayerbooks were even published with Yiddish transliterations of the

Hebrew.[18] Another consequence of the fading influence of the religious establishment in the German lands was the growing passion for magical practices. Itinerant preachers chanted incantations and distributed amulets, small clay objects, which were reputed to heal illnesses and make barren women pregnant. They and their followers fasted and confessed digressions to each other. Men as well as women frequently entered ritual baths for purification. For quite some time Jews had been attracted to messianic figures too. Till Eulenspiegel, a satirical folk hero and writer of the fourteenth century, once "depicted the Jews of Frankfurt as so impatient to know when the messiah would arrive that a Christian swindler deceived them into buying a 'prophecy berry' which they swallowed before realizing that they had been duped; the 'berry' contained excrement!"[19] Those swept up in magical populist practices criticized what they saw as the circular logic of traditional Jewish study, and began to practice a more emotional Judaism.

The trend toward magical Judaism was very much strengthened in 1648, a catastrophic year for the Jews. During the Cossack rebellion against Polish landowners in the Polish-Lithuanian Commonwealth, hundreds of thousands of Jews were murdered in pogroms. Many Jews had prospered in that state, collecting taxes, running taverns and inns, making whiskey, and even sometimes owning land. Those who survived the 1648 pogroms were in despair, and strengthened the support for the messianic movement created by Shabbatei Zevi and his prophet Nathan of Gaza. Shabbatei Zevi was an eccentric, emotional believer in his own spiritual powers, and before he left Judaism in 1666 he had become the leader of a huge sect. The Shabbateans were mystics, ecstatic followers of the cabbala, a secret stream of Jewish ritual and cosmology. They believed that their embrace of the Jewish messiah Shabbatei would lead to a return to Palestine, that "large clouds" would blow through Europe and the Ottoman lands, gathering all Jews together in the Holy Land.

The Shabbatean movement is important for our conversion story in several ways. The sect dramatically attacked the spiritual authority of the traditional rabbis. After Shabbatei converted to become a Moslem, those who followed him became syncretists, seeking to combine their Jewish and their new Islamic identities. This trend disrupted the hitherto rigid borders between Judaism and Christianity, suggesting crossovers and parallels between the two faiths. Altogether the huge initial success of the Shabbateans promoted the notion of changing one's religious identity. The center of the movement was in the Ottoman Empire, but we know from many sources that Shabbatei had supporters throughout the German lands. Glückel von Hameln, a Jewish merchant wife whose memoirs are one of our best sources for this era, was then living with her husband and a houseful of children in Hamburg.[20] Glückel herself was a

Yiddish-speaking Ashkenazic Jew, but Hamburg was also home to Sephardic Jews, who hailed from Spain, Portugal, or Turkey, and enthusiasts for the Shabbatean movement tended to be Sephardim who lived in southeastern Europe and the Middle East. Glückel described in her memoirs how convinced many of her family and friends were that Shabbatei was indeed the messiah. In her words, when letters arrived from Smyrna, his base of operation in Turkey, "the Sephardic youth came dressed in their best finery and decked in broad green silk ribbons, the gear of Shabbatei Zevi. 'With timbrels and with dances' they one and all trooped to the synagogue, and they read the letters forth with joy like the 'joy of the Feast of Water-Drawing.'" She remembered how Jews in Hamburg "sold their houses and lands and all their possessions," because redemption would require them to sail at "any moment" from Hamburg to the Holy Land. Her own father-in-law, who was preparing for such a journey, sent Glückel and her husband Chaim two "enormous casks packed with linens and with peas, beans, dried meats, shredded prunes and like stuff, every manner of food that would keep."[21]

But the movement of redemption almost collapsed overnight in February 1666, when Shabbatei was arrested by the Ottoman sultan, who feared the disruptive consequences of this fast-growing, unpredictable sect and its immensely popular leader. The sultan gave him a choice between conversion to Islam or death. Shabbatei shocked many of his own enthusiasts when he chose to become a Moslem. A minority of his local followers went with him into Islam, claiming all the while that they were actually still Jewish. Most enthusiasts, especially those far away in Germany, eventually declared Shabbatei to have been a false messiah and were devastated by the loss. As for the casks in Glückel and Chaim's house in Hamburg, they stood ready for three years while her father-in-law "awaited the signal to depart." But "at length the old folks feared the meat and other edibles would rot; and they wrote us, we should open the casks and remove the foodstuffs, to save the linens from ruin."

After Shabbatei's conversion, many of his sympathizers became hostile to his movement. Historians have documented the dramatic turnaround, and one account notes that angry rabbis and leaders "began removing all traces of the Sabbatian *madness* from the liturgy and communal records."[22] But small bands of followers, mainly near him in Turkey but also across Europe, remained convinced that even though he was now outwardly a Moslem, Shabbatei was still a Jewish messiah, working to repair the world as a hidden Jew inside his new faith. We see various odd projects taken on after Shabbatei's conversion. One dedicated Shabbatean, Judah Hasid, left Poland in 1700 with thirty-one families, on their way to Palestine. Their circuitous journey somehow took them to Frankfurt, where "they stirred up crowds." Eventually,

Hasid and two hundred of his followers actually settled in Palestine. Yet the Jewish stream in their Shabbateanism was obviously weak, for after Hasid died, some of his followers, while remaining in Palestine, became Moslems, some Catholics, and some Protestants.[23]

Disputes about secret Shabbateanism became virulent in Germany after 1666. The leading rabbi of Hamburg, Jonathan Eybeschuetz, was accused of practicing secret Shabbatean rituals. A convert named Karl Anton who reportedly studied with Rabbi Eybeschuetz published the claim that "beneath the rabbinic façade, Eybeschuetz supported cabbalistic teachings that came close to the teachings of Christianity."[24] Notice the connection between Shabbateanism, cabbala, and Christianity. Another contemporary, a Protestant pastor named David Megerlin, proclaimed that Eybeschuetz was a "secret proselyte" and a "half-Christian."[25] Rabbis in Amsterdam, Hamburg, and Frankfurt am Main issued an explicit threat of excommunication from the community for those exposed as Shabbateans.[26]

But however harshly the rabbis tried to repress the Shabbatean tendency, magical, even messianic Judaism did not die, and indeed took on new forms in eastern Europe as late as the middle of the eighteenth century. One Shabbatean who attracted a large circle of followers was born as Jankiel Lejbowicz, eventually called himself Jacob Frank, and declared himself a "reincarnation" of Shabbatei Zevi. He was born in Podolia, which was then in Poland, in 1727, and as a young adult he lived in Constantinople. There he became an enthusiastic participant in the Dönmeh sect, as the followers of Shabbatei called themselves. Frank began speaking Ladino, the Spanish Jewish dialect, and passed himself off as a Sephardic Jew. When he was 27 he followed Shabbatei into Islam, and then returned with a band of enthusiasts to his hometown in Podolia. One night in 1756 the rabbis, after breaking into a novices' prayer meeting in a small village, discovered them engaged in "acts of debauchery." Tales spread that when the Frankists gathered for secret prayer sessions, they also enjoyed singing, dancing, and erotic sharing of one another's spouses. Frank debated Talmudists in public, and the Catholic authorities looked forward to a sensational mass conversion. Traditional Jews, outraged by the Frankists, attacked them and forcibly shaved off half of their beards as a sign of heresy.[27]

But in the end Jacob Frank and his sect did not find a permanent home in Islam. On the contrary, the Islamic establishment challenged his religious sincerity and excluded his entire entourage, which now numbered 15,000, from the faith. Two years later, in 1759, Frank and a thousand of his followers were baptized as Catholics. Catholic leaders welcomed the Frankists, because they hoped Frank's decision would stimulate a mass conversion of Jews, long desired among Christians as a sign of the return of the Christian messiah. Frank instructed his followers to adopt Christianity outwardly, while remaining secretly Jewish. Their plan was to keep the now-Catholic sect ethnically Jewish, so in the decades and even centuries to come, Frankist Catholics were forbidden to marry Christians by descent. After his arrest by Polish authorities for polygamy, embezzlement, and impersonation of the Messiah, Frank was incarcerated in a monastery. But by 1770, he had been released, and his group settled in a town near Frankfurt, where he called himself a baron and founded a miniature court society, including his own judicial authority and police force. At the height of his influence Frank had 24,000 believers, whose contributions yearly came to a sum larger than the income of the Polish state.[28] After he died in 1791, the sect continued its special way of life under the leadership of Jacob's daughter Eva, until she died in 1817. Conflicting stories of her demise have survived. Some say she was arrested and hanged by the Hessian authorities. Others were convinced that because Eva feared arrest, she fled the Frankist court with her followers.[29] Little is known and much is speculated about the underground survival of the sect in the generations after Eva Frank's death.

Several decades after Jacob Frank died, yet another kind of magical Judaism emerged, also hostile to money, learning, and power, emphasizing how Jews could find God through mystical experiences, song, dance, communal love, and the joys of daily life — the Hassidic movement, which was heir to the cabbalistic and the Shabbatean beliefs and practices. But Hassidism was an entirely Jewish movement in its origins and its sphere of influence, and thus found few enthusiasts in the German lands, where many Jews wished to be less Jewish altogether, rather than more emotionally Jewish.

The Shabbateans and the Frankists blurred the borders between contemporary faiths, and returning Sephardic Jews did so as well. The Shabbateans and the Frankists were entering new religions and all the while claiming that they remained Jewish in some special ways. Other Jews returned to the faith. As time went on, more and more of the descendants of the crypto-Jews from Spain and Portugal who had settled in Hamburg and Berlin resumed a public Jewish life. Because of their sophisticated habits and interests, the crypto-Jews were pioneers in assimilation. They experienced in their bones passing across generations as Catholics and then becoming publicly Jewish. We shall see that converts in the nineteenth century, including Heinrich Heine, would find heroes among the Sephardic Jews of an earlier era. Another way that the boundaries between the faiths were blurring was that more and more German Jews were dressing and talking like Christians; at least we suspect that such behavior was increasing because the rabbis complain about these casual transgressions more and more.[30] One Sabbath morning in Berlin during the year 1738 a man named Jeremias Cohen appeared at the Berlin synagogue without a beard and wearing a wig. His local rabbi was outraged by this iconoclastic look, and he was not allowed to participate in the service.[31]

A far more serious challenge for the rabbis across Germany were the pietist missionaries, who were becoming ever more focused on Jewish conversion in these decades. Pietists resembled the messianic Jews insofar as they craved a more emotional faith and deeper communitarian experiences. Those who created this once-influential Lutheran sect sought deeper intimacies among believers, and they were critical of the authority of parish ministers and church officials. Pietists were enthusiastic to do good, and they did a great deal of it, administering orphanages, workhouses, and a wide variety of schools. An obvious attraction for them were the vagabond Jewish peddlers who had become a familiar sight tramping about on the country roads in these years. For them, peddler Jews represented "a unique combination of all those forms of marginality" which they desired to "redeem and integrate."[32] The poor roaming Jews often gathered at the gates to cities pleading for the right to settle, selling a variety of wares out of their backpacks. Petty trade was intensely competitive in these circles, even though the profit margin was tiny indeed. Across the German lands we find growing numbers of illegal Jews "on the road," without residence rights in any one town.[33]

Some of the pietist missionaries took Judaism very seriously and felt themselves to be sympathetic to the trials of the poor Jews.[34] Johann Jakob Schudt noted in his 1714 book about Judaism how proud he was to have achieved "familiar and open-hearted relations" with individual Jews.[35] To be sure, the goal of the pietist missionaries was to make more Jews into Christians. But still, it is important that they thought they were showing respect for individual Jews. In 1711, a prominent theologian reminded his readers that "the duty of Christian love obliges all Christians to contribute what they can with prayer and just and gentle behavior towards the good of this people, and to take every opportunity to address them in friendship and to inform them of our religion."[36] Missionary activists were both distressed and attracted by the plight of the poor Jews who chose conversion. Johann Georg, a missionary active in Germany during the 1730s, suggested that all the converts from Jewry should be gathered together in an assembly. "It would be a great gathering. Then everyone would see their poverty and say: 'I am astonished that one Jew has chosen to become a Christian.' "[37] It was certainly not new for most converts to be poor. Throughout the medieval centuries it had typically been the most desperate Jews, who were facing excommunication by the rabbis, who chose to convert. Accused criminals, for instance, often chose conversion. But now those Jews tempted by life's fate to become Christians could receive considerable practical aid from the missionaries. In later centuries, young and ambitious Jewish men could make their way in the world by boarding a ship bound for America, or by studying at a university, or by diligent labor in a family business. But in our moment of time none of these three possibilities was easy, if even available.[38] Certainly the Prussian immigration policies show how difficult it was to settle there without considerable wealth. Conversion was therefore the rare chance to make a dramatic change in one's life circumstances.

The pietist missionaries were innovative in how they tried to improve life circumstances after baptism. When they changed their faith, converts usually needed new jobs. Anyone employed in Jewish community institutions could not continue as a Christian, obviously, but even merchants needed to change their occupations, for they would be shunned by still-Jewish colleagues. In many cases converts also left behind their parents, siblings, spouses, and even children. Where could they find employment or love or friendship or community? Let us visit the conversion bureau which opened its doors in Hamburg in 1671 to see some solutions to these problems. Esdras Edzard, a prominent Lutheran pastor in Hamburg, was inspired by Shabbatei's conversion to Islam, hopeful that this event would increase the conversion rate. At his bureau, Edzard taught Judaic subjects to Lutheran preachers from across Europe, and also instructed them on techniques for conversion. He stressed the importance of converts receiving modest, practical occupational training even before the baptism ceremony. Missionary historians estimate that between 1671, when he opened his bureau, and his death in 1708, 148 Jews were baptized at Edzard's local parish. During the same thirty-seven years, one estimate suggests that only 179 baptisms were registered in all of Protestant Germany, making Edzard a central figure in the explanation for who converted during the later decades of the seventeenth century.[39]

After Edzard died in 1708, his son turned to other activities, and his Hamburg conversion bureau eventually closed its doors. It was in Halle, a university town in Prussia, where pietists created a haven for converts that went well beyond what Edzard had accomplished. The mentor of the new institute, which opened its doors in 1728, was August Hermann Francke, a pietist professor of theology at the University of Halle. Francke's patron was King Frederick I, who was interested in the pietists for reasons quite similar to those that had led his father the Great Elector to invite the Dutch, the Viennese Jews, and the Huguenots into Brandenburg. He reasoned that the pietists could soothe the conflicts between the Calvinist crown and the Lutheran population. Moreover pietists were ready to take on various social welfare projects which would stimulate productivity and alleviate acute distress.

Day-to-day administration of Francke's project, soon called the Institutum Judaicum, was in the hands of Johann Heinrich Callenberg, a star student of Francke's at the University of Halle. Callenberg too eventually became a professor at Halle, teaching Hebrew, Yiddish, and Jewish theology. Indeed he learned his Yiddish from a convert. When converts, missionaries, and Judaica scholars sat together to learn each other's teachings, practices, and languages, we see the emergence of a tiny subculture where religions could be compared and contrasted, and changing from one to another became more acceptable. However tiny their numbers, the mix of personalities was volatile and potentially subversive in that time and place. Callenberg's Institute in Halle did not actually sponsor baptism ceremonies, but provided lodging and congenial society for those preparing to leave Judaism and for those who had become Lutherans already. In 1734, just after he had opened his institute, Callenberg proposed the creation of residential communities for converts. In these secluded settlements, former Jews would continue to be part of "a nation separate from other peoples."[40] Callenberg even publicly discussed how these colonies would aid converts in creating an "alternative Jewish identity." It is fascinating to see this open suggestion of syncretism in Callenberg's projects; in his fantasy of the colonies for converts he recommended that some Jewish "rites and customs" should be permitted.[41] To be sure, this plan was not intended to be of service to Judaism or the Jewish people, but rather to add to the number of Jews choosing baptism.

While the notion of a colony of converts remained a fantasy, in their day-to-day work the Institute colleagues wrote and published missionary texts in Yiddish, which their enthusiasts distributed at post houses, inns, markets, and taverns. A favorite site for distributing their tracts was at pietist bookshops and at the Saturday tours of the pietist orphanage in Halle. Although this seems difficult to believe today, missionaries actually entered synagogues during and after prayers, disputing with worshipers. In their reports they were proud to describe how they sometimes were able to "openly rebuke" the rabbis.[42] The twenty traveling missionaries who worked for the Institute during its peak decades during the 1730s and '40s all spoke Yiddish and knew their Jewish theology, both necessary to engage Jews in dangerous conversations. As well as publishing learned articles, their journal also featured diary entries submitted by the itinerant missionaries and reports of daily life at the Institute. Because of the immediacy of its reportage, enthusiastic readers of the journal sent in small contributions to aid in the sacred work of winning Jews away from Judaism.[43]

The story of Joseph Guggenheim's acute ambivalence about converting illustrates just how protracted and painful the transition into Christianity could be. Guggenheim was the *parnas,* a community lay leader, in the town of Ober-Lengnau, and for almost twenty years he pondered whether or not to convert. All during these fraught years, Guggenheim was tutored by the missionary Johann Caspar Ulrich, who used a New Testament in Yiddish provided by Callenberg's Institute, and Christopher Gottlieb, a Jew who had already converted. Guggenheim was concerned to keep his interest in Christianity private from his family and his wider community, even though all the while he hoped to bring them all with him into the Lutheran faith. Once he had decided to leave Judaism, in 1757, Guggenheim suffered a nervous breakdown just before the ceremony was to occur. "He began to scream and bellow like an animal, and to speak in a confused manner." Once the conversion process began he was separated from his family, and "he began screaming for his wife and children night and day." Authorities contemplated ushering him to the baptism ceremony in a straitjacket. After he had officially changed his faith, he drifted in and out of madness for the rest of his life.[44]

During the heyday of the missionary movement, during the middle decades of the eighteenth century, Jewish leaders tried to protect their flocks from the missionary message. Sometimes they banned the conversion pamphlets, but if that tactic failed, they burned the tracts at a public event.[45] The rabbis did have cause for concern, because the innovative techniques employed by Callenberg's staff could be quite effective in attracting curious Jews. Indeed, rabbinical prohibitions were at times ignored when the missionaries came to town. Printed books were apparently a rarity in some of the locations where the missionaries visited, and the free volumes they distributed were sometimes accepted with alacrity. Local Jews took the initiative themselves on occasion, and went out to meet the missionaries at night, or sent their children or their servants to procure their brochures.[46]

One reason for their success in attracting Jewish interest was that Callenberg's traveling missionaries paid close attention to the details of daily life. One of his most dedicated workers, Stefan Schulz, proudly reported that he "spoke Yiddish well enough to be taken for a Jew."[47] Schulz's delight in his ability to pass as a Jew is particularly poignant given that the Jews considering conversion were undoubtedly wondering whether they could ever pass as Christians. Not only were the missionaries trained to speak the proper language, they also made sure to dress the part. In the 1740s two missionaries reported that they deliberately traveled in the poorest of clothes, "because our work demands it; most of the Jews are poor and would shy away from a respectable man."[48] The emphasis on the poverty of the Jews they sought to convert reminds us of how unusual within Jewry the Court Jews were, with their jewelry trade, their private synagogues, and their grand homes.

Just how successful the missionaries were in increasing baptisms is alas not known. Altogether, our quantitative picture of the frequency of conversion in the German lands during the eighteenth century is very sketchy. Primitive evidence suggests that the annual conversion rate was gradually increasing throughout the century, and some even call the phenomenon a "plague of conversions." That such tiny numbers could ever be seen as a plague suggests how much lower the numbers were in the previous centuries. Between 1600 and 1650, roughly 85 Jews across Germany became Protestants, under two baptisms a year. One estimate from the years between 1671 and 1708 suggests that there were 179 converts to Protestantism during these thirty-seven years, which would represent an increase to over four converts yearly. In the fifty years between 1700 and 1750, scholars suggest that "several hundred" Jews became Protestants. If there were as many as 300 conversions over that half century, that would make six baptisms a year.[49] As for Berlin, we can see why it was becoming notorious as a center of conversion. The black notebooks show that 153 Jews became Protestants between 1700 and 1767, or just over two converts a year, *just in Berlin.*

Not only are the numbers of converts very tiny; we know how prone even these figures are to error. Some converts ultimately returned to public Jewish life, and the statistics may also be inflated in the other direction, since on occasion Jews converted more than once, in order to gain the money, lodging, or other assistance provided by a local parish or by the missionaries. But although our numbers are primitive, no one, then or now, doubts that for most of the eighteenth century, most converts were poor when they became Christians and remained poor afterwards. Thanks to the memoirs they wrote and often published in their own lifetimes, we gain insight into their motivations and their experiences. Some distinct trends appear from a close reading of these. Many converts described deep and protracted spiritual crises which became psychological and familial dramas, such as we saw in the case of Joseph Guggenheim. One might expect them to be harsh about all things Jewish, so as to justify the change of faith, but on the contrary, a significant number of memoirists wrote in glowing praise about their Jewish families and their early Jewish education. After the decision to convert, their experiences become more painful, and we read of how hard it was to hide from relatives, friends, and rabbis, as well as their problems finding proper instruction in their chosen faith. The difficult times for converts did not unfortunately end when the baptism ceremony was behind them. Converts who possessed some Jewish learning frequently found employment as professors, teachers, or ministers after they changed their faith. But social integration was much more difficult. Even those who married Christians by birth were reportedly "frequently unhappy."[50]

We see in some of the poignant life episodes of converts that converting did not ensure that one could pass as an authentic Christian. Take the example of the married couple who had both converted, and then opened a confectioner's shop and bought a house. They were hounded out of the regular services at their local church, and their son was called a *Judensau*, a "Jewish pig." The husband noted that the "Christian mob" was harsher toward the converts than they were toward Jews by faith.[51] This truth must have been most uncomfortable for the converts themselves, and suggests that sometimes in their attempts to leave Judaism they suffered more hostility precisely *because* of their change of formal religious identities. A marriage in 1746 suggests, however, that syncretistic practices may have also emerged in more intimate settings, and that conversion did not always lead to loneliness. Magdalena Navrazky's father was a Jew from Posen who had become a Catholic, and he had married a governess, a Christian by descent. Magdalena grew up as a Christian, and she and her first husband became involved with the Moravian Brethren, a mystical Protestant sect. Her second husband, whom she married in 1746, was David Kirchhoff, a Jew who had become a Protestant in Leipzig seven years before. Magdalena and David gave their children Biblical names and preserved rituals from Judaism as well as Christianity. If only we could learn more about their friends and their relations with their families, we might discover whether they participated in a syncretist subculture on the margins of the various faith communities.[52]

We have learned that across the religions, many were searching for more personal, more emotional spiritual experiences. The borders between the faiths were becoming more porous, and within Judaism we see more diversity and dissent. Nevertheless, these shifts did not much affect the rate of conversion to Lutheranism in the German lands. Throughout the seventeenth and through most of the eighteenth century, a tiny handful chose this route, and the Jews who chose baptism were almost always poor. Life in the new faith community was often lonely and impoverished. As we move forward in time to the middle decades of the eighteenth century, we meet richer converts and more extended family conversions. The pietists lost supporters and their institutions closed, but other stimulations and possibilities attracted Jews to become Lutherans. As elite Christian society became more welcoming to wealthy and educated Jews, the advantages of being a Christian became compelling to some. In addition, established theologians pressured distinguished Jewish scholars to convert. The public challenges to Moses Mendelssohn to leave Judaism show us that in these years of optimism and enlightenment, Judaism remained a distrusted, despised religion.

Why Did the Wealthy Begin to Convert?

The example of Philipp Heynemann illuminates the sort of Jews who were now beginning to convert. He was the only son in a family of Court Jews from the town of Weißenfels, in Saxony, born in 1722.[53] As an adolescent, Philipp was sent off alone to study at a yeshiva in Dessau and Fürth, where he became a prize student. When he returned home, his father hired a local theology student to teach him Latin and German. Student and tutor debated furiously about the two faiths, although the father had forbidden such discussions. Philipp's father, Moses, had good reason to fear spiritual debates. His wife had died when Philipp was ten, and because of rumors that she had declared herself a Christian in her heart on her deathbed, controversy erupted about where she could be buried. During the 1730s, Moses's brother, sister, nephew, and niece had also all converted, and a Jewish servant employed by the family had chosen baptism as well.

One day Philipp bought a New Testament, and after long hours reading it, he announced to his family and friends that he had rejected its teachings. But then he changed course, and began planning to convert. One day, while his father was out of town, he escaped to a nearby village, where he lived with a peasant while he studied with a minister to become a Lutheran. He was now 18. His baptism ceremony involved a public debate attended by most of the notables in the area, during which Heynemann successfully answered four hundred questions about Christianity. After his conversion, several of his siblings also converted, and Philipp changed his name to Gottfried Selig. Although his new name meant *happy*, we can well wonder how happy he was as a Protestant. His father disinherited him, which may have been a huge loss, considering his wealth. Selig attended an elite high school, but he was cruelly teased by the other students. He subsequently served as a soldier for a time, worked as an artisan, and eventually became a lecturer in Hebrew at the University of Leipzig. He married one of his cousins whose father had also converted. Because the income from the university was so meager, he had to support his family by traveling about on foot, seeking subscribers for his published writings. He died in great poverty.

Heynemann and his uncles, siblings, and cousins were among the first Court Jewish families to find their lives torn apart by conversion. It would be almost another half century before baptisms of the wealthy and privileged climbed to be almost half of all Berlin conversions. The family experiences among three Jewish extended clans—the Itzigs, the Ephraims, and the Isaacs—show us why those born to wealth, privilege, and power began choosing to convert at this juncture. It was during the Seven Years' War, between 1756 and 1763, that the team of Ephraim, Itzig, and Isaacs came to prominence. We learn much about why some might have hated the Jews then by watching just how they made their fortunes. Prussia's King Frederick had started the war, invading Saxony in 1756. Saxony was an ally of Austria, so the Empress Maria Theresa fumed when she heard of the troops marching in. Maria Theresa's chief ally in her struggle to defeat the Prussian onslaught was Russia, which was more than ready to fight Prussia. These were the decades when Russia and Prussia were beginning a long rivalry over the spoils resulting from slicing up Poland. The Polish state was coming to the end of a long period of collapse and would eventually, by 1795, be completely divided between Austria, Russia, and Prussia.

King Frederick decided to finance the war with a drastic coin inflation, and he enticed the leading Jewish financiers in his capital to aid him in this project. Banknotes were not yet in regular use. Prussia possessed no silver mines and therefore imported silver to produce its coins from points far and near.[54] There was a long tradition of Jews supplying the silver from abroad and managing the Prussian mints. Jewish traders in Poland provided some of the silver needed by the wealthy mint managers in Prussia. Sometimes these roaming traders bought the silver from the Polish nobility, who regularly sold off their plates and coins to stay solvent. The coin inflation was a tidy little way for Frederick to avoid taxing his subjects. And so he decided to vastly cut the amount of silver in the coins minted. The Christian merchants whom the king first asked to do the job declined, in spite of the sizable potential profit. But the Jewish merchants, especially Veitel Heine Ephraim, Daniel Itzig, and Moses Isaacs, agreed to mint devalued coins. They then organized the distribution of the coins inside and outside of Prussia by some of the same peddlers who had bought up the silver in the first place.[55] The contribution of Ephraim and his associates to the war effort was immense. King Frederick managed to raise almost a third of the total war budget by minting the debased coins. But what was good for the king was not at all good for the people, since the debased money caused large-scale inflation. As the war progressed, prices rose steeply; in some locales the price of rye doubled. The Jewish minters were held responsible, and town dwellers expressed their anger by rioting in the streets. A quip of the day summed up the situation: the debased coins were described as "beautiful on the outside, ugly on the inside, Frederick on the outside, Ephraim on the inside."

Even before the war was over, Ephraim and his friends were spending some of their profits on grand new homes and offices. Even for Berlin, where standards were high, the residences which the Ephraims, Daniel Itzig, and Moses Isaacs purchased in the 1760s were supremely lavish. In 1761, when he was 58, Veitel Heine Ephraim spent 16,500 thalers on a mansion on the Mühlendamm, one of the most elegant streets of Berlin.[56] For five years workers labored to rebuild the structure, and once it was finished it became a well-known landmark — which indeed it remains, for it has recently been restored and turned into a museum.[57] Ephraim actually used the building as a business office, and the family lived in a house on the Königstrasse, which he had purchased in 1746. He and his wife Hanna also owned a garden on the Schiff-bauerdamm on the outskirts of the city, decorated by large statues. The Ephraims filled their homes with luxuries both secular and Jewish, with paintings and statues and also with private synagogues and a yeshiva.

We can well ponder the choices faced by Ephraim and his friends when they agreed to serve the crown's bidding by minting and distributing the inflated coins. Some might argue that it would have been better if these families had gone without the super-profits with which they bought their statues and paintings. We can sympathize with the fury of the impoverished Christian population in a time of war and inflation. We do not know enough about what the Jewish minters may have feared would be the consequences of refusing to serve the king in this way. Nor do we know how vehemently the coin devaluation was debated inside the Jewish community. But it would be naïve to ignore how the devaluation, the inflation, and the mansions at prestigious addresses might stimulate hatred and resentment toward the Jewish super-elite. They were, to be sure, victims in a sense, but at a level of well-being that could well have led impoverished Christians to miss the larger point.

The leading Jewish figure of the era actually came to Berlin well before the Seven Years' War to study at Veitel Ephraim's home yeshiva. The year was 1743 when Moses Mendelssohn, aged 14, arrived outside the city gate. The studious Moses, who suffered from a curvature of the spine, had walked to Berlin from his hometown of Dessau, to follow his rabbi, who had been called to teach at Ephraim's yeshiva. Although Moses himself was born in modest circumstances, his patrons were the richest men in the Jewish community, and following his life story will take us directly to their dinner tables. Thanks to the financial and intellectual support of Ephraim and some of his friends, the precocious scholar soon broadened his mastery of the world of learning beyond the Talmud and the Torah. In 1750, when he was 21, he became the tutor for the children of Isaac Bernhard, a silk merchant. He learned secular languages, began publishing essays in German, and made two important Christian friends, the prominent writers Gotthold Lessing and Friedrich Nicolai. Mendelssohn was invited to join his Christian friends at elite reading and discussion societies, but remained an observant Jew. This combination was an absolute novelty for Berlin and Germany and exceedingly rare even in Paris, London, and Vienna.

It was during Moses's time as tutor to the Bernhard children that Veitel

Ephraim invited him to live in his home and also to work in his firm. The offer must have been tempting, because at the time Mendelssohn was earning only 300 thalers a year, a very modest amount in middle-class circles.[58] But Mendelssohn was critical of the coin devaluation and refused to accept Ephraim's offer. In 1762 he wrote to Fromet Guggenheim, his bride-to-be, that "I thank God, be He blessed, that I kept away from the mint. How easily I might have been carried away by the tide . . . everybody blames me for not having seized the opportunity to become a rich fellow."[59] Although he chose not to serve the king by debasing the coinage, Mendelssohn was patriotic, and indeed he wrote a celebratory sermon after the last battle of the war to honor the king's return to Berlin when Prussia was victorious in 1763.

When he was already in his early thirties, just before the war came to an end, Moses and Fromet married. Fromet was descended from the Oppenheimer Court Jewish family of Vienna, and she grew up in Hamburg, enjoying an excellent education and very much up to date on contemporary cultural life. In her quite romantic love letters to Moses, which she intended to "move from heart to pen," Fromet showed how deeply she had integrated popular values and habits with a significant competence in Jewish learning. The content of her letters was utterly modern, although she wrote in Yiddish, and not German. Fromet Guggenheim's life shows us that Jewish women of her generation were expressing secular stances toward love and life without challenging the Judaism they inherited from their parents.[60]

The same strength of character which protected him from the temptation to join Ephraim's mint operation came in very useful in 1769, when Mendelssohn was publicly challenged to convert by a Swiss theologian. He had accomplished much in the 1760s. The crown had granted him a privileged legal status, he and Fromet already had two children, he had won an academic prize for one of his essays, and he enjoyed income and status in his work as a bookkeeper in Isaac Bernhard's silk factory.[61] When Johann Lavater publicly challenged him to convert, Mendelssohn faced a difficult decision, in which the delicate balance he fought to achieve between his religious and his secular identities was severely tested.[62]

Mendelssohn had always been reluctant to articulate his defense of Judaism, and he had always managed to keep private his anger at various insults. For instance, the prominent academic Johann David Michaelis had published an attack on Mendelssohn's friend Lessing's play *Die Juden*. The heroic Jewish figure in the play was reportedly based on Aaron Meyer, Veitel Ephraim's son-in-law.[63] Mendelssohn chose to keep his real views out of the public discourse, but in a private letter he raged to a friend about Michaelis's views. "What humiliation for our oppressed nation! What inordinate disdain . . . from learned people I always expected a fairer judgment . . ."[64] But Mendelssohn's lofty expectations may have been naïve, for Lutheran theologians were convinced that if Mendelssohn could be persuaded to leave Judaism, a "wholesale" baptism of Jews might take place in Berlin. Six years earlier, in 1763, the theologian Johann Casper Lavater had visited Mendelssohn at his home, and they had engaged in collegial conversations about contemporary literature. Lavater became excited when colleagues in Berlin told him that Mendelssohn might be on the verge of converting, and in 1769 he inserted into the preface of one of his books an appeal to Mendelssohn to refute Christian theology, or to renounce Judaism. Mendelssohn was furious that Lavater would publicly demand an accounting of his loyalty to Judaism. But once the gauntlet had been thrown down, he felt duty bound to reply. He spent many weeks drafting his response, the thrust of which was that Judaism, unlike Lavater's version of Christianity, was a religion tolerant of other faiths. He reminded Lavater of how destructive public religious disputation was, and asked for respect for his decision to remain Jewish. As time passed the dispute attracted much attention in Berlin and beyond. One observer noted that "the whole fashionable world in Berlin, and even people who are otherwise hardly interested in the quarrels of scholars and literati in general" talked about Lavater's challenge and Mendelssohn's reply.[65] By the force of his pen and his experiences alone, Mendelssohn mounted a strong defense of Judaism. But unfortunately history did not allow him a real chance to create institutions which opened up new ways to be Jewish. In this book we shall follow the complex destinies of Moses and Fromet and their six children. In spite of the parents' commitment to traditional Judaism, that spirit failed to live on in the lives of four of their children, who ultimately became Christians.

The same "fashionable world" which bought up the copies of the Lavater-Mendelssohn treatises may well have also read a popular novel which appeared in several editions in these years. Johann Kölbele's fictional account of a female convert, entitled *Die Begebenheiten der Jungfer Meyern, eines jüdischen Frauenzimmers von ihr selbst beschrieben* ("The Affair of the Young Meyer Maiden, A Jewish Woman, Told in Her Own Words") shows us how an unsympathetic Christian author imagined the conversion of a well-to-do young Jewish woman. The author explicitly noted elsewhere in his writings that he saw Mendelssohn as the ideal reader of his novel. We see in Kölbele's novel a fictional enactment of the conversion dilemma that Lavater tried to force on Mendelssohn. But unlike Mendelssohn, who mightily resisted conversion, Kölbele's heroine, a well-educated young woman named Ester Meyer, ultimately embraced the Christian faith. Ester came to doubt Judaism because she saw it as superstitious, and she became a deist. She discussed these quandaries with her beloved, a Jewish physician, who shared her critiques of Judaism and who was even ready to convert. But before he could do so, he died. After his death, Ester read his final testimony explaining why he had come to reject Judaism totally. She too became convinced of the truths of Christianity, and began to think of herself as an "inner Christian." She then left home, and roamed about in distress as she faced a series of trials, including courtly intrigues, kidnapping, and escapes. She finally did convert, and she changed her name from Ester to Christiane.[66]

After much opposition to her decision, in the end her parents also converted. But the newly Christian family was nevertheless rejected by members of the dominant society. At this juncture their lives seemed to consist of negative gestures toward their own past. For instance, Ester's father gave up his fortune, which he had come to feel that he had earned "dishonestly." Here we see a sharp critique of Jewish business practices and the overt suggestion that these practices were seen by Jews themselves as a compelling reason to leave Judaism. The Meyer family line seemed to end here. Ester was an only child, "without sensuality," who knew "only love for her parents."[67] Kölbele obviously did not see cross-religious romances as either the cause or the consequence of conversion.

It is difficult to imagine that Kölbele thought Ester's poignant fate would make her a model for Jewish readers considering baptism, though there is much in her story that looks backward to timeworn paths that Jews had traveled toward Christianity. Ester does not come to Christianity through a romantic connection with a Christian man, but rather via the reading of texts written by her Jewish beloved. There is no trace of a search for social advantage in her story. Yet Kölbele's novel looks forward in a very radical way. Although he claimed that he hoped Mendelssohn would be influenced by the novel, the sort of Jew whom Kölbele imagined in his novel was not in fact either a young man like Philipp Heynemann, or a middle-aged prominent intellectual such as Mendelssohn. Rather, Kölbele chose for his imaginary hero a wealthy young woman whose parents had given her a modern education. Just how prescient he was in imagining such a convert will soon become clear.

3

The Coming of Age of Rahel Levin, 1771–1810

"Under the Wing of Frederick the Second," 1771–1786

On May 19, 1771, Chaie Markus gave birth to her first child. She had suffered several miscarriages, and because the new baby girl, called Rahel, was so weak, the doctors predicted a short life for the tiny creature. They wrapped her in cotton wool and kept her in a small box.[1] Against all odds, little Rahel survived, although her health would prove fragile at many points during her life. A year later, her brother Markus was born, and a second brother, Lipmann, arrived in 1778. A sister, Rose, and a third brother, Meyer, followed. Rahel's father was Levin Markus, a prosperous banker and jewelry trader, who had made his fortune working alongside Veitel Heine Ephraim and Daniel Itzig on the coin devaluation during the Seven Years' War. Levin was quite a character. He had not always been the well-heeled patriarch of a bourgeois family. Rumor around Jewish Berlin had it that he had once belonged to a band of Jewish thieves, and that a stigma burned onto his body testified to this special past.[2] But he had made his way in the world, and at the close of the war in 1763 Levin Markus had been granted the "general privilege," which gave him permission to settle his entire family securely in Berlin. Thanks to these advantages, the five siblings enjoyed a luxurious life in their home on the Jägerstrasse. Rahel's brother Markus later reminded her of how they had performed "ballets in [their] stocking feet" on the tapestry carpets of their elegant living room on Saturday mornings.[3] Markus's memory shows that the Markus family was not in the habit of attending Sabbath services. Chaie and Levin spoke German, and they hired tutors to teach their children both German and French. A contemporary portrait of Levin Markus shows him without even a minimal beard.[4] Yet much was indeed traditional about their lives. The family used Yiddish for daily communication, and Chaie, Rahel's mother, covered her hair with a bonnet, the traditional practice for married Jewish women.

Another sign of the Markuses' shifting identity was that even before Rahel was born the family began to socialize with Christians. These relationships emerged out of economic exchanges. In the 1760s, around the time he received his general privilege, Markus began to loan money to actors and aristocrats whose spending exceeded their incomes. And these special clients began to extend their visits to the Markus home, remaining for conversation and shared meals. So Rahel and her siblings learned the languages and the habits of "good society" in the drawing room of their own home.

As she was growing up, Rahel suffered from the complicated emotional dynamics of her family. She was her father's favorite, yet he was harsh. One of her close friends remembered him as "the most spirited and witty despot that one can imagine, and therefore the most wounding." This friend later recalled that "his greatest pleasure was to cause offense."[5] Her mother was emotionally frail, and this annoyed the spirited daughter. This point is of great interest, for we must investigate whether weak ties with a mother made it easier to choose baptism. In spite of all of her alienations, Rahel did not flee the emotional circle of her intimate family. On the contrary, as a young woman and later she was a devoted daughter and sibling.

Once they reached their twenties, Rahel and her Jewish friends began to open their homes to an eclectic circle of friends, and their salons began to be the talk of Berlin and beyond. The salon participants were lucky in these decades, because all the way up to 1806, Berliners enjoyed peace and prosperity, even as many towns and principalities across western Germany fell under French rule. Back in 1792, when France became a republic and began its European campaigns, Prussia and Austria had been united in their opposition to the French. But in 1795, Prussia made a separate peace with France and remained out of the fray for over a decade. The time of peace, which lasted until October 1806, was a fertile, creative era in German intellectual life. Writers, painters, poets, and their friends created a romantic lifestyle and romantic art and literature. During this decade of neutrality, few German intellectuals worried about armies, states, and national destinies. They looked inward and wrote about their feelings and their relationships. Indeed, relationships were highly valued by the romantic intellectuals, who cherished the "elegant passion" of a "solid friendship." They craved intimacy, which they saw as an important emotional resource for creative work.[6] When they chose their lovers and friends to suit their emotional tastes, romantic intellectuals could find themselves flouting social conventions and their parents' wills. Thus the adventures and the heartaches experienced by the Jewish salon women were very typical for their generation.

Rahel Levin was lucky in friendship when she was a child and a young teen. Among her somewhat older friends were Veitel Ephraim's granddaughters Sara and Marianne Meyer, Daniel and Miriam Itzig's daughters Sara, Fanny, and Cäcelie, Moses and Fromet Mendelssohn's daughters Brendel and Recha, and Henriette de Lemos. Her younger friends included Esther Gad, Mirjam Solomon, Amalie Malka Wulff, Fradchen Marcuse, and Pessel and Hitzel Bernhard. These young women enjoyed many luxuries, yet found it daunting to achieve fulfillment in love and work. Sometimes their charisma, their salons, and their romantic enthusiasms brought them celebrity and notoriety without actually making them happy. One outward sign of the dizzying changes they experienced is how often so many of them altered their names. Many received Yiddish names from their parents, and some took on less Jewish first names when still at home or in early adulthood. Thus Brendel became Dorothea, Pessel became Philippine, and Mirjam became Marianne.[7] Later, when they married Jewish husbands, they lost their original family names. And quite a few went on to become Lutherans, divorced, and remarried, changing their family names yet again.[8]

For several of the girls from Rahel's social circle, reading avant-garde novels led to conflicts with their families. In 1776, when she was 13, Sara Meyer fell in love with a young man, probably a Christian.[9] Her beloved sent her a copy of Johann von Goethe's *The Sorrows of Young Werther,* which had been published two years before and was hugely popular among the young across Germany.[10] Sara's tutor at the time was Moses Mendelssohn, no doubt a connection through her grandfather, Veitel Ephraim. In a later letter to Goethe himself, Sara remembered how Mendelssohn "appeared and reproached me bitterly with having forgotten God and religion and whatever else," and then tossed the volume out the window.[11] Meanwhile Sara had responded to her admirer with an ardent letter. But the letter never reached him, because her father intercepted it. She was confined to her room and fell ill with despair. Mendelssohn's friend, the prominent playwright Gotthold Lessing, who was also intimate with Sara Meyer's parents, was critical of Mendelssohn's action and brought the troubled Sara another copy of the novel. But she was not allowed to ever see her admirer again. Two years later, "through the power of Moses and the force of my mother" she would be "married off to a miserable specimen who made my existence a living hell for 10 years," as she later complained to Goethe.[12]

In spite of or because of how much they shared, the young women in Rahel's circles did not always respect each other. Henriette de Lemos, later Herz, who had been a friend of Sara Meyer as a child, commented in her memoir that although Sara was a beautiful woman, "vanity" was her dominant quality. Herz went on to declare that few of their friends were more "stupid" than Sara Meyer.[13] Henriette may have felt superior to Sara Meyer, but she herself was looked down upon by Rahel Levin. Rahel complained in letters that Henriette was "stiff" and "unnatural." Once she commented that "Madame Herz lives dressed, without knowing that one can get undressed, and how that feels." And even more damning was her conclusion that Henriette Herz was *kronen-dumm* and "stupid enough to make one ill."[14] We note with interest that they were often competing over intellect, rather than beauty and men.

Henriette de Lemos was lucky in her looks, her family, and her linguistic talents.[15] Yet we shall see as we follow her life story that when it came to love, enduring friendships, family, and community, she suffered considerably. Her father was a physician, of Portuguese descent. As the eldest child of his second marriage, she was adored by him, although she felt rejected by her mother. Because she was unusually pretty, bright, and charming, as a young child she was often shown off to princes and princesses from the ruling family who had a whim to observe a Jewish wedding or step into a Sukkah, the traditional outdoor hut in which a fall harvest festival is celebrated among traditional Jews. When she was 13, Henriette's parents inquired whether she would rather marry a rabbi or a physician. She chose the doctor, and two years later, in 1779, she was wed to Markus Herz, who was twice her age. He was born as Mordecai ben Hirz Levi to a poor family of Torah scribes, and as a young boy he, like Mendelssohn, studied at Veitel Heine Ephraim's yeshiva. Later he studied medicine at the University of Halle and philosophy with Immanuel Kant at the University of Königsberg. When Henriette married him, Markus was a physician at the local Jewish hospital, where her father was the director. Markus was already an enthusiastic colleague of Mendelssohn, devoted to various projects for the reform of Judaism.[16] The marriage of Henriette and Markus followed a pattern among Jewish physician families in Berlin to marry among themselves.[17]

It would be a stretch to call the marriage a lucky match. Rumors at the time hinted that they did not enjoy a passionate love life, and unfortunately they were not blessed with children. Henriette had been born into a wealthy and cultured Sephardic family, and Markus had worked his way up from poverty. Apparently she was ashamed of his lack of polished manners. Yet for her, the relationship did prove fruitful intellectually and socially. From 1784, for nineteen years until Markus died in 1803, they hosted their famous double salon. In one room he gave lectures on the newest developments in natural science, and in another room Henriette's circle debated about the new novels and poetry. In this charming division of intellectual labor, Henriette and Markus represented in their own home two competing world views, a conflict between rationalism and subjective emotions which was vexing contemporaries across Germany in these years.

A third intimate of Rahel's was Brendel Mendelssohn, Moses and Fromet Mendelssohn's first-born child, whose childhood nickname was Beniken, and who later called herself Dorothea.[18] Ultimately four of the six Mendelssohn children would leave Judaism, two of the sons to become Protestants, and two of the daughters to become Catholics. Brendel's friend Henriette Herz judged that the children grew up with a "religious emptiness," which she attributed to the deistic Christian friends of their father. She thought that the Mendelssohn children suffered because their father's famous friends openly articulated the disturbing notion that Mendelssohn was not actually sincere in his observance of the traditional rituals.[19]

Like her friends Rahel and Henriette, Dorothea was a first-born sibling, considered "clever" by her father and rather critical of her mother.[20] The man her parents chose for her husband was Simon Veit, and they married in 1783, when she was 18. From the perspective of the two families, this was a good match. Veit came from a wealthy family in Berlin. On her side, the modest size of Dorothea's dowry was offset by the immense prestige of her father.[21] In a flowery Hebrew poem read at the wedding, Dorothea was described as "the precious and lovely young lady, the enlightened Brendel, daughter of the famed scholar, who engages in charity and acts of kindness."[22] Mendelssohn would go to his death three years hence convinced that she was happily married to Simon.

One common interpretation of the eventual conversion of so many young women from Rahel's friendship circle is that the Jewish girls of this generation lacked a rigorous religious education.[23] Certainly the reforming intellectuals inspired by Mendelssohn were passionately concerned about Jewish education. But they rarely expanded their efforts to include girls, as we learn from a look at the Freyschule, which opened its doors in 1781, when Rahel Levin was just ten. Because the aim of the school was to teach young Jews secular languages and skills, families like Rahel's might well have found it attractive. Yet the Freyschule could never have changed the lives of Rahel and her friends, for the school was intended for poor boys, Christian as well as Jewish. Wealthy families hired tutors for their children, mainly the sons but sometimes the daughters as well. Indeed becoming a tutor was a classic way for ambitious but impoverished intellectuals, Jewish and Christian alike, to support themselves in their late teens and twenties. The rich boys had their tutors, and the poor boys had the Freyschule.

The founders of the new school were David Friedländer and his brother-in-law Isaac Daniel Itzig. David was born to a well-to-do banking family from Königsberg. He had arrived in Berlin in 1771, joined the firm of Daniel Itzig, and then went on to open a silk factory of his own.[24] Isaac was one of the thirteen children of the coin millionaire Daniel Itzig. Friedländer and Itzig's new school made do with rented quarters for three years, and it was not until 1781 that the Freyschule received permission to purchase a building. Eventually a bookstore and a Hebrew printing press were opened in the same building. Christians were welcome as teachers and students, although most participants were Jewish.[25]

When it opened its doors in 1781, the Freyschule was an extremely avantgarde institution in Germany and even beyond. Precisely for that reason, it was attacked by some and imitated by others, from points far and near. As the years passed, and the reformers founded more schools, published more journals and prayer books, and trained more tutors and teachers, Berlin became the pulsating center of the Jewish enlightenment. One important project was the new edition of the Hebrew Bible, which appeared after a decade of work in 1783. The new Bible was a perfect bridge between the old and the new languages, for it was written in the German language, but spelled out with Hebrew letters. For decades young Talmud students in Germany and beyond would use this Enlightenment Hebrew Bible to master the German language. Because Berlin was so important in the Jewish enlightenment, well into the nineteenth century the reformers in eastern Europe were referred to as the *Berlinshikes*.[26] Traditionalist rabbis complained about the secular pedagogy of the Freyschule, but were certainly not upset that young women could not study there. Years later, the reformers did note the many young women who were choosing conversion, and then they did begin to pay attention to their Jewish education. But their efforts were often too little too late. Judaism was losing the allegiance of girls from the wealthy classes, who began to rebel against the way their parents married them off.

Just five years after the school opened, Berlin's reformers suffered a decisive blow when Moses Mendelssohn died, in January 1786. The circumstances of his death at 57 were much disputed at the time. His health had always been delicate, but he suffered from no obvious long-term illness. That winter he had been absorbed in finishing a short book entitled *To Lessing's Friends,* written to defend his good friend, who had died four years before.[27] Mendelssohn wrote the book because Friedrich Heinrich Jacobi had attacked Lessing as a pantheist and follower of Spinoza, accusations that in the eighteenth century were considered radical and damaging. Mendelssohn was willing to defend deism, the belief that God was the original force which created the universe, but not pantheism, the belief that God can be identified with nature, and he was not willing to allow Lessing's reputation to be sullied with what he saw as a false claim. Mendelssohn pushed both mind and body completing the manuscript, and finally finished the text on the very last day of December 1785. Like all exhausted authors, he was understandably eager to get the manuscript off his desk and deliver it to the printer. Because he was in a hurry he failed to call a carriage, and against Fromet's advice he dashed out without his overcoat. Three days afterwards he felt ill, and on January 4 he died. His friend Markus Herz had been attending him in his last hours, and soon after the death Herz published his medical summary. In his words, Mendelssohn's death "was a natural one and such as occurs very rarely. It was due to an apoplectic stroke from weakness. The light went out because the lamp lacked oil. Given his constitution, only a man of his wisdom, self-control, moderation, and peace of soul could have kept the flame burning for fifty-seven years."[28]

Rightly or wrongly, some historians have blamed Mendelssohn for not reforming Judaism in a way which would have prevented the conversion wave that was already underway in his last years.[29] Obviously, the conversion of four of his six children has encouraged observers to point the finger at Mendelssohn. But we should be wary of blaming one individual for the discontents experienced by the best and brightest Jews in Berlin in these years. We must remember that at the time of his death in 1786, the Jewish enlightenment was still thriving in Berlin. This wide-ranging project of reform inside of Judaism was called the Haskalah. The trend toward radical assimilation was still quite faint, as least as measured by the Judenkartei statistics. In the late 1780s and 1790s, the Berlin conversion rate was still well under ten baptisms a year. For the first time, more women than men began to convert. Perhaps a more important change was the social composition of the converts. In the seventies, the decade when Rahel was born, only a quarter of Berlin's converts were born to privilege. But ten years later, close to half of the converts were wealthy.

The year in which Mendelssohn was so prematurely taken from the historical stage became a turning point in Prussian history, for it was also in 1786 that King Frederick the Great died. The king surely would not have found the symmetry flattering, whereas Mendelssohn might have. We should not be surprised to learn that Mendelssohn's sermons and other tributes to Prussia were not at all reciprocated by King Frederick. The most scandalous episode involved Mendelssohn's election to the prestigious Academy of Science in 1771. Mendelssohn had won the Academy's essay contest in 1763, the year that Immanuel Kant's essay was ranked second. Nevertheless when the members of the Academy voted him membership eight years later, King Frederick vetoed Mendelssohn's appointment by simply ignoring the proposal. The cowardly academicians never even requested a clarification.[30]

Unfortunately, King Frederick's shabby humiliation of Mendelssohn in the affair of his Academy election was entirely in keeping with his often dismal Jewish policy.[31] In principle King Frederick might have been expected to aid the Jews. He was after all sympathetic toward the Huguenot immigrants and the Catholics. And we know how eager he was to have local Jewish financiers mint coins, found luxury manufacturing firms, and supply his army. But in practice King Frederick's rule was harsh for the Jews. It remained difficult for all but the leading families to settle their grown children in Berlin, and during his reign the community was divided into an ever more rigid hierarchy of rights and wealth.

We should not be surprised to find that Jewish and German views of the king diverged. Historians have tended to admire King Frederick, who was after all a smart and industrious monarch. Frederick funded and enjoyed music, ballet, opera, philosophy, and beautiful buildings. And he also strengthened an already vital army and used it aggressively to further Prussia's position in central Europe and beyond. To be sure, posterity's high opinion of Frederick was not always shared by ordinary Prussians. Reports of the mood at his funeral describe his subjects as having been "benumbed without showing grief."[32] Many apparently saw little to admire about Frederick, and were more concerned about the open sewers, the muddy streets full of pot-holes, and the pervasive smell of animal excrement even in front of the royal palace than about ballet and philosophy.

Rahel, however, was enthusiastic about how King Frederick had affected her own life. In December 1808, twenty-two years after his death, she wrote: "until now I have lived under the auspices, in the strictest sense, under the wing of Frederick the Second. Every enjoyment, external, that is, every good, every advantage, every acquaintance I can attribute to his influence."[33] When she changed her name in 1814, she chose Frederike as her second name in honor of the king. Her husband, Karl August Varnhagen, shared this view. For instance, at one point in his memoir he was remembering Rahel's friend Fanny von Arnstein, a daughter of Daniel and Miriam Itzig, who had grown up in Berlin before settling in Vienna. For Varnhagen, Fanny von Arnstein's "freedom of thought and culture" was nurtured during her girlhood in Berlin, "under the blessed influences of the reign of Frederick the Great."[34]

Rahel's gratitude to the king seems baffling. The only way to make sense of it is that she enjoyed considerable social glory in her salon, but cared little about her second-class civic status.[35] But for us, the voice of Rahel Levin must weigh more heavily than the voices of the historians. Rahel's adulatory view of King Frederick teaches us that in these years a wealthy Jewish woman could feel empowered, even though she and her family and friends had no real rights. If one had enough money and a charmed circle of friends, the absence of civic equality was apparently not as crucial as we might think.

The Twilight Years of the Old Regime, 1787–1806

After Frederick's death the institutions which he had cherished and culti- vated deteriorated badly. His successor Frederick William II lacked the austere dedication of the previous two Hohenzollern rulers, and preferred to spend his time with his mistresses, with his obscure mystical cults, and at balls, rather than rising at five to supervise the troops and play the flute. But when it came to Jewish policy there were some modest improvements. Ten more extended families received the right to settle permanently in Berlin, the entrance tax at the town gates was abolished, and Jews were no longer forced to buy surplus porcelain statues from state factories. The king even established a commission to investigate Jewish reform. But the commission did not accomplish much. The main problem was that the king and his advisors were fundamentally opposed to Jewish emancipation. However, even the leaders of the community had difficulty formulating policies, because the gaps between rich and poor and between enlightened and traditionalist were becoming ever wider.

During the creative decade of the 1790s, Rahel and her friends came of age. In salons, clubs, and reading societies, on promenade strolls and at picnics and dinner parties, they forged friendships with prominent Christian intellectuals, some of them born into high noble families. In these years, their futures were open. At the time, they may have imagined a life within their family orbit, but as years passed many embarked on new lives far from the language, the values, and the habits of their parents. Because the new king continued the policy of neutrality in the Napoleonic wars, Prussia was spared the tumult of war, so that intellectuals could ignore politics and create a romantic credo and life- style. In the Jewish world too, politics was often ignored, progress toward emancipation was halted, and many with wealth and power turned away from wider community causes and concentrated on individual escapes from the old ways. Frederick William II continued the policy of rewarding the wealthiest with privileges. The family with the greatest number of privileges was the Itzigs. In 1791, Daniel and Miriam Itzig and their thirteen children received a naturalization patent. At a stroke, their present and future were changed en-

tirely. All male descendants of the family were granted hereditary naturalization, and the daughters and sons-in-law received naturalization for three generations. The Itzig family was now subject to state law and not Jewish law, and
could even purchase land. Daniel Itzig's daughter Margaret and her husband
David Friedländer, however, sought in vain to receive their own naturalization
patent. That they would try for this exemption from the general condition
reveals how ingrained it was to look to the state for exceptional treatment
rather than struggling to change the condition of all Jews.

But neither wealth nor special privileges could guarantee social acceptance
in Christian circles, and the number of young Jews seeking a freer social space
was increasing by the year. We can explore their predicament up close when
we visit one of the new clubs, the Gesellschaft der Freunde, the Society of
Friends, which was founded in 1792. Those attracted to the new Society were
"free-thinkers" who complained that they were "denied access" to Christian
clubs. They came to the new club because they had "a feeling of bitterness"
that they were "treated with repulsion at public places."[36] The Society of
Friends met Wednesday afternoons from three to eight for tea, coffee, smoking, and conversation. In the winter the group rented rooms for its meetings,
and in the summer its 100 members met outdoors in a rented garden.

The club was open to single men of Jewish descent. Why these two qualifica-
tions? When first organized, the Society voted to exclude any of its members
who became Christians. But after five years it was decided to change this rule,
and beginning in 1797, converts were allowed to remain members. The club
now provided a social space where Jews and former Jews could remain
friends. If baptized Jews could remain intimate with their still-Jewish friends,
an important barrier to conversion was removed. We have witnessed the painful isolation experienced by many converts during previous centuries. That
converted men would want to join the Society shows that for some, even the
fateful choice of baptism was not sufficient to achieve real social integration.
Perhaps the converted men who joined the Society would have dispensed with
their still-Jewish friends had they not been "treated with repulsion in public
places" and "denied access to Christian clubs." Ambitions and frustrations
surely made for stressful friendships among the young single men drawn to the
Society.

The restriction to single men was a way of keeping out the super-rich, who
tended to marry earlier than those with more modest resources. The young
men attracted to the enlightenment movement were often single, born to
poorer families, and worked as tutors or bookkeepers for the Veitel Ephraims
of the world. They did not want to spend their leisure time with their em-
ployers. In the words of one of the founders of the Society, "only that section

of the Berlin fathers of families would want to join who were educated and free of religious prejudices." But the problem was that "all these were almost all rich people, full of pride in their wealth and reputation." This was no abstract problem, for "a large number of younger persons including those who were interested in the society from its very beginning were in a subordinate relationship to these men in their private lives . . . for which reason the monied aristocracy was doubly to be feared."[37] Notice how freely they borrowed the term *aristocracy* to refer to their own Jewish elite.

Unlike the serious men who spent their evenings at the garden teas sponsored by the Society of Friends, the handful of Jews who participated in the salons were mixing with the truly prominent. From afar, the Jewish salons seem a sign that hatred of the Jews must have been waning. And even if the numbers involved were limited, there was indeed huge symbolic public significance when famous and well-placed Berliners visited Jewish homes regularly in informal settings. Yet from many sources we can learn that the volatile social mix of salon society led to hurt feelings, anger, humiliation, and self-deception on the Jewish side, and arrogance, condescension, and sometimes explicit antisemitism on the Christian side. For there were definite limits on how many and which Jews could succeed in the salons. And, after all, enjoying a visit to the fascinating and déclassé territory of the Jewish salons was one thing, but marrying a Jewish salon hostess was something else entirely.

Precisely the wide distance between social visiting and intermarriage was the subject of many a discussion between noble salon guests in these years. The correspondence between two friends of Rahel's, Carl Gustav von Brinkmann and Friedrich Gentz, is especially illuminating.[38] One of their recurrent exchanges concerned Rahel Levin's love affair with Karl von Finckenstein, which began when she was 24, in 1795. That she would fall in love with a Christian noble in the first place was not surprising, for we know that her family observed few rituals and socialized with Christians. In her teen years these trends had continued and deepened. To get a flavor of her hostility to traditional Judaism, listen to her irritated tone in 1794, when she went with her mother, her sister, and a male travel companion to visit cousins in Breslau, who were still very observant. It was bad enough, she reported to her brother Markus, that her aunt and uncle, who themselves were "affluent and educated," lived in a noisy street close to "countless chickens and geese and turkeys and ducks." But worse was the next-door synagogue that her uncle had built. One morning during her visit she complained that she had been rudely awakened by "shouting and yelling" in a "mystical language," which she first thought was simply a loud quarrel.[39] An earlier letter to her siblings suggests that she did attend their prayer sessions, but was "almost unconscious" from the "weariness, boredom[,] sadness and fear."[40] At 23, Rahel felt free to express her superiority toward traditional Judaism, but it was not then at all clear where that alienation would lead.

When she met Karl von Finckenstein a year later, Rahel was one of the few among her close friends who was still single. For reasons that are not completely clear to us, her family had never insisted that she marry the Jewish financiers or physicians chosen by most of her friends' parents when their daughters were still in their teens.[41] Henriette Herz married at 15 and Dorothea Mendelssohn at 18. We cannot explain Rahel's failure to marry a Jewish husband by poverty, as her dowry was 20,000 thalers, a rather modest amount in her circles but not so low as to be an obstacle to a Jewish marriage.[42] Rahel and Karl were introduced to each other in the winter of 1795 at a performance at the Royal State Opera House on Unter den Linden.[43] He was somewhat younger than she, musical, moody, a rather handsome blond. For four years, she considered herself engaged to him. Karl von Finckenstein came from a well-established noble family with a lavish estate outside Berlin, and he often vanished from Berlin to spend months at a time there with his family. He felt conflicted between that secure, if boring, lifestyle and Rahel's intellectual enthusiasms and her ironic cynicism toward social norms. In 1799 Rahel ended the relationship, convinced that he would not marry her, much as she desired such a match. Later his friends gossiped maliciously that Karl had never planned to marry her.

For many of these women, personal fulfillment and family happiness proved difficult to combine. Two cousins of Rahel Levin's whose experiences were particularly traumatic were the two Meyer sisters, Sara and Marianne, granddaughters of Veitel Heine Ephraim. Two years after Mendelssohn threw Sara's copy of the Goethe novel out the window, he suggested a match for her, and she was forced to marry an elderly Jewish man, whom she came to detest. She later complained that the marriage had "destroyed her completely."[44] After his death, in 1788, when she was 25 and her younger sister was 18, both were baptized in Wensickendorf, a small village east of Berlin.[45] Very soon thereafter, however, the two sisters returned to Judaism, after some very stormy family scenes. Sara later described the unhappy situation in a letter to King Frederick William III. "My parents," she wrote, "were dissatisfied with the step, and my mother in particular developed a most bitter hatred toward me. . . . I shall never forget the unhappy night in which my entire family persecuted me and my sisters with their imprecations as the objects of their unhappiness, and with no lesser threats than parricide and matricide."[46] "Numb and almost unconscious," she signed a paper which her parents and the local rabbis interpreted as her decision to return to Judaism. Later she claimed that she had remained a Christian in spite of this signature. The case became a public scandal, with some contemporaries questioning the authenticity of her original baptism and others her supposed return to Judaism. The case shows how conversions challenged government and Jewish and Lutheran officials to sort out who could change religions and how.

Nine years after her parents forced the two sisters to resume their Jewish identities, Sara changed her name to Sophie, returned to Christianity, and became engaged to Baron Dietrich von Grotthuß. Pastors and others debated back and forth about whether or not a second formal baptism was required, and in the end she was not baptized a second time before her marriage. Marianne, meanwhile, had entered an arranged marriage after her return to Judaism, but her husband died, and in 1797 when Sophie returned to Christianity, she did the same. That year she hoped to marry Count Geßler, an ambassador at the Prussian court. But later he decided not to go through with the marriage, and the gossip must have been humiliating. Eventually she would marry Prince von Reuß of Austria, but he refused to let her bear his name, and the emperor awarded her the official name of Frau von Eybenberg.[47] The year 1797 was a painful one for Sophie and Marianne's mother Rösel, for their father Aron died after suffering severe business setbacks. Once one of the wealthiest men in Berlin, he died bankrupt. Several years later, two of Sara and Marianne's brothers converted, perhaps to further their careers as inspectors of mines.[48]

Another famous case from these years was that of the two converted daughters of Moses Isaac-Fliess. Their father's will stipulated that no converted child could inherit from his wealthy estate. If they remained Jewish, each daughter was to receive almost 100,000 thalers, a huge fortune. In Berlin at this time a factory worker earned 150 thalers a year, a professor earned 600 thalers a year, and as we have just learned, Rahel's dowry was 20,000 thalers.[49] A year after Moses Isaac-Fliess died in 1779, his two daughters Blümchen and Rebecca chose baptism, and each married a nobleman. Their brothers, who were still Jewish, refused to pay out their dowries, and the case ended up in the civil courts. When Frederick William II became king in 1786, he ruled in favor of the brothers, because parents' rights were a more important principle than the practical project of increasing conversions. The same brothers who successfully denied their sisters an inheritance were in their own ways also displaying the mores that defined the family crisis. One of them, Joseph Fliess, later converted, as did the children of the other brothers. Joseph also enjoyed a long-standing affair with his Christian mistress Louise Luza, whom he married after his wife died. Joseph's brother Beer Isaac remained Jewish, but was the father of two illegitimate children. A third brother, Meyer Moses, was disinherited by their father before he died, because of the son's "style of living," and he too converted in 1787. The tangled webs of family discord, money, and religious conflicts experienced by the Meyer sisters and the Isaac-Fliess sisters were discussed in the newspapers and journals, as contemporaries sought to understand how Jewish law, civil law, and church law regulated the complicated status of converts.[50]

Another conflicted family drama around conversion starred Dorothea Mendelssohn. When we last met her, she was 18, still called Brendel, and newly married to Simon Veit. In the years after her marriage the couple's friends were divided, some thinking that she was contented, and others frankly worried that she was unhappy with Simon.[51] After they had been married for only three years, Brendel and Simon each lost a father. Then two years later, Brendel's mother Fromet and the younger Mendelssohn siblings moved to Neustrelitz, a town some distance from Berlin. Brendel and Simon brought four sons into the world, but only two of them survived, Jonas and Philipp.[52] From a distance, Brendel's family life may well have appeared quite serene and traditional. Yet a closer look reveals that she too was leaving the traditional Jewish world behind while she was still married. She enjoyed friendships with several prominent Christian intellectuals, and she helped found a secret romantic society called the Tugendbund. In 1794 she discarded the too-Jewish Brendel, and began calling herself Dorothea. Three years later, in the summer of 1797, when she was 32, Dorothea first met the writer Friedrich Schlegel. He was then 25 and quite good-looking, with long hair, then a sign of enthusiasm for the revolution in France. Friedrich had already made a name for himself as an intellect, although still in the shadow of his older brother August, a hugely influential professor at the University of Jena.

Luckily for Dorothea, Friedrich was attracted to older women with strong characters, and the two fell in love. As their relationship deepened, Dorothea pondered long and hard about whether she should divorce Simon. One of her confidants was her friend Friedrich Schleiermacher, then 29 and a preacher at the Charité Church, who was also close to Henriette Herz. Schleiermacher was sympathetic to her plight, because he was a sophisticated man, very enthusiastic about women's emancipation. Because of his intimacy with Dorothea and Henriette, both of whom ultimately converted, he has been seen as an advocate of mass conversion. But his thinking about conversion was more subtle than that. If Jews had experienced authentic spiritual transformation, Schleiermacher did favor baptism. But he emphasized the importance of sincere conviction, and he never advocated conversion as a substitute for civic emancipation.

Dorothea's sister Henriette and her childhood friend Henriette Herz both spent hours with Simon, convincing him that Dorothea had really been unhappy in the marriage.[53] Late in 1798 Simon reluctantly agreed to a divorce. He was given immediate custody of the older boy, Jonas, and Dorothea was allowed to raise Philipp, who was then six, for four more years. But, if she were to remarry or become a Christian before Philipp was ten, his custody would revert to Simon. This meant that Dorothea could not immediately wed Friedrich, which left her in the shabby position of a divorced wife with a rather famous lover. Simon was obviously concerned that young Philipp not be exposed at a young age to a Christian socialization. But in spite of his attempt to prevent their becoming Christians, eventually Jonas and Philipp Veit both converted, settled in Italy, and became Catholic painters in the Nazarene style. As for the all-important finances, Simon agreed to provide Dorothea with alimony of 400 thalers a year, which was enough for a modest but still middle-class lifestyle.[54]

After her divorce, Dorothea rented her own apartment. Although they did not live together, she and Friedrich spent their days together reading, writing, and debating contemporary literature and politics. This was a dramatic and troubled time for her. Her closest friends remained loyal, to be sure. But many prominent personalities in and out of her family were shocked by her divorce and by the novel Schlegel published that same year, which was seen as daringly erotic in its time. Thus the radical couple became marginalized even in the avant-garde salon world. Nonetheless, Dorothea, her beloved Friedrich Schlegel, and their mutual intimate Schleiermacher were often joined at lunch by the firebrand Johann Fichte.

Fichte had just arrived in Berlin from Jena, because he had been dismissed from his professorship there. He chose Berlin because of its reputation for tolerance and its lively intellectual scene. Quickly he made quite a name for himself and was even able to support himself by giving lectures in his home.[55] He began as a republican cosmopolitan, but as the French Revolution lost its moral capital inside of the German lands, he became an ardent patriot, with a huge influence on contemporary politics. His followers and perhaps his critics as well could all admire Fichte's personal journey. His father had been a ribbon-maker in Saxony, and as a child Fichte had herded geese.[56] All along his path, he attracted the help of powerful patrons. When he was 30, seven years before he moved to Berlin, Fichte had been appointed a professor at the University of Jena. But he spoke his mind freely, shocking the students when he predicted with joy that "kings and princes would cease to exist within twenty or thirty years."[57] To show his disregard for organized religion, he scheduled his lectures for Sunday mornings, and in those lectures he argued the case for atheism.

The same year that Dorothea turned her life upside down was also a landmark juncture for another prominent Jewish family in Berlin, the Itzigs. Daniel's wife Miriam died in 1791, and eight years later, in 1799, Daniel too passed away. When his will was read out that June, the Itzigs gathered to hear how he had divided his large estate.[58] Up until his death, none of his children or grandchildren had left Judaism. The unique award of naturalization to the family back in 1791 should have made conversion less attractive. That many of Daniel Itzig's grandchildren and great-grandchildren converted shows us that civic equality was not sufficient for those with luxurious personal resources and high social or career ambitions. Immediately after his father was in his grave, one son, Elias Daniel, then 44, made good on his promise "that he would convert to Christianity with his whole family immediately upon the death" of his father. Elias and his wife Mirjam and their children all changed their family name to Hitzig at this juncture.[59] Jakob Salomon, one of Itzig's grandsons through his mother Bella Salomon, also converted very soon after his grandfather died. Jakob made his transformation even more radical, discarding his father's family name Salomon and becoming Jacob Bartholdy. His new last name was a kind of "ancestry by purchase," because Bartholdy was the name of a former dairy which the Itzig family had bought some years before.

A month before his father-in-law died, in April 1799, David Friedländer wrote a small pamphlet that attracted considerable attention. His name was not on the cover, but it was an open secret that he was the author. Friedländer had good reasons to hide his name from the Jewish community, since he was widely seen by his contemporaries as the institutional heir to the Mendelssohn legacy. In this astonishing document he petitioned Wilhelm Teller, a leading Protestant minister, to accept a circle of enlightened Jews into the Lutheran church, under some very special and idiosyncratic conditions. The idea was that Jews would publicly proclaim their allegiance to a deistic version of Lutheranism, which would place them under the umbrella of the church establishment without their actually joining any mainstream church institutions. To no one's surprise, Teller emphatically rejected Friedländer's proposal. Neither he nor state officials wanted a separate sect of former Jews inside the Protestant establishment. After his proposal was rejected, Friedländer did not choose conversion. Nor did he lose his high position in the local Jewish community, which shows that many of his peers who knew he had written the pamphlet sympathized with his plan. Teller's rejection of the plan is certainly not shocking, but the fact that Friedländer continued to enjoy esteem in the community after the plan was rejected is immensely informative. That the public heir to Mendelssohn's values would consider a mass conversion to any form of Christianity shows just how difficult it was to find a way forward between baptism and tradition.[60] After 1799, Friedländer turned away from religious matters, and concentrated instead on the fight for civic emancipation.

But a younger generation of educated Jews did try to create new forms of Judaism in these years in Berlin. Let us now turn to the life of Amalie Wulff Beer to watch one of Rahel's younger friends, born to wealth and power, who committed her energies to the harmonious modernization of Judaism. Although they had much in common when viewed from afar, when we look more closely we see profound differences between these two women. Amalie once referred to Rahel as a *wildgewordene demoiselle,* which we might translate as a "wild and frantic young lady."[61] Rahel could be amazingly catty about Amalie, lamenting that she "lacked the art of living."[62] We shall ponder the contrasting life choices these two women made as the years went by. Amalie Beer's extraordinary wealth made possible choices which the considerably poorer Rahel Levin did not enjoy. Amalie had been born as Malka Wulff, the great-granddaughter of Esther Liebmann, the premier Court Jewish woman of early eighteenth-century Berlin. Amalie's father had been one of the wealthiest men in Berlin, and her husband Jacob Hertz Beer eventually became the single richest man in all Berlin. They married in 1788, when they were both in their late teens. Their four sons, three of whom were fabulously talented, would make their doting parents very proud indeed.

Their eldest, called Meyer when he was a boy, would eventually become the famous opera composer Giacomo Meyerbeer. In 1801, when Meyer was just ten, he gave his first public concert in Berlin. Reports are that "all of musical Berlin" came to hear him, and the reviews were enthusiastic.[63] Soon after the concert, Amalie commissioned Georg Weitsch to paint her son's image in oil. His parents were so proud of their first-born "Jewish Mozart" that they used their various connections in high places to have the Weitsch portrait hung on the walls of the Academy of Art.[64] But not everyone was happy with the image of a Jewish *Wunderkind* up on the wall in public for all to admire. Indeed the Beers' expensive display of their family's high culture backfired, and very soon indeed at that, in a most humiliating fashion. Karl Wilhelm Grattenauer, a prominent Berlin lawyer, made a public complaint, and the Beers retrieved the portrait. From then on it hung on the walls of their large and well-situated home on the Spandauerstrasse, near to the Itzig and Ephraim mansions. But it was not the Academy of Art.

In the coming years Grattenauer would publish a series of unpleasant pamphlets. He took special aim at the young women of Amalie's generation, complaining in print that they "read many books, speak many languages, play many instruments, sketch in a variety of styles, paint in all colors, dance in all fashions, embroider in all patterns, and they possess every single item, that could give them a claim to charm."[65] But for Grattenauer they had no charm at all, for Jews could never cover over their "alien essence." Grattenauer was one of the first to publicly criticize the assimilated Jews who were trying so hard to be less Jewish. As the nineteenth century progressed, critiques of assimilated Jews precisely because they were assimilated would grow more frequent and more intense. This was new, because Jews had long been told to become Christians. Now the visibility and prominence of those converting stimulated those who did not like Jews to focus on new reasons for their animosity. If they had discarded traditional habits and even their formal Jewish identity, the problem became their "alien essence" and their cultural style, rather than their religion. If they read his insulting words or imagined their Christian friends reading his pamphlets, Rahel Levin and Amalie Beer must have felt humiliated indeed. But the subculture Grattenauer was mocking continued to flourish, because more and more drawing rooms, clubs, promenades, and spa hotels provided social spaces where converts, sympathetic Christians, and Jews contemplating baptism could socialize. Indeed it was at a home with such an eclectic mix of guests where Rahel Levin and Karl Varnhagen met for the first time in the spring of 1803. Rahel was then 31, living with her mother in the family home on the Jägerstrasse. After she ended the relationship with Finckenstein in 1795, she had moved to Paris for a few months, where she recovered her spirits. Upon her return to Berlin she enjoyed an affair with a nobleman, the Spanish diplomat Don Raphael d'Urquijo. But that alliance came to a rather quick end, because she realized that he was altogether too volatile and jealous of her social life.[66]

One day during the spring of 1803, she was visiting her childhood friend Philippine Cohen, and was introduced to the Cohen children's tutor, Karl August Varnhagen. Philippine, who was born Pessel Bernhard, was then 27, and had been married for nine years. She had grown up close to the Mendelssohns, because it was her father who had hired Moses as a bookkeeper and eventually the director of his silk firm. Philippine's mother, a widow in 1803, was one of the daughters of Moses Isaac-Fliess who had remained Jewish.[67] Philippine's sister Hitzel had first married a Jewish physician, but they had divorced. Then she changed her name to Wilhelmina, converted, and married a nobleman.[68] As for Philippine, she had married Ephraim Cohen, a Jewish son of a wealthy banking family in Amsterdam, who belonged to the Society of Friends. Because he was one of the first entrepreneurs of his day to use the new English spinning machines in his wool factory in Berlin, he was sometimes called the English Cohen. Four years before, in 1799, Ephraim and Philippine had baptized their infant daughter Sophie, and a year later, in 1800, Philippine and Ephraim, who now called himself Ernst, converted together. Their decision

3.1. Rahel Levin. Artist unknown. Courtesy of the Leo Baeck Institute, New York.

to change their daughter's religion was very much part of a wider trend, for the proportion of converts in Berlin who were five years of age or under was remarkably high for most of the nineteenth century. We know already that 60 percent of all converts in the years between 1800 and 1874 were children under five, and that the years when Philippine and Ephraim took little Sophie to the altar was a decade when infant conversions were at their highest point of the century. Almost 90 percent of the baptisms in this decade were children.

When they met that day in the Cohen drawing room, Karl was more impressed with Rahel than she was with him. That was not really surprising, since she was quite a celebrity around Berlin, while he was a wide-eyed young man of 18 who had come to Berlin to study at the army medical school. His life had not been easy thus far. His father was a physician, and a passionate enthusiast for the French Revolution, who had died some four years before. After Karl spent a few unhappy months living at the army school, one of his professors found him a position as a tutor at the Cohens. Now he could live in more elegant surroundings as he continued his studies.

Even if Rahel had not visited her friend Philippine that day, Karl and Rahel might well have met through her brother Lipmann, who had returned to Berlin from Hamburg three years before. Lipmann Levin was then 25, and by this time he had begun calling himself Ludwig Robert, using Robert as a family name. Like so many of his Jewish friends, he had been trained to enter finance, but he despised the work and the ambience, convinced that no serious intellectual could earn his keep in commerce. Already Mendelssohn's path of clerk by day, intellectual in the spare hours, was becoming problematic for younger Jewish men. When Ludwig Robert returned to Berlin in 1800, he managed to stay out of commerce by drawing on his family inheritance, so that he could spend his days writing plays.[69] Ludwig and Karl were both members of a writers' club they called the Nordstar Bund, the North Star Club, a fascinating circle which included the same eclectic mix of converted and unconverted Jews, nobles, and Christian commoners who frequented the salons. Two of the noble members were Adelbert von Chamisso, an emigré French writer, and Friedrich de la Motte Fouqué. David Koreff, who was beloved in this network, was 21, still Jewish, a medical student, also a poet, composer of operas, and enthusiast for various exotic medical treatments.[70] The leading figure in the North Star Club, also of Jewish descent, was Julius Eduard Hitzig, who was born as Isaac Itzig. He had converted alongside his father Elias and his mother Mirjam in 1799, right after the death of his grandfather Daniel Itzig. At the time of his baptism Isaac Itzig became Julius Eduard Hitzig, and thus he could become a judicial official in Warsaw, then under Prussian control. When we meet him in 1803 in the North Star Club, Julius was 23, back in his hometown Berlin, active as a publisher and a bookseller.[71]

While Karl was living with the Cohens, the family entertained a most interesting cast of characters, who spent their time together in conversations, writing up literary vignettes, sketching, and cutting profiles of each other out of black paper. Varnhagen's best friend at the time was Wilhelm Neumann, an adopted son in the Cohen family, a clerk in their business office, and another member of the North Star Club. Besides Karl and Wilhelm's literary friends, Philippine's sister Wilhelmine and her mother, Fanny Bernhard, visited frequently too. Another regular visitor to the Cohen household was a singer named Frau Seiler, who was enjoying a flirtation with Herr Cohen, according

3.2. Karl August Varnhagen von Ense. Sketch by Wilhelm Hensel. Courtesy of the Leo Baeck Institute, New York.

to Varnhagen's chatty memoirs published much later.[72] That a family such as the Cohens would hire a young man such as Karl as the tutor for their baptized children was a sign of the changing times. They deliberately chose a Christian tutor, and had the connections to find one. He very much appreciated the sophisticated ambience of the Cohen household, but unfortunately his idyllic life as a tutor was cut short just a year later. In 1804, Herr Cohen was forced to declare bankruptcy, and he fled in disgrace back to Holland, leaving his wife and children in Berlin without resources. Philippine could not even pay the legal costs necessary to try to make claims for restitution, and as for Karl, he was obviously in need of another post.[73]

Hermann Eberty, a friend from his club and a descendant of the Ephraim family, came to his aid, and found Karl a new tutoring post at the home of Fanny Hertz in Hamburg.[74] Again, Karl was the Christian presence in a Jewish family that was drifting away from traditional Judaism. Fanny was then 27, and had been married to Jacob Hertz, an older wealthy merchant, for six years. Fanny and Karl fell in love — not a great surprise, since tutors in those years often fell in love with their students' mothers. What was somewhat more unusual, since Fanny was still Jewish and her husband still alive, was that the Hertz family decided to fund Karl's education. Karl revealed in his memoir that Jacob's teenage son from his previous marriage wanted Karl to marry Fanny after his father had died and Karl had become a physician. This episode shows that a struggling lad such as Karl could make his way in the world with the help of wealthy Jewish families who planned the baptism of their own still-Jewish relatives.

In Hamburg during these years, Karl continued to become involved with Jewish friends who were contemplating baptism. In his memoirs he returns again and again to occasions when he tried to mediate in the small crises of everyday life that occur when people from different backgrounds share their lives. Take, for instance, the time when Karl's friend Wilhelm Neumann moved to Hamburg to study with Karl, and arranged to live at Fanny Hertz's home. Shortly before his arrival, friends in Berlin wrote to Fanny about Wilhelm's role in an episode a few years earlier when he had participated in some hostile "mischief" directed against one of his Jewish acquaintances.[75] Fanny was outraged, and reacted by refusing to allow Wilhelm to live in her household. He was allowed only to visit Karl in his room. Karl took a balanced tone in his memoirs. As he remembered the incident years later, he had forgiven Wilhelm for the mistake, but thought Fanny's anger and her punishment of his friend to have been altogether justified.

Another incident occurred in the summer of 1805, just when Karl had decided to leave his tutor post in the Hertz household. His plan was to study full time at a prestigious secondary school in Hamburg and then attend university to prepare for a career in medicine. As he was departing, Karl suggested that Fanny send her young sons to a boarding school. His reasoning was that "in spite of all the care that was taken in the household, there was still too much of the *old Judaism* in it, and the children should remain free of *the old Judaism* at any price."[76] During the next few months, in the fall of 1805, Karl and Wilhelm became involved in the life of another Jewish friend, David Mendel, a fellow student at the Hamburg gymnasium. Mendel had endured a difficult life thus far. His father had been a moneylender in Göttingen, mainly loaning funds to university students. When David was still a little child, his parents had separated, and his mother had raised him alone, in poverty. Karl and Wilhelm invited him to join the North Star Club, which had managed to stay together even though many of its members no longer lived in Berlin. Mendel in turn invited his two new friends to join his local study group, called the Plato Circle.

By the early months of 1806, the three friends were ready to leave Hamburg and begin university. On their meandering route to Halle, they stayed for a time in the home of Mendel's converted uncle Johann Stieglitz in Hannover. It was then that David Mendel became a Protestant named August Neander. Here we see another case where family ties could ease decisions in favor of baptism. Stieglitz was born to influence, and he married influence as well. His father had been the Prince of Waldeck's favored financier, and his wife Sophie was a granddaughter of Veitel Heine Ephraim.[77] Six years before, in 1800, when he was 33, Stieglitz, then called Israel, had converted, and it was then that he changed his name to Johann. Two years later he was appointed the court physician to the court of Waldeck, and he settled in Hannover. Back in his student days at the University of Göttingen during the late 1780s, one of his closest friends had been Wilhelm von Humboldt.[78] Wilhelm and his brother Alexander were two of Berlin's smartest, most progressive, and most influential intellects of their time. During the early 1780s, while they were still teenagers, their tutor had taken them to Markus Herz's lectures. Wilhelm became close to Henriette Herz, and he and his wife Caroline were participants in Dorothea Veit's intimate friendship club called the Tugendbund, the League of Virtue. Because both of the Humboldt brothers became so powerful, their relationship with their Jewish friends is important.

Mendel's new family name, Neander, was a German translation from the Greek for "new Man," perhaps a play on his friend Wilhelm's family name of Neumann. He may well have taken his new first name, August, from his friend Karl's middle name. Before beginning his studies at Halle, the newly Christian nephew moved in with his Uncle Stieglitz in Hannover. Later that spring, Karl and Wilhelm, who were already living in Halle, returned to Hannover for a visit. Karl later remembered how unhappy August became when his father, the moneylender from Göttingen, came for a visit at the Stieglitz home. The new man August, previously David, confessed to Karl how "embarrassed" he was that his father could not "command respect." August had received support and encouragement from his uncle, but still felt ashamed of his father, who remained all-too-Jewish. A few months later, once the three friends were all living together at the university, Karl became impatient with August, whom he found to be too "unkempt and disheveled." Just as the new Christian August was embarrassed by his own father, so too the old Christian Karl distanced himself from his once-Jewish friend, lamenting that he lacked "external cultivation." Neander found another place to live and managed to make some new friends. But obviously converts sometimes had to put up with considerable rudeness even from those who considered themselves to be their friends. One companion from those days wrote to him: "I love you, Neander, however much your looks repel me."[79]

Karl and his two friends had just begun their studies at Halle when Prussia suffered its great defeat, in October 1806. The defeat came after Prussia abandoned its alliance with France, following a decade of withdrawal from the Napoleonic wars. As the years passed, patriots outraged at Napoleon's conquests were becoming more and more angry. During 1805, Napoleon had violated Prussian territory on a number of occasions, but Prussia maintained its neutrality and did not retaliate. In December 1805, the armies of Austria and Russia, fighting together against France, suffered dramatic defeats in the Battle of Austerlitz. Pro-war sentiment was growing across Prussia, and patriots across Germany looked to Prussia, with its well-funded and trained army, to lead the struggle against Napoleon.

The chances that Prussia would turn against the French increased as sectors within the nobility became more ready to join Czar Alexander in the coalition fighting the French. The man facing this fateful decision was King Frederick William III, who had come to power in 1797. Posterity has not been kind to this Hohenzollern king. In one account he was a "devoted, hard-working, mediocre man of distinctly limited intelligence, who was destined to a long reign full of stirring events which he hardly understood."[80] King Frederick William was certainly aware of the growing passion for war among his subjects, because the leading public voice for war against Napoleon was his own wife, Queen Louise.[81] The queen had many enthusiasts for her position. Young officers in the Prussian army "sharpened their swords on the steps of the French Embassy in Berlin," showing publicly their eagerness to fight.[82] During a performance of Schiller's play *Wallenstein's Lager,* the entire audience stood up and sang "up, up comrades to horse, to horse, towards the battlefield and liberty, only on the battlefield can a man show his worth, then his heart will be put on the scales."[83] Finally, in August 1806 the ambivalent king decided to follow the advice of his wife and his advisors, and prepare his army for war. This was a painful moment for a most indecisive man. Late in September, King Frederick William sent Napoleon an ultimatum that if France did not withdraw its troops from Prussian territory by October 9, he should be ready for war with Prussia. Napoleon did not even deign to reply. When October 9 came and went without an answer from him, the king ordered his troops to march westward from their headquarters in Erfurt. Prussia stood alone, because Austria and Russia had both left the fray to recover from their defeat at Austerlitz the year before.

Nevertheless, Prussians had good reason to be confident. This, after all, was the army whose victories had made Prussia into a powerful state during the previous century. No one expected defeat. Yet Prussian soldiers were utterly vanquished on October 10, at the very first battle, at Saalfeld. The king's cousin Prince Louis Ferdinand died in that battle. Louis Ferdinand had been quite a legend in his own time, handsome and debonair, a talented pianist and composer. He had become a passionate patriot, working closely with Queen Louise to arouse patriotism among the jaded nobles of Berlin. Many mourned his death, including Rahel and several of her friends. For Louis Ferdinand had been a close personal friend of Rahel Levin's, and often played the piano at her salon. The prince was also the lover of Rahel's good friend, Pauline Wiesel, a well-known beauty with a rich and varied erotic life.[84]

On October 14, four days after its collapse at Saalfeld, the Prussian army was defeated twice more, at Jena and at Auerstädt. Now the pattern was set, and fortress after fortress fell to Napoleon's soldiers. But such was the faith in the Prussian army that many in high positions still hoped that somehow the trend would be reversed. For instance, on the night of October 17, a "large society" gathered at the home of Christian Wilhelm Hufeland, physician to the king. Hufeland invited his friends for a celebration, because he was so sure that a military victory that day would require a party. But instead of the anticipated good news, Hufeland's guests, including Johann Fichte, were together to commiserate when they were told about another "frightful defeat."[85]

Napoleon himself marched into Berlin ten days later, on October 27. Berliners found it difficult to believe that their soldiers, with their "neat pigtails, white gaiters, and spotless uniforms," had been defeated on the field by these "slovenly and youthful warriors" with their messy hair.[86] In one month, the army of the French Revolution had destroyed the Prussian war machine. The French captured 120,000 Prussian soldiers who became prisoners of war, and confiscated weaponry and supplies. Only one unit was able to flee to East Prussia, safe from French control. The trauma was immense, as illustrated by an episode in the life of Friedrich Ludwig Jahn, soon to become the fiery organizer of the patriotic gymnastics movement. Jahn, who was then 28, later remembered that his hair had turned gray "in a single day" after the battle of Jena.[87]

Soon after his triumphant entrance into Berlin, Napoleon left town to display his new booty at the Hohenzollern palace in Potsdam. The royal family had already departed in haste for points east, so as to avoid capture. While in Potsdam, Napoleon stood in front of Frederick the Great's tomb and told his soldiers: "Gentlemen, if this man were still alive I would not be here."[88] Frederick's tomb was symbolic territory. Back in 1805 Queen Louise, her husband the king, and Czar Alexander had met there to pledge their commitment to the defense of Prussia. An engraving of the three, showing Louise ardently gazing at Alexander, sold briskly at shops in Berlin.[89] The engraving fueled rumors which had been circulating for some time, that the immensely popular queen was in love with Czar Alexander.

Now it was a year later, and the long-avoided war was the new reality. In the fall of 1806, as the queen and her children were in carriages fleeing occupied Berlin, the state of Prussia was hanging by a thread. The old regime had come to an end, and the future was very much up in the air. Napoleon had not yet decided the fate of the once proud state. Jewish life in Prussia too was at a standstill. Discontent at tradition was mounting, yet few had a clear vision of a third way between baptism and tradition.

Under French Rule, 1807–1810

Prussians suffered many privations during that first winter of occupation. French soldiers were housed with local families, firewood became scarce, and many were close to famine. At the University of Halle, Schleiermacher preached rousing sermons in the chapel. That fall of 1806, he was 38, and he had just been appointed professor of theology, a significant promotion after years as a preacher.[90] In his lectures, Schleiermacher pleaded with the students to become active in nationalist projects which would prepare Prussia for eventual military victory over the French. The students at Halle were obviously sympathetic to Schleiermacher's politics, as seen from an incident when Napoleon himself visited the university during the winter of 1807. He was hissed at by the students, who yelled out cries of praise for their own king. French soldiers tried to drown out the patriotic students out with shouts of "Vive l'Empereur," but the students were louder. After this episode, Napoleon ordered the closure of the university.

At various points during the fall of 1806, Schleiermacher, Varnhagen, and Wilhelm Neumann all left Halle, and eventually all three made their way back to Berlin. For all of them, Berlin was a familiar setting, but the historic moment was exceedingly difficult. Many public figures and other persons of means had already left town. The social world of the old regime salons, where thoughtful, clever people talked about books and poetry and plays and each other's private dramas, had passed into history. Karl returned to the study of medicine, funded generously by the Hertz family in Hamburg. The winter of 1807 was a productive time for him, in work and in friendship. He was not planning personal resistance to the French, for at this juncture he was enthusiastic about Napoleon's victories in Prussia, viewing them as "a blow for freedom," a "strike at the heart" of one of "the most autocratic states in Europe."[91] Varnhagen was by no means alone in this line of thinking. Johann von Goethe and Georg Wilhelm Hegel too were initially enthusiastic about how French rule might improve German society.

When Schleiermacher returned to Berlin he became a pastor at the Trinity Church, a stroke of luck for patriots, because with the press censored and French officers keeping a close watch on potential resistance, the pulpit was a rare space for political speeches. No preacher had ever delivered such passionately political sermons as Schleiermacher gave that fall.[92] He played an important role in convincing the hedonistic romantic intellectuals that religion mattered, and he was largely responsible for the Christian strand in nationalist thinking and practices.[93] He also brought Lutheran ministers into politics by convincing them that the nation mattered. For the fate of Prussia, Schleiermacher's integration of religion and politics proved to be a crucial synthesis. Unfortunately for the Jews, the Protestant values of the nationalist movement would make their integration into German life altogether problematic.

Meanwhile, Napoleon and his intimate circle of soldiers were taking control of their newly conquered state, enjoying the luxuries of life in the various palaces evacuated by the royal family. Rumor had it that Napoleon enjoyed rifling through Queen Louise's perfumed letters in search of patriotic missives to Czar Alexander, and that his scruffy soldiers were dirtying the palace floors with their muddy boots. Late in November, King Frederick William and Queen Louise and their children were reunited in Königsberg. A large crowd gathered to celebrate as Louise climbed the steps of the castle. Heinrich von Kleist, a patriotic young writer whom Louise had provided with a pension, was among those waiting to greet her there. In his words, the queen was one of the few who had "grasped all the implications of this hour . . . it is she who holds us all together."[94] Although Prussia continued to lose on the battlefields, the king decided to reject yet another humiliating treaty with France.

Just after Christmas, in the first weeks of 1807, the royal family had to move further east, to the town of Memel, fleeing the advancing French troops. But by March Königsberg was safe again, and Louise and the children traveled over muddy roads on their journey back to the castle. And it was here, in the royal palace in Königsberg, that the royal family would remain until they were permitted to return to Berlin two years hence, in 1809. A peace agreement between Prussia and Napoleon was finally signed in July 1807, with harsh terms handed out to the Prussians. The only consolation was that the Hohenzollerns were not obliterated as a dynasty altogether. Half of Prussia's territories were occupied by French troops, and the state treasury needed to come up with 160 million francs as a forced contribution to the French military campaign. We should not be surprised to learn that at this difficult moment the leading Jewish bankers of Berlin rescued the government from its acute crisis. Amalie Beer's husband Jacob was one of the most helpful. Governments on all sides of the conflict needed large amounts of credit quickly. For financiers prepared to take large risks, the profits could be considerable. As for the state, it had few places to turn in its hour of need. Noble landowners did not necessarily enjoy access to liquid capital, and established Christian merchants preferred to hide their gold and valuables or move them to safe places, rather than make risky loans in wartime.[95] We who have followed the history of Berlin's Jewish financiers in minting and distributing coins should not be surprised to see their descendants responding to the financial crisis of 1807 with generosity. The Rothschild family, based in Frankfurt, was the most notorious Jewish clan to finance various armies and states during the Napoleonic wars.

Even when financiers such as Jacob Herz Beer were only aiding their own state and not offering their largesse to the French, ordinary Prussians who suffered from the occupation resented that anyone became rich while they were enduring hardships. Those such as the highly visible Rothschilds who did make loans to the French made it look as if all Jewish financiers were simply self-interested. As for the Prussian nobles whose wealth was in land, they too were bound to resent the Jewish bankers. Their economy was in crisis. Grain prices fell dramatically once Prussia was truly at war, because one of Napoleon's central means of economic warfare was the Continental Blockade, designed to stop all trade between Britain and continental Europe. So now the English, the major purchaser of rye and barley, could no longer import Prussian grain.

During the two years that Queen Louise and her entourage lived in exile in Königsberg, she hosted a salon. To be a *salonière* had been her goal for some time, but she could never have managed such a private style of being public amidst the rigid pomp of her former life in Berlin. It is a remarkable testimony to the prestige of the Jewish salons that the queen's ardent desire was to host her own salon. The woman at the absolute summit of the social hierarchy was imitating an institution which was dominated in the Berlin setting by women who were very *déclassé* indeed. Queen Louise's Königsberg salons were modest and patriotic. She served only tea, and while they chatted, her guests scraped lint from pieces of cloth, which would be used to dress the wounds of injured Prussian soldiers in a local hospital.[96] The guests included Heinrich von Kleist and another romantic writer living in Königsberg, Achim von Arnim. Arnim and his close friend Clemens Brentano were devoted to various folkloric projects, including a collection of old folksongs, so as to recover the vanishing oral traditions of the common people.

But more and more, the royal couple, like many other exiled Prussian nobles, turned away from fashionable romantic literary passions and began to cultivate their inner spiritual lives. They joined wholeheartedly in the Great Awakening, a revival movement whose participants were called the "perfumed pietists." The queen prayed regularly at Parson Ernst Ludwig Borowski's Moravian church, alongside her friend the Baroness von Krüdener. This high-born lady had experienced a religious rebirth a few years before, when she was living in Berlin and having difficulties in her love life. Imagine how novel it was when her cobbler introduced her to mystical practices. The baroness's daughter Juliette lived with her in Königsberg in these years, serving the poor and the suffering. During that dramatic summer of 1807, the two noble ladies spent their days at a local hospital, singing to wounded Prussian soldiers in Russian, German, and French.[97] Enthusiasts for the Great Awakening organized many projects in these years, spiritual and practical, which brought rich and poor Prussians together, a rare experience in the normally rigid social hierarchy. Young officers in the Prussian army were particularly active among the perfumed pietists.[98] The privations of occupation stimulated another noble, Baron Hans Ernst von Kottwitz, to found a "spinning institute" in the Alexanderstrasse for the growing number of unemployed in Berlin. A year later, the French commandant gave the baron permission to use an empty barracks as a workhouse, with space allocated for families needing shelter. Even the king was moved to donate funds to Baron Kottwitz's projects. Like the pietist missionaries we met in the early eighteenth century, he aimed to initiate projects that would help the poor and underemployed become productive.[99]

One of the patriotic intellectuals who had fled east to Königsberg in the traumatic winter of 1806–07 was Dorothea and Friedrich's friend Johann Fichte. After a semester teaching at the University of Königsberg, however, late in that summer of 1807 he returned to Berlin to join his wife and son. He was then 45, at the peak of his life. Once he was established in Berlin again, state officials asked him to coordinate the planning for the new university envisioned for the city. With this larger project in mind he announced a lecture series dedicated to the theme of culture and politics. The number of subscribers to the lecture series grew too large for the event to take place in his home, so his powerful friends in government helped him arrange to speak at the Academy of Science. Fichte called the series "The Addresses to the German Nation," and eventually these talks would become his best-known and most controversial work. The setting was charged. Although Berlin was still occupied by French soldiers, Fichte did not censor his words. After each lecture he returned home fearing that French officials would haul him from his house and shoot him.[100] But they did not forbid the lectures or imprison or shoot the speaker, and within a year the French government censor even gave permis-

sion for Fichte to publish the text.[101] Fichte's lectures show another way for
German intellectuals to become nationalists. Alongside the religious values
and symbols which Schleiermacher brought to the nationalist movement,
Fichte brought his ardent enthusiasm for the radical Jacobin revolutionaries in
Paris. After the occupation began in the fall of 1806, he became a German
nationalist, but in doing so he refused to abandon his left politics. So by 1807,
Schleiermacher and Fichte and their friends were creating a complex and
timely nationalism that could attract followers from diverse standpoints.

In his lectures, Fichte criticized the selfishness of the educated classes, calling
upon them to identify with the common people.[102] He argued that education
should help individuals find a way to serve those less fortunate and help the
people organize as a nation state. Fichte was convinced of the superiority of
the German people and the German language, views which earned him the
reputation as a founder of modern German nationalism.[103] Over time the
texture and subtlety of the Fichtean message has been lost, and only the most
vulgar version of his nationalism has survived. But Fichte was in truth a complex thinker, and many streams of thought met in his work.[104]

One of Fichte's most ardent listeners on those Sundays in the round auditorium of the Academy was Rahel Levin, who attended alongside her brother
Ludwig. These were painful years for her, because the days of her vibrant salon
life during the nineties and the first years of the new century were over and
gone. Many of her friends had left Berlin, and she was lonely. Fichte's lectures
were a happy exception, and later she praised his contribution, referring to the
lectures as "Fichte's hour, my sole comfort, my hope, my riches."[105] Her attraction to Fichte's message is both thoroughly understandable and deeply
disturbing. Like him, she was an enthusiast for the French Revolution. She too
was a pantheist, critical of organized religion, and socially progressive. Precisely because they agreed about so much, Fichte's patriotic message in his
1807 lectures had a big effect on Levin.

Fichte helped make Levin a Prussian nationalist. But what about his views
about Jews? Unfortunately, we do not know precisely which of his publications Rahel might have actually read. In 1793, Fichte had argued in print
against giving civil rights to Jews. His language still shocks today. He wrote:
"as to giving them civil rights, I see no way other than that of some night
cutting off all their heads, and attaching in their stead others in which there is
not a single Jewish idea."[106] From her letters, we know that although she often
complained about how she was treated as a Jew, Rahel rarely, if ever, expressed herself *as a Jew* when Jews were disparaged. Everything we know
about her life suggests that she might well have made her peace with Fichte's
harsh words. In 1807 she had not yet been baptized, but she had been ready to

do so for at least a decade. As a Jew who had eliminated Judaism from her life, she could easily imagine herself as a Fichtean sort of citizen. In this sense she and Fichte were both anti-Judaism, and Jews who were no longer Jewish could build a new secular society.

During the same season that Rahel and Ludwig were such rapt listeners at the Fichte lectures, she ran into Karl Varnhagen on the street one day. It had been five years since they had been introduced at Philippine Cohen's home. Since that time he had been to Hamburg and to Halle, and was now studying medicine. She, who was now 37, had very often been lonely during the two years since Napoleon marched into Berlin. In a January 1808 letter to Gustav von Brinkmann she complained that "at my 'tea table,' as you call it, I sit alone with my dictionaries."[107] She was, however, making some new friends now. One of her new intimates during these troubled years was Rebecca Fried-länder, an Itzig granddaughter, recently divorced from David Friedländer's son Moses. Rahel became something of a mother figure to Rebecca, and confided her anguish and loneliness to her younger friend.[108]

That summer of 1808 Rahel, who had always loved gardens, rented a house in Charlottenburg, then a small rural village. She and Karl spent their days together sharing their life stories. He was much impressed by her connections to so many influential contemporary personalities, and would return to his room each evening to peruse her precious boxes of letters. They fell in love and became a couple. But they could not marry until Karl had a career and an income. Then there was the problem of his continuing relationship with Fanny Hertz, whose family was still supporting his medical studies. A year hence, in 1809, Karl departed from Berlin to study medicine at the University of Tü-bingen, leaving Rahel behind to suffer a difficult winter. She nearly died of a lung infection and was all the more isolated because of disturbing quarrels with her mother. In the summer of 1808 Chaie had surprised Rahel by moving out of the family home on the Jägerstrasse, and after her time in Charlotten-burg, Rahel was forced to move to more modest housing in town. As for Karl, he became rather bored with his studies, finding the town of Tübingen too sleepy for his taste. Moreover he was turning against Napoleon, and he now wanted to join the fight to oust the French from German soil. In June 1809 he volunteered to fight in the Austrian army. After two years of neutrality, Austria had joined Prussia and Russia in the coalition fighting the French.

During these years of the French occupation, not only had many of the city's leading personalities left Berlin, but values were changing rapidly. Patriots, male and female alike, were rejecting intellectual women and the romantic, erotic freedoms which had previously been enjoyed by salon participants. Male intellectuals did not suffer greatly from the absence of salons, since as time passed Berlin became home to a world-class university, and to more and more newspapers, coffeehouses, political parties, and professional associations. But most of these institutions were closed to women. The predominance of Jewish women among the *salonières* was also increasingly controversial.[109] Salons, some of them sponsored by Jewish women, would return to Berlin after the Napoleonic wars came to an end in 1815. But the Jewish dominance seen during the old regime, in the quarter century before October 1806, would never appear again, and brainy outspoken women of all backgrounds would find it ever more difficult as the nineteenth century went forward to find their place in the public world.

Male intellectuals, on the other hand, gained a prestigious and innovative institution when the University of Berlin opened its doors in the fall of 1810. Because of its many clubs, lectures, academies, and productive intellects, Berlin was chosen as the locale for the new university. As we have seen, Napoleon had closed the University of Halle in 1807. But more was involved in the decision to found a new university in Berlin then than the practical need to educate a new generation, crucial as that was. The extreme political crisis had created an amazing opportunity for reform. The French army was occupying half of Prussia, and the rump state was financially stretched, its meager resources continually depleted by French demands for booty and monies. State officials saw the logic in creating more open institutions, so that Prussians would be motivated to defend a state which was improving their lives. Creating the university had become a passion even for the king, who saw in the endeavor a chance for Prussia to "replace by intellectual power what it has lost physically."[110] All in all the situation was looking up in 1810. In late December 1809, just days before Christmas, the royal family was allowed to return to their castle in Berlin. An ardent patriot, Ernst Moritz Arndt, himself under strict watch by the French, reported how Berliners "shouted and cried" as the couple entered their palace on Unter den Linden, how Queen Louise's eyes were red from weeping as she greeted the throngs of happy Berliners.[111] Alas, the joy of many at seeing Queen Louise turned out to be all too brief, for she died suddenly in July 1810.

Johann Fichte, Friedrich Schleiermacher, and Wilhelm von Humboldt were asked by the king to plan the new university, and their pedagogical vision was innovative. Their dream was to create an institution based on the ethos of the *Bildungsbürgertum*, which we might call the cultivated class.[112] Whereas universities in Germany had hitherto trained clergy, jurists, and officials, here research was to become a goal in itself. Their plan was straight out of Fichte's 1807 lectures. At the university, the academic elite would absorb talent from the lower classes, and the students would go on to challenge the entrenched power of the nobility after completing their studies. But while the vision may have been radical, the institutional setting was modest when the university offered its first classes in 1810, with only 12 professors teaching 250 students.[113] From the very beginning, Jewish students flocked to the new university. Already in its opening year 7 percent of the student body was Jewish, and over the years this proportion would grow considerably.[114]

In 1810 and 1811 Rahel and Karl were each experiencing their own difficulties. Rahel, still in Berlin, was testy and jealous of the life she thought Karl was living. Karl was no longer a soldier in the Austrian army, but serving as the personal assistant to Count Bentheim, his commander from his army days. Bentheim kept Karl busy looking after his problematic finances, and Karl also took on behind-the-scenes diplomatic missions and produced a stream of publications analyzing the latest military developments. As Rahel continued to complain in letters that Karl was enjoying receptions and elegant parties, Karl was losing patience with her demanding tone. Her income on her inheritance had been severely reduced because of family business troubles. At this point, with 800 thalers a year to live on, she was hardly poor; this sum was equal to the yearly income that supported the entire family of a modestly paid professor or civil servant. But she had been far richer when she was younger, and certainly felt poor and adrift in these years.

Karl often felt he had to explain to Rahel that he too was having a rough time. In November 1810 he wrote her that "on the surface it looked as if I was leading a life of ease and luxury." He admitted in the letter that he sometimes traveled in fine coaches, that he did own a few good sets of clothes, although it was probable that the count had never paid the bill for them, and that he sometimes ate at the best tables. But appearances were definitely deceiving, for the truth was that he was "barely able to pay his lad, whom he didn't want to starve, and he could rarely afford light and paper for writing a few letters." He ate with the count only once a day. Otherwise he survived on "bread and beer; he had been able to pay his tailor only recently, although the bill from the previous year was still due."[115]

At this very low moment in their lives, Rahel was almost 40, still single, and socially isolated, and Karl still had no secure income to support a marriage. The best years of the old regime lifestyle were over and past, and Napoleon was firmly entrenched in his rule over central Europe. For better or worse, his successes in dominating German cities and states had turned many against the cosmopolitan values so popular among the eighteenth-century intelligentsia. Now, most Germans who had cheered on the Paris Revolution of 1789 had come to hate the French. Here we see the first emergence of the fatal split between liberalism and nationalism in Germany. France was liberal, Germany was national. This polarity would only become deeper, more bitter, and politically more problematic as time went on. Yet in spite of the smoldering discontent, in 1811 there was certainly no mass movement inside of Prussia opposing the occupation. As for the Jews, they too found themselves at a turning point, with no easy solutions in sight. The token visits to the Jewish salons were no longer fashionable. But reformers within Judaism remained without influence. It was a difficult time to be either a proud Jew or a proud German, and no one knew if Prussia would ever be whole and free again.

4

Emancipation and War, 1811–1813

Itzig's Duel for Jewish Honor, 1811

Rahel and Karl found reasons for hope in June 1811, when they enjoyed a reunion at Bad Teplitz, a spa town in Bohemia, their first time together since Karl had left Berlin two years before. The spa resorts were attractive spaces for a mixed couple such as Karl and Rahel, because social boundaries were more relaxed there than in town. Nothing was going well for Rahel at home. Her mother had died, but she gained no financial autonomy, for her brothers now administered her inheritance, and she chafed at the limits they placed on her yearly allowance. They defended the belt tightening, since the family business was hurting, due to the economic dislocations of the occupation. Rebecca Friedländer, younger sister of Marianne Saaling and recently divorced from David Friedländer's son Moses, was one of her most important friends in these years. Rebecca, also adrift between Jewish and noble society, was trying to publish her novels, with limited critical success. Now, in 1811, she converted and changed her name to Regina Frohberg. The two friends spent their evenings in a circle of French noblemen sent to Berlin to administer the occupation. Rahel grew angry when she became convinced that an unflattering picture of herself appeared in one of Rebecca's novels. Ultimately she would drift away from Rebecca, to whom she felt more than a little superior.[1]

Rahel and Karl had now been a couple for three years, and they were still waiting for him to earn an income suitable for them to marry. Unlike some of her richer women friends, Rahel did not have sufficient family money on her side. By now Karl had abandoned his career in medicine, and it was not clear how he would earn enough to support them. He was, however, constantly busy and peripatetic, working for Count Bentheim to extract lands, castles, and cash allowances from his relatives. All the while Karl was writing industriously and doing his best to meet the powerful, who could help him find a position in the Prussian diplomatic service.

These were dramatic years not just for Karl and Rahel but for German history as well. The War of Liberation which freed Prussia from French domination has long been celebrated in Germany and beyond. But amidst the glories of a successful national uprising of sorts, we note some decidedly troubling developments. We have seen how diverse the strands of belief and practice were that became integrated into nationalism. Folklorist populists, atheistic republicans, and aristocratic landowners could all espouse the same cause, at least during the War of Liberation. But however much these nationalists disagreed about God and the French Revolution, they did seem to agree to exclude Jews from their imagined national community. In this chapter we explore why it became so difficult to integrate Jewish civic emancipation into contemporary nationalist politics. Women too found their roles very much altered, now that the nation needed their services as nurses, wives, and mothers. Ironic distance, witty repartee, and avant-garde opinions were now seen as too French, too feminine, and too Jewish. The values that were now explicit in pamphlets and policies were not entirely new, and sometimes had already surfaced among those who knew the salon personalities well, but despised their values. Thus to understand the nationalist hostility to Jews we need to examine how distaste and discrimination emerged among Christians who were friendly with Jews and former Jews. Exclusion was a devastating reaction to a very unusual integration of a handful of personalities into the summit of Prussian society.

We can see how rapidly values were shifting by following the lives of Rahel and Karl's friend Clemens Brentano and his closest friend, Achim von Arnim. By the time that Rahel came to Bad Teplitz that June of 1811, Clemens was already there, spending an extended visit with Karl. Clemens was a romantic poet and playwright, then 33, a widower responsible for raising his young children. He had recently moved to Berlin to live in the home of Arnim, the poet and folklorist. We last met Arnim back in 1807, during his stay in Königsberg in the entourage of the exiled royal family. During 1811 Clemens and Achim had also become brothers-in-law, when Achim married Clemens's sister Bettina. Clemens, Bettina, and Achim were all superbly well connected in Berlin. A third Brentano sibling, Gunda, was married to Friedrich von Savigny, one of the leading professors of law at the new University of Berlin. The Clemens and Bettina were a fascinating pair of siblings, whose ambivalence toward their Jewish friends is important for our story. They had grown up in a large and socially prominent family in Frankfurt. Their grandmother Sophie von la Roche had been an accomplished novelist, and their father was a wealthy merchant.[2] Ever since she was a young girl, Bettina had been sympathetic to Jews, and once she had even studied Hebrew.[3] Clemens too often had Jews and Judaism on his mind, but his ambivalence tilted toward the negative.[4] Clemens and Achim shared literary and political passions and projects. They were the editors of a popular anthology of German folk songs called *Des Knaben Wunderhorn* ("The Boy's Magic Horn"), a volume dedicated to Goethe, who loved the book and recommended that every German household buy a copy.[5] The collection was a milestone in the emergence of a German cultural identity. Later observers would declare Arnim the "prophet of Prussia's national rise" and credit *Des Knaben Wunderhorn* with sparking the nationalist movement in Berlin.[6]

On January 18, 1811, Arnim called to order the first meeting of the Christlich-Deutsche Tischgesellschaft, the Christian-German Eating Club. The date was chosen because it was the 110th anniversary of the crowning of Frederick I as the first king of Prussia.[7] The Tischgesellschaft members, a group of leisured gentlemen, met every other Tuesday for lunch at a Berlin restaurant. Half of the 46 men invited to join the club were nobles, and even those who were not noble were well placed in establishment Berlin society. Clemens Brentano, Friedrich Schleiermacher, Johann Fichte, Bettina's brother-in-law Friedrich von Savigny, and Rahel's Karl were among the founding members.

That men of the left such as Schleiermacher, Varnhagen, and Fichte would affiliate with conservatives such as Arnim and Savigny shows how eclectic the nationalist spirit was in 1811.[8] The founders saw their new club as a repudiation of the salons, the symbol and the actual space of Jewish and female emancipation, even though the heyday of the salons was actually in the past. Fichte devoted one of his lectures at the Tischgesellschaft to explaining the importance of "the almost unlimited subjugation of the wife to the will of the husband."[9] The nationalism of Arnim and his friends found much resonance among a broad spectrum of the intelligentsia. But their hostility to Jewish emancipation was not received well by all the prominent figures in the Berlin of 1811, and some were shocked when they heard the gossip about what was being said at Tischgesellschaft sessions. Wilhelm von Humboldt, for instance, kept his distance from Arnim's circle. When Humboldt's future son-in-law

August von Hedemann joined the new club, Humboldt was distressed, although his wife Caroline was rather more enthusiastic. Karl Varnhagen recalled in his memoirs that when he spent time with Wilhelm and Caroline, the two men would spar with her about the new fashion for "Fatherland, Christianity, and Womanhood."[10] Karl was clearly conflicted about the politics of the new club, for he soon resigned his affiliation.

At each meeting of the Tischgesellschaft, one member delivered a presentation on a contemporary event. The members were very explicit that neither those they called philistines, women, Jews, nor even those whose families had been Jewish three generations ago could join. By *philistines* they meant crass materialistic persons lacking cultivated tastes. As for their Jewish clause, it was in some ways strange that Achim and Clemens and their friends worried about keeping out Christians whose Jewish ancestors were two or even three generations back.[11] For in strictly religious terms, the child of a baptized Jew was a "regular" Christian, not a convert. But their concern was obviously ambiguous ethnic identities, not religious categories. This astonishing rule reveals much about their fears. Surely they knew that because conversion had been fairly rare in the middle of the previous century, there were few if any descendants of converts living in Berlin in these years. They were obviously worried that the stain of Jewish blood would not be visible, that descendants of Jews would be able to successfully pass as authentic Christians.

The only convert whose situation even faintly approached their third-generation rule was Julius Eduard Hitzig, who had converted in 1799, when he was 19, and their rule may have been framed with him in mind. For a time after his student years Hitzig had served as a judicial official in the French administration in Warsaw; then he returned to Berlin, where he was active as a publisher and bookseller. A few years later, he would be appointed a Court Investigator in the Prussian Supreme Court.[12] Hitzig knew Arnim well, since he published Arnim's newspaper, the *Berliner Abendblätter,* the "Berlin Evening Pages," which first appeared the same year that the club was started, in 1811. Arnim had founded the paper with Heinrich von Kleist, a friend from their days in Königsberg back in 1807. The new paper was innovative for its time. It was only four pages long, it was a daily, and its price was very low compared to the more establishment newspapers. Because of its bold style, the *Abendblätter* was the precursor of the modern tabloid, and all in all it was a huge success. Guards were needed when readers "besieged" its office behind Saint Hedwig's cathedral when copies went on sale.[13] Still, the new paper was not very profitable, and it was forced to close down that same year. Apparently the *Abendblätter* editors were both dependent on Hitzig's largesse and prickly about how he was managing the paper's finances.[14] Thus a nasty stew of dependence and resentment may have been behind their hostility.

But we must return to Clemens and Karl in Bad Teplitz, where the two friends spent a good deal of time arguing about Jews and especially about Rahel. Before she arrived, while the two men were still alone, they quarreled, mainly about her friends and her personality, and at one point Clemens used explicitly anti-Jewish language. Karl, for his own complex reasons, wrote Rahel frequently, telling her about these discussions, even quoting Clemens's hostile words. Again Karl was mediating between a Jewish friend and a Christian friend, explaining each to the other. But this time he was not at all deferential to the Jewish friend, even though she was his lover and intended wife. Rahel reacted with despair and anger.[15] In a letter to her friend Alexander von der Marwitz, she described her feelings: "So murdered, annihilated have I never been, already much more pained and made miserable."[16] That she should be complaining about Karl and Clemens to Alexander was quite remarkable. He was a young nobleman Rahel had met in 1809, and the two would remain intimate until Alexander died fighting in the War of Liberation. That summer of 1811 he was 24, adrift from the officer's life which he was expected to follow, and trying to find his way as an intellectual. Alexander's brother Ludwig was a founding member of the Tischgesellschaft and furious at the way that reformers were threatening noble privileges. Precisely at this historic moment, Ludwig was organizing his fellow noblemen to oppose the new reforms and especially Jewish emancipation.[17] So it was ironic that Rahel expressed her rage to a confidant from one of Prussia's leading noble families.

Long after their summer in Bad Teplitz, Clemens and Karl and Rahel were still quarreling. Eight months later, in April 1812, Clemens and Karl were both living in Prague, while Rahel remained back in Berlin. From Prague, Clemens wrote an unpleasant letter to Rahel, which he showed in draft to Karl and then sent on to Berlin. The letter itself has not survived, but we know that in it Clemens accused Rahel of having "immoral friends," and consistently showing a "lack of tact," and was explicit that both of these defects in her behavior were "Jewish problems." When Rahel received the letter, only then to discover that Karl had not prevented Clemens from sending it, she was furious. Her outrage at both of them was expressed in a letter to Karl. "I didn't think there was such nastiness except in bad books. He speaks to me of a raging desire for my death . . . and, tell, me, where does he get the idea that I am so anxious to be unhappy? He wishes me starvation . . . you must have completely lost your wits to have allowed him to send that letter! Thus do you allow me to be insulted!"[18] She continued with a snide critique of Clemens's masculinity, telling Karl that "I have been insulted three times in my life, once by a man, once by a woman, and once by Clemens."[19] Karl now felt guilty that he had failed to stop Clemens from sending the letter in the first place, and decided he must win back Rahel's good will by taking his revenge on Clemens. He found his chance later that same month, when he was visiting Clemens. Karl boxed Clemens's ears and stole the manuscript of his work-in-progress, a play called *Aloys und Imelde,* as a pawn to "guarantee his good behavior," promising that he would return the manuscript in a year if Clemens proved to be decent to Rahel for the next twelve months.[20]

In another episode from 1811 we see a much more dramatic attack on prominent Jews, which provoked a young student from the Itzig clan to an act of proud self-defense. Not all of Rahel's Jewish contemporaries restricted their bitterness to private letters. Achim von Arnim appears again in this tale, displaying his ambivalence toward wealthy and cultured Jews. During the summer of that year, Moritz Itzig, a university student, tried to fight a duel with Arnim, and although the two never actually fought, Itzig did attack Arnim in public. We are indebted to Karl's summary of the entire episode, which he wrote in 1836, but did not want published until after his death.[21] The first act of the drama began on June 25, during the same month that Rahel went to Bad Teplitz, in the home of Sara Levy, one of Daniel and Miriam Itzig's many children. A childless widow of 48, a loyal Jew and an accomplished pianist, Sara lived in a large and elegant home on Hinter dem Neuen Packhof, today the site of Berlin's National Gallery. As a girl she had been Wilhelm Friedemann Bach's favorite student, and she later became a patron of Wilhelm's brother Carl Philipp Emanuel Bach and his family. Sara was one of a handful of Berlin Jews who had been invited by Karl Zelter to join the Singakademie, the Choral Society, a prestigious performance space and school. She was the Choral Society's first harpsichord soloist, and later donated her entire music library to the Society.[22]

Zelter was a musical dynamo around Berlin, for he also directed the Liedertafel, a men's chorus that performed patriotic songs, and he was a spicy personality whose attitude to Jews was somewhat unpredictable. At times he could gossip maliciously behind the backs of Jewish friends, and he was a member of the Tischgesellschaft. Yet he also went to special trouble to open important doors to various of his Jewish friends, who responded with generous patronage of his projects. Not only did Zelter write music for the temple services; he also welcomed several Jewish families into important local musical institutions. Zelter had been born to a poor family of builders, but his musical talents had changed his life. In his role as director of the Choral Society, he promoted Jewish participation, welcoming Sara Levy, the Mendelssohns, and the Beers to the choir. Zelter's style was anything but polished, and his friends remembered how he would signal his hostility to arty pretension by speaking in "the language of the day laborer or the drill sergeant." When he was in good society, apparently "it was only a question of minutes before Zelter would say something coarse and contrary." Luckily for him, many "saw through the pose and found it refreshing." Zelter was fortunate to count Hegel, Schiller, and our very own "fussy" Varnhagen among his friends.[23]

Sara Levy did not have the intellectual savvy for which Rahel Levin and Dorothea Mendelssohn would become so famous. But as a wealthy widow, she could entertain in style, which Rahel certainly could not do in 1811. Levy had once been quite friendly with both Achim von Arnim and Bettina Brentano. Indeed the new couple had announced their engagement at a party in her garden, and several years earlier Arnim had rented a room in the Levy household.[24] By that June, however, Madame Levy had distanced herself from Arnim, for when she sent out the invitations to the gathering set for the evening of June 25, she invited Bettina alone. The reason seems to have been that her nephew Moritz Itzig, who was living with her at the time, blamed Arnim for one of the more anti-Jewish lectures delivered to the Tischgesellschaft that March. The lecture in question, actually written by Clemens Brentano, had circulated privately before being published in May.[25]

Although he had not been invited to the gathering, Arnim decided to come anyway. He arrived wearing his comfortable day clothing, although the rest of the guests were in formal dress. Madame Levy was "embarrassed and confused," but tried to make the best of the situation.[26] Arnim, who was known about town for his tendency to utter "tactless and frivolous" antisemitic witticisms, stayed for several hours, all the while making "disparaging fun" of the guests. By the time he finally left the Levy home, the other visitors were outraged. Madame Levy felt herself "insulted and ridiculed" in her own home by a guest she had never invited. Her nephew Moritz Itzig took it upon himself to demand an apology from Arnim. Moritz was then 24, a student of Johann Fichte's at the University of Berlin. He had been living at his aunt's home for five years, since the death of his father, Isaac Daniel Itzig, in 1806.[27] During the 1790s, Isaac had begun supplying the French army with horses. But in 1796 the French defaulted on a loan, bankrupting Itzig. Ten years later he died, an impoverished and broken man.[28]

After Arnim left that evening, Moritz sat down and wrote him a "serious and measured" letter requesting that Arnim "answer for his behavior." Instead of a swift apology, Arnim responded in a letter full of "sarcastic derision." It was then that Itzig challenged him to a duel. Arnim was furious to think that a Jew would teach him what was "decent behavior," and especially that a Jew would take the initiative in challenging him, a nobleman, to a duel. Itzig's challenge *was* a bold gesture in two respects. For one thing he was appropriating behavior that had once been exclusively noble. Even more audacious was Itzig's attempt to use the duel to defend his injured honor *as a Jew.* This was cultural adaptation with a powerful twist of pride.

Arnim took Itzig's letter to his exclusive noble club, called the Casino, where he collected a list of signatures from his aristocratic friends, who agreed that no nobleman should have to defend his honor in a duel with a Jew. He appended the signatures to a long letter of his own, rejecting Itzig's challenge. Itzig was not intimidated. In Varnhagen's subsequent summary of the incident, Itzig's response was a "righteous rebellion."[29] Moritz Itzig wrote back to Arnim that whoever "refused the sword" in such an "ignoble and cowardly" fashion must expect to "meet the blow of the club." Arnim's response was nonchalant. He laughed about the incident to his friends, and considered the case closed. But Itzig meant what he said about the blows of the club. One evening Arnim was visiting the public baths on the Kurfürstenbrücke. Suddenly he felt powerful blows, accompanied by the words, "Base scoundrel! Dishonorable coward!" His attacker chose words such as "ignoble" and "dishonorable" to shame Arnim. At the literal level he was accusing Arnim of failing to act according to the moral code which Arnim himself had argued was reserved for those of noble birth. Arnim called for help, and passersby restrained Itzig. Itzig openly identified himself by name, explaining to anyone who would listen that Arnim was a nobleman who was ready enough to insult others, but not ready to defend himself on the field of honor. Arnim was incensed, and decided to turn to the law for his revenge for the beating.

In his brief to the court, Arnim demanded protection from Itzig, who he claimed was deranged. But the court disagreed, finding Itzig very rational. He was given a light punishment of a short time in jail for attacking Arnim. At this point Moritz's first cousin Julius Eduard Hitzig enters the saga. Somehow, Julius obtained the court records and shared the details with his sister and other friends and relatives. Reading between the lines we can be confident that Hitzig was probably Karl's "deep throat" source for his 1836 report of the entire affair. So although Julius had been a Christian for well over a decade, he obviously remained intimate with his still-Jewish relatives and friends, and seemed to have sympathized with Moritz's defiant gesture. Ludwig Robert, Rahel's brother, was also well informed about Itzig's plight. He expressed his outrage in a letter, where Robert asked the recipient of his letter to "picture the devil as slave-driver and you have a feeble image of the figure Arnim cuts in the trial. He asks, after he has received the beating [from Itzig], he asks the Supreme Court to protect him from the insane *Jewboy* who from an early age has been sick and hypochondriac — how base [and] cowardly!"[30] As time went on, Arnim began to lose respect among his noble peers. While some of them initially sympathized with his refusal to duel with Itzig, once he went to court they began to see him as a coward. As for Moritz Itzig, in Varnhagen's words, he went about Berlin "unembarrassed and dashing" after his release from jail. Indeed, a circle of prominent noblemen who had jointly written Itzig a harsh public indictment when the case first appeared on the court docket withdrew their missive and distanced themselves from Arnim.

To modern eyes the duel certainly appears to be a silly way to risk one's life. Our revenge for insults is often the lawsuit. But when dueling became widespread among aristocrats in sixteenth-century Italy, it was an improvement over the inter-familial blood feud. Since a duel only involved two individuals, the quarrel would end when the duel was over. From its very beginning the practice of dueling was a privilege of noble males.[31] Indeed one of the most important functions of the duel was to show publicly that only nobles could demand satisfaction when their honor was insulted. Certainly Arnim's refusal to fight a duel with Moritz Itzig fits this model. Yet as with many other once exclusively noble practices, over time the noble caste often lost its exclusive monopoly. We are familiar with this pattern over the centuries, as nobles lost their exclusive rights over land and state offices. So too with the duel. Thus Moritz Itzig, the student ready to fight a duel, was typical of his era. Just then across Germany, students were eager to share in the special honor that came with being *duelfähig*, a word that meant one was "able" to duel, that one belonged to the magic circle of those whose honor, if injured, could be defended with a sword or a pistol. During the early nineteenth century, over half of the 2,000 duels fought yearly in Germany were engagements between two university students.[32] Yet not everyone involved saw the spread of duels as a positive development. The radical students of this era, who created nationalist fraternities, condemned duels as a decadent aristocratic ritual, silly and reactionary, and nationalist intellectuals disagreed about whether the duel was a ritual worth preserving in the new Germany they were creating.

Johann Fichte faced a very different duel fracas, also in 1811, just four months after he became the first rector of the University of Berlin. Fichte resigned his post after an episode in which several hostile Christian students challenged a Jewish student to fight them in a duel, but he refused. This was the reverse of the Itzig-Arnim situation. Unlike Itzig, who wanted to use the duel as a *defense* against anti-Jewish hostility, in this case the Christian students wanted to use it to *express* anti-Jewish hostility. Fichte was furious that the Christian students were not expelled. Interestingly enough, Friedrich Schleiermacher, who was now a professor at the new university, defended the Christian students.[33] Some observers of Fichte's Jewish politics argue that his stance at this juncture shows that he had become more pro-Jewish since 1792, when he had argued that cutting off Jewish heads was the only way to remove Jewish ideas from contemporary discourse.[34] During these years, men of a certain class position could expect to challenge or be challenged in a duel. Several of our personalities, including Wilhelm von Humboldt, Heinrich

Heine, and Karl Marx, had to decide whether or not to accept a challenge at one time or another. Precisely because the duel was a practice just then spreading beyond the aristocracy, it became a metaphor for conflict in these years. Just two years after Itzig challenged Arnim, a contemporary would describe a battle during the War of Liberation by noting that one needed to imagine "6,000 educated, honorable men walking with determination to a *duel of life and death. . . .* "[35]

Some may conclude that Itzig's campaign against Arnim was a folly, that the duel was already an antiquated gesture in 1811. On the other hand, he expressed his defiance against Arnim's anti-Jewish hostility in a very secular and a very German way. The inner synthesis of his Jewish and his German identities is remarkable, and vividly illustrates the noble-Jewish alliance of the old regime era, even as that alliance was rapidly becoming frayed and brittle, and indeed passing into history. All in all, Moritz Itzig's rare combination of affiliations is immensely illuminating, because he had integrated his Jewish and his Prussian identities. He died two years later, in the Battle of Lützen. As for Arnim, he may have imagined himself a patriot, but the reality was that although he applied to serve in the Landwehr, the militia inside the army, he was rejected, and so he spent the war years on his landed estate at Wiepersdorf. In the end, at the moment of truth, the nobleman failed to serve when needed, whereas the Jewish soldier gave his life for Prussia. A wry observer who obviously knew them both, the official Friedrich von Staegemann, contrasted the two in a quip: "Itzig and Arnim remained behind, Itzig on the battlefield of Lützen, and Arnim behind the stove."[36]

Itzig's stance was very different from that of our leading personality Rahel Levin. She craved noble society, even if the price was insult and humiliation. Itzig's defense of Jewishness in a public gesture would never have occurred to Rahel and her friends who were determined to achieve assimilation. Of course, being a Jewish *woman* may have made it much more difficult for Rahel and her circle to integrate a Jewish and a patriotic identity. Although Arnim rejected his petition, Itzig could at least imagine using a male gesture to revenge the insult to his aunt. Achim von Arnim's position was as nuanced as was Itzig's, albeit over different issues altogether. His decision to go to the Levy home uninvited shows he was attracted to the social scene at the Jewish salons. Yet once there he was hostile, and when challenged to the duel by a Jew, he acted strictly according to caste norms which held that only those who belong to the noble caste could determine who was eligible to fight a duel. Yet completely in contrast to his own principles, when he submitted his brief against Itzig to the court, Arnim relied on state institutions in an utterly modern fashion. When he turned to the court for revenge against Itzig, we see writ small a crucial transition from caste power to state power. And it was precisely this transition which was dividing the Prussian nobility in 1811.

The episode of the Itzig duel shows that the old regime alliance between the Jewish elite and the nobility was unraveling rapidly. Even during the 1790s only a handful of nobles and Jews shared cultural tastes and leisure pursuits which created a chance for friendships and romances. Still, the noble-Jewish alliance remains our best explanation for the remarkable success of the old regime Jewish salons. Now, in 1811, these two closed castes still had some minimal mutual interests. Indeed the new emancipation law of 1812 can well be explained as the last hurrah of the noble-Jewish connection. But the French occupation and the new nationalism it provoked was making it hard for individual nobles and individual Jews to share a common vision of Prussia's future and to sustain relationships across this large divide. From the noble perspective there was more economic logic to their hostility to Jews than meets the eye initially. Reformers demanded more sacrifices from nobles, just when their agricultural economy was collapsing. Taxes rose dramatically, and landowners were asked to extend the mortgages on their estates to raise cash to pay Napoleon's fines. Since most estates were heavily mortgaged to begin with, many noble families endured bankruptcies, and some even were forced to sell their land. Arnim's estate, for example, had not been well managed, and he decided to become a gentleman farmer so as to support Bettina and their growing family. We cannot be surprised that Jewish financiers were poised at this moment with the funds and the desire to buy the noble estates, but this outraged the nobles, who often blamed the state for policies which seemed to make the Jewish elite so rich. Again we see the wider trends within a personal story, for Moritz Itzig and his father Isaac were the proud owners of a landed estate.[37] Another arena for tension between nobles and Jews was the prestigious and competitive civil service. One way for down-at-their-heels nobles to retain their family status was to send their sons to university and then on to careers in the bureaucracy. But who was competing for those plum appointments? The super-educated and refined young men of Jewish descent, of course.

With this background in mind, we can grasp why the Prussian nobility was divided about the new reforms. On the one side were those nobles committed to systematic change. The two leading reformers, the *Reichsfreiherr* Karl vom Stein and Chancellor August von Hardenberg, were themselves born to noble privilege. On the other side, Arnim and his friends raged against the reformers, arguing that if prestigious careers were opened to talent, and if commoners could buy landed estates, the entire aristocratic system was at risk. What was good for the state and what was good for the noble estate were now at odds.[38] During 1811, the noble rebellion against the state went so far that Friedrich

August Ludwig von der Marwitz and Count Friedrich Ludwig Karl Fincke von Finckenstein were charged with conspiracy, and locked up in the Spandauer Citadel for five weeks.[39] When they stormed against the reforms, the angry nobles sometimes fumed that Prussia was becoming a *Judenstaat,* or a Jewish state. Certainly not all Jewish families prospered in the dicey times of the Napoleonic Wars. And we shall see that the Jewish emancipation which the reformers granted in 1812 contained significant loopholes. But myths and prejudices are rarely informed by the nuanced detail of actual circumstances. Rightly or wrongly, the dissident nobles identified the Hardenberg reforms as an adoption of *Jewish* economic practices.

Truth be told, the angry nobles so worried about the strong Jewish presence in the economy did have cause for concern. In 1803 when the new Stock Exchange opened its doors, two of the four directors were Jewish, and four years later, the new Directory of Industry included 30 Jewish and 22 Christian bankers. In the years between 1812 and 1815, among the 32 top banking houses, 17 were owned by Jews, 6 were owned by converts, and only 9 banks were owned by Christians. Moreover, by 1814, 60 percent of those whose fortunes were worth 200,000 thalers or more were either Jewish or formerly Jewish.[40] Thus the crisis of the agricultural economy coincided with an expansion of the money economy, and nobles rightly feared the integration of the two kinds of wealth. Once estates were available for purchase, the closed circle of exclusive noble land ownership, political power, and consummate status was breached. Angry nobles were correct to point to the leading reformer, Chancellor Hardenberg, as a serious enemy, for he was searching for ways that capital could penetrate the agricultural sector. His plan was for Jewish financiers to purchase estates which belonged to the state, and thereby bolster the collapsing budget.[41] Certainly we can see how shocking it was for nobles to face the symbolism and the reality of Jews owning landed estates.

In addition to these dramatic developments, many Prussians were convinced that the war against France was lining Jewish pockets. War had long provided a useful opportunity for Jewish merchants to prosper. We understand this reality better by looking closely at one of the premier Jewish families in Berlin then, the Mendelssohns. Like his sister Dorothea, Abraham Mendelssohn would also eventually become a Protestant. But although both siblings ultimately chose baptism, Abraham's life was much more harmonious than his sister's, both before and after his baptism. When Abraham was 21, in 1797, he had been sent to Paris to work as a *kassierer,* a lowly banking assistant, known as a *kommi* in contemporary slang. But while his rank may have been modest, the setting in the prominent Fould banking house was impressive. His sister Henriette, who was then 26, also had a position with the

Fould family as the governess for their children. This was during Dorothea and Friedrich's wandering years as they migrated from Berlin to the little university town of Jena, and then, beginning in 1802, to Paris. Dorothea's younger son Philipp still lived with them. Because Friedrich continued to find a secure income elusive, Dorothea began editing volumes of medieval French texts, all published under Friedrich's name. But still they were short of funds, and so in 1803 she decided to approach her brother Abraham and her sister Henriette, who were also living in Paris then. With a certain amount of bad faith she promised them that she was planning to leave Friedrich, and that therefore she should receive her share of the family inheritance even before their mother Fromet died. Abraham and Henriette did not believe her, and refused to help. A year later, on April 6, 1804, Dorothea would finally become a Protestant, and she and Friedrich would marry.[42]

Early marriage to a Jewish merchant, scandalous divorce, and the bitter struggle to support her child and mate did not add up to a happy mode of emancipation for Dorothea. Henriette was spared some of these pains because she never married at all, and found productive ways to support herself. After her stint as a governess for the Fould children, she founded a boarding school for aristocratic girls in the garden house owned by the Foulds on the Rue Richer.[43] She counted the Humboldt brothers, Madame de Staël, August Schlegel, and other cultural leaders among her admirers. Sometimes her so-called friends could be spiteful behind her back. Karl Zelter wrote to Goethe in Weimar that he found it most "peculiar, when a Jewish girl from Berlin is welcome in the best Parisian society, although she has no personality, and no competence in the language, customs, and conduct" of Paris high life.[44] By some accounts it was Henriette who introduced Abraham to his future bride, Lea Salomon, when he returned home to Berlin for a visit. Others are convinced that Abraham and Lea had met in Berlin before Abraham ever left for Paris, at a meeting of the Gesellschaft der Freunde.[45] When they fell in love in 1803, Lea was 28, living at home in Berlin, the cultured daughter of a wealthy family. Like so many of the Itzig women, Lea had received an extraordinary education. She spoke several languages, sang beautifully, played various musical instruments well, and could even read Homer in the original Greek.

Just as Dorothea's path in life alienated her from many Mendelssohn family members, so too Lea had a sibling who became estranged from their mother, Bella. Both stories show how stormy and controversial conversion was among the most assimilated families. Two years after Lea and Abraham fell in love, her older brother Jacob decided to convert. Their mother was so outraged by Jacob's baptism that she cut off all contact with him. Besides becoming a Protestant, Jacob and another brother, Isaac, had added the name Bartholdy

4.1. Lea Mendelssohn. Sketch by Wilhelm Hensel. Courtesy of the Leo Baeck Institute, New York.

to their family names.[46] We can be quite sure that Daniel Itzig would not have been happy about the direction his descendants' lives were taking, only a little more than a decade after his death in 1799. Lea's wealthy parents opposed the match with Abraham, because they did not want their daughter marrying a mere *kommis*. They finally agreed, on the condition that Abraham would quit his lowly post in the Fould firm and the newlyweds would move to Hamburg, where he and his older brother Joseph would found their own banking firm.

4.2. Abraham Mendelssohn. Sketch by Wilhelm Hensel. Courtesy of the Leo
Baeck Institute, New York.

Abraham was reluctant to leave France, because at that moment, in 1804, he
was enthusiastic about how Napoleon was reforming French society. Back in
1791 the Revolution had granted the Jews a very radical emancipation, in
contrast to the still-dismal situation back in Prussia. But Abraham and Lea did
as they were asked and moved to Hamburg, where they lived in a charming
home on the outskirts of town. Their first three children, Felix, Fanny, and
Rebecca, were born during their Hamburg years. Abraham and Lea were

committed to a rigorous intellectual and artistic education for their progeny, who were awakened early in the mornings to begin their pedagogic routine.

Their firm thrived, but the war situation complicated their lives. Hamburg was occupied by the French, and under the heel of that domination Lea and Abraham were becoming less sympathetic to the Napoleonic system. Because the occupation in Hamburg was riddled with corruption, the Mendelssohn brothers conducted a lively business importing spices, coffee, tea, sugar, and tobacco. Under the table, many French officials were quite happy to accept the bribes offered by the Mendelssohns and others.[47] Had the Continental Blockade been enforced, Hamburg's shipping trade would have been entirely ruined. Not only were all English imports forbidden to enter German lands, but even items from England stored in warehouses were supposed to be confiscated. Moreover any German ship carrying British goods could be seized by the French as well. Not everyone profited under such chaotic conditions, and indeed many firms collapsed in exactly the same era. To prosper, Joseph and Abraham needed a combination of "burning aggression" and "cool calculation," qualities also shared by the much more famous and eventually much wealthier Rothschild brothers.[48]

The main reason that the Mendelssohn brothers became high-end smugglers was because they became agents for the Rothschild brothers in Hamburg. Mayer and Gutele Rothschild, the parents of this epic clan, themselves born in the middle of the eighteenth century, were the proud parents of ten children, five sons and five daughters. Mayer had begun as a modest rare coin dealer living in the Jewish ghetto of Frankfurt, and eventually he became the financier of Prince William of Hesse-Hanau, his local ruler. By the time Napoleon's empire was in place, Mayer and Gutele's sons were ready to be sent out into the world to establish the Rothschild banking house. Nathan settled in London, Salomon in Vienna, Carl in Naples, and James in Paris, and Amschel remained in Frankfurt. The family profited from war because they were rogue capitalist traders, ready to share insider political information, exchange currencies, hide assets, and take huge risks in all their endeavors. Their means of communication from London to Paris to Frankfurt were designed for rapid relay of information and secrecy. In their letters they called London Jerusalem, and when the destination of the letter was a public post office, they used different colored envelopes to indicate to waiting spies the content of the letter. When a letter was not the right medium, they commissioned boats and runners, as well as using their famous carrier pigeons.

When Nathan arrived in London in 1804, he bought not just cotton but also "foodstuffs, colonial wares and every other kind of goods," none of which could be exported to the continent.[49] Observers at various British ports noted that suddenly all of Nathan's accumulated "bales and boxes" would disappear, to reappear shortly on the docks of Hamburg. Abraham and Joseph Mendelssohn then distributed the "cotton goods, yarn, tobacco, coffee, sugar, and indigo" across Germany. Abraham and Lea became rich, because "famine prices" were gladly paid for the rare commodities. From the patriotic point of view, smuggling British goods into the Continent was a blow to France and its policy of ruining the English economy. But they were also making fortunes while many poor Germans could not afford the high prices. The paradoxes of the coin millionaires of an earlier era come immediately to mind. But after the Mendelssohn firm had enjoyed seven years of good fortune, in 1811 the French occupation officials in Hamburg became serious about enforcing the ban on exports, and Abraham and Lea decided to flee the city incognito. Later chroniclers note that they arrived in Berlin not as "impoverished refugees," but rather as loyal Germans who had "staked their fortune" in the struggle against Napoleon.[50] But for those who suffered poverty and misfortune during the occupation, any war profiteering was problematic, even patriotic profiteering.

When they arrived in Berlin after a decade away, the nationalist movement had become a significant presence. The new gymnastics society was attracting young men to the nationalist cause. The patriotic gymnasts did their exercises in a field outside of town, next to the army rifle range at Hasenheide, a woodland area that had been enclosed by the Great Elector in 1678 for the breeding of hares.[51] The dynamic organizer of the Hasenheide gymnastics scene was Friedrich Ludwig Jahn. In the five years since Prussia's defeat, Jahn, now 33, had roamed about Germany visiting various universities, where he collected around him a circle of devoted patriots. Jahn's spirit and energy can be seen in many nationalist projects of the time. While living in Königsberg in the entourage of the royal family, he had founded the Deutscher Bund, a secret organization committed to the expulsion of French troops not just from Prussia but from all German lands. In 1810 Jahn published his *Das Deutsche Volkstum* ("The German People"), which would later become the indispensable text for patriots in those years.[52] Jahn was especially talented at creating new practices, performances, and symbols. For years he had dressed in a black medieval-looking outfit that was called the *Alt Germanische Tracht*, the old Germanic costume. He emphasized the importance of using only German, and refused to speak or write a word of French. One of his fantasies was to dig a huge pit on the French-German border, which was to be filled with wild animals, and thereby discourage any Germans from even visiting France!

Jahn's gymnastics events proved very popular, and soon Berliners began to stop by to watch the "songs, trumpet playing, short speeches, and holy flames" that were also part of the Hasenheide scene.[53] The training space was near the

4.3. Friedrich Jahn and the Gymnasts at the Hasenheide Field, 1818. Engraving by Gottfried Kühn. Stiftung Stadtmuseum Berlin.

village of Tempelhof, where Berliners often went on Sundays to enjoy meals at the local inns and refreshment tents. But there were no such pleasures for the gymnasts. Soon Jahn became unhappy with the tourist observers, and moved his training grounds to a more obscure spot in the woods.[54] A contemporary observer later remembered that "I was taken as a child to see Jahn at his open-air gymnasium whither the youth of Berlin flocked at that time . . . A cleared area of a few acres in extent, screened by fir-trees . . . The athletes had declared war on every kind of softness; only the simplest body-building food was permitted, and every sort of spirits, cakes and sweetmeats was vigorously banned."[55] The movement caught on like wildfire, and managed to attract men from the lower orders, a novelty thus far in the nationalist movement. Jewish gymnasts were welcome to join in, and we do not see signs of overt hostility to Jews at this juncture in the movement. Seven years later, by 1818, in Prussia alone there were already at least one hundred gymnastics clubs, attracting at least six thousand gymnasts. Across all of Germany the number involved was twice that.[56]

Participants believed that gymnastics could integrate body, mind, and spirit, and thereby prepare men for war against Napoleon. Like the Tischgesellschaft, the exercise movement was an exclusively male affair. In the words of a contemporary, the thinking behind the project was that whatever "is memorable in history is renewed through the spectacle of *masculine* power."[57] Jahn's vision went beyond preparing male bodies for national conflict, for he advocated a change in the young men's sexual habits as well. He and other patriots sought to combat what they saw as a homoerotic tone then pervasive among male friendships. It was certainly not outside the bounds of acceptable behavior under the old regime for men to enjoy sex with other men, without being forced to take on a homosexual identity. But many nationalists were passionately opposed to homoerotic friendships and also to adultery, and attacked both practices as decadent, French, and effeminate. Their sexual ideal was the heterosexual couple and the warm, cozy, domestic family nest.[58] Jahn exhorted his followers to "belong to one fatherland even as they belonged to one household, and have one true love in their lives."[59]

Jahn's legacy has been controversial since the Nazi era, because for him entrance to the magic circle of the nation was by ethnic ancestry.[60] In one harsh evaluation, Jahn's ideology and the institutions he created show that "German national consciousness was unmistakably and distinctly racist from the moment it existed."[61] Indeed some see a connection between his xenophobia and his disdain for women, homosexuality, and adultery, and blame him for influencing German culture in the deepest way, for many decades into the future. Other scholars disagree, arguing that it is unfair to blame later racist movements on Jahn.[62] Jahn's success in attracting young men eager to build their muscles on the Hasenheide gymnastics teams showed that in the five years since the defeat at Jena, nationalist enthusiasms were spreading beyond the intelligentsia. We have seen how Friedrich Schleiermacher brought religion and romanticism to the nationalist cause, and how Johann Fichte brought a radical political spirit into the nationalist consensus. But those who listened to Schleiermacher's sermons and Fichte's lectures were often well born or at least well educated, and certainly the members of the Tischgesellschaft were very privileged, while the gymnasts building their muscles for all to see on the Hasenheide were often from the lower classes, crucial if the movement was to spark a widespread military resistance to the occupation.

The year 1811 ended with a somber death, the suicide of Heinrich von Kleist, on November 21. Kleist had several reasons to take his life, especially his difficulty earning an income from his writing. In the autumn of 1811, Kleist was 34, a man in despair. He had rejected a military career, and since his family monies were scarce, he tried to support himself as a writer, a journalist, and a publisher. But when his plays were produced they often failed miserably, and much of his fiction remained in the drawer. To be sure, Kleist brought some of his troubles upon himself. In the pages of the *Abendblätter* he made little jokes about August Wilhelm Iffland's preferences for male lovers. His public attacks on Iffland were self-destructive, because Iffland was the Director of the National Theater, and he retaliated by refusing to stage any of Kleist's plays.[63] Kleist was especially depressed that fall, because the previous spring the government had closed down the *Abendblätter*. The paper was popular, even with the king himself, but Hardenberg, the liberal chancellor, was angry that the articles often took aim at the new reforms. Kleist resolved to kill himself, and found a partner in death, Henriette Vogel, who was suffering from terminal cancer. Suicide had acquired a romantic aura since Goethe's hero in *The Sorrows of Young Werther* had taken his life because of his despair in love. After Heinrich's and Henriette's bodies were found, dead by pistol shots, on the shores of the Wannsee lake, friends and acquaintances and strangers far and wide tried to comprehend the tragedy. Ironically, Kleist's spectacular death brought him greater renown than his writing brought him while he was still alive. Soon after the suicide the *London Times* carried a detailed report.[64] Many local intellectuals interpreted Kleist's suicide as a "symbolic act of despair at the continued humiliation of the nation."[65]

Rahel Levin was one of his most passionate admirers, although she had scarcely known Kleist. Observers of the contemporary scene noted that both were outsiders, "she through birth," and he through "spiritual decision." Two days after his death she wrote her friend Alexander von der Marwitz, "with bitter tears streaming down her face," that Kleist's "godly virtues" could never die "after a pistol shot."[66] How should we interpret Rahel's sympathy for Kleist? We wonder if she would have identified so passionately with him had she known that in 1802 Kleist had written to his sister that "I am seldom out in Society. Jewish Society would be my favorite, if the Jews did not act so pretentiously with their cultivation."[67] Even when we remember her enthusiasm for Johann Fichte, whom posterity has judged harshly for his view of Jews, we must find her identification with Kleist ironic. She was still Jewish in 1811, yet quite ready to sympathize with the troubles of individual noblemen, just at the moment when many of these privileged gentlemen or their relatives opposed Jewish emancipation. Rahel felt responsible only to herself and her existential state. Other Jews, however, had taken on a responsibility to history, at a peak moment in the saga of Jews in the German lands.

The Gift of a Fatherland, 1812

In the first months of 1812, the leaders of Jewish Berlin were eagerly waiting to hear good news from Chancellor Hardenberg. Six years into the occupation, Jewish fortunes were still very much needed to bolster the sagging state budget. Fate had given the Jews of Prussia an excellent moment to press their case. At the time when a major law, the 1812 Edict, was formulated, the Prussian treasury was still in deep arrears, with a debt of 200 million thalers.[68] Not only did the state still require their fortunes, but should Jews be allowed to become soldiers, the entire community might thereby prove their patriotism in battle against Napoleon.

In 1812 no one knew what exactly would happen to Prussia. For two years, since Christmas of 1809, when the royal family had returned to the city, the number of French soldiers in Berlin had declined sharply. But recently Napoleon's troops had reappeared in strength, en route to invade Russia. King Frederick William's subjects were increasingly restive, and many feared an uprising. Whatever support the French had enjoyed back in 1806 had long since disappeared, during six years of hardship, impoverishment, and humiliation. But Paris was not the only target for angry Berliners, who were "disgusted" that their king had supinely agreed to allow French soldiers back into Berlin. Napoleon had also coerced Prussia into providing him with 20,000 Prussian soldiers to aid in the Russian campaign. As the French troops arrived, the population was irate. When the French soldiers celebrated Napoleon's birthday with a parade, they faced a mob of Berliners throwing stones, and bayonets were needed to clear their path.[69]

The month of March 1812 proved, however, to be a golden moment in Jewish time, if not yet in German time. For the two years since Hardenberg had become chancellor, the community leaders had relentlessly petitioned government officials for some radical improvement in Jewish status. The salon women had created a place for themselves at the summit of Berlin society and enjoyed "trophy friendships" with the prominent. Yet even for the lucky salon Jews, the disparity between their social glory and their political humiliations remained wide. At the time, Jewish emancipation was very much a topic of contemporary debate. Under Napoleon's rule in the western German cities and little states, many Jewish communities had been granted significant emancipation. By 1812, Jews in Westphalia, in the Grand Duchy of Berg, in Frankfurt am Main, in Baden, and in the Hanseatic towns had been released from various restrictions and taxes. But the problem was that many saw Jewish emancipation as a French policy. Thus it was rather touchy to favor Jewish emancipation in Prussia at precisely the moment when Prussians were becoming more and more set against all things French. Contemporaries, especially ardent patriots, wondered whether Jews in Prussia would be ready to fight the French when it was the French who had done the most to help Jews.

But the doubters were wrong. On the contrary, many Jews in the Prussia of 1812 were eager to demonstrate their loyalty to their state, now in its darkest hour. Rahel Levin expressed this mood in a letter to Karl: "just God, how easy and natural it is to love one's fatherland, if only it loves you back just a little!" Then she added the key second sentence: "you do it even without counter-love."[70] Rahel summed up the struggle to become patriotic as if Prussia were a man with whom she was in love. She had no fortune to give for her nation, and as a woman she could not sacrifice her life on the battlefield. The financiers with means were ready to show their love with loans and donations, but they expected that civic emancipation would be the just reward for loyal services rendered.[71] The man whose name has gone down in history as the leader of this struggle was David Friedländer. He was now 61, and had recently been honored as the first Jew to be elected to a position on the Berlin City Council. In the urban ordinance issued in 1808, protected Jews could vote and hold honorary municipal offices, as long as they owned a home or a business. Later Abraham Mendelssohn would also serve proudly on the Berlin City Council.[72] Friedländer was born to wealth, owned a profitable silk manufacturing firm, and was one of the twenty richest Jewish men in Berlin.[73] As with so many Court Jews from the previous centuries, Friedländer's high status inside the Jewish world was matched by extraordinary connections with powerful statesmen. He was at once friend, banker, and financial advisor to Wilhelm von Humboldt and his brother Alexander, the natural history scholar.[74]

Contemporaries were then and historians are now rightly perplexed as to whether the successes of these latter-day Court Jews were a boon or a barrier to the wider emancipation effort.[75] From our place in time, even to ask whether persecuted minorities desired equality sounds absurd. But we know well that the privileged Jews of Berlin had achieved the equivalent of a private civic equality. Since the time of Israel Aaron and Esther Liebmann, the state had rewarded extraordinary wealth with special rights. But those rights had been granted to families, not to the wider community. Precisely because his own family was so lucky, the verdict on Friedländer's efforts at this juncture is very much contested. One harsh judgment holds that he was a "slave, cringing before the dominant race and religion, both on his own behalf and that of his people."[76] Others disagree sharply, arguing that his activism shows that "he was not just a selfish spokesman for his class," and he did not "abandon the welfare of the majority of the Jews."[77] In Friedländer's behalf we must note that he had retired from his firm so as to devote himself to the emancipation project. Then there was the controversy over his "dry baptism" proposal from 1799. Remember that after church officials rejected his plan, Friedländer did not choose "wet" baptism as his solution. Nor did the local community, which knew of his role in the project, refuse his continued leadership. Thus we must conclude that his vision of a post-Jewish sect within the Lutheran church must have been seen as plausible by other powerful community leaders.

Now it was twelve years later. Friedländer and his peers could take pride in some minimal improvements in the Jewish situation. The much-hated requirement that Jews purchase unsold porcelain figurines from the state factory had been rescinded. In 1800, the law which made the entire community responsible for any Jews who went bankrupt was also canceled. When we follow the fate of the Itzig family we see clearly how privilege insulated the super-rich from the needs of their poorer fellow Jews. Readers will recall that back in 1791 the entire Itzig family had been granted "all rights possessed by Christian citizens." Yet some of these descendants were obviously not entirely satisfied with the rights and obligations of their position at the summit of Berlin Jewry. During the 1790s we find Itzigs who were failing to pay their community taxes, and we know well that more and more Itzig descendants were choosing baptism.[78] For us the converted Itzigs are a portent of the future. Because they already enjoyed a sort of quasi-citizenship *before* they chose conversion, they experienced at an earlier juncture what thousands of Jews would face *after* the 1812 Edict.

To grasp the deeper meaning of the converted Itzigs, we must recall the moment in 1995 when Jürgen Habermas walked out of the lecture hall during Martin Walser's speech on the occasion of the Scholl prize. Remember that Walser had provoked Habermas by declaring that conversion was a kind of emancipation. Many readers will surely side with Habermas, finding Walser's stance hostile to Judaism. Now that we are familiar with the texture of Jewish politics back in 1812, we can see that Walser was echoing the policy of the Prussian state in these years. That policy was to award only a partial emancipation and repress the reform of Judaism, leaving baptism as the only way to gain a kind of functional, immediate emancipation. Many will be elated that Habermas opposed this problematic Prussian policy that so constrained the lives of many personalities in our story. But anger at Prussian policy must be balanced by awareness that it was often those with the most privileges who chose baptism.

When Friedländer petitioned state ministers for a comprehensive emancipation, they were surprisingly explicit about how important money was in the fight for Jewish rights. Just as financial needs had motivated the Great Elector to invite Israel Aaron to settle in Berlin back in 1663, so now too money was linked to rights. Sometimes Jewish communities were asked to pay directly for their emancipation, as in Frankfurt am Main. In December 1811, Frankfurt's mayor, the Archduke Dalberg, made it clear to the Jewish leaders that more rights would be granted only if a tidy sum was paid for the privilege. The amount requested was 440,000 florins, twenty times the amount of the annual tax bill paid hitherto by the community. In the Frankfurt case the underlying logic of the exchange was laid bare for all to see, not a pretty picture for posterity, but apparently quite normative for the year 1811.[79] That Jewish elites seemed to be able to buy rights for the wider community helps us understand why critics from the left were sometimes cynical about Jewish emancipation.

In the Berlin case we see no direct payment for emancipation. Nevertheless anyone who went looking for the role of money behind the scenes no doubt found plenty to gossip about in Berlin. Hardenberg was the central figure in these backstage negotiations. We find Hardenberg everywhere, supporting Jewish emancipation and the careers of individual Jews. At the time of his divorce from his first wife, when he was dangerously in arrears with his creditors, he was offered a loan at very low interest rates by the Westphalian financier Israel Jacobson.[80] Later Jacobson would represent the Berlin Jewish community in the negotiations for the 1812 Edict. The friendship between Jacobson, the well-heeled Jewish banker, and his supremely influential noble client Hardenberg blossomed, and the two men remained intimate for over a quarter of a century.[81] Closer to home in Berlin, Hardenberg dined weekly during these years with Amalie and Jacob Herz Beer.[82] We see a parallel in Vienna, where Prince Klemens von Metternich enjoyed a close relationship with his banker, Leopold von Herz.

In 1812, when Friedländer called on his help, Jacobson was 44, and for four years, since 1808, he had funded and organized modern elementary schools and prayer services in towns across Westphalia. Jacobson's standing as a latter-day Court Jew must have been enhanced by his "ancestry by purchase," for he and his brother each owned a landed estate in the little state of Mecklenburg, and were even invited to become representatives in the Mecklenburg estates assembly.[83] When Friedländer sat down to write his appeals for emancipation, he did not promise an explicit payment, but he certainly pointed out the financial implications of the current crisis. In an 1809 letter to Hardenberg's colleague Wilhelm Anton von Klewitz, Friedländer pointed out that if emancipation was not granted, wealthy Prussian Jews might choose to leave the country, depriving Prussia of their funds, skills, and connections. Obviously trying to parry a familiar line of attack that Jews were sympathetic with the French occupation, Friedländer denied that French rule had in any way benefited the Jewish economy. On the contrary, he argued that because many Jewish Berliners had departed town after the 1806 defeat, closing their stores and businesses, the community tax base was depleted. Between 1806 and 1809, of the 405 Jewish families living in Berlin, the number of truly poor families had increased from 135 to 175. Another 130 families were not doing well enough to pay their Jewish taxes. And even among the 100 richest families, many were not able to keep up with their obligations to the community.[84]

Friedländer was concerned that the increasing rates of conversion were draining the community coffers. Three years later, in January 1811, Friedländer sent Hardenberg a list of the names of fifty families who had lost relatives to baptism. He knew in his bones what we have learned from the Judenkartei statistics, that a *family crisis* was depriving the community of so many of its young, its best, and its brightest minds. David Friedländer experienced the losses in his own extended family. His daughter-in-law Rebecca, Rahel's friend, had divorced his son Moses and converted. Several of his wife's Itzig cousins were already baptized, and several more would make the same choice in the coming years. In his letter, Friedländer stressed that because so many of the converts were wealthy, their departure from the community tax base had deprived Berlin Jewry of 10 percent of the budget during the single year of 1809.[85] He reminded Hardenberg that many Jewish parents were secretly converting their children, as well. His point was that if emancipation were not granted, more Jews would choose baptism, and the community would find it more difficult to aid the state financially. In the end, the state would suffer from Berlin's conversion wave. The logic of money and emancipation was apparently so obvious to all involved that Friedländer felt comfortable arguing that the state should want Jews to stay Jewish so they could pay more taxes.

Thanks to the Nazi genealogy project, we can amplify Friedländer's details about the huge spike in rates during these years. Until the closing decades of the eighteenth century the number of converts had been well under ten a year. The trend at the outset of the new century, as seen in Graph 1 of the Appendix, was choppy, but upward. Graph 2 shows that a huge proportion of the converts were infants, and more and more of these children were born to wealthy families. Parents wanted to spare their children conflicts later in life, to have them grow up thinking of themselves as Christians. It is doubtful if such households continued to practice Jewish rituals. Still, parents who remained Jewish could probably retain smoother relations with their own parents and extended families. The burden of deception and secrecy in various directions must have been considerable, and the legacy passed on to the children was obviously intricate.

Friedländer's open reference to the nexus of money and conversion would certainly not have shocked Hardenberg and his staff. Government documents also refer openly to financial aspects of conversion and especially of intermarriage. One plan discussed in these years was to institute civil marriage, which would mean that a Jewish partner marrying a Christian would not need to convert. In 1808 State Minister Leopold von Schrötter wrote a memorandum emphasizing how desirable such intermarriages were from various angles. Remaining Jewish would allow the Jewish partners to inherit, which we know from the saga of the daughters of Moses Isaac-Fliess was sometimes a problem for converts. Moreover, he stressed, "Christian society would receive an influx of some of the Jewish capital which has been accumulated in commerce."[86] If wealthy Jewish daughters could take their parents' wealth into a civil marriage with a nobleman, this would be an elegant way to infuse the troubled landed economy with Jewish capital. Schrötter's proposal was actually optimistic, because he was assuming that Christians, especially noblemen, were willing to marry Jews or former Jews. This is notable, since no one was clear at the time how much of a burden the Jewish stain could become. Schrötter's opponents, who feared that washing the stain clear would be difficult, should not be discounted lightly. Would they have been pleased to learn that a century after their deaths the Nazi genealogy bureaucracy went about unmasking the Jewish ancestry of hundreds of thousands of Christian Germans?

A converted Jewish bride rather than a converted Jewish groom lessened the burden on the noble family. In her name and in the legal descent of her children, her Jewish identity could be removed. In their private relationship, life might be easier for the couple themselves if the wife was the mate with the inferior descent. When a woman marries above her station, her subordination is double, as a woman and as lower caste. In the other direction the inferior man has to cope with a socially superior wife, and the children bear the Jewish stain in their family name. Moreover, a converted Jewish husband might purchase a noble estate and in this way threaten the privileges meant only for that caste. To be sure, if the mother was born Jewish, even if she converted, her children might well be seen as religiously Jewish, since according to tradition identity is determined by the mother. But it is doubtful that this consideration would be troubling to Christian families.

Thanks to a set of marriage records for the first half of the nineteenth century included in the black notebooks, we can investigate these trends in more detail. As we move into the 1820s and 1830s, as we see in Graphs 3 and 4 of the Appendix, the general trend was for men to overtake women among the converts and among those who married out. We can explain the shifting proportion of Jewish women entering intermarriages by the eclipse of the Jewish salons. Salons provided an ideal setting for romances across the religious divide. But during the Napoleonic Wars Jewish salons all but disappeared. And the statistics show clearly that the proportion of Jewish women choosing baptism and being chosen for ethnic intermarriages continued to lag behind the male pattern as we move forward in time. So even though there were distinct advantages to the Jewish mate's being the woman, this trend was fading. The rate of intermarriage did not sink, but the gender match of the mixed couples was more often reversed.

As the saga of the Itzigs has illustrated, more and more converts had been born to wealthy families, but their ample resources were not always providing a buffer against baptism. Moreover, even a fortune plus the grant of quasi-citizenship that the Itzigs received did not succeed in keeping all of the younger Itzig cousins Jewish. But as we see from the choices made by the Beer family, there were also distinct advantages to loyalty. Hosting Chancellor Hardenberg on a weekly basis was possible for the Beers because they were the royalty of the Jewish community. We now turn to how and why some activists born into such wealthy loyalist families found the will and the vision to create new ways to be Jewish. Now, in 1811, Amalie and Jacob were at the summit of their power as *the* avant-garde power couple of the Berlin Jewish establishment. Jacob had become one of Berlin's richest men, and was prominent both in the Jewish world and in finance, as one of the four directors of the Stock Exchange and an Elder in the Jewish community.[87]

The Beers were central in the emergence of a religious space between tradition and baptism, a space well described as harmonious modernization. They certainly look modern in hair and dress. In the portrait of Amalie Beer painted by Carl Kretschmar in 1802, when she was 20, she wears neither a wig nor a bonnet, and feels comfortable showing quite a lot of cleavage. In 1812 both Beers changed their first names, when Malka became Amalie, and Juda became Jacob.[88] Their oldest son, the *Wunderkind* composer, was given the name Jacob at birth, although he was called Meyer by his family. Eventually he created his own family name, Meyerbeer.[89] He also later changed his first name from the still quite Jewish Jacob to the Italian Giacomo. One younger brother was given the Jewish-sounding Wolff at birth, but later called himself Wilhelm. Heinrich was originally named Henoch, and only the youngest son, Michael, seems to have used the same name during his entire life.

4.4. Amalie Beer. Painting by Carl Kretschmar, 1802. Courtesy of the Leo Baeck Institute, New York.

Changing one's first name was a public way to show belonging in mainstream society. Amalie and Jacob spoke German to each other and to their children most of the time, but did speak the German Yiddish dialect, called *Judendeutsch,* at the occasional more intimate moment.[90] Speaking German at home was a step toward speaking proper German in public, and may also have helped them see themselves as truly German. We see from Amalie's letters that her command of written German was far from perfect, a common failing among the Jewish women in her circle. The tutors the Beers hired to teach their sons show how they balanced the Jewish and the secular. Christian tutors taught the boys music, history, German, French, and geography. Their parents also hired bright young reformers, called *maskilim,* who taught them Hebrew and other Jewish subjects, and these tutors escorted the privileged young Beers on their study abroad trips.[91] For many years the boys' head tutor was Aaron

4.5. Jacob Herz Beer. Painting by Johann Heinrich Schröder, 1797. Hans-Luise Richter Stiftung/Stiftung Stadtmuseum Berlin.

Wolfssohn, whose previous post was as director of a modern Jewish school in Breslau. Wolfssohn's official title was *Haushofmeister,* or "courtly tutor." That the Beers would use a noble phrase to describe a tutor actually teaching Jewish subjects shows how French they wanted to sound when they mentioned their children's pedagogy.[92] Because of their lavish resources, the Beers could provide substantial patronage to those in their orbit. Eduard Kley, a Jewish student at the University of Berlin, lived with the Beers for eight years, from 1809 until 1817, and gave the sermons at their domestic temple which they opened in their home in 1815.[93]

None of the four Beer sons converted, and the three who married found

Jewish wives. Because Giacomo chose a career in music, worldly success and loyalty to Judaism were not entirely polarized. Composing operas was not a career which at least explicitly required conversion. Yet a caricature of Giacomo which appeared after his death suggests that he stayed Jewish so as to receive a fortune from his grandfather. The publication of this drawing in a prominent humor magazine shows that he was a cultural icon whose Jewish identity was of interest to wide circles of readers. In the picture Giacomo is sitting in a boat in the Jordan River. To his right is a noble insignia and a harp, representing high culture and aristocratic identification. On his left we see his grandfather's will and bags of money. The satirist suggests that whether or not to convert was a weighty decision whose outcome was unpredictable. The association of money with the grandfather's will was not a sinister fantasy of the satirist's. Because Giacomo was the first male heir to be born in two generations, when he was born his grandfather provided for a lavish inheritance, under the condition that the first name Meyer not be abandoned. When that grandfather lay on his deathbed in 1812, Giacomo, then 21, promised he would never convert.[94] This cynical interpretation of Giacomo's quandary shows that both remaining Jewish *and* converting could be viewed cynically by unsympathetic observers. The association of money with Jews obviously transcended the question of conversion. Just as the right to settle, marry, or become a citizen were rights granted for payment, so both conversion and Jewish loyalty might involve a financial calculus. The message of the caricature was that nothing a Jew or even a former Jew did was ever authentic.

In the same year that his grandfather called Giacomo to his deathbed, the culminating moment of the Jewish struggle for civic emancipation was approaching. After so much labor by so many, on March 11, the 1812 Edict was finally pronounced. On the very next day, the Berlin community leaders wrote an effusive thank-you letter to Hardenberg, expressing their "deepest gratitude" for his role in this "incalculable act of charity." Notice they did not use the words "justice" or "equality." A week later the community representatives were invited to meet the chancellor in person, and declared their thanks for receiving the "gift" of a Fatherland, to which they felt bound by feelings of "respect, love and the deepest gratitude."[95]

The new law created the category of local *residents,* sometimes referred to as *denizens.* Whereas individuals gained freedoms, the Jewish community as a state within a state lost rights. Judaism now became one of the tolerated religions in Prussia, and special taxes were abolished.[96] Jews could change their residence, work at previously closed occupations, and purchase any property, including land. In order to earn these privileges, Jewish men were expected to serve in the army, each family had to choose a family name, and

4.6. Giacomo Meyerbeer's Dilemma. From the *Kladderadatsch*, 1860. Bildarchiv Preussischer Kulturbesitz/Art Resource, NY.

community records were to be only written in German. The power of the rabbis to control community behavior was radically curtailed. As the famous phrase summed it up, "to the individual Jew everything, to the community, nothing."[97]

On the burning question of whether educated, modern Jews could take on civil service positions as professors, judicial officers, or ambassadors, the Edict was blatantly contradictory. In one paragraph these enticing opportunities were promised, but another paragraph left open whether Jews could ever be appointed to public offices.[98] Ambitious young Jewish men after 1812 would find it difficult to choose careers, not knowing how far they could advance without baptism. The continuing temptation to convert so as to become a professor, lawyer, or diplomat deprived the Jewish world of many of its best and its brightest, precisely the men who might have devoted themselves to reforming Judaism. Because the 1812 Edict was contradictory about whether the ambitious could obtain prestigious posts without becoming Christians, baptisms spiked upward, as we have seen in Graph 1. Moreover it was cruel and confusing to demand that Jews modernize their religious practice as a condition for complete emancipation, and simultaneously seduce their brightest intellectuals to leave the faith altogether.

This was not the total equality which France had granted its Jews in 1790 and 1791, or the emancipation which Wilhelm von Humboldt had advocated for Prussia, of equal rights for equal duties. Rather, the ethos of the 1812 Edict was a partial and conditional emancipation. The new law did ameliorate the worst contradictions in the Jewish situation, but its omissions and contradictions left serious problems for the future. The spirit of the new law was that if Jews became modern and served the state loyally, eventually a wider equality *might* be granted. Were the community leaders correct to celebrate the terms of the new law? Later generations remained immensely proud of the long fight for emancipation. One proud historian later wrote that unlike the peasants and the town dwellers, who received their emancipation as a gift from above, Jewish leaders worked in a "determined" and "manly" way to obtain their equality.[99] We immediately think of Itzig's determination to fight Arnim in a duel when we hear the emancipation struggle called a masculine effort. We note that nationalists then called Prussia their Fatherland, not their Motherland. Citizenship was a status fought for by men, and the Jews' new identification was with a masculine place. For their part, state officials knew full well how important emancipation was for Jewish communities across Prussia. While at work on the many drafts of the new law, one of the officials involved observed that "the Jews will feel as if the Messiah has come after the new Edict will become law."[100]

The timing of the 1812 Edict was exquisite. As a result of it, almost 70,000 Jews in Prussia became residents of the state. But what is important is how small this number was, not how large. Because it was a very small Prussia that existed in 1812, only the Jews living in the provinces of Brandenburg, Saxony, Pomerania, and East and West Prussia received their emancipation. Thousands of Jews in provinces which had been Prussian before Napoleon's victories in 1806, and which would return to the large Prussia that emerged later, *were not included* in the new law.[101] Each party to the deliberations which resulted in the 1812 Edict could be pleased with this result. Statesmen with little sympathy for Jews were happy because so *few* Jews had been emancipated. The Jews were lucky that Prussia was in a crisis from 1807 onward, so that the generosity of the Jewish financiers was needed, which created an obvious obligation fulfilled by emancipation.

The new law mandated some changes which many Jews had already adopted. Take the important identity marker of names. Bureaucrats had long been frustrated by the instability of family names among Jewish families, since first and last names moved between the generations in a most confusing manner. Obviously many Jews agreed, for even before 1812, over four hundred families, almost a quarter of the Berlin Jewish households, had already chosen a new family name.[102] After the Edict was announced, 325 families chose new family names. The point is that close to half of the Jews in Berlin altered their family names to fit their new civic status.

But amidst all this celebration of the Edict, what about the voice of Gershom Scholem condemning its terms as a false start to Jewish modernity in Germany? To be sure, Prussia's new law was the most progressive Jewish legislation of the epoch across the German lands. And the Jews themselves seemed pleased, for we find no voices expressing anger about the loss of religious and judicial autonomy.[103] As a sharp judgment from afar, Scholem's lament may contain much wisdom, but it is not a sentiment that was prominent at the time.

As for Jewish women, although the wealthy *salonières* had certainly done their part in stimulating pressure for emancipation, they profited little from the Edict. Their salons had been a marvelous, exceptional demonstration that prominent intellectuals valued Jewish minds and Jewish sociability. Everyone was aware that Jewish wealth had made the salons possible, but money had not bought charisma, or friendship, or shared cultural passions. And now that the new law harmonized social glory and civic status, only men were rewarded.[104] Neither the privilege of dying on the battlefield for Prussia nor the dream of a civil service career was meaningful to Jewish women then. Just as the revolutions of the era were fought by men and men gained more rights, so too with Jewish emancipation.[105] Moreover, before very many years had passed, the liberal agenda would be repressed, and what had been ambiguous in the Edict was never granted. Nevertheless, for all its shortcomings, few could disagree that the 1812 Edict was a major milestone in the struggle for Jewish equality. The new law established a platform on which future Jews could fight the good fight for truly equal citizenship. Itzig's battle against Jewry's enemies could go forward, not with the aristocratic gesture of the duel, but with military service and careers open to talent.

We have no evidence that Rahel Levin was pleased with the Edict. It was not that she expected more rights *as a woman*. Rather, she was indifferent to the Edict because her passion was to escape Judaism, not to improve the status of loyal Jews. But to escape Judaism in style she had to marry Karl, a goal which was still elusive. As 1812 came to a close, Karl was eager to leave his employment with Count Bentheim and return to Berlin. Prussian patriots were now eager to pick up guns to oust the French, but their king was still doing the bidding of Napoleon. In February 1812, King Frederick William had signed the Treaty of Paris, binding Prussia ever more tightly to France, and Prussia had even abandoned its alliance with Russia. German patriots like Karl who had been serving with the Austrian army now saw Russia as the prime mover in the fight against Napoleon. Rahel had been pleading with Karl for months to return to Berlin, as she felt lonely and was eager to have him by her side. Yet they quarreled in letters. At one point he was so frustrated with her demands that he predicted that "when I come to Berlin, it shall be as if I didn't know you were there, or that the sun shines."[106] Finally, in August 1812, he was discharged from the Austrian army and was soon back in Berlin. But the next months proved very trying. That winter turned out to be one of the coldest of the entire nineteenth century, and Karl was literally penniless. He moved in with Rahel and her maid Dore, certainly not the way they intended to begin their life together. Moreover his public stance as a patriot put him in real danger. French officials were keeping close tabs on Schleiermacher, Fichte, Hitzig, and Karl as well. But he kept up the round of appearances and tried to hide his threadbare situation. Indeed it was in these months that he convinced Goethe to publish several of Rahel's letters, which appeared anonymously in a prominent literary journal.[107] More important for his own career, he obtained an interview with Chancellor Hardenberg, who promised him a commission in the Prussian army and eventually a diplomatic post. Meanwhile Karl bided his time, waiting for history and his fate to turn.

Her relationship with Karl did not protect Rahel from humiliations as she struggled to make her way in high society. This we can learn by listening to one of the dreams she recorded in her diary during the year 1812.[108] The dream is uncannily modern, reflecting intimacies between three women and a complex stance toward emotional pain. In it she lies on a bed next to her friend Bettina von Arnim and to the Mother of God, whose face resembles Friedrich Schleiermacher's wife Henrietta. The bed is perched "close to the edge of the world," and from this perch the three women can watch the people of the world working. "Our business on this bed . . . was to ask each other what we had suffered—a kind of confessional!" The Mother of God watches with sympathy and weeps as Bettina and Rahel take turns asking the other one if she had suffered particular injuries. First Rahel asks about mortification, then about the sufferings of love, then about injustice, and then about "murdered youth." As Bettina confirms the shared pain to Rahel, "the particular form of suffering we were speaking of was rent from the heart, the pain multiplied a hundredfold: but then we were rid of it forever and felt wholly sound and light."

But once the four troubles that she and Bettina share are already purged, Rahel feels her heart to be "still filled with the heavy burden of earth." And she wants her last burden lifted, and so she asks: " 'do you know — disgrace'? Both shrink away from me as if in horror, though with still something like pity in their gesture . . . and try, in spite of the confined space, to move away from me. In a state bordering on madness I scream: 'I have not *done* anything. It's nothing I have *done*. I have not *done* anything. I am innocent!' " Bettina and the Mother of God do not understand her. " 'Woe,' I cry out, weeping as if my heart were threatening to melt away, 'they do not understand me either. Never, then! *This* burden I must keep; I knew *that*. Forever! *Merciful* God! Woe!' Utterly beside myself, I hastened my awakening." Her disgrace, we are told by one interpreter, was her Jewishness.

Jews as Patriotic Soldiers, 1813

Just after Karl returned to Berlin, in the fall of 1812, Berliners could see with their own eyes that Napoleon's campaign in Russia was failing. Back in July, when his troops invaded Russia, Napoleon had been at the height of his power. Indeed, the sheer number of soldiers involved in the Russian campaign made this "the largest and most intimidating invasion force in history."[109] But it soon became clear that Napoleon had overstretched his good fortune. Russian generals ordered their troops to retreat to the east, which strained French supply lines. Nevertheless the French army did push forward, reaching Moscow in September. But when the population of Moscow began burning huge tracts of their own city, French soldiers in need of supplies and shelter were forced to reverse course and retreat westward. Still, they suffered terribly from the same record-breaking winter temperatures that made Karl so miserable in Berlin. By December 1812 almost 100,000 of the 600,000 troops which had sallied forth to conquer Russia were back in eastern Prussia, and they were "ill-equipped, wounded, and scattered."[110]

Napoleon's failures provided Prussian patriots with precisely the moment for which they were waiting. Officially, Prussia was still allied to France. But more and more Prussians were fed up with occupation and war. Napoleon's fate hung in the balance now, and the actions of the German states would be decisive. On its own, Russia would have difficulty defeating France. But if Prussia and Austria joined in the struggle, Napoleon's empire in central Europe would be in serious danger.[111] For Friedrich Jahn and his followers, the time was now, and the gymnasts began to attack French guards and sabotage their supply boats passing through Berlin's canals.[112] On the diplomatic front, it was a powerful noble general who ultimately forced the king to declare war on France. Just as 1812 was coming to a close General Count Ludwig Yorck von Wartenburg took history into his own hands. Yorck was the commander of the Prussian army in West Prussia, and Napoleon had chosen him to lead the 20,000 Prussian troops the king had committed to the invasion. But alas for Napoleon, his choice of General Yorck for this task turned out to be altogether unfortunate.[113] For Yorck was a passionate patriot, and moreover he was ready to mobilize the local population for war against France.

It was on December 30, 1812, that General Yorck signed the Convention of Tauroggen with Russia without royal permission, promising joint military campaigns against the French invasion of Russia. For months now, he had been pressuring King Frederick William to take up an alliance with the Russians. But the king, indecisive as usual, failed to respond, and so Yorck worried. Would the king accuse him of high treason if he made a secret alliance with Russia? Would he be thrown into prison, or worse, be executed? Two weeks after he signed the pact with Russia, Yorck described his complicated emotional state: "now or never is the time to regain liberty and honour. With a bleeding heart, I tear the bonds of obedience and wage war on my own."[114] General Yorck's fellow Prussians, rich as well as poor, agreed. Sympathetic army friends and state officials protected Yorck from arrest. Before the king had time to mobilize against his rebellious general, the leading reformer, Baron vom und zu Stein, arrived in East Prussia. Without the king's approval, Stein called for a meeting of the Landtag, the aristocratic assembly. The Landtag delegates met and organized a militia, called the Landwehr, and the new militia put out a call for able-bodied males between 18 and 45 to take up arms against France.[115] Ironically, it was a circle of activist nobles who created a people's army, so long a dream of liberals and radical republicans.

It comes as no surprise to learn that the king was not at all pleased with General Yorck's bold alliance with Russia. Indeed for some time after Yorck signed the Convention of Tauroggen, Prussia remained allied with France. There were reasons for the king to fear that once Prussia left the French alliance, Napoleon might respond by the "outright elimination of Prussia as a state."[116] But gradually, Frederick William's advisors convinced him that General Yorck was right, because Prussia had much to gain by signing a clever treaty with Russia. They argued that the fall of the French empire was inevitable, and if Prussia was on the winning side, victory could mean a return to its former size and even an expansion. And so on February 26, Prussia formally joined its fate with Russia. In addition to these convincing arguments for self interest, King Frederick William was pressured by an increasingly restive population. General Yorck's December agreement with the Russians roused huge enthusiasm in Berlin. When the king and court departed Berlin for Breslau, many saw the move as a sign that the king would expand upon Yorck's treaty with Russia and truly declare war against France. Yet the politics of the moment were most confusing, for Prussia remained formally allied to France.

Patriots had good reason to ponder "for whom and against whom" a war would be fought.[117] Amidst this policy confusion, the Berlin police were finding it increasingly difficult to restrain the locals from harassing French troops. There were noisy demonstrations, and French soldiers suffered verbal and bodily attacks. It was becoming obvious that failure to harness this rage would be risky for the king's own rule.

The spirit of resistance among Berliners was strengthened when an advance guard of Russian soldiers entered the city on February 16 and 17. On the day when 300 Russian Cossack soldiers arrived at the Alexanderplatz, "there were clashes and fire was exchanged especially near the castle where the artillery stood. By the Schleusen bridge a cannon was looted and thrown into the Spree river. A crowd of thousands surged through the streets. The city was like a boiling cauldron."[118] A week later, when General Yorck and his troops arrived, the mood in town became ever more jubilant. Then, just days later, Baron vom und zu Stein arrived, ready to end the alliance with France once and for all. Events moved quickly. On March 17, Stein presented the king with a call to arms, instructing him to: "sign, or abdicate!" The ever fearful Frederick William signed, all the while "white as a sheet and trembling."[119] The call to arms invited patriots from across Germany "to fight for our independence and the honor of the *Volk*."[120] Before the ink was dry on his signature, thousands of Prussians were already equipping themselves for battle. The numbers of conscripts swelled, because men from the propertied classes, including university students, were now required to serve. Most of the student volunteers joined the Free Corps, whereas noble volunteers joined the Landwehr, the new civilian militia. A third way to aid the war effort was to join the Home Guard, which mobilized younger and older men to police their local hometown streets. As the months of battles continued, close to 300,000 Prussian men fought in the War of Liberation. Reformers were thrilled, because this was the total mobilization of the population of which they had dreamed.[121]

Even those Prussians who were not of the right age or sex to march off with rifles in hand found ways to support the war effort. Money was scarce, but donations were high. Nearly two million thalers flowed into the state's coffers that spring to pay for the war effort, and Prussians of all ages and classes donated their silverware and jewelry to melt down for arms production.[122] The business community raised a loan of 1.2 million thalers, and the women of Berlin took special responsibility for collecting jewels. The treasury received 160,000 rings, earrings, and necklaces.[123] Across Prussia, local Jewish communities did their share, and often in very public ways. An article in the *Vossische Zeitung* noted that Jewish children were bringing their little savings banks and family silverware into their synagogues. We read of one Jewish

4.7. The Volunteers' Departure in 1813. Woodcut by L. Pietsch, after an oil painting by Gustav Graef. In the foreground Jewish parents bid their son farewell. Bildarchiv Preussischer Kulturbesitz/Art Resource, NY.

butcher who "had thrown in his golden wedding ring as a sign of gratitude for his newly won citizenship."[124] In Potsdam the rabbis and community leaders melted down Torah scroll decorations and *kiddush* cups for the war effort.[125] Melting down *kiddush* cups to pay for uniforms and cannons shows how dramatically values were shifting among Prussian Jews. This was hardly the behavior of an isolated minority living as a "state within a state."

The pacing of events could not have been more perfect. Now Jewish men could take up rifles to show that the emancipation granted the previous year had been just and timely. A long-term complaint against the Jews was that they were not sufficiently manly, so bravery on the battlefield was the ideal gesture to redeem the reputation of the Jewish minority. Civic emancipation and military service were constantly linked in words, deeds, and public performances. In the days when the War of Liberation was beginning in March 1813, Jewish communities across Prussia marked the first anniversary of the Edict. In Breslau, local volunteer soldiers were invited to participate.[126] A lithograph from Breslau shows a Jewish father bidding his soldier son goodbye. The father is wearing a top hat, scarcely the traditional Jewish head covering, and the new soldier bears a white cross on his hat.

The goodbye we see in the Breslau scene was repeated many times across Prussia, since somewhere between 700 and 800 Jewish soldiers fought in the War of Liberation.[127] In Berlin, a stronghold of patriotic sentiment, one estimate suggests that half of the eligible Jewish men fought in the war.[128] Our statistical picture remains sketchy, because religious affiliation was not always recorded by military authorities.[129] About half the Jewish soldiers, close to 400, joined the Free Corps. Because soldiers in this division had to pay for their own uniforms and guns, these young men must have enjoyed the support of their families. We see a romantic image of such a family in the famous painting by Moritz Daniel Oppenheim called *The Return of the Jewish Volunteer*. The parents and siblings welcome home their beloved soldier, who is still dressed in his uniform. Oppenheim's painting portrays a powerful synthesis of Jewish piety and patriotic pride.[130] The mother in the painting looks too traditional to be a Sara Levy, but the exhausted returning soldier well fits our imaginary image of Moritz Itzig. Another portrait by Oppenheim depicts Baruch Eschwege, a Hanau businessman who was a volunteer in the War of Liberation.

Now that the Edict had generated the duty and the war itself was providing the opportunity, rabbis did not oppose Jewish soldiers going to battle. Their silence at this juncture was altogether remarkable, since for many years there had been much debate inside and outside Jewish circles about traditional Jews maintaining ritual observance while on the battlefield. All in all, Jewish participation in the War of Liberation was a huge success, as measured by the many *unconverted* Jewish soldiers who were promoted to officer rank, and the 71 Jews who earned the Iron Cross.[131] Jewish physicians cared for sick and wounded soldiers, among them Karl's brother-in-law David Assing, who lived in Hamburg. Assing was a convert, a published author as well as a physician, and married to Karl's sister Rosa.[132] Many Jewish soldiers reluctant to convert must have been relieved that army service did not require baptism. But when we examine the story of Menno Burg, we see that any ambitious military man who refused the price of conversion would nevertheless face daunting obstacles. Burg was 24 when the war broke out, and later remembered how "the youths . . . tore themselves from the arms of their weeping loved ones and climbed onto the open wagons, and how, as the long column began to move, they swung their caps high in the air to shout a hurrah for Prussia . . . "[133] Alas, Burg was frustrated that he was never sent to the front, but spent the war years teaching geometry at the Artillery Training School. His superiors proposed him for a promotion to lieutenant after his first year, but the proposal was

4.8. The Return of the Jewish Volunteer from the War of Liberation. Painting by Moritz Daniel Oppenheim, 1833/34. The Jewish Museum/Art Resource, NY.

turned down by his superior, Major von Bardeleben, because Burg was Jewish and committed to remaining so. Eventually he was promoted to second lieutenant, thanks in good part to the aid of his well-placed patron, Prince August of Prussia, a nephew of Frederick the Great. He continued to teach in the Artillery School, but he was never allowed to lead troops in the field, because he was not a Christian. Burg was repeatedly asked to convert so he could be promoted, and over the years the king and Prince August quarreled back and forth about Burg's stubborn refusal to leave Judaism. Finally, when he was 58 and still Jewish, he was promoted to major.

Meanwhile, as Prussians were buying uniforms and donating their silver to aid the war effort in the early spring of 1813, Karl was still in Berlin, searching about for a position. He was elated when Baron von Tettenborn of the Russian army marched into Berlin, because he knew him from his years of service with

4.9. Baruch Eschwege, Volunteer Marksman in the War of Liberation. Portrait by Moritz Daniel Oppenheim, 1817/18. Copyright: Historisches Museum Frankfurt/Main. Photograph Horst Ziegenfusz.

the Austrian army. Now Tettenborn offered Karl a position as a captain, which he accepted with alacrity. His tasks were to serve as secretary, press officer, and director of medical care in the baron's unit. Again he had found a way to use a military appointment to supply himself with insider news for his publications, and again he found a noble patron to rescue him from thread-bare gentility and boost his status. In March, Karl was on hand when his division liberated Hamburg from the French, and when the Hamburg Senate donated a sum of money to his unit, he received a generous share. Karl was filled with joy. He had just founded a successful military newspaper, and Hardenberg was still promising him a post in the Prussian civil service when the war was over.[134] He wrote to Rahel: "What happiness! My dear Rahel, we are finally living through beautiful times!"[135]

By early summer many hoped that a French defeat was imminent. But still, as the fighting raged in and around Berlin, those who could left town. On May 9, 1813, Rahel departed for Breslau, accompanied by her servant Dore, her old friend Nettchen Marcuse, and her brother Markus and his family. Nettchen Marcuse had been close to Rahel since childhood, and had led an emancipated life in the same noble bohemian circles in which Rahel traveled. Ten years before, Nettchen had enjoyed a love affair with a prominent nobleman, Wilhelm von Burgsdorff, and a child had been born from this relationship. At one point when she was living in Paris, Rahel had helped Nettchen care for the baby.[136]

Rahel, Dore, and Nettchen chose Breslau because Rahel's uncle lived there. But upon her arrival, Rahel was insulted that her relatives did not invite the three of them to live at their home, forcing her to rent a room in town. She was strapped for cash, because the funds Karl had given her from his Hamburg windfall had begun to run dry. Moreover her uncle insisted that she give him her silver to sell, so as to procure additional funds for her support.[137] Once her brother Ludwig arrived in Breslau too, the two siblings decided to move on to Prague. Because Prague was already quite full of refugees, Rahel appealed to Karl to contact his patron Count Bentheim to help her find housing. And so it was that on June 1, Rahel, Ludwig, and Dore arrived at the rented rooms of Bentheim's current lover, Auguste Brede. Brede was an actress from Berlin, and she and Rahel had several mutual friends. One of Auguste's other tenants that summer was Carl Maria von Weber, the composer. Rahel was delighted with the society she found in Prague. She and Auguste spent many evenings at the theater and the opera, and chatted at length about art, literature, and the lives of their various friends. She reported to Karl that "I am healthy here, and funny: and very lively."[138] Away from Berlin, in the midst of war, she had found a way to recapture the special pleasures of her life before 1806.

Gossip among her set became spicier as several old Berlin friends also arrived in Prague that summer, including Clemens Brentano. It had been a year since Karl had stolen the manuscript of Clemens's play. Now, perhaps because he was truly sorry, perhaps because he wanted his manuscript back, Clemens tried to make amends to Rahel. The two spent a great deal of time together that summer in Prague, attempting to repair their relationship. Like so many in the romantic generation, both Karl and Clemens highly valued intimacy. Nonetheless, after long consideration, Rahel decided to make a final break with Clemens. Karl, for his part, kept his promise and returned Clemens's manuscript. In this episode Rahel was not at all obsequious, but instead defended herself and was prepared to cope with the social consequences.

Late that summer, the war provided Rahel with a chance to publicly demonstrate her patriotism and her as-yet untapped talent for organization. In August, Austria finally joined Russia and Prussia in the fight against France. Prussian soldiers wounded in the battles of Kulm and Dresden filled the Prague hospitals, and injured men lay dying in the streets. Rahel initiated a massive nursing project, funded by her wealthier friends. Lea Mendelssohn, Lea's brother Jacob Salomon Bartholdy, and Caroline von Humboldt all sent funds. With their contributions Rahel bought blankets, bandages, medicine, and food.[139] She marshaled 150 local women to help her visit the wounded and organize their care. In a letter to Karl, then marching on Bremen in Tettenborn's unit in the Russian army, she exulted: "I am in touch with our commissariat and our staff surgeon: have a great amount of lint, bandages, rags, stockings, shirts; arrange for meals in several districts of the city; attend personally to thirty or forty fusiliers and soldiers every day; discuss and inspect everything."[140] Moreover her activity gave rise to utterly modern sentiments about women and war. She wrote to Karl, "in my heart I carry a kind of plan, to call upon all European women that they will never participate in war and will all help those who suffer: then we could be *calm,* from *one* side at least, I mean, us women."[141] Her efforts, however glorious, depleted her always precarious health. When she wrapped up the nursing project during the fall of 1813, she collapsed with a severe case of rheumatic palsy and remained bedridden for several months.

We can imagine how pleased Rahel must have been that Caroline von Humboldt, the wife of Wilhelm, was eager to fund her nursing campaign. Patriotic philanthropy provided Jewish women with a way to show their nationalist passions and to deepen their relationships with Christian women in a very public way. Amalie Beer, for instance, was invited to join an otherwise all-noble circle of women organized in Berlin who solicited contributions for the war effort.[142] In gratitude, three years later, in 1816, she was given the Queen Louise Award for her good works. The king himself graciously intervened to make sure that the shape of the actual award was a simple gold medal rather than its usual form, a cross — an amazing consideration shown to Amalie Beer's proud Jewishness.[143] Editors of the enlightened journal *Sulamith* were thrilled. In their journal's pages they exulted that this award showed that patriotism could indeed be consistent with loyalty to Judaism.[144] On the occasion of the award, the king also presented Amalie Beer with a bust of Queen Louise. Her husband Jacob was also active in nationalist causes. After the war was over, he helped found the Luisenstift (the Queen Louise Foundation), which awarded stipends to children whose fathers had died on the battlefield during the War of Liberation.[145]

In Vienna, Fanny von Arnstein and her niece Marianne Saaling also joined prominent women in philanthropic projects. Even before Austria entered the coalition Fanny had been the only Jewish woman voted onto the steering committee of the Society of Ladies of the Nobility for the Promotion of the Good and the Useful. All the other women chosen were princesses or countesses.[146] Over the years of occupation Fanny and her husband Nathan gave generously to help wounded soldiers, and their good deeds were very public, often reported in local newspapers. Fanny was among the wide circle of family who were devastated when her cousin Moritz Itzig and his brother were wounded on May 2, at the battle of Lützen. Moritz died of his wounds eleven days later.[147] It is regrettable that we shall never know how Moritz Itzig would have coped with the difficult challenges of the coming years.

Moritz Itzig's saga, from would-be duelist to fallen soldier, was played out at the highest reaches of Berlin society. But we see from the story of Esther Manuel that the war also created astonishing opportunities for a poor and oddly ambitious Jewish woman.[148] Esther Manuel was born in Hanau in 1785. In her early twenties, she married an artisan who changed his name from Müller to Grafemus, and they had two children. Her husband was a Christian, but there is no record of Esther's baptism. Grafemus abandoned his family in 1808, and she heard rumors that he had joined the Russian army. Esther eventually traveled to Berlin to find some charity to support her, and because she was too poor to afford the postal service carriage, she dressed as a man to travel on horseback. Once in Berlin she appealed for funds to the Jewish charities, but to no avail. In a patriotic gesture, after Queen Louise died in 1810, Esther changed her name to Louise. She was still very poor, frustrated in her continuing efforts to locate her husband. Eventually, sometime in the fall of 1812, using connections in the Jewish community, Louise went to the king's son and daughter-in-law, Prince William and Princess Maria, and told them of her desire to join the army. Touched by her predicament and by her passion to fight, they purchased her a horse, a uniform, and a gun, and arranged for her to enter the army, dressed as a man! She was not the only female fighter motivated to take up arms for Prussia. Berliners just then were celebrating the heroism of Leonora Prochazka, a disguised woman soldier who had just died in battle, with popular songs and poetry.

By March 1813, in the first days of the War of Liberation, Louise Grafemus was already in battle, on her horse with rifle in hand, and although she was quickly wounded, she kept on fighting. One day that spring, during a battle, by some astonishing fortune, she chanced to meet her long-lost husband, who was indeed a soldier in the Russian army. In front of all the soldiers, she tore off her uniform and revealed her identity as a woman in disguise, causing a huge sensation. But fate took away what it had just delivered, and Herr Grafemus died the very next day. Louise then left the army, and wandered to St. Petersburg, where she worked for a Russian nobleman. In time she returned to Berlin, where she spent her days writing appeals to the government to receive a pension as the widow of a fallen soldier. When the king did give her a tiny pension of two thalers a year she became a most modern publicity seeker, finding journalists to tell her story. The owner of a porcelain factory even ordered cups made bearing her image! Her family back in Hanau refused to help her, because they were angry that she had continuously neglected them as well as her two children. Eventually she married a German publisher in Russia and settled in Riga, where she died in 1852, at the age of 67.

Louise Grafemus invites comparison with our most rebellious women such as Dorothea Mendelssohn or Rahel Levin. Yet the differences matter. With good reason we may doubt that any of the salon women would ever have wrapped up their breasts, urinated in the bushes, or ridden a horse in battle. The difficulties endured by the salon women required psychological and cultural resources, not physical bravery. The life of Louise Grafemus teaches that there were various ways to depart from establishment roles.

Those enjoying more resources did not always choose to risk their lives for Prussia, and some were haunted by that choice. We last met Rahel's brother Ludwig in the spring of 1813, as the two siblings left Berlin for Breslau. He spent the war years in a peripatetic drift, moving between Vienna, Paris, Berlin, and Prague. Because the family business had suffered losses during these years, Ludwig's annual interest payments from his inheritance were insufficient for his support. His dream was to make a living as a playwright, but as of 1812 this dream was still a fantasy. He refused to work in commerce, then the dominant Jewish occupation. During the war years, he supplemented his inheritance with income from a post as private secretary to a Russian count.[149] We are reminded of Karl's services to Count Bentheim, and can only empathize with struggling intellectuals and their forced dependence on aristocratic patrons. With less expensive tastes it might have been possible to live more modestly and independently. Ludwig never did fight for Prussia, and after the war he was still pondering why not, and explaining himself to Rahel. "A soldier I *cannot* become: I don't ride and on foot I would be in the sick bay within the first eight days; and even if I were healthy and vigorous enough, I still could not go along. I have examined myself carefully and earnestly. It is impossible for one, after he has been forbidden as a Jew for 35 years, suddenly to have courage — I mean *this* kind of courage — I have *another* kind — I wouldn't let myself be insulted without fighting [a duel] — ."[150]

We who have followed the twists and turns of Moritz Itzig's struggles to duel with Achim von Arnim read Ludwig's words with high passion. We learn much from his distinction between the two kinds of courage. Aristocratic honor can beat in a Jewish heart, but the new status of Jewish citizen is not a felt identity for him. His readiness to fight duels shows that the noble-Jewish alliance is very much alive within him. But he is not ready to die because of a passionate identification with the Prussian state, and he knows that he does not have the bodily qualities necessary for that physical courage. Here we see a complex identity indeed. At least in his own mind, Ludwig Robert was proud to announce that, like Moritz Itzig, he possessed the aristocratic and manly courage to defend himself on the field of honor. But he could not have been more clear that his longtime lack of rights as a Jew made it impossible for him to imagine sacrificing his life in a war for Prussian independence.

The Beer sons experienced the war in very different ways. Wilhelm fought in the war, and Michael, who was only 13 in 1813, later remembered making bandages at home for the wounded soldiers.[151] But Giacomo's experience was somewhat parallel to Ludwig Robert's, although he found less to say in his own defense. Not only was Giacomo away from Prussia during the worst of the conflict, but he was in Paris, the heart of enemy territory. After the war, during the summer of 1815, Giacomo, back in Berlin, chanced to meet an old friend on the street. Once this friend had been a *bon vivant* who loved his daily pleasures, and had been decidedly aloof from military enthusiasms. But in the war this young man had gone into battle for Prussia, and when they met in 1815 he was still wearing his army uniform. Meyerbeer suffered when he compared his easy life in Paris to his friend's military service. He lamented in a letter: "oh, how his gaze pained and humiliated me! Indeed, what plausible reason could I give for my failure to fight, where neither my age nor my position in society excluded me? Devotion to my art? How would my conscience be punished by my lies?"[152] We can only wonder what he meant by his "lies." We know that Giacomo was very sensitive to the possible antisemitic motives of his critics. Thus when his own behavior fit the stereotype that Jews were cowardly weaklings lacking patriotism, his pain was great.

But soon the long years of fighting, which had begun in 1792, finally came to an end. During the fall of 1813, as Rahel lay ill in her bed in Prague, and Karl fought in his Russian unit, Napoleon and his Grand Army were in serious trouble. He had rejected the proposal of an armistice, and Austria had now joined Russia and Prussia in the allied coalition. Every week more and more German soldiers who had been forced by the French occupiers to fight in

Napoleon's army defected to one of the three allied armies. Then, during three long days in October 1813, Napoleon's troops suffered a dramatic and traumatic defeat at the Battle of Leipzig. Six months later, on April 6, Napoleon had lost not only the battle for Europe, but power in France.

At this blessed moment in German time, Karl's spirits were high. General von Tettenborn had allowed him to keep a collection of gold coins his unit had uncovered in a post office in Bremen. He was finishing off a book analyzing key battles in the war, and his new newspaper was doing very well. He managed to arrive in Paris just when Napoleon was forced from power and King Louis XVIII was called to the throne of France. One of his puzzling moments that jubilant spring was when Rahel's old friend Pauline Wiesel, who was also in Paris, tried to seduce him. He was reportedly indignant, and wrote to Rahel about the incident. She told him that she laughed when she read his letter, lighthearted about the entire matter. We see here another example of how alive old regime permissive values were in her heart. She wrote Karl that Pauline wanted only "a taste of Rahel's man, like iced punch."[153]

Karl was satisfied with his life at this juncture. Fate had handed him another peak experience about which he could write and publish. Now he was truly poised to take on the diplomatic post which Hardenberg had promised would be his. By the spring of 1814 Rahel had recovered her health, and was ready to leave Prague. Karl and Rahel spent several weeks in Bad Teplitz, preparing their future. In the end the war had been good to both of them, and the moment had come when they could join their destinies in marriage.

High Culture Families and Public Satire, 1814–1819

Rahel and Karl Marry, 1814

Formalizing her relationship with Karl was Rahel's first priority when she met him in Bad Teplitz that July. Karl remained in an exuberant mood, and perhaps as a sign of his confidence in his destiny he had taken to calling himself Varnhagen von Ense.[1] One day when he was doing some family research in a library in Munster for his patron, Count Bentheim, Karl had discovered in a volume of genealogy records some long-lost Varnhagens with a von Ense added to their family name, and appropriated this much more prestigious name for his own use. His new title, even if a very shirt-tail kind of nobility, was attractive to Rahel, who had always wanted to marry an aristocrat. Rahel and Karl were both hoping that Chancellor Hardenberg would invite Karl to join the Prussian delegation to the Vienna Congress, due to open that fall.

Now, finally, the moment had come when they could marry, the moment when her baptism was necessary. She had stopped using Levin back in the 1790s, preferring the adopted family name Robert. In 1812 several Levin siblings officially took the family name of Robert-Tornow.[2] But a change of religion was more complicated. Since the 1812 Edict did not make it possible for a Jew to marry a Christian in a civil ceremony, Rahel would have to become a Christian in order to marry Karl. Her brothers had no objections at this point. Indeed, before many years had passed all three of them would also be baptized.[3] Moreover, they had long been looking forward to her marriage, as they were eager for Varnhagen to begin paying for her upkeep. Just how Rahel felt about Christianity at this juncture remains unclear. At the time and later, many judged that her motives for baptism were entirely pragmatic. But scholars now question this assumption, arguing that before her baptism in 1814 she had begun to believe in a Christian God.[4]

After their reunion in Bad Teplitz, by early September Rahel was back in Berlin living with her brother Moritz, arranging the details of the baptism. First she approached their long-time friend Julius Eduard Hitzig for help. Hitzig was now 34 and, following years of work as a publisher, had just been appointed to a post in the judiciary. He arranged for her to see Johann Jakob Stegemann, a preacher at the Jerusalem Church and the New Church, both Lutheran parishes. Stegemann was known as an enthusiast for Jewish conversions. Indeed Rahel's friend and Julius's first cousin Lea Mendelssohn and her family had been renting an apartment which Stegemann owned for three years, since their return from Hamburg in 1811.[5] Two years after he officiated at Rahel's baptism, Pastor Stegemann would baptize the four Mendelssohn children.

Pastor Stegemann was a perfect choice for Rahel and Karl. They wanted the baptism kept as secret as possible, which was one reason why they did not seek out their friend Friedrich Schleiermacher to preside over the ritual. By 1814 Schleiermacher was a very prominent figure in Berlin, as a pastor at the Trinity Church, a professor at the University of Berlin, religious advisor to the Ministry of the Interior, and president of the local section of the Reformed Calvinist Church. If he had become involved, discretion and privacy would have been out of the question. Yet we wonder whether they really expected to keep her change of faith a secret. After all, everyone then knew that to marry a Christian one had to be a Christian, and Rahel was a very well known personality in Berlin. The day that she first met with Pastor Stegemann, Karl happened to be out of the city for a few days. She wrote to him full of pride that "he received me, as if Spinoza wanted to be baptized: so crushed was he with honor."[6] Then, having secured Pastor Stegemann's help, Rahel went about accumulating the necessary letters and affidavits.

It was on Friday, September 23, that Pastor Stegemann baptized Rahel in the home of her brother Moritz. She knew it was a special honor that Stegemann would agree to perform the ritual in a Jewish home. In her baptism she took the two new first names Frederike Antonie, in a tribute to King Frederick the Great. She explained how important new names were in a letter she wrote a year later to Ernestine Goldstücker, a friend who was about to convert. "I consider this changing of names important. You thereby become to some extent outwardly a different person; and this is especially necessary . . . "[7] Four days after her baptism, Pastor Stegemann married Rahel and Karl. Henceforth she would be called Frederike Varnhagen von Ense. The frail baby who had entered the world as Rahel Levin in 1771 had traveled quite a long road.

And so, at 43, Rahel began her life as a married woman. She was elated and felt that she was treated with a new esteem, both by her family and by her wider social circle. Perhaps it was for the better that she did not know the ugly comments circulating behind her back. In October, a few weeks after her wedding, Wilhelm von Humboldt wrote to his wife Caroline: "I was told that . . . [Varnhagen] has now married the little Levy. Thus, she is able now to become an ambassador's wife and excellency. There is not anything which cannot be achieved by a Jew."[8] Humboldt was not the only acquaintance of Rahel's who was mulling over her marriage. Dorothea Schlegel was living in Vienna in the fall of 1814, and there she heard the rumor that Rahel and Karl were about to marry. She wrote her son Philipp in Rome not to tell their old friend Henriette Herz, also in Rome that year, about a possible marriage. Dorothea's reasoning was that "I believe that it will happen as little as you do. Varnhagen is fearful enough to want it and to work for it. Rahel however is fearful enough *not* to want to marry, and to thwart his push for a marriage."[9] But Dorothea's prediction was wrong, since Rahel and Karl married two days after she wrote that letter. The social advance that Rahel's marriage to Karl represented made her an obvious *parvenu,* or social climber. But the truth was that both were willing to conform to social conventions to improve their status.[10] He was a pretend nobleman, and she was, at least in the eyes of some, a pretend Christian. Yet both were critical of the monarchy, of aristocratic privilege, and of many social conventions.

Rahel and Karl's compromises were rather intricate. Not only were they an intermarried couple, but both were also republican patriots with aristocratic friends and aristocratic tastes. Their political passions would be severely tested in the repressive years following the Vienna Congress. The contrast between their parvenu status and their politics did not make them especially hypocritical for their times, or even for ours. If we were able to talk with them now, they might well justify the noble title and the baptism by reminding us that as a noble Christian couple they could better fight for liberal, even republican causes. Unlike some other men in their circles who had married an older intellectual woman, Karl showed a high regard for Rahel's intellect. Sometimes his adoring habits were laughed at by their friends. He occasionally asked those with whom she had just spoken at social gatherings to repeat her *bons mots* so that he could note them down in a little book.[11] Comic moments notwithstanding, his pride in his wife's talents can well be contrasted to what seems to have been Friedrich Schlegel's attitude. Dorothea was bold when she divorced Simon and followed her heart to live with Friedrich. But once they were married, her behavior became quite subservient. At various junctures in their lives she supported her family with her literary work, yet none of her reviews, essays, poems, translations, or text editions, or even her novel *Florentin*, appeared under her own name. Rather, Friedrich's name was on the title page as the "editor" of these many works.[12]

During the nineteen years of their marriage, Karl put much time and thought into preserving Rahel's work for posterity.[13] His dedication to her talent has allowed us to reconstruct her life and the lives of her friends. Because her letters and notebooks once considered lost have been found again in Poland, we have learned that she was sometimes ambivalent about what she had achieved in the marriage. She was certainly happy to be the wife of a noble official. But at the same time she was self-possessed enough to sometimes feel "humiliated" with the status she had "bought so dearly, so painfully."[14] As unhappy as she had sometimes been in the years before her marriage, she remained proud of what she had accomplished in those years. As time went on she complained that it was "intolerable" that "now I have to behave toward people as if I were nothing more than *my husband*; in the past I was *nothing*, and that is a great deal."[15] On another occasion she summed up the balances in the marriage by referring to it as "the upside-down crown upon my fate; and I am *grateful to the bargain*."[16] The upside-down metaphor was strong in her thinking, for she reminded Karl in 1809 of how he had compared her "to a tree that has been torn out of the earth, and then had its top reburied instead; yet its nature is too strong! The treetop takes root, and clumsily the roots become a treetop. That, my love, unfortunately! unfortunately! is me. This is the measure of my life."[17] The idea was that she had ripped herself away from her Jewish roots, but had with some difficulty, as an upside-down person, created a place for herself in the tough soil of Christian society.

Soon after their wedding, the newlyweds met up in Vienna, where Hardenberg had appointed Karl press secretary for the Prussian delegation to the Vienna Congress. Vienna that year was crowded with kings, princes, envoys, and their "secretaries, clerks, followers, servants," as well as the "pickpockets, courtesans, portrait-painters, caricaturists, commission-agents, scandalmongers, doctors, confessors, prophets and charlatans" who surrounded those with real power.[18] Many of Rahel's old friends found their way to Vienna during this decisive year. Friedrich Schlegel, Wilhelm von Humboldt, and her on-again-off-again friend Friedrich Gentz all had official positions at the meeting, Gentz especially powerful as the chief of protocol for the Congress and intimate of Count Klemens von Metternich, the Austrian head of state.

Reunions in Vienna in 1814 were often troubled. Across the years, there had been intrigues, deceits, and broken love affairs. Sometimes matters of the heart were at stake, but the complex politics of the era also strained relationships. Some from Rahel's old circle remained loyal to the ideals of the French Revolution, still hopeful that Prussia might become a constitutional monarchy or even a republic. Other old friends had become much more conservative, and identified with Metternich's program of keeping the old regimes intact. Besides politics, power itself divided former friends. In 1814, Rahel's friends from the 1790s were in their forties and fifties. Some at the summit of their careers were now reluctant to socialize with the same fascinating outsiders whom they had found so attractive a quarter century before. The pleasures of a miniature utopia were in the past. During and after the Vienna Congress those pleasures were replaced by both real social progress and real backlash. Wilhelm von Humboldt's complex stance vividly illustrates what had been lost and what had been gained over the years. Alongside his friend Gentz, Humboldt did work for Jewish emancipation in Vienna in 1814. But in doing so, he felt released from his social obligations to his Jewish friends. In an 1810 letter to Caroline he wrote that "he was working with all my might to give Jews civil rights so that it would no longer be necessary, out of generosity, to go to Jewish houses."[19]

Rahel and Karl may have been spared some possible insults that year because neither was well connected enough to be invited to the most important balls and dinners. And we know how important balls and dinners were for the negotiations at the Congress. Indeed, the universal lament that year was that "the congress dances well but it does not work."[20] One home that was open to the parvenu couple was that of Fanny and Nathan von Arnstein, who lived in the Hoher Markt, a prestigious Viennese neighborhood. Fanny was Daniel and Miriam Itzig's eighth child, a decade older than Rahel and her circle, and had departed Berlin to marry Nathan von Arnstein in 1776, when she was 18. Now Fanny's two sisters also lived in Vienna, Cäcelie, wife of the ennobled Jewish financier Bernhard von Eskeles, and her younger sister Rebekah, whose life journey was much rockier than Fanny's or Cäcelie's. Thirty years before, Rebekah had married David Ephraim, a grandson of Veitel Heine Ephraim. After their marriage David went bankrupt, then converted, changed his name to Johann Andreas Schmidt, and moved the entire family to Vienna. Eventually Rebekah and their two children, Jette and Julius, also converted.[21] From the windows of their home, the von Arnsteins could see a fountain depicting the marriage of the Virgin Mary to Joseph. It is intriguing to speculate whether they found this statue symbolic of how many of their family and friends were passing from Judaism to Christianity.[22]

Gossipy visitors were certainly attentive to the religious status of the Arn-

5.1. Cäcelie von Eskeles. Portrait by Friedrich von Amerling, 1832. Germanisches Nationalmuseum, Nürnberg.

stein family. In October, while he was serving at the Congress, Friedrich von Staegemann wrote a letter home to Berlin that summarized the hidden complications of an evening with them. On the night in question, he was surprised to meet an Italian diplomat, Cardinal Consalvi, at the Arnsteins' lavish house. Staegemann recounted that at first "all were merrily engaged in discussion." Then Rebekah, Fanny's younger sister, made some mocking remarks about Catholics. Another guest, a Countess Engel, "suffered greatly," he reported, from Madame Ephraim's comments. Staegemann added that the cardinal and his assistant were obviously very disoriented, for they had no idea when they chose to visit the Arnstein home "that the family was not a Christian one."[23] The religious status of the Arnstein family continued to concern Friedrich as the evening went on. He left their house with August von Hedemann, a member of the Christian German Eating Club and the son-in-law of Wilhelm von Humboldt. Hedemann was hostile to Jews and shared his feelings openly. Later Friedrich reported on the conversation to his wife Elisabeth, and she wrote back that "after all, such sentiments were no longer an opinion about which one must feel shame."[24]

Karl may not have been present on the evening Friedrich described, but he would have been intensely interested in the gossip about who said what to whom. During his years as a soldier in the Austrian army, Karl had already become acquainted with the elegant comforts of the Arnsteins' hospitality. This comes as no surprise, since we know he had an affinity for wealthy Jewish families, who often had become his patrons and friends. Fanny opposed baptism for herself, because she saw herself as a follower of Moses Mendelssohn. She has been described as a "true daughter of the Enlightenment," who could look with "serenity" on both traditional Jews and converts.[25] But we must wonder how difficult it was to maintain this serene balance. She and Nathan clearly intended to keep the family line Jewish, and therefore went to great trouble to arrange the alliance of their only daughter Henriette and Heinrich von Pereira, heir to a wealthy Portuguese Jewish family. But we see that Fanny often had to face conflicts between her own loyalty to Judaism and the choices made by her relatives. Henriette and her husband decided to baptize their son in 1805, and five years later the couple also became Catholics. Reportedly Fanny was at peace with these decisions.[26]

Old friends who met again in Vienna during the year of the Congress experienced awkward reunions. Dorothea and Friedrich Schlegel had been living in Vienna since 1808, the year that both of them had become Catholics. Friedrich's politics had moved steadily rightward, without any obvious worldly rewards. Like Karl, he tried to improve his standing by discovering a noble great-grandfather from the seventeenth century.[27] Back in 1804 he had received a well-paying position in the Austrian civil service, but soon he lost this job too. During the Congress year Dorothea was short of funds as usual, and she and Friedrich accepted Fanny's gracious invitation to live in the Arnsteins' palace. Perhaps Fanny's wealth and prominence compensated for her still being Jewish. Yet in spite of her ongoing money troubles, these were happy years for Dorothea. After many lonely times, she had found real intimacy with a few Catholic noblewomen. It was at the Arnstein home that Dorothea and Henriette Herz had a chance to size each other up after many years apart, for

Henriette too spent several months during the Vienna Congress living at the Arnsteins'. In the eight years since her husband Markus had died, her life had also been difficult. She lived modestly on a small pension, working as a tutor in music and English, and one solace was her continuing friendship with Friedrich Schleiermacher. She had turned down offers of marriage and governess posts which would have required baptism, because she sought to spare her mother that pain. Henriette was unhappy in Vienna, reportedly because she was jealous of Fanny's special place in Viennese high society, and she soon returned to Berlin.[28]

One of the vexing issues facing the delegates when they continued their deliberations in the fall of 1815 was the future of Jews in various states. By June 9 the Congress had drawn a new map of central Europe and created a new political body in the German Confederation. Remaining tasks were postponed to a follow-up session in Paris that would convene in September. There had been a huge pressure to complete the work, because in March Europe had again been thrown into war. Napoleon refused to accept his exile on the island of Elba, and on March 1 he and a small army had returned to France, with a plan to again conquer central Europe. But Napoleon's dream died on June 18, at the Battle of Waterloo. This time his demise was final. Soon he would find himself in truly far-off exile on the island of Saint Helena, where he would live until his death in 1821.

Delegates at the Congress faced complex debates about Jewish emancipation. The new Confederation of German States included 35 states and four cities, and the status of the Jews varied widely from place to place.[29] Wilhelm von Humboldt and Chancellor Hardenberg both argued for the radical solution of granting equal rights for equal duties, on the French model. And even Count Metternich and Friedrich Gentz, who were to the right of Humboldt and Hardenberg on most questions, stood with them in support of full emancipation. So many episodes recounted here contributed to this moment. There was the dramatic success of the old regime salons, where Jewish talent and modernity were displayed. The political agitation of David Friedländer had provoked government figures to take the issue seriously. Then too Hardenberg and other colleagues felt obligated to the Jewish financiers whose loans and donations saved Prussia in its darkest hour. Moreover, shared enthusiasms for high culture and nationalist projects had deepened the relationships between powerful Jews and powerful Christians. Personalities such as David Friedländer, Israel Jacobson, and Jacob Hertz Beer were at once bankers, intellectuals, patrons of the arts, gracious hosts, and pillars of the Jewish community. Humboldt and Hardenberg's commitment to full emancipation should never be forgotten, precisely because in the end their position did not become the policy of the new Confederation. The proponents of a radical French-style emancipation met stiff opposition, and in the end the new constitution of the Confederation specified that only laws which had been issued *by* the local governments would be valid, not those issued *in* the various states. Because of the tiny word *by,* cities and states could retract the radical emancipation granted by the French. The city of Frankfurt am Main retracted the emancipation which had already been granted, and Bremen and Lübeck actually expelled their Jewish communities in 1816.

In September, as the Congress was winding down its deliberations in Paris, Karl was at Hardenberg's side, in his job as press secretary for the Prussian delegation. Rahel spent the summer with the Arnsteins at their summer home in Baden, and then moved on for a long visit in Frankfurt, where she had many friends. She was not eager to return to Berlin, as her memories of the unhappy years during the French occupation were still all too fresh. Even now, as a Christian wife, she still found that the higher she climbed, the greater was the motivation to pillory her. Moreover, the timing of her social ascent was terribly unlucky. For wherever we turn in Jewish Berlin in these years, we shall see that hostility to Jews was becoming more acceptable, just as Elisabeth Staegemann said: "after all, such sentiments were no longer an opinion about which one must feel shame."[30]

Rahel's most painful insult in Frankfurt came from Caroline von Humboldt. Once upon a time, they had been intimate enough to call each other *du.* For years they had not seen one another, but finally, when they met up again at a party that fall, in the company of several mutual friends, Caroline spoke to Rahel using the formal *Sie.* Caroline had chosen "a very simple way to wipe out an old, now embarrassing friendship."[31] But in the same months Rahel also enjoyed shining moments when her ascent seemed right, validated, confirmed, especially the day in June when Goethe paid her a visit. In her salon days in the 1790s, when she was in her twenties, she had been a devoted reader of Goethe's novels. Now, when he was beginning to attract critiques from a younger generation of writers, Rahel remained devoted. Alas, because of the early hour and his failure to announce his visit ahead of time, she was not formally dressed when he arrived. But she suppressed her vanity, so as not to keep the supremely important Goethe waiting. Thus she received him in a black quilted housecoat.[32]

Rahel was elated at Goethe's overture, somewhat shabby as it was. Later that day she exulted in a letter to Karl in Paris that "Goethe was here this morning at a quarter to ten . . . this is my patent of nobility."[33] That she would equate Goethe's visit with an aristocratic title suggests an easy translation between cultural and social status. Although he was born into a merchant family from Frankfurt, after huge successes as poet and novelist and courtier in the Duchy of Weimar, Goethe had been ennobled. His life story was an inspiration for everyone who felt themselves to be gifted, and eyed the rewards which princes and aristocrats could bestow upon the talented.

Finally, in the summer of 1816, the couple settled in Karlsruhe, where Karl had been appointed the Prussian ambassador to the new state of Baden. They were thrilled to be able to live in style, thanks to his salary of 3,000 thalers a year, quite an increase considering that during recent years he had been living on no more than 500 thalers. Rahel, too, was overjoyed, for she had felt poor living on 800 thalers a year since her mother died. Moreover, now she was finally the wife of a noble diplomat. Alas, the higher she climbed, the more vulnerable she became. During her four years in Karlsruhe she was never once received at court. Still, she would later remember these as some of the happiest days of her life.

The New Reform Temple, 1815

During the same years that Rahel fretted about not being invited to court in Karlsruhe, back at home in Berlin a circle of her peers worked to create an alternative Jewish practice to prevent conversions of those alienated from tradition. There was reason to worry. Observers at the time commented that the religious situation in Berlin was "chaotic," and that the "synagogues were empty."[34] Protestant pastors also worried about empty pews in their churches and tried to adapt their faith to the changing times. The sacred time for common worship had become contested among Christians, as seen in angry protests when Johann Fichte delivered his academic lectures on Sunday mornings.

The reformers and the rabbis were not the only observers aware that conversion rates were spiking upwards in dramatic fashion. Friedrich Leopold von Schrötter remarked in 1800 that if conversion continued at its current pace, "there would be no more Judaism in twenty years."[35] As we see in Graph 1 of the Appendix, by 1815 conversion rates were very high, at almost 100 converts per year. This comes as a surprise, because in principle the 1812 Edict should have made baptism unnecessary. But as the story of the Itzig family has shown us, conversion offered advantages which civic improvement alone did not offer. Indeed, the deep historic connection was between emancipation and reform, not between emancipation and conversion. Both in principle and in practice, emancipation made reform possible. The gist of the new edict was that Jewish communities in Prussia were losing their status as self-governing "states within the state." Rabbis could issue bans on new reform projects, but their power was waning.[36]

The two faiths were changing in opposite ways. Judaism was becoming less of a civic religion just when Protestant Christianity was becoming more of one. As time went on, Judaism would become lighter and fainter and altogether less defining in the lives of many Jews. Once a total way of life, Judaism would become a thin, partial identity, and sometimes much less than that. This was precisely the goal of the state officials. The autonomy lost by the rabbis was exchanged for limited civic rights. In a phrase, to the individual Jew, everything, to the community, nothing. The word *Jew* came to stand for ethnicity and difference and the past. *Mosaic* and *Israelite* were the new terms which expressed the modern way to be Jewish. Protestant Christianity, in contrast, was adding on more meanings and functions and becoming an altogether thicker identity. The result was that at this historic moment many of the best and the brightest Jews saw baptism as indispensable in their struggle to become more German on the inside as well as on the outside. Improved conditions for Jews as Jews could not compete with the advantages of baptism.

Would a successful reform alternative in Berlin have reduced the number choosing conversion? To explore this question, we must visit the reform services initiated by Israel Jacobson, who left Westphalia for Berlin in the spring of 1814. He was already supremely well connected in Berlin, as we remember from his role in negotiating the terms of the 1812 Edict. Because of its reputation as the vibrant home to the Jewish enlightenment, Berlin was the obvious destination for Jacobson at this juncture. Still, as modern as Berlin's Jewish elites were, we should not imagine that the *Haskalah* activists completely dominated Jewish life in Berlin. At least half the Jews who lived in Berlin were poor, and those with the most meager resources tended to be more observant. In these years Berlin still had three rabbis and a yeshiva with forty students.[37] But the wealthy, who could afford to pay for others to study and pray for them, were quickly losing interest in traditional community activities. Jacobson's plan was brilliant, because it had the potential to keep the wealthy and their resources within Judaism at a moment of real crisis.

Whereas in the time of Moses Mendelssohn the rich had been funding both the old self-help societies and the new enlightened books and schools, they were now abandoning the traditional institutions. Some even questioned whether they should fund the reform projects. Berlin's upper crust were spending their fortunes on paintings, salon entertaining, patriotic philanthropy, and the Choral Society rather than on *yeshivot* and dowry funds for poor girls.

Jacobson's first home in Berlin was an apartment suite within the residence of the Itzig family on the Burgstrasse, where he entertained David Friedländer and his other prominent friends in the community.[38] But not all those alienated from traditional practice were so eager for Jacobson to succeed in Berlin, as we hear from Rahel's reaction to his arrival there. In June 1814, while she was still in Prague, friends informed her of Jacobson's move to Berlin. As soon as she heard the rumors, Rahel wrote in anger to her brother Ludwig: "I only hope that Jacobson with all his money does not succeed in bringing about a Jewish reform here. I am afraid the vain fool will." In the same letter she declared that "people like us cannot be Jews."[39] Her comments show a sharp divide emerging between those who aimed to disappear as Jews and those committed to modernizing their faith. Others who we might imagine would take on the work of reform stood on the sidelines, especially David Friedländer, who was conspicuous in his absence. In 1815 Friedländer was 65, and his years as a well-placed lobbyist for civic emancipation were behind him. In spite of its limitations, the 1812 Edict had been a tremendous victory. But what next? Friedländer had been pushed toward religious activism by Provost Teller himself in his reply to the 1799 proposal. Teller had asked Friedländer directly: "why do you not remain satisfied for the present with having separated the pure gold of your original Israelite creed from the ignoble parts later added to it?"[40] But Friedländer declined to follow Teller's advice, and by 1815 he was depressed about Jewish progress. He was quite the radical, for his idea was to eliminate the "specific Jewish character of the synagogue" and "reduce Judaism to a simple system of morals."[41] At this juncture, Jacobson's moderate plan was more appealing to dissatisfied Berlin Jews than Friedländer's vision.

The first ceremony to which Jacobson invited the wider Jewish public was in the spring of 1815, on Shavuoth, a spring harvest festival, when he organized a confirmation celebration for his son.[42] Every Saturday morning after that, Jacobson led services in his home for two hours. The new services were much shorter than usual, although the language of prayer remained Hebrew. The room was ablaze in candles.[43] The men's heads were covered, and the sexes sat separately. What was radically new was the choir, composed of Jewish as well as Christian students at a local Berlin school directed by Jeremias Heinemann. Heinemann was then 36, and had worked alongside Jacobson at the new school and temple in Westphalia. He was a prolific reformer, editor of a renewal journal called *Jedidja*, and the author of pedagogical pamphlets, school texts, and literary criticism on contemporary German poetry.[44] Heinemann's students sang in German and Hebrew, accompanied by organ music. Heinemann was also quite an enthusiast for improving women's position in Judaism. During his Berlin years, he welcomed girls in his school, and he also conducted an annual "religious fest" as a kind of confirmation service for girls as well as boys.

The sermon at the new services was in German, delivered either by Jacobson himself or by one of the university students who worked with him on the new services. For a time, Jacobson covered all of the expenses. Later, a fee was charged for tickets, at least on the Jewish New Year. Surviving reports suggest that the services fulfilled deep spiritual longings among their participants. One observer noted that some men "after twenty years of alienation from Judaism spent the entire day at the services; men thought to be above religious feeling were shedding tears of devotion."[45] Their tears are fascinating, since critics at the time and later complained that the atmosphere at reform services was "cold" when compared to traditional Jewish worship styles. While the services were still meeting in Jacobson's apartment suite the number attending was high, reported up to 400.[46] Because of the crowds, in 1817 the home temple moved to the residence of Amalie and Jacob Herz Beer. During the next six years, close to 1,000 participants attended services at the Beer home on one Saturday or another.[47] This meant that well over a third of the Jewish adults in Berlin were showing at least some interest in the new prayer style.[48] Those attracted to the new Jewish practices tended to be richer and younger than Berlin Jews who did not attend.[49]

The Beers spent 7,000 thalers renovating their mansion, by constructing three connected rooms, decorated with "golden tassels, gold-covered columns, and curtains embroidered with images of golden crowns."[50] And the Beers also recruited their children and friends to contribute to the services. When the services moved to their home in 1817, Giacomo was living in Paris, but he sent back music for the services at least once, and Christian acquaintances, including Karl Zelter and Bernard Anselm Weber, also composed religious scores.[51] Here Zelter was influenced by Karl Fasch, his own teacher and the founder of the Choral Society, who had set Moses Mendelssohn's texts to music and also written Chanukah music for his friends.[52] That Christian friends of the family contributed to the new services forces us to question a common critique that the reformers had relied too heavily on Protestant values and practices.[53] Perhaps here is the rare example of the mutually respectful religious symbiosis often sought by historians. Another prestigious Christian friend of reform was Friedrich Schleiermacher, who took a keen interest in the new services and attended on at least one occasion. If only we knew what he and Henriette said about the new services when they took their walks in the Tiergarten Park. Although Henriette was still Jewish in 1815, she was openly hostile to the new services in her letters to friends.[54]

A contemporary once described the Beer home as "the most glamorous house in all Berlin," and it was altogether fitting that the temple services would be held in a large home.[55] In these years, the difference between a private event and a public event was not *where* people gathered, but rather *who* participated. Homes were of course the private setting where families gathered for meals and celebrations. But if the family was wealthy and hospitable, homes could also be very public spaces where strangers met, chatted, courted, competed, and enjoyed each other's good company. Because Jewish communities did not always possess the right to erect public synagogues, home prayer groups had long been common in Berlin, as elsewhere. Indeed, the politics of home synagogues ran in Amalie Beer's blood, as it were. We recall her great-grandmother Esther Liebmann, who hosted a home synagogue back in the early years of the eighteenth century. And Amalie's father Liepmann Meyer Wulff, known as one of the most pious Jews in the community, had been the patron of a domestic synagogue. Now, in 1815, a century after Esther Liebmann's death, many observant Jews in Berlin still preferred to pray in private homes, although since 1714 they could have attended Berlin's main synagogue on the Heidereutergasse.

We can well imagine that sometimes it was tricky for the Beers to separate the private from the public. What was private to one person in the family could seem public to another. In February 1814, when he was living in Paris, Amalie wrote to Giacomo, responding to his complaint that she had shared his letters with her *Hausfreunde*. She assured him that "I have never done this, except perhaps when you have enjoyed a lucky success in your art."[56] The term *Hausfreunde* captures how public the Beers' life was. "Friends of the house" did not mean intimate friends and family, or Giacomo would not have been so sensitive at having his "private" letters read in the "public" setting of the Beer home. We note that the proud mother felt no qualms about bragging of her son's accomplishments, even when he was trying to be modest. The new reform services can be understood as a continuation of Moses Mendelssohn's legacy. Neither Joseph or Recha Mendelssohn, the only two of Fromet and Moses's children to remain Jewish, took on the labor of Jewish renewal. Because they were very public in their Jewish identities and also prominent in mainstream society, the Beers were very much in Mendelssohn's tradition. But now, three decades after his death, they had ventured well beyond what Mendelssohn and his circle had accomplished. On the Jewish side their new services went far beyond Mendelssohn's careful critiques of traditional Judaism. And their prominent activity on the high culture scene was far more stylish and luxurious than Mendelssohn's modest tea-times with Lessing and other intellectuals.

We see much of the tradition of the Court Jews in the Beer lifestyle, but we must attend to the historic shifts at both ends of the exchange. For in a few short decades, there had been enormous progress in what the state delivered in return for Jewish financial aid. Now the prince who dined weekly at a Jewish home was a liberal state official, and in return the wider Jewish community received the gift of the 1812 Edict. In their home life, the Beers not only hired a *Hofmeister* to organize their sons' education but also enjoyed the services of a *Gesellschafterin,* a noble social secretary. Antoinette von Mantalban was an impoverished noblewoman who lived in their home and provided advice on etiquette, and she may have aided with social connections as well.[57] While it was true that one could not purchase friendship any more than one could purchase creativity, being the kind of family with whom an Antoinette von Mantalban would want to live was surely helpful in prompting the right people to accept one's invitations.

There is much to admire in the way the Beer family balanced their commitments to creating a modern Judaism with their secular high culture projects. Yet we also need to imagine how they were seen by those less well endowed with money, talent, and connections. Often their children's talents were displayed at public events which they themselves were funding. With their expensive tutors, their lavish home concerts, and their generous philanthropy, the Beers may well have been seen by some as trying to buy not just emancipation but also high culture. The prominence of the Beer family in contemporary public life surely rubbed some the wrong way. Sometimes critiques of their style were voiced by friends, including those whose fate seemed similar. One of Veitel Heine Ephraim's great-grandsons, Felix Eberty, left us a revealing picture of the Beers in his memoirs. Eberty was himself a convert, trained as a jurist, and in time became a professor of law at the University of Breslau.[58] He remembered that "the old Beer provided a sparkling hospitality. He and his benevolent wife were constantly in a good mood, and they had none of the pretentious arrogance of money-proud financiers. They made sure that everyone who visited felt well, and because of their admirable qualities, one overlooked the lack of authentic cultivation in the Beers." Eberty concluded that "this lack was, in the eyes of their guests, overcome through the great honor and respect which the excellent sons showed their parents."[59] The key phrases here are *pretentious arrogance* and *authentic cultivation.* Eberty is really competing with the Beers as he writes his memoir. He insinuates not too subtly to his readers that he possesses authentic cultivation, and can therefore notice when other Jews are not quite so cultivated.

The Beer temple was a notable effort to create a new Jewish institution, a spiritual space for alienated Jews. But as Rahel's 1814 letter shows, a sharp divide now emerged between those who were trying to leave their Jewish identity behind and those who were working to create a new Jewish identity. As our story continues, we need to examine why some families dedicated themselves to reform, while others chose to leave the Jewish world entirely. Much was at stake. Each individual entered the moment of decision with particular commitments and particular financial and social resources. Those inclined to judge Amalie Beer a heroine must remember her enormous privileges. Like their own ancestors, Amalie and Jacob were very much the queen and king of the local community. If the chancellor was a regular dinner guest at one's table, the rush to leave Judaism behind may not have been so intense. The Beers did not need parvenu marriages and careers open to talent to make their way in the world. On the contrary, by converting the Beers would have lost their supreme position at the summit of Berlin Jewry.

During the six years that the services met in her home, Amalie Beer enjoyed a distinct public position in her domestic temple and her salon. She selected the boys' tutors, planned their daily work schedule, and organized their public performances. She felt comfortable in this role because she herself had been trained by Vincenzo Righini, the conductor for the court.[60] Berlin reformers were concerned with attracting women to reform, and in 1817 a book appeared entitled *Religiöse Gesänge für Israeliten, insebesondere das weibliche Geschlecht,* "Religious Songs for Israelites, Especially the Female Gender," which Amalie may have helped to compose.[61] Amalie Beer's life helps us understand the contradictions of women and reform. For although reformers wrote articles promising to improve women's standing in Jewish life, historians have complained that they actually accomplished little for women.[62] But although the male reformers did not deliver on their promises, at least one real woman was living out their message, or perhaps was even the inspiration for their promises.

We see in the journal *Sulamith* how much attention reformers paid to women's issues, at least in print. The editors of the little journal chose a woman's name for the title of their publication, and on its cover was a picture of a woman.[63] We often see that in moments of national awakening men choose to represent their new movement with a female image. Authors who wrote for the *Sulamith* wrote about the problem of *agunot,* women abandoned by husbands without an official divorce, and complained about how inadequate religious education was for Jewish girls.[64] Reformers proposed that sermons be delivered in German, and advocated confirmation ceremonies for girls as well as boys. Their credo was that a more aesthetic service would enhance women's loyalty to Judaism.[65] Another of their ideas, very much in tune with wider trends, was for mothers to attend more closely to their children's education. Moreover beyond the services, reformers created a few public settings in which women participated, such as the lectures and classes organized by a preacher, Leopold Zunz, in the Beer temple.[66]

Amalie Beer's life story shows that women in Berlin then could play an important role in creating a new way to be Jewish. High culture was her expertise, not finance or commerce. Unlike Glückel of Hameln, Esther Liebmann, or Gutele Rothschild in their time, Beer did not sell seed pearls, provide the king with jewelry, count receipts in the family bank, found lace workshops, or travel to the Leipzig fair.[67] Like so many among her well-to-do peers, Amalie Beer was not a *business wife,* but rather a *high culture wife.* The salon women often mastered some kind of art themselves, or helped train their children in music, literature, or art. When they rejected commercial roles, they were actually fulfilling a dream of many reformers, who were embarrassed by the reality and the image of Jewish women working in commerce. Reformers then and later saw in women's public labor an example of how Jewish family roles were distorted. Their ideal was the leisured Christian lady. Indeed some reformers saw Jewish women's public work as a sexual danger. The writer Ayzik Meyer Dik, for instance, complained that "the women of Israel and their daughters sit selling all kinds of silk and linen and everyone who comes to buy wants to try out the taste of a virgin."[68]

With their concerts, tutors, and songbooks, Beer and her high culture women friends show how women's lives were changing. By the early nineteenth century many women preferred religious and cultural activism to unpaid labor in family enterprises. Productive labor departed from domestic space, women worked less often in family businesses, and husbands worked less often at home. Well-to-do families left the cities and built homes in the new suburbs. But their homes were not at all isolated enclaves, but could be very public spaces.[69] This is how we should view Amalie Beer's work in the temple. She preferred to hire her sons' tutors, draw up guest lists with her social secretary, and plan the music for the temple rather than keep the books for the family business and ride in a carriage on a bumpy road to the Leipzig fair.

A walk in the Orthodox neighborhoods of Brooklyn or Jerusalem in our own times shows that in some corners of contemporary Jewish society the business wife is very much alive. In the centuries before Amalie Beer, wealthy Jewish women too had often worked publicly in family businesses. Amalie's great-grandmother Esther Liebmann was a shining example of this distinctive pattern. From today's vantage point we may find the business wives a more attractive model than the high culture wives, for the public labor of the business wives may well have enhanced their influence at home. In our time we are perhaps less likely to romanticize the high culture wives, since their investment in the accomplishments of their sons grates on our contemporary feminist sentiments. But from a historical view we must see that the high culture mother role also provided women with autonomy, public recognition, and power within their families.

"The Company We Keep," 1815–1818

In the fall after the temple services began, a short one-act play opened in Berlin. *Unser Verkehr* ("The Company We Keep") had its premiere at the Berlin Opera House on September 2, 1815. The satire was written by a Breslau physician, K. A. B. Sessa. Sessa himself was decidedly obscure, for this was his only published work of literature, the first edition was anonymous, and he died the year it opened in Breslau. Although the setting was a poor Jewish village and not urban Berlin, the performance of this play was bound to wound families like the Beers. We know that the Beer sons were distressed by Sessa's drama. When the play opened, Michael Beer, then 15, wrote to his brother Wilhelm that *Unser Verkehr* showed "how the hate of the Christians has manifested itself in a most abominable fashion."[70] Three years later, the brothers were still agitated about Sessa's satire; an 1818 letter from Giacomo to Michael expresses hurt and anger about it.[71] The play had first been performed in Breslau in February 1813, was published anonymously in 1814, and had been scheduled to open in Berlin in the summer of 1815.[72] But Chancellor Hardenberg forbade the performance, arguing that it might provoke riots against local Jews. We must wonder whether he discussed this problem over dinner at the Beer home. But in private settings, Berliners found a way to enjoy snippets from *Unser Verkehr*. The lead actor, Albert Wurms, gave readings of the play in various homes around town, including one performance at the celebration of the Royal Princess Charlotte's birthday with the royal family at court.[73] Public pressure mounted, and eventually Hardenberg reversed the ban. So the play opened on September 2.

Set on the street of a Jewish village, the play recounts the story of the Hirsch family, who are ambitious for their children to succeed. Abraham Hirsch sends his son Jacob "to wander in the world," and Jacob departs the village carrying a sack of counterfeit coins. Those who knew of the past reality of Jewish coin manipulation could feel the sting in this detail. After a time, Jacob volunteers to fight in the War of Liberation. Jacob increasingly sees himself as successfully assimilated into German society. He declaims, "Ich will werfen den Juden bei Seit, ich bin doch aufgeklärt — ich hob doch gor nicht Jüdisches an mer!" In an English that preserves the mock dialect, Jacob has just announced proudly that "I vant to trow the Jew in me by the vayside. I'm enlightened, no — don't have nothin' Jewish in me."[74] The message and the medium were so far apart that audiences would howl in laughter at Jacob's self-delusion. As the farce continues, Jacob turns out to be a coward on the battlefield. After the war, he returns to his village. There the drama shifts to an episode in the life of one of his childhood friends, Isachar Morgenländer. Sessa's choice of names here was

5.2. Images of Jews from the play *Unser Verkehr*. Bildarchiv Preussischer Kulturbesitz/Art Resource, NY.

thoroughly malicious. Morgenländer means *Oriental,* a way to brand Jews as permanent outsiders in the German nation. Sessa's choice of Morgenländer may also have been a slap at David Friedländer. Jacob's old friend Isachar has now become Isidore, and is studying at a nearby university. Isidore and Jacob Hirsch now compete for the hand of Lydie Polckwitzer, who is cultured and modern as well as rich and beautiful. Jacob tries to win the competition by lying to Lydie's father, announcing that he has won the lottery, but the family discovers his lie and cancels the engagement.

Throughout the play, Sessa's Jewish characters are utterly calculating and insincere. Sessa mocks their language, their commercialized marriages, and how all encounters and relationships seem to involve financial competition. The play exposed some of the touchiest problems of contemporary Jewish life, and many were undoubtedly pained and humiliated. Throughout *Unser Verkehr* the characters speak a comical German that was a carefully constructed fake Yiddish. All in all, Berliners found the farce hilarious. It is ironic that the lead actor, Albert Wurms, had apparently learned how to speak mock Yiddish from various Jewish friends.[75] This episode reveals the painful truth that there were Jews in Berlin willing to help Wurms satirize other Jews. Wurms also offered a popular home performance featuring his imitation of a Jewish woman who entertains her guests with the recitation of a classic German poem. At first she pronounces the words correctly. But by the end of the poem she becomes quite flustered, and closes her performance in Yiddish.[76] The message is clear: proper German is only a cover for a truer, different, self, a self whose Jewishness is expressed in Yiddish. In Wurms's satire, language defines ethnicity.

That Wurms learned his mock Yiddish from Jewish friends suggests that not all contemporary Jews were appalled by Sessa's farce. One contemporary Jew who understood precisely the behavior Sessa was mocking was August Lewald, a convert born in Königsberg, an editor and theater director, who in 1836 published a novel called *Memoiren eines Bankiers,* "Memoirs of a Banker." In this autobiographical novel, Lewald's narrator asserts that Sessa's play was a "masterpiece," because the characters were "utterly true to type."[77] Well into 1816, *Unser Verkehr* was still being applauded by audiences in Berlin. Portraits of the play's characters, whose satire even now is quite effective, were sold by local street vendors, who found many buyers.[78] The wild popularity of the play showed government officials how strong popular sentiment was against Jews who were becoming more mainstream in dress, language, and public behavior. All in all, 1816 was turning out to be a rather bad year for the Jews. Minister of the Interior Friedrich von Schuckmann formally proposed that year that the 1812 Edict be retracted altogether. The Ministry of Finance issued a proclamation that "all civil rights must be linked to their [the Jews'] conversion . . . as long as a Jew remains Jewish, he cannot obtain a position in the State."[79] The equation of emancipation and conversion became ever tighter in the coming years.

In the months when *Unser Verkehr* was drawing huge crowds and the promises of the 1812 Edict were fading, more and more books, articles, and pamphlets devoted to the topic of Jewish emancipation were filling the bookstores. A few authors, including Johann Ewald and Heinrich Paulus, did argue in favor of continued emancipation, at least for wealthy and educated Jews. But Ewald and Paulus were definitely tilting against the trend. For just as Sessa did in *Unser Verkehr,* most of the pamphlet authors attacked the very Jews who already looked and talked like Christians. Imagine how the Beers and the Mendelssohns must have felt when and if they read what Garlieb Helwig Merkel wrote in his book *Über Deutschland* ("About Germany"). "Previously," Merkel asserted, "Berlin Jews had only been permitted to live on the other side of the River Spree opposite the Palace." He was distressed that "now the Jews bought up every house for sale in the main streets and filled the city with their shops." He complained that "now, they lead in occupations such as the book trade, which had previously been closed to them. Almost all the country homes on both sides of the Tiergarten, the Berliners' only place of recreation, had passed into Jewish hands." Merkel was incensed to find "these mobs of aliens," who "sit on the lovely summer evenings in the doors of their homes watching the citizens walking in sand and slush."[80] It cannot have been pleasant to own a prestigious home on the Tiergarten and find oneself described as belonging to a "mob of aliens." And Merkel was not the worst. To see a much more dramatic attack, we must explore the pamphlets that appeared for sale in 1816, penned by a historian from the University of Berlin, Friedrich Rühs. Rühs had been recruited to join the history faculty by Johann Fichte, and he was a prolific academic, publishing mainly in medieval German history but also on a variety of contemporary topics. Rühs was convinced there was a deep and permanent division between the Jewish minority and the wider German society.[81]

For Rühs, as for his mentor Fichte, to belong to a nation meant not just living on a defined spot of land, but also sharing a religion, a language, and habits of dress, hair, and food. Rühs saw the Jews as a separate nation, and he wanted Jews to retain their distinctive habits, even to wear a special ribbon to distinguish themselves, which would be called the Badge of Shame.[82] The point of distinctiveness was exclusion. Even without the ribbon, Rühs hoped that "a German, even if he be deceived by looks, behavior, and speech, can recognize his Hebrew enemy."[83] Just as Sessa showed in his satirical play, it was precisely the Jews who could pass as Christians who were disturbing to hostile observers such as Professor Rühs. The rage to become more German clashed painfully with the hostility which the most successful assimilation evoked in intellectuals such as Rühs.[84] How should we view Rühs's public hostility to newly emancipated Jews? Few readers will be surprised to learn that since the Holocaust, the pamphlets from these times have been seen as a significant step on the road to the Nazi genocide.[85] The question of how antisemitic writings in 1816 affected later tragedies is a central preoccupation in this book, and we cannot help but see the shadow of Auschwitz extending back to events in the early nineteenth century. But we must avoid a too-easy determinism. We must use our historic distance from 1816 to evaluate Rühs and his fellow nationalists in their own time, not ours. It was no easy task to define Germanness at that moment. Rühs and his colleagues were unable to construct real geographical boundaries or a coherent political system for a united Germany. They despaired because their chance to create their state was disappearing. By 1816 they realized that King Frederick William III would not deliver on his promise to grant Prussia a constitution. The link between anti-semitism and nationalism was then and continued to be troubling, but in its larger aims nationalism itself was certainly a plausible and attractive stance in 1816.

Perhaps because the geographic boundaries were so fluid, Rühs looked to Protestant Christian identity to define who was a German. Yet it is crucial for our story that he allowed converts to enter the magic circle of the German people.[86] Contrast Rühs on this point with another pamphlet author from 1816, Jakob Friedrich Fries, who refused to allow baptism as an entry point into the German people. Fries was then a respected 43-year-old scholar, who just that year had been called to a professorship in philosophy at the University of Jena. Fries reviewed Rühs's book, and soon his review appeared as an independent book. Moreover Fries's views mattered, because he often hosted his students in his home, he was active in student politics, and his little book from 1816 was actually read aloud in public taverns.[87] In its pages he sought to justify denying Jews, even converted Jews, any civil rights. Fries agreed with Rühs about much, but they parted ways over conversion. Unlike Rühs, Fries had a wholly ethnic view of nationhood, so for him conversion was not suffi-cient to make Jews into Germans. Just how prominent Fries was then becomes clear when we learn that Georg Wilhelm Hegel had been immensely jealous of Fries some years before.[88] Hegel's jealousy is ironic, since he ultimately became hugely influential, whereas Jakob Fries languishes in obscurity. In 1816, how-ever, Hegel had just been appointed to a long-sought professorship at the University of Heidelberg, whereas Fries had already been a professor for some years. Hegel was then 46, and was delighted with his new post, because he had been frustrated with his position as the rector of an academic high school in Nuremberg. Hegel had despised Fries for years, going back to their years on the faculty of the University of Jena. Hegel, always the rationalist, despised Fries's emotional stance toward all subjects.[89]

Our exploration of these two pamphlets reveals dramatic shifts in how the antipathy to Jews was cast. It was new for critics to ignore Jewish texts and practices when they criticized Jewish life. Undoubtedly, in the wider world, beyond the pages of the pamphlets, religious passions continued to motivate hostility to Jews and Judaism. But the nation, not religion, was the big prob-lem for Rühs and Fries. Creating ethnic borders inside the society was one way to imagine a nation at a time when a unified state remained a distant dream. It was also in the year 1816 that the Mendelssohns decided to baptize their four children, although they themselves remained Jewish for the time being. When we last crossed paths with Abraham and Lea Mendelssohn, in 1811, they had just returned to Berlin from Hamburg. Now, five years later, several more relatives had converted, including Abraham's brother Nathan and his sister Henriette, and Lea's cousins Marianne Saaling and Rebecca Friedländer. Neither Lea nor Abraham showed evidence of a spiritual affinity for the Lutheran faith, a telling fact which Lea herself admitted in a letter in 1799, when her cousin Julius Eduard Hitzig converted. She remarked that "it would be a blessing if we could dispense with all this hypocrisy. But given the desire for a more elevated occupation than that of merchant, and the prospect of those many affectionate friendships which induce young people to befriend members of another religious community, there is really no other option."[90] For our interests the key phrase is *all this hypocrisy,* a revealing admission from an important personality. Given their elevated status in Berlin, it would seem unjustified to argue that the Mendelssohns baptized their children in 1816 to gain civic equality.

Now Abraham and Lea had good reasons to be unhappy with policies that can be seen as a functional retraction of the 1812 Edict. But in Abraham's own life we see little evidence of political exclusion, since by 1816 he was actively involved in local and national politics. Three years before, he had joined David Friedländer on the Berlin City Council. Moreover in the very year he and Lea baptized their children, Abraham had been sent to Paris to help negotiate the details of the final peace settlement between France and Prussia. Careers for their children are a most plausible explanation of their decision. Felix was only seven in 1816, and long before his parents agreed to let him pursue a musical path, their plan for him was a career in the law, which definitely required baptism. Good evidence is the letter which Abraham wrote to Fanny in 1829, explaining that they decided to baptize the children in 1816 because that was the year that the Prussian state decided to enforce "religious requirements." He and Lea feared that they could no longer raise their children in a "neutral way."[91] Abraham was likely referring to the 1816 decision to remove unconverted Jews from the Prussian civil service. Here a comparison with the Beer family is illuminating. Giacomo's success as a composer and conductor shows that at least in Paris, baptism was not required for a musical career. The two families shared so much, yet on the issue of conversion there was obvious disagreement. There must have been heated and searching conversations on this point, for in 1816, Abraham's niece Betty, who had already converted, returned to Judaism to marry Giacomo's younger brother Heinrich.[92]

Lea and Abraham's decision must have required much soul-searching, considering Lea's mother Bella and her militant opposition to baptism. Remember that she had cut off all contact with Lea's baptized brother, Jacob Salomon

Bartholdy. They kept the children's status a secret, a situation that must have become much more complex to maintain in 1820, when Lea and Abraham moved their family to an apartment in Grandmother Bella's home on the Neue Promenade.[93] Given her treatment of Jacob, they may have feared that she would cut off the considerable Itzig inheritance if she knew the truth.[94] To safeguard their secret, Lea and Abraham must have kept their family relationships quite separate from their social life with Christian friends. Baptism could not be used to help one socially unless it was known that one was now a Christian.

Another of our key personalities was also baptized in 1816, David Koreff, Karl's friend from the North Star Club. Like Karl, Koreff had studied medicine at the University of Halle before the 1806 defeat. During the war years he had lived in Paris, practicing medicine, composing operas, and writing poetry and musical reviews. A lavish family inheritance enabled Koreff to offer his professional services gratis to selected patients. One of them was Caroline von Humboldt, and gossipy friends were convinced that at one point she and David Koreff had even become lovers.[95] We can only imagine how Rahel must have reacted to the gossip about this affair when she heard of it, as surely she must have. In 1816 Koreff was 33, and had just been appointed a professor of medicine at the University of Berlin. His star was rising, thanks to the ever-crucial patron Chancellor Hardenberg. In 1816, Koreff expected Hardenberg to appoint him the director of a new medical clinic. After the cabinet order appointing him to the professorship had already been announced, Hardenberg reportedly asked Koreff if he was still Jewish. Since the answer was "yes," Koreff was told that the moment had come when he must become a Christian. He left Berlin for the ritual, which was performed in a small town near Dresden. Koreff's story teaches us that baptism was not always the public turning point which it sometimes seems from afar. To us, Hardenberg's question to Koreff seems incomprehensible, since Koreff was the chancellor's private physician, and cared for his body on a daily basis. Our presumption would be that if he had converted, Koreff would have confided or bragged or hinted to Hardenberg that he was now a Christian. At any rate, after his baptism, Koreff's life flourished. He lived in an elegant home in the center of Berlin, busy with many love affairs. He was a great favorite in the salons, now reviving after years of occupation and war. Hardenberg further rewarded him with a prominent professorship at the new University of Bonn. But some at the university resented Professor Koreff's rapid climb to power, and his students humiliated him by smoking during his lectures.[96]

A year later, Henriette Herz, now 53, finally became a Lutheran, the last of her circle to leave Judaism. Henriette had long been convinced of the truths of

Christianity, but she waited until her very religious mother died in 1817.[97] Once she had made her decision, her friend Schleiermacher tried to persuade her to let him preside over the ritual at his church in Berlin. She rejected this idea and, like David Koreff, chose to have the ceremony in a small town outside Berlin. After her baptism, Henriette spent several years in Italy, living with Dorothea and Friedrich Schlegel, who had left Vienna that year so as to be close to her sons in Rome. Here, tensions flared between Henriette and Dorothea. Viewed from a distance, these two fifty-something converted women had much in common, yet Henriette was jealous of Dorothea's integration into Catholic society in Rome. For by 1817 Dorothea was going to Mass daily, and her two grown sons were now both painters in the Nazarene movement, whose enthusiasts dressed in the garb of the historic Jesus. Dorothea enjoyed a close relationship with her brother-in-law Jacob Salomon Bartholdy, who was also living in Rome as Prussian consul. Indeed Bartholdy commissioned Dorothea's sons to paint frescoes of Bible scenes on the walls of his villa.[98]

Henriette Herz did not change her life in any radical ways after her baptism. She was a bright woman whose life was interesting enough, yet she left neither novels nor a full memoir nor diaries nor correspondence behind for us. Her intellectual work seems to have depended very much on her relationships, as did the timing of her conversion. Her memoir ends when she was only 17, and she burned her entire correspondence with Dorothea Schlegel. She wrote drafts of two novels, but after Dorothea reacted with merely weak praise, she destroyed both manuscripts.[99] Of the three childhood friends, it is ironic that it is Rahel, who never saw herself as a real author, whose words have survived and who has become by far the best known of the three. Karl's dedication to saving her every word made it possible for us to know her thoughts today.

With Henriette's conversion at age 53 we see yet another way that Jewish daughters from Berlin balanced their desires to become Christian with their ties to their mothers. Hers was the path of the dutiful daughter, who postponed her baptism until after her mother died. Dorothea, in contrast, was the first to convert, and broke many of her close family ties at the time of her divorce from Simon Veit. Rahel too chafed at the constraints of traditional Jewish marriage practices, but by the time she converted, her brothers supported her decision and her parents were already dead. The sharp polarity between Dorothea's stormy exit from Judaism and Henriette's deference to her mother illuminates Lea Mendelssohn's compromises. Lea truly tried to "have it all" in her relationship with each generation, by baptizing her children first, then herself and Abraham, and all the while keeping the baptisms a secret from her own mother. Of course there must have been a high psychic cost to this complex family strategy.

As time went on, the disappointments in the wider world continued, and we see difficulties in every corner of Jewish life. There was the humiliation of *Unser Verkehr* and the scurrilous pamphlets. Morale suffered when prominent converts left the Jewish world. Traditional Judaism suffered too, when two of the rabbis from the community synagogue died.[100] Meanwhile, internal tensions divided the fragile new alternative temple from within. Some of those who were writing sermons and prayerbooks began to criticize the elitism of the temple. In the fall of 1817 Isaac Markus Jost, then a teacher in a Berlin school, planned to bring some of his students to the Beer temple for Rosh Hashanah, and requested that the students be included in his ticket. He heard a rumor that those who tried to enter without a ticket of their own would be sent away by the police. He brought his class anyway, but they were asked to leave, and Jost later departed in a huff.[101] Later, he complained about the elitism of the temple, especially about the seats reserved up front for the wealthy. In response, the temple leadership consented to set up a section for "the learned" near the seats reserved for the wealthy. So *Bildung,* or cultivation, achieved some parity with *Besitz,* or property. Jost was right to be outraged, because the Beers and Jacobson were certainly not acting in the democratic spirit.

More important in the long run, however, was the increasing hostility of the state and the crown to the reform project. Indeed, after the services had been moved from Jacobson's apartment to the Beer home, officials were plotting to close down the popular domestic temple. Only five years after the 1812 Edict, emancipation and reform had become hotly disputed inside ruling circles. Alas for the reformers, the king himself had taken a special interest in the question, and he was vehemently opposed to the creation of new religious sects. Two years after Jacobson began the services, in 1817, the king issued a ruling forbidding them. Hardenberg intervened, however, and the reform services were allowed to continue. The official rationale was that they were a temporary measure, allowed only so long as renovations of the large public synagogue were not yet complete. From the king's viewpoint, if Jews could experiment with an alternate variant of Judaism, political dissidents might organize too. We find it difficult to think that the reform services threatened social revolution. But we can better understand the king's fears by considering the increasing unity among varieties of Protestant practice. Many in and out of power were pleased in 1817 when Lutherans and Calvinists joined together to create the Evangelical Church of Prussia. For over a century, the Hohenzollern dynasty which ruled Prussia had been Calvinist, whereas the population was mainly Lutheran.[102] Schleiermacher had labored long and hard on this project, because he believed that religious union was a step toward national union. Here is yet another example of how Protestantism then was becoming a thicker civic identity. Nationalist organizers also aimed to merge the two Protestant faiths, although their draft constitution included an explicit ban on Judaism, which they regarded as a "creed" which was "detrimental to the causes of mankind."[103]

Besides working on their draft plan for a future German state, the fraternity students experienced a heady few days during the fall of 1817, when members of the Burschenschaften climbed the Wartburg mountain for bonfires, songs, speeches, and prayers. Close to five hundred students from ten universities attended, almost 5 percent of the German university population.[104] Most were Protestants, but Catholic students were there too, even though their universities had not been invited by the planning committee and although the very choice of a place to meet was profoundly Protestant. The Wartburg Festival would long be remembered as a high point of the nationalist youth movement from the era of the War of Liberation. The date of October 18 had double historic significance, as the fourth anniversary of the Battle of Leipzig and the three hundredth anniversary of Martin Luther's posting of his theses on the door of the Wittenburg church that began the Reformation. Later Luther had lived in the Wartburg castle while he translated the New Testament from Latin to German, and even threw ink at a vision of the devil.[105] In the Wartburg Festival as in other celebrations from these years, faith and nation were symbolically connected. Since the Prussian triumph at the Battle of Leipzig, public commemorations on October 18 had become a tradition. The ceremonies in 1815, for example, were celebrated around a "pillar of fire" on various mountaintops, or at altars built in town squares. Some of the participants decorated themselves with oak leaves, because the oak tree had become a symbol of the German nation, and the festivals often closed with a church service.

The radical fraternity activists who met on the mountaintop aimed to create a nationwide organization of political fraternities, and they worked closely with the gymnastics organizations from Berlin and elsewhere. Since 1811, when Friedrich Ludwig Jahn organized the first gymnastics club on the Hasenheide exercise grounds in Berlin, hundreds of gymnastics clubs had been organized all across Germany, drawing in thousands of participants.[106] The gymnastics clubs attracted students as well as artisans, an unusual mix. And at least up until 1817, Jews *who were still Jewish* could join the radical fraternities as well as the gymnastics clubs, and some Jews did indeed march up the Wartburg mountain on those two historic days in October 1817.

The explicit integration of Christian symbols and practices in the nationalist projects of the day had long been planned by Jahn and other nationalist intellectuals. In spite of their deep antipathy to all things French, Jahn paid careful attention to how revolutionaries in France had constructed their new national festivals. The French had celebrated the national festivals on the holy days in

5.3. The Wartburg Festival. Colored wood engraving, 1817. Bildarchiv Preussischer Kultur-besitz/Art Resource, NY.

the Christian calendar, but the celebrations had been militantly secular. Jahn's vision was much more Christian in every respect, for he planned the new German festivals to occur on a holy Christian day and be Christian in form and content. Moreover the plan was to engage their participants directly in German history by commemorating specific events in the German past. For instance, Jahn's colleague Ernst Arndt organized the Deutsche Gesellschaft clubs, which sponsored holy festivals in the name of all Germans.[107] Jahn and Arndt celebrated the wild success of the Wartburg Festival as the realization of their dreams.

Many students who climbed the Wartburg mountain that October wore the radical dress of the day, the traditional German clothing which had been popularized by Turmvater Jahn in Berlin. The outfit was a black medieval-looking suit, with a long jacket. As one student reported, with the suit the students often wore "a broad white collar, over which hung our long hair. On our heads we wore velvet berets with silver crosses."[108] The students carried the black, red, and gold colors of the old imperial order which had been held high in October 1813 by the soldiers at the Battle of Leipzig. One episode at the festival that has proven controversial since 1817 is the bonfire of books and symbols from the old regime. Debate continues regarding whether the auto-da-fe was planned by the main organizers of the festival, and how many student activists actually participated in the bonfire. Among the burned items were a corporal's cane, a military corset, and a wig pigtail. The books which were dashed into the flames included the Napoleonic Code, Saul Ascher's book called *Germanomania*, and a work of history by August von Kotzebue.

Ascher was one of the rare Jewish intellectuals who explicitly attacked the xenophobia of the student nationalist movement.[109] Unfortunately we know little about Ascher's life. He was a journalist and scholar and gadfly whose actual occupation continues to elude scholars. The poet Heinrich Heine lived in Berlin in the early 1820s, and there he got to know Ascher. Heine later remembered that they would discuss topics such as "what is fear?" They debated whether fear arises from reason or emotion. "On this question I argued so often with Dr. Saul Ascher when we met by chance at the Café Royal in Berlin . . . Towards the end of his sermon he used to look at his watch, summing up with the sentence: 'reason is the highest principle! — Reason!' Whenever I hear this word nowadays, I remember Dr. Saul Ascher with his abstract legs, his grey, tight and transcendental coat and his brusque cold features which might serve as a copperplate to a geometry textbook. This man, well into his fifties, was a personified straight line . . . "[110] It is unlikely that Ascher attended the Wartburg march, but he surely heard reports of how his book *Germanomania* was burned on the mountaintop. One of the book's targets was none other than Friedrich Rühs. Ascher rejected Rühs's attempt to define Germanness by reference to Christian identity, and was angry that Rühs wanted "to promote the conversion of Jews to Christianity, so that they be transformed into Germans!" Ascher retorted that it was not "as if Christianity were an indispensable condition of Germanhood! Which reminds me, that the Germans as Tacitus describes them . . . were quite brave Germans without being Christians."[111]

But for Jewish students who saw themselves as patriotic, the festival became rather problematic. Jewish students who watched Ascher's book burn may well have felt most uncomfortable. One Jewish radical who was at Wartburg that October later remembered that "never in my life have I been asked so often, so intensively, so persistently, about my being a Jew, as during the last week . . . Some pitied me for being doomed to be a Jew, others accused me;

some insulted me, others praised me for it . . . but all my comrades were constantly aware of it. Oh, how deeply was I disappointed, how deeply wounded, frustrated, humiliated, how much in pain, in despair — and now, ever since then, how perplexed, how bewildered, how hopeless am I."[112] We leave the students on the mountain now, to explore the tribulations of one of the best and the brightest sons of German Jewry, who tried to integrate his Jewish past with a socialist future for himself and indeed for the wider society.

The life story of Ludwig Börne, born Baruch, shows how tricky it was to integrate a patriotic republican politics with a Jewish identity in those years. To trace his journey we must depart Berlin, which would have made him happy, since he feared humiliation by the sophisticated, competitive, and judgmental salon circles there, and avoided the town for years. Börne converted in 1818, a year after Henriette Herz did, somehow fitting since the two had been linked for decades. Back when he was a teenager, in 1802, his parents sent him to Berlin to live with the Herzes, in order to prepare for a career as a physician.[113] Börne fell in love with Henriette. Considering his age and her personality, few of their mutual friends were surprised that she did not reciprocate his feelings. Still, they would remain close friends in the years to come.[114] After Markus Herz died, Börne left Berlin, and he later decided not to become a physician. Eventually he earned a degree in political economy at the University of Gießen, an unusual accomplishment for a young Jewish man then. For most of his adolescence and early adulthood, the city of Frankfurt was under French control. In 1811, when he was 25, the French granted the local Jews their full civil rights in exchange for a large payment. Börne was at the right place at the right time, and secured an administrative post in the local police. But unfortunately for the Jews of Frankfurt, and thus for Börne, when the French were ejected from German cities during the War of Liberation, the town council canceled all the new freedoms. After four years in his post, in 1815, at the close of the Vienna Congress, Börne lost his position. For some time after his dismissal, he searched for an alternative career that would provide financial support, intellectual stimulation, and a public intellectual role. This combination of ambitions was a tall order, because although Börne needed the finer luxuries in life, he felt too cultured to take up any of the careers then open to Jews that would support such a lifestyle. Moreover in spirit and in body he was frail, and throughout these years and later he often felt "lonely and depressive." His friends observed, perhaps lacking sympathy, that he often collapsed in episodes of "self-indulgent hypochondria." Occasionally he had "fits of melancholy," and sometimes he even talked of suicide.[115]

Three years after his dismissal, in the spring of 1818, he changed his name from Louis Baruch to Ludwig Börne. He had already left his first name behind some years earlier, when he abandoned Löw for Louis. Now, he felt he needed to change his family name because he was convinced that Christian readers would not read his new theater journal if its editor could easily be identified as Jewish.[116] Once the Senate of the City of Frankfurt approved the change, he announced his new name in a notice in the *Frankfurter Intelligenzblatt*.[117] That he would call attention to it in the newspaper shows that he was not trying to use the name change to "pass" as a Christian. Moreover, considering the similarity between his old and new names, we can well wonder if strangers would truly think that the journal was edited by a Christian by descent. Many contemporaries surely knew that he was Jewish.[118]

The public way that Börne changed his name was very much at odds with the puzzling secrecy of his conversion to Christianity. He was baptized three months after he changed his name, on June 5, in a church in the town of Rodelheim, near his home in Frankfurt.[119] Again, a convert chose privacy in a small-town location. For at least two years after the ceremony, he was convinced that neither his parents nor his friends knew that he was no longer Jewish. Of course Börne's discretion on the topic may well have been one of those secrets which are known but not discussed within families. According to most accounts of this juncture in his life, Börne's conversion only became known after the police mistakenly arrested him in 1820. After his arrest he was forced to fill in a form, and in the space for "religion" he listed himself as Christian.[120] To convert in the Frankfurt of 1818 was quite different from converting in the last decades of the previous century in Berlin. In Frankfurt, even the richest and most cultured Jews rarely socialized with Christians, whereas in Berlin participation in salons encouraged baptism. Without the friendships and love affairs that already bound Jews to Christians, the drawbacks of conversion may well have outweighed its attractions.

Börne must have tried to keep his baptism secret from his family because he was sure that they would have disapproved. He had many motives for a passive-aggressive rebellion against his parents. His relationship with his mother had always been distant, and over the years, he had come to see his father as "cold and patriarchal."[121] They had quarreled about a career in medicine, about money, and about the politics of German nationalism. Gradually Ludwig had become more patriotic and a radical leftist, whereas his father maintained the stance of a Court Jew. Another reason for Börne's secrecy about his baptism was his relationship with Jeanette Wohl, a divorced Jewish female friend in Frankfurt. She was an accomplished and sophisticated woman with leisure to devote to his career, and in time she became his patron, accountant, editor, muse, and daily correspondent. How the two enjoyed their evenings alone is mysterious. Her mother was observant, and Jeanette was in her own way loyal to Judaism. This mattered, because in these years Börne was a daily guest at the home of Jeanette's family.[122]

Why, then, did he take on the burden of a secret identity in 1818? Over the generations those fascinated by Börne have contemplated his possible impulses. None of the motives we have seen so far for the other converts in his generation seem appropriate in his case. He did not seem to want a Christian wife, and as a lonely soul, he did not seek a better social life in Christian circles. His only romantic entanglement, if we might call it that, was with Jeanette Wohl. Ironically, after his baptism became known he may have been even lonelier than before, since his still-Jewish friends in Frankfurt ostracized him once his Christian status was made public. An episode from the winter after the baptism underscores that he did not intend to use his baptism to improve his social position. That winter Börne applied to join one of the local reading clubs in Frankfurt. The club's officers rejected his application, because they thought he was Jewish. Yet, when Börne responded in a letter to the club, complaining about their exclusionary policies, he chose not to reveal that he had in fact become a Christian. This is certainly not the behavior of someone committed to self-promotion and radical assimilation.[123]

Nor can we find any obvious career motives to explain his decision to convert in 1818. Unlike his younger contemporaries Eduard Gans and Heinrich Heine, Börne did not do it to become a professor.[124] If career had been his motive, it would have been more likely for him to have converted immediately in 1815, so as to keep his position with the police. There is no evidence that he sought employment at a university or in a civil service post after he became a Christian. Indeed, with journalism as his career goal in 1818, it is not entirely obvious why conversion was necessary. For it was precisely in these decades that unconverted Jews were beginning to publish in mainstream newspapers and journals. Among the most prolific and prominent were Leopold Zunz and Saul Ascher. Other Jewish journalists of the time included Aaron Bernstein, Moritz Veit, and Lazarus Bendavid. In the first half of the century, historians have identified at least seventy Jewish men who earned a living as journalists, writers, or publishers in towns across Germany.[125]

As for a sincere religious awakening as a Lutheran, nothing points in that direction either. The simplest way to sum up his conversion motives is that Börne saw Christianity as integral to his identification with German national culture.[126] In this sense he was a living summation of what Friedrich Rühs wanted, a fusion of national and Christian rituals, symbols, and identities. His example suggests that insofar as conversion was a way to enter the German ethnic nation rather than a faith, such converts were not hypocrites, because they did not view baptism as a religious act in the first place. A thicker, politicized Protestant identity was more attractive than a thinner, less civic Judaism. Börne was certainly not alone in his quest to deepen his affiliation with German national culture, but because of his strong left commitments and his solitary ways, he took on the outsider status of an engagé activist in the left, and so we can well see him as the first secular left convert. Just because he did not disdain all particular identities, and saw himself as *German* rather than cosmopolitan, his decision to convert can look rather inconsistent. German was a desirable ethnicity, but Jewish was not. Becoming a *Christian* German was not just a matter of effectiveness in the public world, but also an inner state of mind.[127] He may have been unusual among our converts, but on the broader canvas of his times he was very much "a typical creature of the nineteenth century, whose sense of self resided in the search for non-local, non-traditional identities." Contemporary "notions of ethnic pride and cultural sensitivity" should not blind us to the reality that Christian and Jewish intellectuals alike sought to leave behind their cultures of descent.[128]

Jews Are Attacked on the Streets, 1819

We have seen that each year that passed since 1815 brought additional humiliations for those Jews who wanted a new life without becoming Protestants. We can imagine how distressing it must have been to hear everyone talking about Sessa's play and about the hostile pamphlets, or to witness Saul Ascher's book going up in flames on the Wartburg mountain. But 1819 turned out to be more painful for contemporary Jews than any other year since the Napoleonic Wars had ended. Moreover, 1819 was a watershed year for the young nationalist movement as well. It has been aptly labeled "the year of misfortune in the nineteenth century."[129] In utterly different ways the year saw setbacks for the student radicals, for the emergent left movement, and for Jews as well.

The first episode took place in March, initiated by a young man named Karl Sand. He had grown up in a pietist family in Franconia, which had been occupied by French troops for seven years after the 1806 defeat. Sand had been a volunteer in the War of Liberation, and after the war he became a fraternity activist, one of those enthusiasts who marched up the Wartburg mountain in 1817. Indeed he brought with him his own personal manifesto, inscribed with the lines "The German language rise up! The true knighthood come to bloom! The German land be free!"[130] After the festival, at the University of Jena, he became an active gymnast, and came under the influence of Wilhelm Leberecht de Wette, a theologian who saw Jakob Friedrich Fries as his mentor. While at Jena, Sand also became an intimate friend of Karl Follen, one of the most memorable personalities caught up in the student movement. Follen was a charismatic young intellect with a huge influence on the student radicals. He argued that any act, including murder, was justified in the struggle to achieve a true republican democracy.[131] Throughout 1818, Sand and some of his friends organized acts of self-sacrifice for liberal and national causes. The fraternity movement in Jena "began to discuss daily who should be 'corpsed' for the sake of freedom." Metternich was of course the chief enemy in these circles, but because of his high position he was difficult to assassinate.[132] Sand chose as his target August von Kotzebue, who was universally hated among the patriotic students.

The student radicals saw Kotzebue as an enemy of democracy, German unity, and the moral domestic life they were seeking, suspected him of being a Russian agent, and had burned one of his books on the Wartburg mountain. In 1819 August von Kotzebue was 57 and living with his second wife and child in Mannheim. For decades he had been a furiously productive playwright, editor, and novelist, whose works were translated and performed widely. He knew the theater from the inside, because he had also worked as an actor and a director.[133] The radicals' hatred for Kotzebue came from several directions. For one thing, his sympathetic and sexually experienced female characters were precisely the sort of women the radicals disdained. His plays often depict women who violate bourgeois sexual norms, and suffer for their freedoms. But in the end they tend to be forgiven and indeed to triumph. Like their mentor Johann Fichte, who argued for banishing women from civil society, many radicals hated female intellectuals and the sexualized aristocratic subculture of the old regime. Many felt unsympathetic to Jewish emancipation, and found Kotzebue's support for that cause problematic. After Saul Ascher published a critique of the Wartburg Festival, Kotzebue came out in print supporting Ascher.[134]

Kotzebue's popularity with the court also irritated the radicals. During the years he lived in Berlin, in the very beginning of the new century, when he was in his early forties, Kotzebue had achieved a "peculiar and uncomfortable status" in the republic of letters.[135] The royal family in Prussia adored him, as did the public, and indeed, contemporaries regarded him as a phenomenon because both rich and poor flocked to see his plays. It was widely known that Kotzebue was in the employ of the royal courts in Vienna and Saint Petersburg, although few knew exactly what he did in return for the payments. His publications during the War of Liberation showed that although he opposed Napoleon, Kotzebue was very much on the right, for he publicly defended the old regime courts and attacked the radical students and the gymnasts. He complained that their values and practices were "incompatible with his own

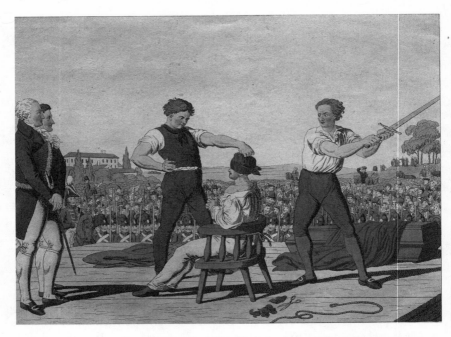

5.4. Karl Sand's Beheading. Lithograph. Bildarchiv Preussischer Kulturbesitz/Art Resource, NY.

deeply held values of order, tolerance, and humility."[136] In short, Kotzebue was an ideal target for Sand's passionate opposition to the contemporary realities of 1819.

On March 23, in the early evening, Karl Sand found his way to Kotzebue's door. Once in his living room, Sand thrust his dagger into Kotzebue, while shouting, "I take no pride in you at all. Here, you traitor to the fatherland!"[137] After Kotzebue died of his wounds, Sand tried to kill himself, but he failed. He soon found himself in prison, where he was operated on to heal his wounds. He was also allowed books and the occasional visitor. Sand's assassination of Kotzebue caused a huge crisis among his supporters, and divided the liberals from the radicals. When Wilhelm von Humboldt heard of the assassination, his conclusion was "now a constitution is impossible!"[138] Because government officials believed that the Kotzebue killing was a conspiracy, they arrested scores of fraternity students, and their mentor Fries was fired from his professorship. Follen tried to organize student radicals to march into Sand's prison and liberate him, but his appeal fell on deaf ears.

On May 20, 1819, Sand was beheaded in Mannheim. His death was scheduled for early in the morning, because the police hoped to prevent public support demonstrations. But word circulated quickly, and a sympathetic crowd gathered. Enthusiasts for Sand's image and for his act "grabbed pieces of the blood-stained scaffolding to keep as relics."[139] The executioner himself sympathized with Sand's cause, and took home the pieces from the scaffold, which he used to build a memorial cabin in his garden, where members of the Heidelberg fraternity met regularly in the decades to come. Debate about Sand's act and its consequences continues to this day. Even in a book from the 1980s we read that Sand delivered "justice" to Kotzebue with his dagger.[140] The entire episode made governments queasy about social upheaval, with good reason. The Prussian and Austrian police pursued the student radicals, "seizing books and papers, making arrests, and conducting secret examinations."[141] That July, another angry patriot, Karl Löning, tried to kill President Ibell of Wiesbaden, but failed. Once in prison, Löning committed suicide by swallowing bits of glass.[142]

Moreover beyond the desperate protests by the student radicals, artisans too began to complain loudly about their rising price of food. Three years of bad harvests, which had begun in 1816, drove up the price of bread, and the food shortage hit just at a time when unemployment among artisans in the towns was already high. The cause was, ironically enough, the demise of the Napoleonic system. Napoleon's Continental Blockade had been a great boon to the artisans of Germany, because the absence of British cotton exports helped local weavers sell their cloth at good prices. But after the wars were over, English fabrics flooded German markets, throwing thousands of artisans out of work. The impoverished artisans turned their wrath on the Jews, blaming the Rothschilds and other Jewish financiers for the profits earned by outfitting armies, smuggling British goods, and lending money to various governments. During the long years of war, merchants who could tolerate high risk were needed to transfer funds between states, exchange currencies, and help the wealthy hide their assets. To be sure, when the Rothschilds and the Mendelssohns smuggled British goods into the Continent they were sabotaging the French system. But they were making fortunes during a time when most Germans were suffering. Hostile observers may well have known the history of the mint leasers and coin millionaires of the previous century.

Those who blamed Jewish financiers for their sufferings may well have become only more incensed if they believed that Jewish emancipation was purchased with wartime profits. Rumors had circulated in 1815 that the Rothschilds were paying Friedrich Gentz and other supporters of Jewish emancipation to plead the Jewish cause during the Vienna Congress. We know that some Jewish merchants did very poorly in the dicey economic conditions of the times, but the simplistic logic was that some Jews were getting richer while the artisans were becoming poorer. We see here the very beginnings of the slippage between anti-capitalist and antisemitic sentiments, a conflation that had tragic resonances all the way forward to the Nazi era.

That August, all of the pent-up anger was expressed in the *hep hep* riots which erupted in towns across southern Germany. Some argue that the phrase *hep hep* was derived from a Latin saying which was first used during the Crusades. Another interpretation posits that *hep hep* was an evocation of the sound goats make, and that Jews were associated with goats because of their beards.[143] The first incident occurred on August 2, in Würzburg, Bavaria. The occasion was the return to Würzburg of Professor Joseph Behr, the local deputy to the Bavarian Assembly of the Estates, which had begun its sessions in February 1819 in Munich. At its most recent session Professor Behr had defended the extension of Jewish emancipation in Bavaria, a proposal initiated by Solomon Hirsch, a prominent court banker to King Maximilian Joseph I. Hirsch was hated by those to whom he loaned money, including many students and other citizens.[144] The angry rioters called out "hep hep" as they went marauding through Würzburg's Jewish neighborhoods. Soon the *hep hep* cries could be heard on the streets of Bamberg, Frankfurt am Main, Darmstadt, Karlsruhe, Leipzig, Dresden, and Heidelberg. Danish towns were also the scene of riots in Jewish neighborhoods that August. Jews often fled town, sometimes living in tents some distance away, but even flight could prove dangerous. Late in September, the highways of the Grand Duchy of Baden were still filled with Jewish families who had fled their homes weeks before. Guards were stationed on the roads to protect the Jews from "the insults of the peasants."[145] It remains unclear to this day whether any Jewish lives were lost that August and September.[146]

Prussia was one place where the *hep hep* spirit was almost altogether absent. To be sure, in May, two months before the rioters took to the streets in Bavaria, a "royal prince" stopped ten-year-old Felix Mendelssohn on the street, spat at his feet, and called out "hep! hep! Jew-boy!"[147] We who know his family's history must find this particularly poignant, for in 1819 Felix had been a Christian for three years. But two months later when the riots broke out in southern Germany, the Prussian streets remained quiet. In the words of Friedrich von Staegemann, "our Jews heard little *Hep-Hep* . . . if it were not for the cursed so-called free cities, the Jews of Germany would be assimilated within fifty years."[148] Historians have explained that because the merchant class in Berlin was not as dominated by Jews as was the case in southern German towns, there was less hatred toward them there. Moreover, the movement toward a free trade economic market was further advanced in urban

Prussia than in the southern states, and the power of the guilds had been definitively broken back in 1808 by the reforms of Stein and Hardenberg. Our intense focus on Prussia from the inside has shown the gradual retraction of the 1812 Edict, the repression of reform, and the massive pressure for conversion as the functional replacement of emancipation. Nevertheless, in comparative perspective, Prussia was also a modern state with much to offer contemporary Jews.

After calm had been achieved, the August riots were "delicately suppressed" as a topic of discussion during the 1820s and beyond. Some contemporaries discounted their importance by arguing only "despicable ruffians" were involved.[149] Even inside the Jewish world silence was the rule, at least insofar as historians can measure from reading what was published at the time. Contemporary Jewish journals like *Sulamith* and *Jedidja* avoided the topic altogether. Editors apparently feared that such discussion might "weaken" their "co-religionists' love" for their "Christian fellow citizens."[150] Their silence makes it difficult for us today to understand why local Christians rioted against Jews in August 1819. One analysis was penned by Ludwig Börne, whose perspective was altogether controversial, then and now. He condemned the riots in no uncertain terms, but he also tried to understand why so many angry Christians went on the rampage against their Jewish neighbors that August. He argued that the riots were a protest against the leading Jewish merchant bankers and the conservative princes they sometimes served.[151] Börne, like his so-similar peer Heinrich Heine, truly hated the Rothschild family. Other contemporaries focused on the ideological campaign against emancipation. Rahel blamed the nationalist intellectuals and their pamphlets and plays. She wrote to her brother Ludwig about the riots in September, after she had spent the summer in Karls-ruhe, a scene of serious upheaval. In Karlsruhe posters had been affixed to the walls of the synagogues as well as to the banking house of a local Jewish financier, calling for the extermination of the Jews.[152] In her letter, Rahel claims that she was not surprised at the outbreaks. She interprets them as a displacement of protest away from the hated "regimes." In her words: "for 3 years I have been saying: the Jews will be attacked . . . *This* is the German courage of rebellion." In her view, previous generations of Christians had been permitted to "hate, despise and persecute [the Jews] as inferior beings," but "a few wise German rulers and much time . . . put an end to this license." Here she was surely thinking of King Frederick the Great and her own special connection felt to him in childhood. Rahel went on to blame the riots on "the new hypocritical love for the Christian religion." This new Christianity incited the people into the "*only* terror they *can* still be provoked into, because they remember having been permitted it as of old! The pogrom." She took many others to task for causing the riots: "the professors Fr[ies] and Rü[hs], and others, whatever their names. Arn[im] Brent[ano], our crowd; and even more highly positioned persons full of prejudice." Her reference to "our crowd" seems surely to refer to the Sessa play, with its title *Unser Verkehr.*

In addition to the hostile rhetoric emphasized by Rahel we must also consider the backlash against the ways even minimal emancipation had changed Jewish life for the better. One recent analysis points to the hostility evoked when Jews increasingly "live[d] in places where they had hitherto been forbidden," and their positions in occupations previously closed to them. Altogether, the radical changes which resulted from emancipation "created resentment among the common people." In that summer of 1819, the "common people" found support for their hostility to Jews in "intellectual circles," whose complaints and slogans "stirred the masses to hatred and destruction. Thus matters erupted in violence."[153]

If large numbers of students participated in the riots, that would strengthen the case for the influence of nationalist intellectuals. Students would read what Fries and Rühs published and debate their views at fraternity or gymnastics club meetings. However, the proportion of students among the rioters in the summer of 1819 has become the subject of debate. Scholars find considerable differences across the towns where rioting occurred. In Würzburg, for instance, university students did join in the attacks. But in Heidelberg, in contrast, 200 students, "armed with swords and sabers, under the leadership of two professors, restored the crowd to order."[154]

We bid goodbye to the year 1819 with a look at an engraving of the *hep hep* riot in Frankfurt. The two large muscular women on the left, one with a broom and one with a pitchfork, fit our story neatly. They are angry women of the people, whose husbands worked as artisans or shopkeepers or in manufacturing. But the attacker on the right is obviously from a different social station entirely. He could be an extremely well-dressed student, a government official, perhaps a leisured noble landowner. His presence in the picture shows clearly that the 1819 riots brought rich and poor against the Jews. The well-born gentleman's victim we might call the *jüdischer Elegant,* who appears in other caricatures of the time. The satire is funny and cruel, because his body cries out from under his clothes: "I don't fit in here!" That he would have the funds and the good taste to cover this body with gentlemanly clothing is understood to be touchy and somehow offensive.

But individual stories consistently remind us that everyday life for individuals was not always as harsh as the satirical visual images might suggest. In the same summer as the riots, Julius Jolson was 18, and one evening that August

Hepp ! Hepp !

5.5. The *Hep Hep* Riots in Frankfurt am Main, by Johann Michael Volz, 1819. Germanisches Nationalmuseum, Nürnberg.

he walked into a pub in Erlangen to eat a meal.[155] He was from Munich, a graduate of the Gymnasium and an activist in patriotic student politics. Jolson had just arrived in Erlangen to begin his university studies there. Apparently the students in the pub discovered that he was planning to become a Lutheran. They loudly mocked his intentions, and he pondered "how to defend his honor without humiliation."[156] Their mockery is disturbing, because from our vantage point they should have seen his conversion as the surrender of ethnic separateness, a decision to make himself German in religion as well as in politics. Jolson's dignity was saved by a fortuitous event, the arrival in the pub of Hermann von Rotenhan, a leisured young nobleman also about to enter the university. Jolson sensed an "instinctive affinity" with Rotenhan, a feeling that he could "hope for protection" from the noble gentleman. Indeed Rotenhan did intervene on behalf of Jolson in a "chivalrous manner," and soon the taunting ended. Jolson and Rotenhan became close friends, and soon afterwards Jolson was baptized. In time he would become Friedrich Stahl, a conservative professor and church activist, known for his opposition to allowing unconverted Jews to hold civil service posts. We bid goodbye to Jolson and to the tumultuous second decade of the new century, and turn to the 1820s, when the harmonious modernization of Judaism ground to a halt.

6

The Entrance Ticket to European Civilization, *1820–1833*

"Berlin Does Not Enchant Me," 1820–1821

The summer of 1819 was also a troubled time for Karl and Rahel, after (four contented years in Karlsruhe, the capital of the southern German state of Baden.[1] Karl chafed at the constraints of his official position representing Prussia abroad, and Rahel was insulted that court society rejected her. Baden was the rare German state to receive a constitution in 1818, but Karl's radical politics were nevertheless seen as troublesome both by Baden's Grand Duke Ludwig and by Karl's superiors back in Berlin. Alas, he overplayed his hand, and late in July he was recalled from his post. His republican enthusiasms had long irritated King Frederick William III. Moreover his patron Chancellor Hardenberg was rapidly losing power in Berlin. Karl was offered a position as the Prussian envoy to the United States, but he declined, as Rahel's health was too frail for such an uprooting. And so the couple returned to Berlin. While Karl awaited word on what he hoped would be another assignment somewhere in Germany, they rented a furnished apartment on the Französiche Straße.

Rahel's reluctance to return to Berlin seems to have been quite rational. Indeed, she found the social scene which awaited her there disappointing. She wrote her old friend Gustav von Brinckmann that "Berlin . . . does not enchant me . . . Death, aided by the war, has taken its toll among our friends . . . at every corner, where *our kind* used to live, there are *strangers*." She continued her lament, noting that "the whole constellation of beauty, grace, coquetry, liking, love affairs, wit, elegance, cordiality, urge to develop ideas, true earnestness, uninhibited calling on each other and visiting, good-humored jest, is dissipated."[2] It is true that in the Berlin of the early 1820s, coquetry and love affairs were disdained in favor of simplicity, domesticity, and family intimacy. We have arrived at the era which has come to be called the time of Biedermeier. Herr Biedermeier, the source of the term, was a caricature from a column in a humor magazine called *Fliegende Blätter*. In later years, he was a target of satire, but in the 1820s his values were idealized and admired.[3] The value contemporaries placed on cozy experiences among intimates was reflected in their interior furnishings, designed for comfort and friendship, rather than grand display. The living room of the home, called the *Wohnzimmer*, typically included a sofa and comfortable chairs, surrounded by small tables holding sewing equipment, bird cages, or plants. The piano was indispensable, as a source of pleasure and sociability as well as a symbol of refinement.

As the proliferation of pianos demonstrates, the peace and prosperity of these years made it possible for more Germans with enough funds, leisure, and education to cultivate the arts at home. Contemporaries were so enthusiastic about cultivation, or *Bildung*, that they used the word frequently, to describe people and experiences. In this era and later, the term *Bildungsbürger* designated the kinds of persons who wanted and acquired cultivation. In the closing decades of the old regime era, a small circle of lucky women had displayed their hard-won cultivation in salons. What was special about the salons was that they took place in private homes, yet were well known to the wider public. Now that the years of occupation and war had finally come to an end, salon-style socializing had resumed in Berlin. Indeed observers were convinced that by the 1820s, there had been a sharp increase in the number of bluestocking women who possessed the ambition to host a salon.[4] Some historians argue that by that time across Germany, salons had become "commonplace events" among circles of intimate friends and relatives.[5] Precisely because ever wider circles of Berliners had the money, time, and skills to chat in salons, attend the theater, read books and journals, visit museums, and play and listen to music, it was becoming harder to restrict high culture to the well born.

Moreover, salons were no longer the unique cultural institutions they had been a half century before. Now newspapers, museums, theaters, coffeehouses, and the new University of Berlin provided public spaces for the cultivated. Unfortunately, few of the new public spaces provided leadership positions for women. Salons remained a unique space for women, but defining just what was and what was not a salon vexed contemporaries. Observers mocked the pretentious style of hostesses who thought they were "running a salon" when they were "merely running a restaurant."[6] Here we must explore all possible variations of socializing. We can certainly distinguish between different styles of entertaining, depending upon whether invitations were issued, whether a woman was the host, just how many or what kind of visitors attended, or how intellectual the discussions were. But we avoid such categories here and use the word *salon* in a colloquial manner, so as to survey the broad horizon of contemporary Berlin social life. When intellectuals mixed socially, sometimes they spoke of weighty issues and sometimes they laughed and gossiped and were frivolous. Some gatherings were formal, and other times friends arrived at the same home without elaborate planning. We need a wide landscape of the past so that we can chart what was changing as time passed.[7]

After the Vienna Congress, Jewish women were less often prominent as *salonières,* as Fanny Lewald learned the hard way. Fanny was born into a well-to-do Jewish merchant family in Königsberg in 1811, and she was bright, well educated, sensitive, talented, and ambitious. But when she was a single daughter in her twenties, living in her family home and strictly supervised by her parents, she was painfully unhappy. Fanny's father David had a complex stance toward baptism. He feared that if he himself converted he would alienate his traditional Jewish business associates in eastern Prussia, but he and his wife Zipporah favored conversion for the younger generation. Thus the parents agreed that Fanny and her brothers could convert when they were teenagers. After years of struggle against her father, who was convinced his family would be humiliated if she became a published novelist, Fanny did begin to earn her living by her pen. She eventually moved to Berlin in 1845, when she was 34. Her cousin August encouraged her writing, and in time she became an established, prolific, and popular author of novels and political essays.[8] Fanny's heroine was Rahel Levin Varnhagen, and even after she began hosting her own salon, she envied Rahel's circle during the old regime years. In her novel *Prinz Louis Ferdinand*, published in 1859, Lewald reconstructed the atmosphere of Rahel's first salon, complete with imagined exchanges on the subject of conversion between Rahel and Dorothea Veit Schlegel.[9] What Fanny Lewald knew in her bones was that in the Biedermeier years, salon hosts were more and more often born to noble privilege. Among salon hosts, the proportion of Jews to nobles had now reversed itself. Back in the old regime years, 9 of the 16 gatherings called salons were hosted by women who were either Jewish or of Jewish descent.[10] Now, in the 1820s and '30s, 12 of the 16 women hosting salons were noblewomen, including one princess and two countesses.[11] Still, it would be a mistake to attribute this shift only to caste privilege, important as caste was. For now Berlin was home to a string of noble *sa-lonières* who were remarkably accomplished and charismatic.

The most prominent was Elisabeth von Staegemann, whose husband Frie-drich belonged to the Tischgesellschaft and was an ironic observer of the Itzig-Arnim dispute.[12] By 1819, Friedrich had been ennobled and was the editor of a government newspaper. An ardent liberal, he was outraged as Chancellor Hardenberg began to buckle under Metternich's repressive policies. Elisabeth, now 58, was graced with natural beauty and artistic sensibilities and talents. After a divorce in her early years, she had hosted her own salon, and when she married Friedrich in 1796, they continued the tradition, enlivened by the talented friends of Elisabeth's two daughters. Antoinette was a gifted pianist, and Hedwig published her poetry while still a young woman. Later Hedwig would marry Ignaz von Olfers, the director of the Royal Museum in Berlin. When Elisabeth fell ill in the late twenties Hedwig hosted the Staegemann salon, and later she and Ignaz would host an important salon, carrying on the family tradition.

Every Friday the Staegemanns sponsored their *jour fixe,* a regular open house, attended by prominent noble Berliners, who chatted while playing cards, making music, or reading novels and poetry aloud. Several notable personalities in our story were regulars, including Chancellor Hardenberg, the two Humboldt brothers, Achim von Arnim, his wife Bettina, and her brother Clemens Brentano. This was a prestige salon, and Jews and former Jews must have been eager to feel welcome there. The lucky ones included Regina Froh-berg, David Koreff, Jacob Herz Beer, Eduard Gans, Julius Eduard Hitzig, and Rahel Varnhagen. Koreff must have been gratified that the conversation at the Staegemanns' frequently turned to his obsessions, such as mesmerism, me-diums, and magnetism. Koreff was also a frequent guest at the salon of Henri-ette von Crayen, a beautiful French noblewoman whose visitors chatted in French.[13] A portrait of Henriette from 1783 shows a confident woman, wear-ing pearls, satin, and fur. By the 1820s Madame von Crayen was in her sixties, but still enjoyed her pleasures. Some of her habits were decidedly racy for staid Berlin. She collected her love letters in a *musée d'amour,* a "love museum," and enjoyed reading selected bits aloud during her salon evenings. Henriette had many friends at court, and several Prussian princesses were frequent guests. Her politics were strongly conservative, and in his memoirs Karl Varnhagen went so far as to accuse her of being a paid spy for the conservative Minister of the Interior Baron Kaspar von Schuckmann.

Another remarkable noble *salonière* was Elise von Hohenhausen, who moved to Berlin in 1820, when she was 31.[14] What fascinating role reversals we see in her life. Elise supported her husband and three children with her prolific labors as a translator and journalist. Meanwhile, her husband Leopold, also a writer, spent his days lounging in the Konditorei Stehely on the Gendarmenmarkt, canvassing his friends to help him nab a position in the government, a goal he never achieved.[15] At one point Leopold turned to his wife's friend Professor Koreff to help him in his search for appropriate employment. So the noble wife supported the family with her literary labors, while the noble husband turned to the converted professor for aid in landing a job.

Obviously, times had changed, and now Jewish women faced stiff competition from such sophisticated noble salon hosts. The wider shifts in public opinion mattered too, and as Jewish emancipation became both more real and more disputed, those looking to spend an evening in society may well have preferred the noble homes. Moreover, many of the former Jewish *salonières* were either no longer living in Berlin or no longer in a position to entertain in style. Henriette Herz had returned to Berlin in 1819 after two years in Vienna and Rome, and was now a Protestant. But this change in religious affiliation did not much improve her rather restricted social life. She remained too poor to entertain in the style she had enjoyed while her husband was still alive, although she did occasionally host more modest affairs which contemporaries called *Teegesellschaften,* or tea societies.[16] Fanny Lewald, who so wanted to be a *salonière,* visited Henriette in her sparsely furnished apartment on her first visit to Berlin in 1832 and found her a poignant figure. Lewald later remembered how Herz sat underneath a portrait of herself as a 14-year-old, "her aged countenance still bathed in the afterglow of the momentous days gone by."[17] Now Henriette no longer felt welcome at Berlin's more prestigious salons. Certainly, her isolation had nothing to do with a loyalty to Jews or Judaism. Indeed, after her conversion she was rather derisive about those she referred to as the "unlucky enlightened Jews."[18]

Neither of the two Meyer sisters, Sophie or Marianne, had lived in Berlin for years. It will be recalled that both had converted in 1788, when Sophie was 25 and Marianne 18, but were then forced by their parents to return to Judaism. For the next years Sophie, now a widow, traveled a great deal, often to the spas in Bohemia, where she became friendly with Goethe, who encouraged her intellectual pursuits. Unfortunately few of her writings survived. Nine years later, in 1797, Sophie and Marianne both revived their Christian identities, and Sophie, then 34, married Baron Dietrich von Grotthuß. The couple lived in Berlin and hosted a very exclusive salon, whose guests included several princes. But in 1806, the baron lost his entire fortune, and they moved to the small town of Oranienburg, where he became the local postmaster. Marianne, meanwhile, who had married a count the same year that her sister married the baron, became estranged from her noble husband, but was allowed to use the title Frau von Eybenberg. She moved to Vienna, but died fifteen years later, when she was only 42. Alas, her memoir has been lost.[19] Sophie outlived her younger sister by sixteen years, and died in 1828, when she was 63.

Vienna had become a common destination for other Jewish salon women whose early years had been spent in Berlin, including the Itzig granddaughters Marianne Saaling and her two sisters Julie and Rebecca.[20] Marianne had been living in Vienna for years with her aunt Fanny von Arnstein. In 1815 she became a Catholic, in preparation for a marriage to Count Marialva, but he died before the wedding. Gossip circulated that he had actually changed his mind about marrying her before his death. In the 1820s Marianne returned to Berlin and lived with her sister Julie. Her inheritance came in handy as she created a social role for herself as a philanthropist, especially with her annual Christmas fair, which raised large amounts for charity. Dorothea Schlegel, after two years in Rome, had returned to Vienna. Now, during the '20s, after years of anguish and struggle, she felt beloved by a circle of Catholic friends, and Friedrich was at last settled into a government career. As time had passed Dorothea had achieved greater peace with her Jewish origins. Just before Simon Veit died in 1819, she wrote him a poignant letter, asking his forgiveness for the wrongs she had committed at the time of their separation.[21] She had become close again with her younger sister Henriette, now in Paris after years in Vienna. The religious terrain for these sisters was nuanced indeed. When Dorothea became a Protestant in 1803, and then five years later was baptized as a Catholic, Henriette drifted away from her sister. Yet in 1812 Henriette too was baptized as a Catholic, so as to obtain a post as a governess for a Catholic family. When her young student in Paris married, however, Henriette found herself rather alone in the world, and in 1824 she returned to Berlin to live with Abraham and Lea.[22] During her Paris years Henriette enjoyed a lively social life, but she never hosted her own salon, and she was rarely in Berlin during the 1810s.

Several Jewish women then living in Berlin did enjoy the background, values, and tastes which often made for successful salon careers, but for one reason or another did not host salons. For instance, by 1811 Lea Mendelssohn was back in Berlin after her years in Paris and Hamburg. However, she and Abraham and the four children were living in rented quarters, and their years of lavish hospitality lay in the future. Another personality from the old regime years, Philippine Cohen, was now too poor to host a salon in the grand style, after the bankruptcy and departure of her husband from Berlin.[23]

And so it was that when Rahel and Karl returned to Berlin in the fall of 1819, the social scene was greatly altered, and only a few Jewish homes sponsored open houses in the old style. One small salon was hosted by Henriette

Solmar, a distant relative of Rahel's, who had also become a Christian and had changed her name. Single throughout her life, she lived with her mother, who was well connected socially, and after her mother died, Henriette lived with her widowed sister and her niece. Solmar was a talented singer and pianist and a solo performer in the Choral Society. Her guests included several of the most prominent noble salon women in Berlin, and she enjoyed a warm friendship with Rahel and Karl. Solmar had a reputation among her friends for stimulating exciting conversations at her salons without appearing to dominate.[24] Another minor Jewish salon was hosted by the well-to-do merchant Philipp Veit and his wife Caroline, who lived on the Neue Promenade. They called their regular gatherings the Donnerstag Abende, the Thursday Evenings. The Veits' son Moritz, still a teenager in the 1820s, would later earn a doctorate from the University of Berlin and become a bookseller and reform activist in the Jewish community.[25]

But neither Henriette Solmar nor the Veits were hosting salons on the grand scale. Indeed, during the 1820s only two of the women from Rahel's original circle continued to entertain prominent Christians in style, Sara Levy and Amalie Beer. Neither had been intimate with Rahel when they were all younger, and fate had not brought them closer. Both were heir to enormous fortunes, unlike Rahel. Moreover, Sara and Amalie were committed to the modernization of Judaism, rather than to Rahel's path of radical assimilation. Their integration into elite Christian circles may well have been eased because music, not words and ideas, was the passion of both women. Because it was a universal language, a revealing accent or grammatical error could not embarrass a composer, a conductor, or a pianist.

In 1820, three years after the Beers had renovated their home to make a space for the temple services, they moved to a large villa near the Tiergarten Park.[26] In 1817, state officials had threatened the closure of their home temple, but it remained open until December 1823. The Beers maintained a remarkable division between their Saturday morning temple events and their salon, which attracted a very different circle. In the salon, Amalie seems to have played the leading role. Their youngest son, Michael, who was at this point a student at the University of Berlin, noted that his father tended to be withdrawn on social occasions, happy to sit silently and "brood over his drink."[27] Michael's new friend Harry Heine, who arrived in Berlin to attend the university in March 1821, was one of the very few guests at the Beer salon who also attended the services. Otherwise, none of the hundreds of Berlin Jews who prayed at the Beer home on one or another Saturday morning seem to have attended the salon gatherings. The Beers were in fact among the few Jews present at their salon concerts who were still Jewish. They must have been very proud that almost a quarter of the fifty-odd guests who came regularly to their salons were of noble birth.[28] Chancellor Hardenberg was still their weekly guest for dinner, and Wilhelm and Caroline von Humboldt as well as various prominent ministers and diplomats visited regularly. At their musical salons the Beers also provided performance space for many pianists, conductors, and singers, including their own *Wunderkind* Giacomo.

The few guests of Jewish descent who came to the Beer salon were almost all baptized or soon to be baptized. One of them was Rahel herself, and she and Karl were altogether malicious behind Amalie's back. Karl later wrote that Rahel found her "stiff" and "lacking the art of life."[29] Other Jewish or formerly Jewish guests at the Beers' salon included Rahel's brother Ludwig, David Koreff, Lea and Abraham Mendelssohn, Eduard Gans, and Ignaz Moscheles, a pianist. Another of Rahel's nasty comments about the Beers makes it absolutely clear that she preferred settings where there were few others of Jewish descent present. She once reported in a letter that she had enjoyed an evening at the Beers because on that occasion the gathering was less "mixed" than was usually the case.[30] She felt justified in complaining when the Beers let in too many former Jews, even though she herself may well have been seen by some as one of the riff-raff.

Although she felt comfortable insulting Amalie Beer, Rahel could be stung when she was the victim of someone else's snobbery. An incident from the winter of 1819, just months after their return to Berlin, shows how deeply she suffered when social success seemed out of reach, or available only at a high emotional cost.[31] What so irked Rahel that December was that although she specifically asked Karl to procure her an invitation to the Staegemanns' for New Year's Eve, he was invited alone. They cannot have been entirely surprised, given that Karl very much admired Elisabeth, and Rahel and Elisabeth had never been intimate.[32] Still, she was stung and admitted the "annoyance," though she consoled herself by noting that she would sometimes be insulted "if I cannot act according to my own ways and my own choice." Moreover Rahel was angry with herself for even being upset, since the Staegemanns were really "people whom I would not otherwise have wanted to see." She disdained those who insulted her, but still suffered from their rejection. But painful as such moments were, in the same diary entry where she lamented the New Year's Eve insult, she also clarifies that more was at stake than her personal suffering. She went on to write that former acquaintances, even friends, were changing their values. She complained about the "great poisoning of all insight and outlook, of which they are so proud!"[33] Here she surely meant the hostility of many nationalistic intellectuals toward the romantic, cosmopolitan lifestyle of her set during the old regime years. Her conclusion was that "the deadly, nameless annoyance because of the visits at the Staegemanns" will probably "soon kill me." Yet survivor that she was, she took heart by reminding herself that "I did not learn anything" from this episode, other than that "one can remain alive afterwards."

During the same season when Rahel and Karl were settling into their new routines on the Französische Straße, a circle of Jewish university students reacted to the recent *hep hep* riots with a commitment to renew Judaism. Ironically, the founding meeting of their club took place on November 6, 1819, one day after Friedrich Stahl converted.[34] The circle of students called their new venture the Verein für Cultur und Wissenschaft der Juden, the Association for Jewish Culture and Scholarship. The charismatic leader of the group was Eduard Gans, one of the guests at the Beer salon. Gans had just recently returned home to Berlin after receiving his doctorate in law from the University of Heidelberg. The journey through life of the supremely talented and ambitious Eduard is a poignant one, that must evoke sympathy from any modern-day intellectual free from the cruel choices he faced. His life story is important for us because his fate turned on the touchy decision of whether or not to convert. Gans proved to be a star student in the history of law and aimed for a professorship. Some optimists interpreted the fine print of the 1812 Edict to mean that a Jew who was still Jewish could achieve an academic career without baptism. But there were distinct loopholes in that law, and Gans's story illustrates how frayed the promises of 1812 were becoming a decade later. As baptism was almost a sure-fire solution to the problem, the temptation to undergo an inauthentic baptism was enormous.

Eduard had been born to wealth and power, and his father Abraham had loaned funds to Prussia back in 1807. During the occupation, Abraham had sold supplies to the French force, but in 1813, when Prussia started to prepare for war, he began to provide horses and uniforms to the Prussian army. Yet, for all of his power and prominence, when he died suddenly in 1813 Abraham left his wife and children with debts rather than assets. Moreover, three years later, Friedrich Rühs attacked him in print, accusing him of having been a war profiteer. An insult from Rühs in print could be serious, considering the influence of his work at this decisive historical moment. In order to restore Abraham's lost fortune, his widow Zipporah, born into the prominent Marcuse family, wanted her first-born and very bright son Eduard to become a financier too. She herself had impressive connections at court, as demonstrated by the prestige of having been a maid of honor at the wedding of Queen Louise with Frederick William III.[35] But already in his teen years, Eduard had adamantly rejected a career in finance. Eventually the family agreed that he should study law, so that he could help his family win the lawsuits necessary to recover Abraham's lost fortune.

In addition to the public insult of Rühs's attack on his father, Eduard was

6.1. Eduard Gans as Professor. Portrait by Wilhelm Hensel, 1829. Collection The Israel Museum, Jerusalem. Photo © The Israel Museum, Jerusalem.

embarrassed that he had not volunteered to fight in the War of Liberation. He went to the extent of lying about his birth year to make it seem as if he had been too young to serve.[36] Here we see a dilemma which many young intellectuals of Gans's generation faced. If they had been born into wealthy families, their fathers might well have profited by supplying the French army during the occupation. If the son then did not fight in the War of Liberation, the humiliation was double.

We know that not all Jewish merchants made money during these times, that Christians too profited from supplying the French army, that noble nationalists such as Achim von Arnim sat out the war on their landed estates, and that Jewish patriots such as Moritz Itzig died in battle. Then too Jews were involved in public patriotic philanthropy, such as the war charity work of women including Rahel, Amalie, and Fanny von Arnstein. But however complex the reality, the public perception was that Jewish financiers were especially successful in these troubled times. The high-profile maneuvering of the ubiquitous Rothschild family certainly contributed to popular misconceptions. Pity poor Gans, caught up in the swirling currents of his time.

In previous years, before he migrated to Heidelberg, when he had been a student at the University of Berlin, Gans suffered from what he described as a "social boycott." In 1816, he had complained about the problem to Wilhelm von Humboldt. Humboldt was then living in Frankfurt representing Prussia at the newly established Diet of the German Confederation, but he returned to Berlin regularly and maintained a lively interest in the politics of the university.[37] He suggested that Gans seek comradeship among "those with the same inclinations and the same age, on the margin of the student subculture."[38] In other words, it was a prominent noble statesman who suggested that Gans cultivate his relationships with other Jewish students. Gans took this advice to heart, and that year he and several friends founded the Wissenschafts Zirkel, the Scholarly Circle. At their regular meetings, members delivered mini-lectures to each other on philosophical themes from Plato to Hegel.[39] Many of those involved were also longtime members of the Society of Friends and surely familiar with how conflicts over conversion were often straining relationships among friends and families. Observers later noted that for some couples "what one would regard as sacred became the butt of ridicule for the other." Food and holidays were obvious sites of tension. Sometimes "parents were unable to eat at the tables of their adult children, while the children were embarrassed to visit their parents."[40]

When some of those in the Scholarly Circle founded their new Verein in November 1819, they excluded converts altogether, and the leading figures pledged never to give in on this key point.[41] This circle of young intellectuals shared ambitious goals to reform the reality and the image of contemporary Judaism. Like Mendelssohn, Gans and his group opposed the common use of Judeo-Deutsch, the dialect of Yiddish spoken in Germany. They also opposed "huckstering, senseless customs, tyrannical rabbis, bad schools, superficial cleverness, uncouth manners, discrimination against females, and apostasy."[42] They aimed to spread their new approach widely among young Jews across Germany and eastern Europe through publications, lectures, and schools. The challenges they took on at this difficult moment were bracing. Many of the leading intellects of the time, Jewish and Christian alike, often saw only two choices, either traditional Jewish practice, or radical assimilation through conversion and intermarriage. Many agreed with Friedrich Schleiermacher, who once opined that Judaism "is long since dead," and called it "a mummy."[43] Another contemporary declared that "Jewish history had come to an end."[44] In the words of an 1818 regulation, "the Jews were not at all to be regarded as a religious party but simply as 'the rubble of a ruined people.' "[45]

But the thirty-five founders of the new Verein tried to create a third path between tradition and radical assimilation.[46] Among the older members were David Friedländer, who was now 69, and Israel Jacobson, still active in the new temple, who was now 52. Other stellar figures in the new club were Lazarus Bendavid, the director of the Freyschule, Aron Wolfssohn, a tutor for the Beer children, and David Fränkel, editor of the *Sulamith*. The brainiest men in the Verein were still in their early twenties, including Leopold Zunz, a preacher at the Beer temple, Immanuel Wohlwill, a university student, Moses Moser, a bank clerk, and Isaac Markus Jost, who until recently had been the director of a local school.[47] In five short years before the Verein collapsed in 1824, the engaged activists accomplished a great deal. They founded a library, published several weighty scholarly volumes, sponsored a school for Jewish youth in Berlin, and recruited corresponding members from Hamburg, Frankfurt, and beyond. One of their honorary members from New York City was Mordechai Manuel Noah, who became notorious because of his plan to found a Jewish colony in Buffalo, New York. The joke around Berlin was that the new colony might be named Ganstown. Happily, the Verein members knew how to enjoy themselves, going out for beer in local pubs after their sessions and spending vacation days out in the sunshine at favorite fish restaurants on the outskirts of town.[48]

After the Verein activists had been at their task for three years, in September 1822, a new recruit joined their club. He was Harry Heine, the friend of Michael Beer's and a student at the University of Berlin. To posterity his first name was Heinrich, but at the time everyone called him Harry. When he joined the Verein, Heine had already been living in Berlin for a year and a half, having come from Göttingen.[49] He drifted into the Verein when he met Joseph Lehmann, an active member, at Hegel's lecture course at the university. Unlike the leaders of the Verein, most of whom had received a serious Jewish education, Heine had a minimal Jewish background and identity. He was convinced that his parents expected their children to convert.[50] That someone from his alienated background would enter the Verein showed that the club activists had found a way to attract young intellectuals estranged from their heritage.

During his Berlin years, Heine lived with Eduard Gans and Moses Moser, gave lectures at the Verein school, and helped to plan a women's auxiliary, working with Amalie Beer.[51] Heine remained in Berlin for less than a year after he joined the Verein, but even after he left town he remained involved with his friends from this circle. We know he attended services at the Beers, and he must have returned for visits even after he left Berlin, because in a letter from 1823, he mentioned that he was "awaiting" Leopold Zunz's next sermons.[52] The contrast between Heine's actual participation in the Verein and his public mockery of the reformers is yet another example of his astonishing ambivalence toward all things Jewish. For when he published his *Briefe aus Berlin* ("Letters from Berlin") in 1822, he denied that he had ever been to the Berlin prayer circle.[53] In print and in his private letters, he criticized reform efforts and praised traditionalists. In a letter to Immanuel Wohlwill, Heine mocked the Verein and other reformers for trying to create "a little Protestant Christianity as a Jewish company." He criticized his colleagues for making "a tallis out of the wool of the Lamb of God," joking that they made "a vest out of the feathers of the Holy Ghost and underpants out of Christian love, and they will go bankrupt and their successors will be called: God, Christ, and Co."[54] He condemned his own friends for their commercial approach, although he himself was constantly obsessed with money.

Heine's critique of reform was expanded in other letters to his Verein friends. In another letter to Wohlwill, he lamented that the reformers were "chiropodists" who "have tried to cure the body of Judaism from its disagreeable skin growth by bleeding, and by their maladroitness and spidery bandages of rationalism Israel must bleed to death." At this time he was obviously still committed to reform, because he complained to Wohlwill that "*we* no longer have the strength to wear a beard, to fast, to hate, and to endure out of hate; that is the motive of our Reformation." When he joined the Verein, Heine was 24, and had already burned through a potential career in business, a disaster as an apprentice financier just like his father. Indeed his father Samson's business disasters had brought his Uncle Salomon into Harry's life as a problematic surrogate father figure. In his late teens Harry already knew that he wanted to study literature and write poetry. But it was well known that writers then could never live off their words, and so Uncle Salomon had sent a 17-year-old Harry to business school, followed by various apprentice positions. For a time he even lived with his uncle in Hamburg, and worked in his banking house. Then Uncle Salomon set him up in his own firm, selling English yard goods. But the dreamy and delicate Harry despised this life, mocking the Hamburg residents for looking like "walking numerals," and his creditors rarely found him available.[55]

Just as his own business career was floundering, his father went bankrupt and was declared mentally incompetent by Uncle Salomon, who also shut down young Harry's business as well. For decades to come, Heine would look with both hatred and hope toward his uncle — hatred because of the way his uncle had treated his father, and nevertheless hope that Uncle Salomon would support his own talent with his fortune. Heine's difficulties with his uncle were compounded when his uncle's daughters each in turn rejected his marriage proposals. As a teenager in Hamburg he had fallen in love with his cousin Amalie, but she rejected his interest. Later some surmise that he experienced another unrequited passion for Amalie's younger sister Therese. Observers then and later gossiped that by marrying one of his female cousins, Harry might have seen a way to benefit from his uncle's fortune. Heine's vicious views about reform may have been stimulated by his simmering anger at his uncle, who was a leading patron of reform in Hamburg. But before we begin to empathize too much with Harry's rage at his uncle, we should remember that Uncle Salomon was donating 200 thalers a year to Heine's support in the years when he lived in Berlin, not enough for a very grand lifestyle but sufficient to live modestly as a single man.[56]

By the time he arrived in Berlin in March 1821, Heine was already a published poet and essayist. His conflict between the law and writing continued, exacerbated by his outrage at the conservative stance of several of his professors. When Professor Theodor Schmalz "began fulminating against human rights" during his lectures, Heine reported that "his feet instinctively began to tap out French revolutionary marches."[57] Outside the classroom he was immediately welcome in literary circles, delighted to find editors and publishers eager for his work. He was much appreciated by Karl, who proved useful because he was known then and later as "somewhat of a bear" in society, and Rahel, who helped to "polish his manners."[58] Karl became an important friend to Heine, providing him with positive reviews of his work, introductions to prominent acquaintances in and beyond Berlin, and wise counsel in many of his difficulties in the years to come.

Heine also became friendly with the Beers, whose home offered quite different pleasures from those he found at the Varnhagen salon. At the Beers he found larger crowds and musical entertainments and friendship with two of the Beer sons, Giacomo and Michael. Friends noticed that he appreciated Amalie's sense of style. She loved yellow, and chose it for the walls in her drawing room. Heine too loved yellow, and he considered it a dramatic contrast to the "brownish complexion of the forefathers."[59] Indeed in their love of the color yellow, Harry and Amalie were both showing their allegiance to romantic fashion. Goethe had dressed the title character in his novel *The Sorrows of Young Werther* in yellow, and yellow remained popular for decades later.[60] Heine was quite the romantic in his dress, often sporting "velvet jackets, dandyish, open Byronic collars, and a fashionable wide-rimmed high felt hat known as a Bolivar."[61] The Beers ordered their clothes at the Jordan and Heese haberdashery, which made the most sophisticated clothing in Berlin. The shop was in the center of town, located next door to the Café Josty, where shoppers could treat themselves after a fitting to hot chocolate with whipped cream and florentine cookies.[62] Heine was so enthusiastic about the sweets sold at this restaurant that he mentioned how grand they were at the beginning of his *Letters from Berlin*, exclaiming "and here we find Josty! You gods of Olympus, I shall spoil your Ambrosia if I describe the sweets which are displayed there."[63]

We depart the year 1821 with the image of the Beers and Heine drinking hot chocolate at the Café Josty. In the thirty-five years since Mendelssohn's death in 1786, we have seen a realization and even an expansion of his vision of Jewish modernity. We shall now see how the king and his ministers derailed, curtailed, and repressed the emergence of this third path. As we have learned, the decade after the Edict of 1812 was a special time for a handful of lucky Jews in Berlin, who had found a way to combine Jewish renewal and avid participation in high culture. To begin the day listening to Professor Hegel lecture at the university, spend the afternoon in a committee of the new Verein, and in the evening pay a visit to Elise von Hohenhausen's salon required multiple identities, passions, and commitments. As we move into the year 1822, we shall see just how vulnerable and fragile the project of harmonious modernization was becoming. Government officials were busily closing down the options, making conversion the only possible road away from traditional Judaism.

Heathens in the Fatherland, 1822

One day in January 1822, a group of prominent middle-aged Berliners gathered at the home of General Job von Witzleben.[64] That day they founded the Berlin Society for the Promotion of Christianity Among the Jews. This modest little gathering was most significant for our story, because Witzleben and his friends were hugely influential. When they turned their attention to conversion, their actions mattered. Their aim in 1822 was to make conversion a condition of civic emancipation, and in this goal they were smashingly successful. They intervened in the conversion problematic just as the family crisis was beginning to ebb. For it was just in the years close to 1830 that we see an upsurge in young adult male converts, who outpaced the Jewish women choosing baptism and intermarriage. The new trend, spurred on by the Witzleben circle, was careerist conversions. Witzleben's circle were pietists, and we know how important conversion often was to pietist activists across the generations. We recall the practical pietist missionaries of the early eighteenth century, dressing shabbily, learning Yiddish, and organizing homes, jobs, and charity for the small number of mainly poor Jews who chose to become Lutherans. Their calculated masquerade as poor Jews was not a far fall down the social hierarchy, since missionary activists at that time tended to be rather marginal, rarely born to privilege. From the perspective of Jewish fate the work of the pietists is altogether problematic, because across the generations they tried to convince Jews to abandon their faith. Yet their social welfare projects and their vital communities help us understand why pietists attracted participants to their version of Lutheranism.

But now, in the Biedermeier years, pietism had changed, and so many wealthy and powerful individuals became enthusiasts that they were called the "perfumed" pietists. Among those at the Witzleben home that January day in 1822 were Court Chaplain Ludwig Theremin, minister at the Cathedral of Berlin, Georg Nicolovius, director of religious affairs in the Ministry of the Interior, and Johann Ancillon, former tutor of the king. Their politics were solidly on the right. Ancillon's books were among those burned by radical students during the Wartburg Festival in October 1817, and he was especially despised by Hegel, Schleiermacher, and Humboldt. Witzleben and his friends would certainly not learn Yiddish and dress in shabby clothes to persuade poor Jews to become Protestants. They were at the summit of their careers, several of them intimate with King Frederick William III. Because they could transform their convictions into state policies with ease, "their religion was political and their politics were religious."[65] Their successes in influencing state policy shows how quickly the policy choices regarding conversion were changing. It was now only ten years since the wondrous "gift" of the 1812 Edict, and already a sharp conflict had emerged about conversion. The framers of that law had opposed requiring baptism as a condition for civic equality, but now Witzleben and his friends lobbied for the much harsher view that only Jews who were no longer Jewish could enjoy secular rights. Gans was their ideal victim.

Their initial goal was to influence policy from above, but they also organized practical projects, such as distributing free copies of the New Testament, recruiting missionary agents, and opening schools for Jewish children. Their Berlin Society even attracted artisans and shopkeepers eager to participate in missionary activities.[66] The activists in the Berlin Society emphasized that they did not want to induce Jews to convert "in name only." They denounced inauthentic baptisms and were proud to declare that they would not offer "earthly advantages" to potential converts.[67] This shows a pervasive contemporary worry that spiritual transformation was becoming an ever more rare motive for baptism. The missionary cause was reviving not just in Germany but also in England. The London Society for Promoting Christianity Among the Jews had been founded back in 1809, and was a well-funded and ambitious organization, publishing booklets and journals, organizing schools, and helping the mainly poor Jews prepare for life as a Christian.[68] The London Society made a difference in Germany, because the missionary homes and schools which pietists had founded more than a century before in Hamburg and Halle had long ago closed their doors.

The converts involved in the Berlin and London operations were altogether peripatetic, often beginning their missionary careers with a baptism in Germany, a move to London, affiliation with the London Society, and then a return to Germany to do missionary work.[69] These networks could compensate for broken family ties, and they provided a space for intimacy with other former Jews and with sympathetic Christians. One of the London Society's most active convert missionaries during the 1820s was Julius Anton Eduard. Eduard had been born into an impoverished family in Posen, and as a boy he was attracted to Christian practice and doctrine. He converted at 16, and later studied theology at the University of Berlin. Eventually Eduard became affiliated with the London Society, although his base was in Breslau, where he served for decades as a pastor. He remained single, and perhaps it was some consolation to him that he was immensely loved by his parishioners.[70]

The most prominent of the convert missionaries to affiliate with the London Society was Joseph Samuel, born in Franconia. When he was 28, Samuel became a Protestant and took the name Friedrich Frey. After some time studying in a Lutheran seminary in Berlin, he departed for London, where he became an activist in the London Society.[71] Frey was ambitious about the missionary project, but erratic and sexually rather irresponsible. By 1816 he had been dismissed by the Society for adultery, a turn of events which cannot have been altogether surprising, since one of his lady friends was the wife of the leading patron of the Society. Eventually he left Europe, settled in New York City, and later became a professor of Hebrew at Michigan State University in Pontiac, where he died in 1850.

Considering his opposition to reforming Judaism, it is no surprise to find King Frederick William III very enthusiastic about the Society's aims, and happy to fund its work. Although in its published rhetoric the Berlin Society vehemently opposed opportunist baptisms, it registered no opposition when the king presented each convert with a generous financial gift. The wider politics of the project becomes even more clear when we learn that Witzleben and his friends saw their work in the larger European perspective of empire. This sounds surprising indeed for Berlin in the year 1822, but the evidence is clear. In a speech delivered at the founding celebration in February 1822, Sir George Rose, the British envoy in Berlin, was astonishingly frank about the imperial context of the conversion project. He empathized with the "pious Christians in Germany" who until then had been "almost excluded from that field of heathen-conversion to which only seafaring nations have direct access." But they should take heart, he urged, and "be comforted in directing their glances upon those missions of the old People of God who live amidst them or in their immediate vicinity."[72] The notion that making all Jews into Christians could somehow compensate for the lack of an empire sheds a very disturbing light on later tragic events in German history.

While General Witzleben and his friends concentrated on influencing state policies, they inspired various younger activists to work on the day-to-day projects. One of the most industrious was Friedrich August Tholuck, in 1822 a newly ordained pastor and a lecturer at the University of Berlin.[73] Tholuck represented the London Society in Berlin, and was kept busy translating, editing, and writing tracts used by both missionary societies. At the university he taught rabbinical literature, attracting Christian as well as still-Jewish and formerly Jewish students. In later years, when he taught in Berlin, Rome, and Halle, Tholuck surrounded himself with a series of young Jewish men who ultimately converted. Perhaps the most notable of his students was Sontheim, whom Tholuck baptized in 1820. Sontheim had been born in Breslau, served as an officer in the War of Liberation, and then wandered about until arriving in Berlin in 1819. Later he became an active missionary in the town of Thorn.[74] Tholuck had experienced considerable trouble with his first appointment at the University of Berlin, because the powerful Friedrich Schleiermacher found his theological politics too conservative.[75] Schleiermacher did have his favorites, especially August Neander. The "new man" Neander had much to show for himself. His mother and all of his siblings had eventually converted too, and his academic career had prospered. A lifelong bachelor, he had his sister for companion and housekeeper. With the immensely helpful patronage of Schleiermacher, Neander was now a professor of theology at the University of Berlin, a prolific scholar, and influential in the missionary world too. Although he is obscure today, an 1830 portrait of the most notable intellectuals of Berlin includes him, alongside the two Humboldt brothers, Schleiermacher, and Hegel.

Unfortunately for the missionaries, David Mendel's metamorphosis into the "new man" August Neander was not a very common story during the 1820s. They were intensely aware that few converts were motivated by a spiritual

DAS GELEHRTE BERLIN.

1. W. v. Humboldt
2. Hufeland
3. A. v. Humboldt
                                                4. C. Ritter
                                                5. Neander
                            I.   *6. Schleiermacher*
                            7. Hegel

6.2. Leading Learned Men in Berlin. Clockwise from the top: G. W. F. Hegel, Frie-drich Schleiermacher, Alexander von Humboldt, Wilhelm von Humboldt, Christoph Wilhelm Hufeland, August Neander; Carl Ritter is at the center. Lithograph by Julius Schoppe, ca. 1810. Bildarchiv Preussischer Kulturbesitz / Art Resource, NY.

rebirth into the new faith. In the words of the reformer Isaac Markus Jost, "the proselytizers here are fools because they try to achieve with lots of money and noise a goal which will come of its own."[76] Yet when we study the difficult choices faced by Eduard Gans and his friends, we see that careerist conver-sions were not rising "on their own." Rather, as the family crisis ebbed and career conversions became more frequent, we see how a harsh government policy advocated by the Witzleben circle affected the skyrocketing rates. Now, a decade after the Edict was issued, what had been ambiguous in that law was made crystal clear. During the past ten years, the Edict had been attacked from several directions, but it had not been withdrawn. But in August 1822, when King Frederick William III issued the so-called Lex Gans, the Gans law, the chance to become powerful and influential while remaining Jewish was becoming well-nigh impossible. Shortly after he received his doctorate in Heidelberg in 1819, Gans had gamely applied for a position in the history of law at the University of Berlin. Chancellor Hardenberg and Baron Karl von Altenstein, the minister of religious and educational affairs, both supported his application. But Friedrich von Savigny, chair of the law faculty in Berlin, was dead set against appointing Gans. Savigny aimed to make Prussia into a Christian state, which meant excluding Jews who were still Jewish from positions of influence and power. Savigny was one of the founders of the Tischgesellschaft, was married to Bettina von Arnim's sister Gunda, and passionately despised the liberal politics of his rival Hegel. Hegel had been teaching at the university in Berlin since 1818, and Gans was his prize student. By the late summer of 1822, Eduard had been waiting for three years for the government to make a decision about his candidacy.

Gans had thrown his hat into the ring at a moment of throbbing turmoil in German intellectual life. Since Karl Sand's murder of Kotzebue three years before, the Carlsbad Decrees had silenced the radicals and liberals. Overt political dialogue in newspapers, journals, literary societies, and even sermons from pulpits had become decidedly dangerous. When they gathered in coffeehouses and at dinner parties and salons, angry radical intellectuals fumed about contemporary politics, but because of the strict censorship, when they sat down at their desks to write their books and articles, debate became constrained and disguised. We must read between the lines so as to grasp the passions of the moment. Untangling those passions is difficult, for debates divided contemporaries in complex ways. Liberals and leftists fought conservatives, romantics fought rationalists, and from every perspective contemporaries debated Jewish emancipation. Yet none of these alignments were at all clear-cut, and among the liberals were rationalists like Hegel as well as romantics like Schleiermacher. Hegel's politics were closely watched, much debated, and especially complex, because he was opposed from both the left and the right. Radical intellectuals such as Jakob Fries criticized Hegel's affiliation with the powerful figures of the Prussian state, while from the right, Savigny despised Hegel as a liberal.

In the conflict between reason and emotion, Schleiermacher played a key role. He was now 47, a professor of theology at the university and prominent preacher. His politics were decidedly left, so much so that at the time of the Kotzebue murder the Berlin police were monitoring his sermons. Schleiermacher was distraught when three patriots, Christian De Wette, Ernst Moritz Arndt, and Jakob Fries, were dismissed from their academic posts after the Carlsbad Decrees, and he blamed Hegel for not defending De Wette.[77] The conflict between rationalism and romanticism made for strange bedfellows. For although Schleiermacher was very much on the left and Savigny was very much on the right, because they were both romantics they both despised Hegel's rationalism. Jewish politics also made for odd alliances. For example, Hegel advocated Jewish emancipation without conversion and campaigned in support of Gans's right to become a professor *as a Jew*. As an ardent rationalist, Hegel wanted the state to be thoroughly secular. On the other hand, romantics like Schleiermacher and Savigny, who valued tradition and historic customs, insisted that the state should be Christian. The odd turn was that although Savigny and other conservatives vehemently opposed emancipation, leading Jewish reformers shared their romantic approach to history. Leopold Zunz, for instance, viewed Judaism as a historically evolving civilization.

In the four years since he had arrived at the university, Hegel had become immensely popular as a lecturer and gentleman around town, in spite of his obscure and difficult philosophy and his slow and halting lecture style. Outside of his study and the classroom he savored good wine, costume balls, and games of cards with his pleasure-loving friends. One of these was Heinrich Beer, who was unlikely to appreciate the finer points of his intellectual creations. Giacomo's younger brother Heinrich was the only one of the four Beer children who did not become accomplished in some field. In fact Heinrich, who married Abraham Mendelssohn's niece Betty, was eventually declared insane by his family and placed under guardianship. Sometimes he wasted money on silly expenditures, such as the day he spent 6,000 thalers on walking sticks. Heinrich very much admired Hegel, and was known to "follow him like a shadow." They were such an unlikely pair that none of their contemporaries quite understood their relationship. Reportedly "everybody in Berlin was continually surprised by the intimacy of the profound Hegel with Heinrich Beer."[78]

Alas for Gans, in the rough and tumble of academic politics at the university, Hegel was not as powerful as was Savigny. However, in spite of Savigny's powerful opposition to Gans, Chancellor Hardenberg ardently supported Gans's case, and continually requested that his like-minded friend Baron von Altenstein proceed with appointing Gans to the faculty. Because he was caught between Hardenberg and Savigny, Altenstein's solution was to stall. Finally, in August 1822, the king himself stepped in to settle the case. Government policy was clarified to mean that only Christians could become state officials. Gans was awarded a 1,000-thaler grant, and it was diplomatically suggested that he go abroad to pursue his academic career. Many of his friends expected him to leave Berlin in 1822. But he remained in town, still the president of the Verein, and lived off his family inheritance while he wrote a massive and erudite history of Roman law. Sadly for him and for Jewish fate, the great patron of Jewish progress Chancellor Hardenberg died that November. Now liberals were truly in despair, for Hardenberg was the protector of many with democratic politics and had been an influential advocate for Jewish emancipation.

A good reason for state officials to want to require conversion for prestigious careers was that so many university graduates were flooding the job market. Keeping out the still-Jewish Jews limited the competition for scarce positions. The German population was growing at a rapid rate, and the institutions of higher learning had expanded to meet the demand. The number of university students across Germany tripled between 1800 and 1820, from just over 5,000 to over 15,000.[79] Available posts in the professions with prestige were definitely not keeping pace with the supply of trained candidates.[80] Therefore, many graduates spent a decade or more as tutors, clerks, or high school teachers before they could obtain a fully salaried position. Several of our personalities suffered this fate, including Fichte and Hegel. Those opposed to Jews becoming professors may well have fretted that the University of Berlin was becoming a magnet for ambitious Jewish students born in the eastern provinces. At this juncture the number of Jewish students across the German lands was still tiny; less than 3 percent of university students in these years were Jewish.[81] But the University of Berlin was becoming more and more attractive to Jewish students. The borders of Prussia had expanded greatly to the east at the Vienna Congress, and thanks to the 1812 Edict, Jews could now move from the provinces to the capital city. Already in 1810 7 percent of the students at Berlin were Jewish, and by 1834 the *Sulamith* editors exulted that "several hundred" Jewish students were enrolled there.[82] This change was notable since the Jewish population of Berlin was scarcely increasing at all in these decades.

During the same months that Gans and other ambitious young Jewish intellectuals were pondering the pros and cons of a pragmatic baptism, Lea and Abraham Mendelssohn joined their children in the Lutheran faith. Both of them experienced much drama and conflict about conversion in their extended family networks. Just before his baptism in 1822, Abraham retired from the banking firm he had founded with his brother Joseph. The stated reason was to spend more time organizing his talented children's education, but Joseph may have insisted that he leave the firm when Abraham shared his plan to become a Christian with his brother. We know from the story of David

Lewald that there were practical reasons to keep converts out of a family banking firm. On Lea's side of the family too, baptism was much debated. Living so close to Grandmother Bella after converting their children must have been tense for Lea and Abraham, so we can imagine that they thought long and hard about the decision to proceed with their own baptism in 1822. The moment came that fall, while the extended Mendelssohn family was on a grand tour through Switzerland and southern Germany. When they left Berlin during the summer, the entourage included Lea and Abraham and the four children, their tutor Karl Heyse, and cousins Julie and Marianne Saaling. Indeed it was on this journey that Julie and Karl fell in love.[83] All in all, Lea reported in a letter that they felt as if they were "traveling like princes — poets, artists, and princes all in one."[84] On October 4, in Frankfurt, Abraham and Lea became Lutherans, officially adding Jacob's new family name Bartholdy to their last name.

Some scholars have surmised that Lea and Abraham waited until Grandmother Bella died before they converted, so as to ensure their inheritance.[85] But that interpretation is certainly wrong, because Bella remained alive for two more years after their baptism. We can definitely rule out a spiritual impulse. Abraham's letters to his children defending the family baptisms show no trace of even a perfunctory religious sentiment. Rather, Abraham explained their decisions in vague secular terms; his explanation to Fanny was that "we have educated you and your brothers and sisters in the Christian faith because it is the creed of most civilized people today."[86] There were probably other issues on their minds, including career plans for their sons, the social reputation of the entire family, and a desire to feel more German on the inside. Whatever the complex stew of impulses that motivated their decisions, what was new in the history of conversion was that Abraham made no pretense whatsoever of religious motives.

Three days after their baptism, the Mendelssohn party arrived in Weimar, where they visited Johann Goethe. The year before, Karl Zelter, one of Felix's music tutors, had taken the young Mendelssohn to Weimar to play for Goethe.[87] A picture of Goethe and Felix painted years later depicts the older genius looking away while the young pianist gazes admiringly at him. The body language of the two figures is a dramatic representation of the utter lack of mutuality between talented Jews and high culture. On that October day in 1822, Fanny played for Goethe too, and he told the proud parents that she was "as gifted as her brother."[88] Years later, when the correspondence between Zelter and Goethe was published, the Mendelssohns were rudely informed about what was said *behind their backs*. Remember, Zelter had been an early member of Arnim and Brentano's Tischgesellschaft, and many of his best

6.3. Felix Mendelssohn Plays the Piano for Goethe. Painting by Moritz Daniel Oppenheim, 1864. Jüdisches Museum Frankfurt am Main/Private Collection.

friends were leading activists in patriotic circles. Just days before he arrived with Felix in Weimar, Zelter wrote Goethe that Felix "admittedly" was "the son of a Jew but he is no Jew . . . for once it really would be *eppes rores,* the rare event, if a Jewish boy were to become an artist."[89] Zelter's use of Yiddish to make a hostile comment shows the complexity of his feelings toward his Jewish friends. He certainly helped his Jewish friends advance their musical careers, and they knew how to reciprocate with their lavish donations to his projects. The irony was that here Zelter was insulting the same Jews whom he was helping, in the language which they refused to speak.

As the talented Mendelssohn children grew to adulthood, there were times when the parents wanted to be more assimilated than the children. Abraham and Felix disagreed over the years about the crucial marker of the family name. During the 1820s, as his star was rising, Felix took to eliminating the Bartholdy altogether, listing himself on his concert programs as Felix Mendelssohn. Abraham was outraged, and reminded Felix in an angry letter that "a Christian Mendelssohn is an impossibility." The name Mendelssohn, he reminded Felix, "would always stand for a Judaism in transition."[90] He continued, "you can not, you must not carry the name Mendelssohn . . . A name is like a garment; it has to be appropriate for the time, the use, and the rank, if it is not to become a hindrance and a laughing-stock . . . There can no more be a Christian Mendelssohn than there can be a Jewish Confucius. If Mendelssohn is your name, you are *ipso facto* a Jew."[91] We must ponder what Moses and Fromet might have thought of their newly Christian descendants. In later years Abraham and Lea would try to explain that just as Moses had changed his life dramatically by coming to Berlin in 1743, they were following in his footsteps by changing their lives in another way. Surely it was a complicated psychic task to leave Judaism when one's father had been Moses Mendelssohn. But let us bid goodbye to that lucky family now, and return to the mounting problems of those who sought to change Judaism rather than to depart from their community of fate.

Closing the Temple and "Crawling to the Cross," 1823–1825

As Gans was pondering how to pursue his professorship and the Mendelssohns were absorbed in music, the reformers were experiencing serious difficulties from within and without. In September 1822 Leopold Zunz quit his paid position as the preacher for the Beer temple, complaining that "preaching in the face of official arrogance and communal apathy was incompatible with his honor."[92] Zunz's decision to opt out of the fragile reform services illuminates the class tensions dividing the reformers from their patrons. Zunz and his friend Isaac Markus Jost may have been especially sensitive, since both grew up in an orphanage in Wolfenbüttel, "amidst poverty, filth, and disorder," where they endured a "heartless regimen of talmudic studies."[93] But whatever their personal dramas, we can justly wonder whether the hostility these intellectuals felt toward the Jewish super-rich was an indulgence. They seem to have been cutting off their noses to spite their faces. After all, the Beers and Jacobson were funding the most avant-garde Jewish institutions of the day, and any young intellectual determined to contribute to this renaissance needed patronage from somewhere.

Within a year after Zunz's resignation the entire episode had come to an end. In September 1823, the government tried to close the temple permanently. Reformers rallied and organized a short additional service with German hymns and a sermon at the community synagogue on the Heidereutergasse. But because these services were so popular, the traditionalists appealed to the king in protest. In December the king ruled that the only Jewish ritual practice allowed would take place in the community synagogue, "without the slightest innovation in language, ceremonies, prayers or hymns, wholly according to the established custom."[94] The reformers were frustrated and powerless. They had been betrayed not just by a king and a state officialdom hostile to Jewish emancipation in the first place, but also by their own religious leadership.

The repression of the new reform movement recalls Scholem's lament about the false start to the modern Jewish era. The logic of Scholem's position is that the reformers were themselves partly responsible for the debacle, because they aimed to create a Judaism which was more Protestant, more rational, more *German*. Yet his critique is too harsh, and ultimately unhistorical. It was simply not in the spirit of the times for reformers *in that place at that time* to emphasize the ethnic and national dimensions of traditional Judaism. In Scholem's own time, a full century later, a handful of thoughtful Jewish intellectuals did find a way to feel deeply Jewish and deeply German. But this dual ethnic identity was fragile and rare then, and was quite impossible in 1820.

Less than a year after the services were closed, in May 1824, Gans's Verein held its last meeting. Their academic journal, their lecture classes, their European-wide network, all their labors of the last five years had collapsed. Now, within two years, the project of modernizing Judaism had suffered two huge, one might even say lethal, blows. Berlin was known far and wide as the capital of the Jewish enlightenment, and the Verein and the new temple were each immensely innovative. Those pondering conversion must have felt the pendulum shift further from Judaism. As we have seen, the best and the brightest young Jewish men from the eastern provinces continued to flock to Berlin to attend the university, read newspapers, and chat in the coffeehouses, and, if they were lucky, gain a place at a home concert or a prestigious salon. But without the Verein and the Beer temple, the Jewish community institutions were frozen in time, stuffy and old-fashioned. The varied life that Heine had enjoyed in Berlin in the early 1820s was disappearing, and the choices now became much more polarized.

At this painful juncture, lay activists struggled to keep the reform alternative alive.[95] They found some solace at the yearly Leipzig fair, where reformers organized modern services during the fair weeks. For several years the Leipzig services, which were held in an auditorium at the university, attracted over 200 participants from cities as far away as Amsterdam and Bucharest.[96] And when a new community school opened in Berlin in 1829, traditional Sabbath prayers were followed by a supplemental reform service, including a sermon in German and songs by a student choir. Government officials looked the other way.[97] On occasion families celebrated holidays and life cycle events with modern services in their homes. But it would take another thirty years, until 1854, before a new reform congregation opened its doors in Berlin.[98] In Hamburg reformers fared much better, and even created an enduring "Temple Association" as early as 1817.[99] Heine's Uncle Salomon was one of the sponsors of the Hamburg temple, and Heine himself attended services from time to time, critical and edgy as ever in his reactions.

Many at the time and later saw reform as a perilous enterprise designed to keep Jews from converting, as seen in the humorous cartoon published decades later, in 1903, where a reform rabbi walks a tightrope above the baptismal waters. In the 1820s and '30s, the rabbis and the officials both opposed reform, but they did so for completely opposite reasons. The officials feared that successful reform would lower conversion rates. Their analysis matched the reality uncovered in the Judenkartei notebooks. Rates in Berlin declined during the eight years when the temple was open, and rose after it was closed. In their view, reform and conversion were alternative paths away from traditional Judaism. If Jews could alter Jewish rituals, they might be less likely to convert. So their policy was to close down reform so as to stimulate more conversions. The rabbis, in contrast, had a linear model, and viewed reform as one step away from tradition, and baptism as a further step on that same path. Like Jacobson, most reformers were lay activists, whose analysis was the same as the officials': that reform would be an alternative to conversion. The rabbis, in contrast, were certain that reform had already led to the spurt in conversions. Notice that the rabbis had to work with the state to oppose the reformers, because the 1812 Edict had transformed the meaning of excommunication. The religious establishment was increasingly dependent on the state, at the same moment that the state was opening up its ranks to accept individual Jews as citizens, albeit with a very second-class status. This situation brings to mind the way Achim von Arnim was forced to appeal to the state to retaliate against Moritz Itzig. Was it obvious to many at the time that the rabbis purchased a short-term victory over reform by a very dubious alliance with a very cynical state system with no sympathy for Jews or Judaism?

In order to understand how the conversion pattern was changing in these years, we need to consult Graph 5 of the Appendix, which contrasts the absolute numbers choosing baptism in any given year with the total population of Jews in Berlin. It was in 1815 that the highest proportion of Berlin Jews chose baptism. Until the 1830s the Jewish population of Berlin did not grow much at

Unsere Zukunft liegt auf dem Wasser.

Ein Zuschauer: O Gott, o Gott, ich hab' immer so Angst, daß er mal 'neinplumst.

6.4. Reform Rabbi in Danger of Falling into the Baptismal Waters. Originally published in the satirical journal *Schlemihl*, 1903.

all, and thus during the 1810s, when the absolute numbers were on the upswing, the numerator of the base population remained low. During the years immediately after 1815, both the absolute number and the proportion of Jews choosing baptism fell. Graph 1 clearly shows that during the years after 1815, when the services were open, the number of baptisms dropped sharply. Not only did rates drop while reform flourished, but after the services were closed down by the government in 1823, rates rose again. What we need to examine in the coming pages is whether the opening of the Beer temple explains the drop in rates after 1815.

When we examine the converted population to ask which Jews were making this choice, we see that the gender of the converts switched in a quite dramatic fashion. Before 1820, as Graph 3 shows, either women and men had converted in equal proportions, or marginally more women had converted than men. After 1820 we never see a year when more women converted than men. Indeed, during the 1820s the gap between the high number of male converts and a much lower number of female converts was wider than at any other point during the nineteenth century. We saw in Graph 4 that during the same years that the men began converting more than women, the proportion of converted women who married Christian men also dropped. Indeed conversion rates and intermarriage rates for women moved very much in tandem, as we see in Graph 6. This graph shows clearly that there was a much tighter connection between female conversion and female intermarriage than there was for the men. A higher overall number of men converted and married out, but a greater proportion of the women who converted went on to marry Christians by descent. Graph 4 shows that the intermarriage rate itself was increasing, which was an important change within the Jewish world of Berlin. For when men and women from the same ethnic group choose to marry outsiders, we have a good hint that the morale of that group is low.[100] We must, however, handle these statistics with care. For the marriage listings of the black notebooks include marriages between two converts, which were really not ethnic intermarriages. Ten percent of the marriages included in the notebooks fall into this category.

Converts who married each other show that baptism was not always a step on the journey to true social integration. We remember couples such as Magdalena Navrazky and David Kirchhoff, both of Jewish descent but both Christians, who had married in 1746. One of the most notable marriages between two converts during this era joined Lea and Abraham's youngest son Paul with Heinrich Heine's 22-year-old cousin Albertine. In her wedding picture from 1835 Albertine is wearing a large cross, and a church is visible from the window of her room. Both Paul and Albertine had been baptized as children, Paul in 1816, when he was only four, and Albertine in 1825, when she was 11, alongside four of her siblings and her father.[101] Several other personalities in our story also married across religious borders. Rahel's beloved brother Ludwig married Friederike Braun, and Karl's sister Rosa married David Assing, a physician from Hamburg. Felix Mendelssohn would marry the daughter of a Protestant pastor, Cécile Jeanrenaud, in 1836. Heine too married a Christian woman, Crescene Mirat, after he left Germany for Paris in 1831. Heine's friend Karl Marx, who was baptized by his father in 1824 when he was six, married his childhood sweetheart, Jennie von Westphalen, indeed with her father's blessings. Many converted Jewish women married Christians, including Dorothea Mendelssohn, Sophie Meyer and her sister Marianne, Fanny Lewald, and Julie Saaling. Lea and Abraham's oldest daughter Fanny married the painter Wilhelm Hensel, and their younger daughter Rebekka married the mathematician Peter Dirichlet. Therese Schlesinger, daughter of a Jewish music publisher, married Felix Mendelssohn's close friend, the Christian singer Eduard Devrient.

In addition to the drop in female conversion and female intermarriage, we

6.5. Albertine Heine on Her Wedding Day. Portrait by August Theodor Kaselowsky, 1835. © Jewish Museum Berlin. Photo: Jens Ziehe.

see other signs that the family crisis among the wealthy Berliners was less
intense by the 1820s. We see more adult male converts born in the eastern
provinces from modest families, who replaced wealthier converts who had
been born in Berlin. This era likewise saw a reversal in the ages of converts, as
shown in Graph 7. We have already learned that infant conversion was shockingly high throughout the years covered in the black notebooks. Now we learn
that the highest decade for child converts was early in the new century, when
almost 90 percent of those baptized were five and under. In those years only

6 percent were in their twenties. As time passed, the proportion of converts who were so young began dropping, and during the 1820s only 41 percent were infants, a low point in child conversion. Now, a third of the converts were in their twenties.

If we can identify which Jews were converting, we can better explain why rates were rising in the 1820s. The most obvious explanations, which of course are not at all exclusive, include the work of the missionaries, the suppression of reform, the lure of a prestigious career, intermarriage, desires to feel more German, and changing socializing patterns allowing converts to remain intimate with Jewish family and friends. Although the timing is suggestive, both contemporary observers and scholars have been adamant that Witzleben's society did not recruit very many alienated Jews to become Lutherans.[102] It is ironic that missionary work in Prussia had revived just in the years when fewer converts were motivated by spiritual rebirth. Yet, although the new missionary society did not motivate many individuals to convert for religious motives, the group did affect conversion rates. Like the rabbis and like Achim von Arnim, if they wanted to make a difference they had to work through the state. For the Witzleben circle agitated to close the loophole in the 1812 Edict that had been ambiguous about the need to convert for high-status careers. The decision against Gans in 1822 dashed hopes that the doors to such careers would be open to Jews who were still Jewish. The conversions of many of the most intelligent and ambitious of the times, including several personalities in our story, can be explained by the burning passion to achieve a career worthy of their talents.[103] The career motive goes some distance in explaining the class and age pattern too, since the poorer young men converting in the 1820s and '30s chose baptism during or after their university studies. Moreover, the careerist motive could affect the behavior of parents too. Parents chose to convert their children, so as to spare them the inner conflicts of making the decision later, when they would be applying for positions open only to converts.

Another likely influence on shifts in the rate was the eight-year experiment in reform Judaism. Perhaps some of those who converted after 1823 had considered baptism earlier, but remained Jewish because the new services provided them with an alternative way to be Jewish. We know that Leopold Zunz considered baptism in 1823, although he ultimately decided not to take this step.[104] If a Jew with as much education and conviction as Zunz thought of converting, how tempting it must have been for those whose ties to Judaism were much weaker. We know that the participants in the services tended to be young adults, and we suspect that many if not most of these young adults were men. And yet, statistics are tricky. The apparent correlation between the closing of the services and the increase in adult male conversions could be a misleading coincidence. Just because there were many young men in the services, and just because there were many young men among the converts after 1823, we cannot assume that these were the *same* men. For this conclusion we would need to match the names of the converts with the names of those attending the Beer temple.

Moreover, another reason to question whether reform could halt the rise of conversions is the downward shift in the class position of the young male converts. We know that the men who were baptized after 1830 tended to be poorer than earlier converts, a change from the peak years of the family crisis. That means that they were unlikely participants in the new services, who tended to be from the richer families.[105] By the time the family crisis ebbed, many wealthy extended families had already left Judaism. We can track the same trend by watching occupations. Rather than the financier or merchant converts who had been rather common in the years before and after 1800, now more and more converts were students or teachers. The point for our tale is that even if the services had not been closed in 1823, rates might still have increased anyway. We have good reason to doubt that the poorer young men who converted after they moved to Berlin would have been eager to participate in the reform subculture.[106] We know how intellectuals such as Zunz and Jost resented their dependence upon the Beers of the world.

Yet another possible explanation for a rise in the conversion rates in these decades was that loyalist Jews were more willing to accept converts into their intimate social and family circles. We know well that fear of loneliness had been a very good reason for alienated Jews in previous generations to remain Jewish. In the 1820s, several social spaces existed where former Jews and those still Jewish could mix in a relaxed setting. Precisely because they eventually decided to accept converted members, the Society of Friends was a special destination for former Jews to mix with still-Jewish Jews. Moreover, several Jewish couples welcomed converts to their homes and found a way to remain close after such a decision. Even though Leopold Zunz decided not to convert, he and his wife Adeleid were obviously quite open-minded.[107] Karl Varnhagen was friendly with Leopold, and Adeleid enjoyed relationships with several Christian women. There were, however, limits to their tolerance toward converts. Adeleid apparently "resented Rahel's apostasy," and we do not know whether Rahel was ever a guest at their home.[108]

Social life was complicated indeed. Whereas Rahel was reconciled to inviting to her home some people who would never reciprocate, the characters in August Lewald's semi-autobiographical novel *Memoiren eines Bankiers* refused to do as she did. Lewald's novel was set in an east Prussian town during the 1820s. The narrator and his wife become Catholics in the years after the War of Liberation, but they are dismayed when the prominent Christians whom they invite to their home do not invite them back. They decide to socialize among a circle of converted Jews and Jews considering conversion.[109] That such a network could exist even in August Lewald's imagination suggests that conversion did not necessarily result in utter loneliness.

Another possible reason for the rise in baptisms was the impulse to piece together a new inner identity that was felt to be national or cultural rather than religious. Becoming a Lutheran was a profound way to feel more German on the inside, reinforced by the Christian values of the nationalist movement and of state institutions. Both from the right and the left, from rational secularists and from romantic conservatives, Protestant affiliation was increasingly seen as necessary for civic affiliation and identity. Ludwig Börne was the best example of this trend, as the first secular leftist convert. To deepen our understanding of the conversion problematic, we must enter the lives of three individuals, Daniel Lessmann, Harry Heine, and Eduard Gans, who converted in these years, in order to view up close the complexity of individual choices. Lessmann arrived in Berlin in 1824, when he was 28. His father had been an ardent *maskil* who changed the family name from Lewin to Lessmann, perhaps in honor of Mendelssohn's friend Gotthold Lessing. Daniel was one of the rare Jewish intellectuals of his circle who fought for Prussia during the War of Liberation and had even been wounded in the cause. While recuperating in a small village, he fell in love with a Christian woman, but they never married, and he remained single throughout his short and rather unhappy life. Lessmann was trained as a physician, but he never practiced medicine, and instead wrote and published prolifically, producing works of history, novels, literary history, and journalism.[110]

During his twenties Lessmann was peripatetic, wandering from Vienna to various towns in Italy, before he finally settled in Berlin. He had friends who were active in the Verein, and indeed Zunz had nominated him to become an associate of the club back in 1821. The same year he came to Berlin, Daniel was baptized, and his friends later speculated that he waited for this step until his father died.[111] After his conversion, Daniel did not cut ties with his Verein friends, nor did they break relations with him. Moses Moser later remembered his reaction to Lessmann's decision as a turning point in the significance of baptism. In a letter to his friend Immanuel Wohlwill, Moser wrote that "there was a time when I would have considered such a step a reason to terminate a friendship. Now I find nothing spiritual within the Jewish community worthy of a noble battle. Amidst this universal dismemberment every individual has to see how he can come to terms with the particularities of family ties, etc. which may shackle him."[112] Even though he was able to keep his friends after his baptism, Daniel enjoyed little serenity, and seven years later he took his own life, by hanging himself from a tree.

Another of Lessmann's colleagues in the Verein also had baptism on his mind in 1824: Heinrich Heine. To understand Heine's fate we should examine his story in tandem with the troubling history of his close friend Eduard Gans. Heine had departed Berlin in May 1823, to live with his family in Lüneberg, where they had moved the previous year. Harry was sarcastic about Lüneberg, calling it "the capital of boredom."[113] Restless as ever, he soon left for the University of Göttingen, where he had studied before coming to Berlin in 1821, determined to complete his law degree. While at Göttingen he wrote several chapters of a historical novel set in the medieval era called *The Rabbi of Bacherach*. Those who read the novel today find Heine's voice full of "richness and understanding" for the Jewish situation of the time. Yet the novel remained unfinished, and at the time and later some speculated that he could not finish the book because his personal quandaries about Judaism were too intense. By May 1825 Heine finally passed the preliminary law examination, albeit with a mediocre grade. While he was pondering how to plot his future, his friend Eduard stopped off in Göttingen for a visit. Since the 1822 ruling that baptism would be necessary for him to become a professor, Gans had been living with his mother, busy with his mentor Professor Hegel, planning various projects to spread Hegel's liberal views. But Gans was fretting, because productive days at his desk, good reviews, coffeehouse dialogues, and even Hegel's support were hardly a professorship. After the Verein closed down in 1824, there was one less reason to remain in Berlin, and the following May Gans left for Paris. His support was provided by the two-year stipend for study abroad which Hardenberg had secured him back in 1822. Apparently many of his friends thought he would never return to Berlin.[114]

On his way to Paris, Eduard stopped in Göttingen to visit his friend Harry. During that visit, the two men discussed the need for baptism if they were to become professors of law. Gans's mother was still pressing him to work in commerce, which meant remaining Jewish was an advantage or perhaps even a requirement. Heine, on the other hand, was sure that his family actually wanted him to convert and enter an academic career.[115] Two years before, while he was writing his law thesis, at home with his family in Lüneberg, he wrote to a friend in Berlin: "as you might imagine, they are talking about baptism here. No one in my family is against it except me."[116] Still, during their reunion that May, both expressed loyalty to the values of the Verein, and they promised each other that neither would "crawl to the cross."

But only weeks later, once Eduard had moved to Paris, Harry reneged on his promise, although he was ambivalent about the decision. In 1823 he had written to Moses Moser that "I consider it beneath my dignity and honor to convert to Protestantism in order to get a job in Prussia! . . . These are sad times we live in. Scoundrels have become the best we've got, and the best we've got have all turned into scoundrels."[117] At some point in the spring of 1825, presumably after Eduard left for Paris, he began to study the Lutheran faith with Gottlieb Grimm, a pastor in Heiligenstadt, a small town close to Göttingen. On June 28 he was baptized, receiving the name Christian Johann Heinrich Heine. Reports tell that he was "pale," that during the lunch afterwards he "hardly spoke."[118] Why did Heine decide to become a Lutheran at this moment in time? His most famous remark about his baptism was that it was "the entrance ticket to European culture."[119] Here he was idealizing his own motives, for the baptism was meant to be his "entrance ticket" to his own career as a law professor. As the years passed, his careerist stance grew increasingly ironic, for although Heine "bought the ticket," he never succeeded in becoming a professor of law. During the five years after his baptism, while he was still in Germany, Harry envied his friends who could live as gentlemen scholars from their family monies. In his own mind he justified his baptism by his need to work for a living. Later he wrote his friend Moser that "if the laws permitted stealing silver spoons, I would not have had myself baptized."[120] Here he was thinking of his friend Eduard, or perhaps of Giacomo and Michael Beer. This was obviously a difficult juncture in his life, for he considered suicide in the winter of 1825, six months after his baptism.[121]

He was conflicted about his Jewish identity for decades after the baptism. In a letter to Moser in January 1826, he admitted that "I regret very much that I had myself baptized; I cannot at all see that things have gone better for me since then, on the contrary, I have since had nothing but misfortune."[122] Yet for years after the event he certainly rarely sounded sorry. Five years later, when he was sitting for a portrait with Moritz Daniel Oppenheim, the painter, a committed Jew, asked Harry if he had converted. Heine brushed the question aside, and quipped that "it was vastly more painful nowadays to have a tooth pulled than to convert."[123] And a decade after his baptism, when he was already in Paris, he declared that "he did not belong to the Jewish religion and that he had never set foot in a synagogue."[124]

In the meantime, Eduard, now in Paris, set to work on the third volume of his tome on Roman legal history. He was delighted that David Koreff and Alexander von Humboldt were also in Paris then, as was the publisher Johann von Cotta, who encouraged him to return to Berlin to edit a new liberal journal. Eduard told Cotta and his friends that he could only take on this venture if he could finally become a professor at the university. Seven months after arriving in Paris, he followed in Heine's footsteps, and was baptized into the Lutheran faith, on December 12, 1825. None of his friends thought he was motivated by any religious impulses whatsoever. Gans freely admitted to friends that "if the state is so stupid as to demand that I profess something that the responsible minister knows well that I do not believe, well then — it shall have its way."[125] Soon he made plans to return to Berlin, and by March 1826 he was appointed a professor at the university, to Hegel's delight and Savigny's outrage. Gans's decision agitated many. Heine sat down and wrote a poem, "To an Apostate," full of cruel insults to Gans. He must have been ashamed of the poem for he never published it, and Eduard never read it. Some of the lines would have hurt him badly, such as "yesterday you were a hero; look how low the mighty fall."[126] He was fully aware that in the poem he was projecting his own guilt onto Eduard, for he wrote Moser that "I think so often about Gans because I do not want to think about myself."[127] In wider Jewish circles Gans's decision caused despair. Because of his public prominence as a reformer, his conversion was seen as a "depressing blow to hopes for Jewish emancipation."[128] He returned to live with his mother, who was reportedly at peace with his baptism, although sometimes she teased him about his new religious status. Just how he maintained his relationship with former Verein friends is ambiguous. He remained in contact with Leopold Zunz, but contemporaries also gossiped that Gans "could not bear to see Jews any more."[129] It may well have been painful for Zunz to watch Gans begin his climb to the top of local academia. His dictum that "baptism degrades the Jews in the eyes of the same government which desires it" may well have been formulated in response to Gans's baptism.[130]

Now that he was a Lutheran, Gans could begin to realize his political and academic goals. In the middle of the summer of 1826, Gans and Hegel called a meeting at Hegel's home to found the journal which Cotta had proposed in Paris. The plan was to establish a "counter-Academy" to rival Berlin's prestigious Academy of Science, which had long refused Hegel's appointment because Schleiermacher opposed him so passionately. Gans was appointed the General Secretary of the new institution, called the Society for Scientific Criticism. The plan was to meet weekly to discuss articles proposed for publication in its *Yearbooks for Scientific Criticism,* a journal advocating liberal, even radical politics, intended to have broad appeal, with no dry scholarly articles. Should we be surprised to learn that Gans not only was the organizer but was also occasionally the patron as well? At one point when the funding for the new project was scanty, Gans contributed 2,000 thalers to keep the journal afloat.[131] In spite of his status as a new Christian, there are parallels between his new project and the now defunct Verein fur Cultur und Wissenschaft des

Judentums. It is obvious that Gans enjoyed creating alternative institutions with broad mandates to change the world. Now that he was no longer Jewish, the intellectual program of his new organization was wider, and now his colleagues were among the premier intellects of the day. Yet the function of the project in his day-to-day life was remarkably similar to his work with the Verein during the early 1820s, and some of the personalities funding the Society were already in his orbit, including Moritz Veit and Lea and Abraham Mendelssohn. Here again we see wealthy Jews donate funds to an avant-garde cultural institution, and they in turn find a social space to shine in high society.

Exploring the lives of the Mendelssohns, Daniel Lessmann, Heinrich Heine, and Eduard Gans shows us that careers, social advancement, and new national identities drew these men to the cross. When their siblings, parents, cousins, and friends converted too, or at least continued to socialize with them, the emotional costs of baptism were vastly reduced. But did their baptisms bring them what they sought? Was Heine right that the best had become scoundrels, and if he was correct, were those scoundrels at least happy? These are our important questions now as we move into the final seven years of our journey.

The Dark Side of the New Identities, 1826–1833

Because of their high-profile accomplishments, converts such as Rahel Levin Varnhagen, Eduard Gans, Heinrich Heine, and Felix Mendelssohn were watched from near and far with a huge range of feelings, from admiration to jealousy to critique. Sometimes those facing similar predicaments found ways to support each other. But as Heine's poem about Gans shows clearly, parallel predicaments did not always lead to solidarity. Among obscure converts as well as among the notorious, we see expressions of great hostility, in private and in public, to a peer also born to Judaism who was somehow more visibly Jewish. In the frantic struggle to escape the Jewish stigma, bonds of family and friendship sometimes snapped and broke. Take, for example, Rahel's younger brother Ludwig Robert. Robert did not enjoy easy success in his chosen profession of playwright. In 1819, at 41, he too became a Lutheran, so as to marry his beloved Friederike Braun, who was Christian, and also in the hope of improving his theatrical career. Four years before, in 1815, during a performance of one of his plays, "stones were hurled in the streets, and one could hear cries of 'slovenly scribbling by a Jew!' "[132] In spite of such attacks Ludwig was committed to the theater as a forum for social critique. He and Rahel often discussed the problem of their Jewish descent. Just months before his baptism, during the fateful summer of 1819, the two siblings exchanged letters about the *hep hep* riots. That summer found both of them in Karlsruhe, one of the settings where Jews and Jewish property were attacked. Ludwig complained to Rahel that *other Jews* did not take the hostility of the riots seriously enough. That phrase is all the more remarkable since four years before Rahel had included the phrase "people like us cannot be Jews" in one of her letters. Ludwig was not entirely at peace with his decision to be baptized, but he tried to convince her, who had already been a Christian for five years, that he *was* convinced of the necessity of the act. "Since you know me well, you will also know that I am taking this step as earnestly as I have earlier refused it," he wrote.[133]

Although he saw the theater as a forum for social critique, Ludwig chose not to address the Jewish problematic directly in his plays. Like Michael Beer with his play *The Paria,* or Giacomo Meyerbeer with his opera *The Huguenots,* he found that one way to express anger yet avoid too much notoriety was to create a work of art lambasting prejudice toward *another* minority group. Indeed Robert's most successful drama, *Die Macht der Verhältnisse* ("The Power of Relationships"), was the story of a nobleman who refused to fight a duel with a commoner. In the play, the son of a pastor is outraged that his honor has been violated by a noble official. The insulted man challenges the nobleman to a duel, but when the noble refuses to duel, the insulted man decides to shoot the officer in cold blood. Many were sure that the play was based on the Arnim-Itzig affair, but Robert always denied this.[134] In another play entitled *Jocko,* Ludwig took aim at another man of Jewish descent rather than an arrogant nobleman. *Jocko* was a slapstick version of a short story by the fantasy writer E. T. A. Hoffmann, who lived in Berlin in these years. In the play, the owner of a real-life pet monkey has dressed his pet in fancy clothes and introduced him into good society. But as the story proceeds, the true identity of the monkey is revealed. When *Jocko* played in Berlin, as soon as the dressed-up monkey appeared on stage, the whole theater was filled with waves of laughter and joyous cries of "Saphir! Saphir!"[135] Who, we must ask, was Saphir? Unlike most of the other converts from these years, Moritz Saphir received a thorough religious education, and even published some of his early works in Yiddish. He grew up in Lovasbereny, a small village near Budapest. When he was ten, his mother died. In his early years he was a star yeshiva student, destined for a life as a rabbi. While studying at a yeshiva in Prague, he became acquainted with a priest who introduced him to secular learning. He quickly mastered German, French, English, and Italian. Peripatetic and ambitious, he roamed from Prague to Budapest to Vienna.

In 1825, when he was 30, Saphir found his way to Berlin. There he began publishing two controversial newspapers, crammed full with biting satire.

Ironically enough, one of his most eager readers was King Frederick William III. Saphir himself wrote many of the articles, famous for their jokes, sexual innuendos, roguish anecdotes, and pointed satire about local and national politics.[136] The king's enthusiasm was all the more surprising, considering that Saphir took aim not only at radical nationalists, but also at monarchists and monarchs, militarism, and press censorship.[137] Saphir was appreciated by some of Berlin's major personalities, and even convinced Hegel himself to write for his papers. One of his funniest projects was a society dedicated to "tomfoolery" called the Inverted World. Moritz was known for his extravagant outfits and sometimes went around town wearing a curly blond wig. He was very public in his hatred of Henriette Sontag, an immensely popular singer, which did little for his own reputation. Sometimes he also attacked other Jews, including Ludwig Robert and Heinrich Heine. Perhaps Saphir was seeking revenge for the way Robert had mocked him in *Jocko*. Yet on the other hand Saphir could also be a proud Jew. He celebrated humor as a Jewish trait and emphasized that laughter was "the defense and the weapon of the oppressed."[138] Throughout his life Saphir would "react to anti-Semitism fiercely" and "fought it courageously," and he once explained that antisemites were "sick individuals" for whom Jew-hate filled a "psychological need."[139]

Considering his leftist politics, it comes as no surprise that Saphir was enthusiastic about Gans's new Society for Scientific Criticism. But Saphir was too isolated to participate in Gans's world, as revealed by an incident in May 1826. One of his friends had organized a gathering at a restaurant, aiming to reconcile Saphir with his critics, and during the dinner, conversation turned to praise of Henriette Sontag. Saphir shared his plans to publish yet another parody of her. Karl Schall, a Breslau publisher, began shouting obscenities at Saphir, then stormed out, and was followed by all the guests at the party, leaving Saphir alone at the table. On another occasion in their troubled relationship, Schall challenged Saphir to a duel, and friends wondered who would be Saphir's "second" in case he was killed. "Finally, a taxi-coach pulled up bearing Saphir's second, and out stepped, of all people, Hegel!" Hegel actually saved the day by convincing Schall to apologize to Saphir, and thus preventing the duel from taking place.[140]

After four years in Berlin, Saphir's public demands for freedom of the press began to irritate the king, and in 1829 he lost his temporary residence permit to live in the city. He was not protected by the 1812 Edict, because he had never become a citizen of Berlin. He wanted to resolve the crisis by converting, which would have made it possible for him to remain. But because of his inferior status in the city, he needed official state permission to change his religion, and his request was rejected. This decision brings nuance to our story, for it suggests that not every decision about Jews made on high was driven by the simple goal of increasing conversions. But here again we see the long arm of the state determining religious matters. Saphir soon left for Munich. Three years later, after his father died, he became a Lutheran. He never married. Let us leave him with his father's testament, in which he asked a younger son, not his first-born son Moritz, to recite the Jewish mourning prayer, the kaddish, in his memory.[141]

Debate about Saphir's work and his politics obviously agitated his friends and enemies. When Ludwig Börne arrived in Berlin in the spring of 1828, his friends warned him to avoid Saphir. Börne, whose politics were similar to Saphir's, ignored this advice, and during his weeks in Berlin Moritz and Ludwig met often for walks in the Tiergarten. Ever the malicious gossip in his letters back to his intimate friend Jeanette Wohl in Frankfurt, Börne acknowledged that Saphir was "widely hated and scorned."[142] In 1828 Börne had been a Christian for a decade, and had become the successful editor of a journal of theater criticism, convinced that such writing could rouse public anger against the harsh repression which so stifled German life in the 1820s. Contemporary radicals and liberals were delighted with his work, convinced that he was "the most effective scourge of the universal public outrage that modern Germany had ever seen." Even now, almost two centuries later, readers find his satirical writings "immensely funny," and some find it impossible to read him "without laughing out loud."[143] Ludwig was also motivated by sheer financial need. Like Heine, he raged against a father figure who denied him the funds to be a gentleman scholar. Because his father so strongly disapproved of his son's politics, Ludwig's inheritance after his father died in 1827 was much less than what he had expected.[144] But unlike Heine, who liked champagne with dinner and trips to the seaside when he felt despondent, Börne was an ascetic and could live on the cheap.

In his personal life, Ludwig's attachment to Jeanette Wohl continued to be close, but lacking in the normal trappings of bourgeois life. Both lived in Frankfurt for many years, and they traded several letters back and forth every day. Back in 1822, Jeanette had proposed that she and Ludwig move to Berlin and set up a joint household with Ludwig's old friend Henriette Herz. But Ludwig haughtily rejected this plan. Now, six years later, when he finally made a long-postponed trip to Berlin, he was the one to propose a real marriage with Jeanette. But his conversion back in 1818 now proved to be a serious barrier to their union, because in order for them to marry he would have had to return to Judaism, or she would have had to convert. But Jeanette was too loyal to her family and to Judaism to make this step, even if she *had* passionately desired a marriage with Ludwig. She lacked confidence in her passions and in his sincerity, and he was conflicted about commitment and daily intimacy. They sound so modern in their discontents. So the year 1828 passed without their union, and the chance never came again.

Ludwig's letters to Jeanette were full of spicy gossip about other personalities he met or wanted to meet during those spring months in Berlin. He decided not to seek a meeting with Schleiermacher, whom he had admired from afar when he was a student at the University of Halle in 1805. They had not become intimate then, and now Ludwig was sure that the famous theologian "could not stand him," because for Schleiermacher Börne was too much the militant secularist and rationalist.[145] We can sympathize with his desire to meet Hegel, whose politics were more to his liking, but the occasion never came to pass. Once he had been in love with Henriette Herz, when she was 37 and he was 17. Now that she was 64 and living alone in modest circumstances, Ludwig was most unsympathetic. He noted to Jeanette that "her wrinkled face looked to me more like a curtain, behind which was hiding her previous beauty. I moved the curtain away, but nothing was behind it."[146]

Rahel and Karl's home on the Mauerstrasse was an obvious destination for Ludwig Börne. After they returned to Berlin from Karlsruhe in the early fall of 1819 they had lived in rented quarters, but in 1826 they had finally purchased their own home. Visitors described the "large and airy" rooms painted light blue, with the "simple but elegant" furnishings. In the living room was a bust of Prince Louis Ferdinand and one of Friedrich Schleiermacher.[147] At first glance Rahel, Karl, and Ludwig shared many mutual friends, radical politics, and a complex stance toward Jewishness. Rahel and Ludwig agreed that baptism was a positive and necessary step, but none of the three was indifferent to anti-Jewish hostility. Still, in spite of their affinities Ludwig did not spare Rahel and Karl his critical eye. He saw himself as the principled leftist, irritated with their worldly compromises. He wrote to Jeanette that Karl was so eager to remain in the diplomatic service even after he lost his appointment in Baden that he ingratiated himself with the ruling elites. He was even angrier at Rahel for her search for prestigious connections.[148] Although Ludwig told Jeanette he admired her intellectual acuity, he did not appreciate those same qualities in Rahel, complaining to her that Rahel was a "superkluge Frau," a super-clever woman, who made mistakes because of her "Superklugheit."[149] Ludwig's absence of sympathy with the dilemmas of a smart woman lacking his opportunities for productive political engagement is troubling, though we know that his critique of Rahel's obsequious social climbing was well justified. Ironically, Rahel never knew how Ludwig was insulting her in his letters to Jeanette. She wrote to a mutual friend that "she worshipped him." In a letter she wrote to Ludwig, she volunteered to become "his flag bearer, his drummer and trumpeter, his field chaplain, as well as his laundress and canteen woman."[150]

While he was in Berlin that spring, Ludwig also visited Abraham and Lea

Mendelssohn. For three years now, the Mendelssohns had been living at Leip-zigerstrasse 3. Their new home was near the Potsdam Gate, surrounded by a large garden, and had once been part of the Tiergarten Park. Lea was delighted when they moved there in 1825, writing to a cousin that "a whole row of rooms opens on to a garden, which is itself surrounded by other gardens." Further beyond was a "large meadow" and even a small farm that provided the family with fresh milk and butter.[151] Conversion in this special extended family did not always lead to estrangement.[152] Shortly after the family moved in, Abraham's sister Henriette, now 44, returned to Berlin from Paris and settled in with the family. She had become a devout Catholic back in 1812, while working as a governess for the Sebastiani family. Relations were not so warm between Abraham and his still-Jewish brother Joseph, but Joseph's wife Hinni tried to preserve some connection with Lea and Abraham's family, and several of their children were quite intimate. By 1825 it had been three years since Abraham had retired from the family bank. Joseph and Hinni's son Alexander eventually joined the Mendelssohn bank, and he was one of the few grandchildren of Moses and Fromet who remained Jewish. Abraham's other still-Jewish sibling, Recha, a divorced and rather sickly woman, was close to Abraham and his family.

Their first years in the new home were later seen by many affectionate observers as the family's "happiest hour." Fanny, the oldest sibling, was now 20, a talented pianist and composer, and prominent soloist in the Choral Society. Abraham, however, was adamant that she could never enjoy a public career in music, because few well-to-do families allowed their daughters to publish books or perform on stage. Body was also a painful issue for Fanny. She had lovely large eyes and powerful, musical hands, but lamented that she was too plump and too petite and had inherited her grandfather Moses's crooked back.[153] In love, however, she was lucky. In 1821 Fanny had met Wilhelm Hensel, a painter, whose specialty during this time was designing *tableaux vivants* or "living pictures" for court society. In these performances, actors would assume fixed poses to illustrate a story, with elaborate costumes, set designs, and music. Wilhelm had been born to a poor Brandenburg minis-ter but was making his way up in the world.[154] In 1823, the Berlin Academy of Art had awarded him a study trip to Italy. Before he left, Wilhelm proposed to Fanny, and her parents seemed to agree, but asked for secrecy because of Grandmother Bella. The plot then thickened when Lea and Abraham dis-covered that Wilhelm was considering following his sister Luise into the Cath-olic Church. Abraham and Lea were adamant that they did not want their Protestant daughter to marry a Catholic, and so they forbade Fanny to even see Wilhelm. To us their concern seems odd, considering that Abraham's two sisters were both Catholic, and one of them was living in their home. More-over, their opposition to the match cannot have been so vehement, since Abra-ham sent funds to Rome to support Wilhelm while he was on his study trip there. Wilhelm later reciprocated the kindness, by helping to settle the estate of Lea's brother Jacob, who died in 1825.[155] In the end Wilhelm decided not to change his faith, and when he returned from Italy in 1828 he resumed his ardent courtship of Fanny. Grandmother Bella had died in 1824, and Fanny and Wilhelm married five years later.

When the Mendelssohns moved into their new home, Felix was 16, and his career as a composer was flourishing. He had already written more than one hundred musical compositions, and was much admired for his overture for Shakespeare's *Midsummer Night's Dream,* performed to great acclaim in Stet-tin in February 1827. But a few months later Felix suffered a serious setback when his comic opera *The Wedding of Camacho* closed after opening night. Because opera was then the most prestigious musical form, Felix felt that a failure to compose a great opera was a huge stain on his reputation.[156] He escaped from public humiliation by embarking on an extensive walking trip across Germany, including long stays in Frankfurt and Heidelberg. When he returned to Berlin that fall, Felix entered the University of Berlin, because Abraham and Lea insisted on a fine education while he was pursuing his musical career. One of his favorite professors, and indeed a close friend of the family, was the newly appointed Eduard Gans. Gans was a regular visitor at the Mendelssohns and just then was hoping to marry Felix's younger sister Rebekka.

As Felix's career began to dominate the lives of the other three siblings and their parents, tensions boiled beneath the surface and sometimes erupted. Abraham's moody irritability was a problem for the entire family. Fanny was very devoted to Felix, but also jealous of his public success. Because her par-ents refused her a public life, her only performance space was her family concerts. While Fanny envied Felix, Rebekka resented Fanny. Later she la-mented that "my older brother and sister stole my reputation as an artist. Next to Felix and Fanny, I could not aspire to any recognition."[157] The brothers had their conflicts too. Felix later wrote to Paul about the time he threw him off a chair, and Paul responded by scratching him.[158] Just how the secret baptisms and family intrigues affected these family dramas we cannot know.

Once they had moved into the Leipzigerstrasse home, the Mendelssohns' musical programs every other Sunday afternoon became important social events. Paul Heyse, the son of Julie and Karl, remembered the gatherings in rosy hues. "The hall was like a shrine, in which an enthusiastic congregation absorbed every tone with the utmost attention."[159] And the participants in the "enthusiastic congregation" were a who's who of Berlin in 1825, including Leopold Ranke, E. T. A. Hoffmann, Hegel, the two Humboldt brothers, Karl and Rahel, and Ludwig and Friederike Robert. Many from the musical world came too, including violinists, conductors, choral society directors, and editors of musical journals. The Mendelssohns supported high culture in many different ways, including their patronage of the Choral Society and the Society for Scientific Criticism. They also built a copper hut for geomagnetic observations by their dear friend Alexander von Humboldt, who returned to Berlin in 1827 after years abroad.[160] That same year Alexander offered a series of public lectures on geography, held at the new quarters of the Choral Society which were open to women, a novelty at the time. Fanny attended, exulting that "gentlemen may laugh as much as they like, but it is delightful that we too have the opportunity given us of listening to clever men."[161]

From our distance in time we might well conclude that this wealthy and talented family had traveled quickly and elegantly away from the Judaism of their grandfather Moses. Yet when we look behind closed doors we see how malicious some of their Christian friends could be. During these years, one of Felix's most intimate friends was Adolf Bernhard Marx. Marx was called the Abbé by the Mendelssohn children, a nickname derived from the sound of his two first initials. His father was a physician in Halle, and he had come to Berlin in 1822 to study law, had converted, and was now editing an influential musical journal. Friends of the family could be most critical of Felix's relationship with the Abbé, noting that Marx "gained an ascendancy over Felix such as no one ever exercised over him."[162] Abraham liked Felix's friend, apparently because the Abbé loved to argue, and "the elder Mendelssohn was very fond of contradicting, and of being contradicted."[163] Karl Varnhagen, who visited the Mendelssohns often, was horribly rude about Marx behind his back. He complained that "he immediately impressed me as unpleasant through his common appearance and coarse manner. He crawled like a cockroach before Felix, uttered obsequious admiration for him. . . . [Marx] was so fat and short, so overly plump, so unpleasantly pungent and suffocating . . . 'man as bug,' one said of him."[164] Karl did not use the word *Jewish* to describe Marx, but the insinuation is quite obvious. And this is all the more remarkable, since Karl saw himself and was seen by many as a friend of the Jews. He endangered his career when he married a woman of Jewish descent, and he surely considered himself an ardent supporter of Jewish emancipation. Others could be even harsher toward poor Adolf Marx. Zelter wrote to Goethe that Marx "may have been baptized with salt-water, for his excrement has a gray-green-yellow color."[165] Truly, it is astonishing how hated some converts were, even or especially by their friends.

The year 1829 proved very eventful for the Mendelssohns. For musical history, the significant event was the performance of Bach's *Saint Matthew Passion,* which took place on March 11. For two years, Felix and Fanny, their friends Therese and Eduard Devrient, and a circle of singers and musicians had been working through the music privately at the Mendelssohn home. It is surely ironic that Grandmother Bella, who owned the score of the music, had presented it to Felix as a gift back in 1823. Some scholars have claimed that the present was given at Christmas. We cannot know whether this little detail was true or not. How amazing were it to be true, that the grandmother from whom so many baptisms were hidden would have celebrated Christmas with her extended family, who were *secret* Christians. It is surely more plausible to imagine that the gift was for a Hannukah celebration!

Felix's friend Eduard persistently pressured Felix to beg Zelter to arrange for the public performance of the work. Eduard had been born into a famous theatrical family, and decided when still a teenager to become an opera singer. He was now 27, a singer in the Berlin Royal Opera, and for five years he had been married to Therese Schlesinger, the converted daughter of the musical publisher Adolf Martin Schlesinger. Because her family had been poor when they first moved to Berlin and she was quite talented, Zelter had generously waived the fees to teach her music. Through Zelter, Therese had met the Mendelssohns, and during these years she and Eduard lived in rooms in the Mendelssohn home on the Leipzigerstrasse.[166]

According to legend, it was on a cold January morning in 1829 when Felix and Eduard called on Zelter in his office at the Choral Society's new building, off Berlin's premier avenue Unter den Linden. Felix, wearing a blue jacket and a pair of new yellow gloves, tried to persuade him to lend the Choral Society facilities and singers for a public performance.[167] Zelter was an enthusiast for Bach, yet he hesitated to agree that the Choral Society should perform the ambitious and long-neglected work. One of his fears was that the established musicians from the Royal Berlin Orchestra would be outraged that Felix would conduct the music, considering that he was "a rich man's son and an amateur who did not have to earn his living by music."[168] Zelter in fact resisted mightily, calling Felix and Eduard "snotty-nosed brats," but in the end he agreed.[169] The event was a spectacular success for Bach and for Felix. The night of the performance, the house was sold out within ten minutes, but the hall only held room for one thousand, and more than a thousand enthusiasts tried in vain to enter. The king and his family, Schleiermacher, Hegel, and Rahel Varnhagen were among those listening. The performance was a sensation, talked about across Berlin, and "at a stroke, Mendelssohn had become one of the leading figures in the historical performance movement, indeed, one of Germany's most celebrated conductors."[170] Zelter wrote to Goethe about the performance, and Goethe responded "it was as if I heard the roaring of the sea from afar."[171] Amidst all the celebration there were more than a few comic moments. Later that month, at a select dinner at Zelter's home in honor of the performance, Therese Devrient was seated next to a gentleman who "continuously tried" to talk her into "drinking more wine," and "so annoyed her with his gallantries" that she turned to Felix and asked him to inform her "who this dumb goofball is beside me." Felix replied that "the dumb goofball beside you is the famous philosopher, Hegel."[172]

Few at the time failed to note the paradox that a convert from Judaism helped restore a great work of Christian music. The year 1829 was precisely a century after Bach's church music was written *and* a century after Felix's grandfather Moses had been born. Six months after the Bach performance, on September 10, the family and the wider public celebrated Moses Mendelssohn's centennial. Jubilee celebrations with a thoroughly civic, nonreligious tone were organized across the German lands, in Berlin, Dessau, Frankfurt, Dresden, and Hamburg. In Berlin the memorial was staged in the hall of the Society of Friends, and Jews as well as Christians attended. Speakers lauded Mendelssohn's German publications, not his stature as a Jewish philosopher, and they toasted the health of the Prussian king and the city of Berlin. Verses to the memory of Mendelssohn were sung to the tune of a Beethoven song. In short, Mendelssohn's memory was constructed to fit into the "canon of classical German poets and thinkers."[173] All in all, such a tone must have been comforting for the converted descendants of Mendelssohn. In subsequent years, Felix's friends and enemies pondered the ironies of his legacy and his public stance as a Christian composer and conductor. Almost twenty years later, Heine wrote to Ferdinand Lassalle that "I cannot forgive this man of independent means that he sees fit to serve the Christian pietists with his great and enormous talent. The more I admire his greatness, the more angry I am to see it so iniquitously misused. If I had the good fortune to be Moses Mendelssohn's grandson, I would not use my talents to set the piss of the Lamb to music."[174] We can easily see the hypocrisy in Heine's private attack on Felix, as well as his intense jealousy of Felix's wealth.

At the close of that momentous year, on Christmas eve, Lea and Abraham celebrated their twenty-fifth wedding anniversary. The program included a play written by Eduard Gans, a poetry recitation by Ludwig Robert, and performances of music composed by Fanny and Felix.[175] Surrounded by their successful children and a wide circle of friends, clients, hangers-on, admirers, and secret enemies, Lea and Abraham must have been convinced that their baptisms had been the right choice. They would never have acknowledged any dark side of their new identities, at least not in 1829.

While Felix was struggling to make a name for himself in Berlin, Giacomo Meyerbeer, then 38, was living in Italy, and enjoying a huge success as a composer of grand operas in the Italian style, leading his admirers to worry that his music was insufficiently German. Giacomo was not a hardy type; indeed "his nervous afflictions, real and imagined," multiplied as the years passed. Wherever he was staying, he kept in close contact with his family back in Berlin, reporting dutifully on his "nervous exhaustion and all manner of stomach ailments, digestive problems, headaches, and painful skin rashes," which propelled him to flee to various spas to recover his equilibrium.[176] We know that Lea Mendelssohn and Amalie Beer were rather competitive about the very different talents of their sons. In 1818 the two families had become joined by the marriage of Abraham's niece Betty and Heinrich Beer. Betty was the only child of Abraham's older sister Recha, one of the two Mendelssohn children who remained Jewish. Betty's life had not been easy, for after a few short years of an arranged marriage, her mother had divorced Betty's father Mendel, and she supported her daughter working as headmistress of a boarding school for girls near Hamburg. Betty had converted, but returned to Judaism to marry Heinrich.[177] The couple had one child, who died when he was only ten years old. The third Beer son, Wilhelm, entered the family firm but took scientific and musical work very seriously indeed. He was an accomplished singer and a dedicated astronomer who published his research and had his own planetarium. Wilhelm married a Jewish woman, but their daughters all converted and married into the French nobility, although their only son remained Jewish.[178] Amalie and Jacob's youngest son Michael was a quite successful playwright, a wanderer from Paris to Munich to Berlin and back again, who remained single and died young.[179]

The Beers gave Giacomo quite a bit of freedom to sow his wild oats, but were adamant that when it came time to marry, the wife would be appropriate to their elevated station. He was the first born but the last to marry, in 1826, when he was 33. Amalie went to considerable effort to find the right mate for the family, and when a match with an Ephraim descendant did not come to pass, the woman selected was Giacomo's first cousin, Minna Mosson. The marriage was apparently without major conflicts, although what with Giacomo's many musical journeys away from Berlin, the two do not seem to have spent a great deal of time together.[180] All of Giacomo and Minna's children converted. So for all their efforts to reform Judaism and keep their sons Jewish, the Beers were survived by only one Jewish grandchild.

While the Beers and the Mendelssohns were absorbed with the romances and the careers of their children, our converted bachelors were more concerned with politics and revolution. By 1830, Prussians had been enduring the restrictions of the Carlsbad Decrees for a decade. Whereas Berlin had been a lively culture center during the old regime years, now, a quarter of a century later, contemporaries complained that the city had become a sleepy backwater town. In 1834 one resident complained that Berlin was a "dead city," where "grass is growing between the cobblestones." Smoking was permitted only on the main street which led to Charlottenburg.[181] Few streets were paved, and it was the rare avenue lit up by gas lamps at night. Rats reigned supreme, and 200,000 buckets of night soil were collected every evening by a squadron of women who deposited the fecal matter in the river each morning.[182]

But the spirits of German liberals revived dramatically during the summer of 1830. On August 3, the birthday of the king was being celebrated in a large auditorium at the University of Berlin, where Professor Hegel was delivering a speech awarding the yearly prize of the Academy of Science to the writer Karl Gutzkow. Suddenly, during his lecture, a "fire storm of excitement" broke out in the room, as news published in a special edition of the newspaper circulated: Paris was engulfed in revolution, and King Carl had abdicated![183] Heine was living on the island of Helgoland on the River Elbe that summer, enjoying a love affair with a soprano from the Hamburg opera. Since he had received his law degree and become a Protestant, his poetry and prose publications had made him quite famous. But he had yet to find financial security, professional recognition, true love, or inner serenity. Mail came to Helgoland once a week, and one morning on the beach while reading the latest newspaper, he was elated to discover that a revolution had erupted in Paris. Later he remembered the moment as "sunbeams wrapped in newsprint."[184] He rushed back to Hamburg, where he followed news of the spreading revolt, which was sparking upheavals in Belgium, Spain, Greece, Parma, Modena, the Papal States, and Poland. But the good news for the liberal movement was not necessarily good news for the Jews across Germany. In Hamburg the windows on his Uncle Salomon's home were broken by angry rioters, and he must have been dismayed to see that rioting citizens posted handbills across Hamburg reading "Down with Jews, the Police, and Taxes." Pamphlets included complaints that Jew-boys "monopolize newspapers in the coffeehouses on their *Shabbes*."[185] Rioters hostile to Jews also gathered in Hessen-Darmstadt, Karlsruhe, Breslau, and Munich.

From our vantage point, to see economic anger focused on wealthy Jews is disturbing. But Heine and Börne focused their attention on events in Paris, not the anti-Jewish behavior of their own neighbors. That July, Ludwig Börne was healing his gout at a resort in the Taunus Mountains, and every morning he walked down the country road to meet the postman halfway, so that he could hear the latest news from the papers early. When he read about the revolution, he immediately abandoned his cure and rushed home to Frankfurt, then onward to Paris. Ludwig's *Letters from Paris,* which originated as communications to Jeanette Wohl, made his name in Germany and beyond. Heine, meanwhile, was also eager to find his way to Paris, but still he lingered in Hamburg, because he was trying for an appointment as a legal official with the Hamburg Senate. By February 1831, however, that dream had died. He and Ludwig Börne had become friends back in 1827, and now, in letters, they discussed various radical political publishing ventures. But nothing came of their plans. In April Heine wrote to Karl Varnhagen in Berlin that "every night, I dream that I am packing my suitcase for Paris, to breathe fresh air."[186] A week later, Harry was appointed the Paris correspondent for a liberal German newspaper, which was at once a solution to his money problems and a useful political niche. He departed for Paris, and would never live in Germany again. At 34, Heine had arrived at his happiest time. After he had been in Paris a little less than a year and a half, he wrote to a friend that "if a fish were asked how it felt to be in water, it would say: like Heine in Paris."[187]

Harry and Ludwig enjoyed a vibrant German political community in Paris, and many of the German expatriates were Jews or former Jews. Personal relationships were sometimes stormy and on occasion remarkably malicious. Here again we see the dark side of the new identities. Felix Mendelssohn arrived in Paris in 1831, after two years in London and various cities on the Continent. His musical success in Paris was not quite as resplendent as it had been in London. He openly disliked Heine, covering all bases with his double critique that Harry not only "maligned everything that was German," but also spoke "bad French."[188] Felix also disliked Giacomo Meyerbeer, whose ambitions were certainly closer to his own. When Felix was told that he resembled Giacomo, "he had his hair cut and arranged differently to cancel the resemblance."[189] Soon Felix left Paris, after recovering from a slight case of the cholera epidemic then raging across Europe. So again this young man enjoyed superior good fortune.

Meanwhile, as the years passed, Heine and Meyerbeer were experiencing a difficult relationship. A decade before, when he had arrived in Berlin to study at the university, Harry had been welcomed graciously by the Beers. The same year that Harry came to live in Paris Giacomo arrived as well. He was now at the height of his powers and popularity, but because he spent his own fortune on his art and on a fine lifestyle, gossips were relentless that he was somehow buying his fame. Meyerbeer was generous to the ever-needy Heine, providing him with "opera tickets, dinner invitations, and a proposal to set some of his poems to music."[190] In return, Meyerbeer hoped Heine would aid him with positive reviews, in France and of course back in Germany. Heine was eager to function as Meyerbeer's press agent, and there were episodes where Meyerbeer did pay him to bribe a hostile journalist. We know Heine well enough not to be surprised that he resented his own dependence on Giacomo, and behind his back he criticized his friend's music as "colicky and hemorrhoidal" — exhibiting the same sort of dependence and resentment he always showed toward his Uncle Salomon.[191]

While Heine, Börne, and Meyerbeer were each in his way enjoying the glories of Paris, Felix was drawn back to Berlin. The circumstances which called him there turned out to be highly unpleasant, not just for his career but for the entire Mendelssohn family. The episode began when Karl Zelter died in May 1832, which meant that his post as director of the Choral Society was now free. His assistant for almost two decades had been Karl Friedrich Rungenhagen, who was the inside candidate for the post. Lea and Abraham were understandably eager to have their *Wunderkind* Felix assume this esteemed job, and as long-time patrons of the Choral Society they may well have expected that their generosity and the generosity of Lea's aunt Sara would be repaid at this juncture. Felix himself did not necessarily want to return from his wandering life and settle in Germany, and he was also reluctant to promote himself as Zelter's successor. Nevertheless, Abraham persuaded him to return to Berlin, and by the end of June he was again installed in the garden house on the Leipzigerstrasse.

Later that summer the delicate negotiations began. Schleiermacher proposed that Rungenhagen and Mendelssohn share the directorship, but nothing came of that idea. For months the directors of the Choral Society debated, and when the dust settled Mendelssohn lost decisively, gaining slightly over half as many votes as his rival. Felix was in despair, and later described his defeat as the "severest trauma of his life." By the spring of 1834 he departed Berlin for good, first for London and then to conduct a festival in Düsseldorf. Meanwhile, the Mendelssohns withdrew from the Choral Society, an especially severe loss for Fanny, who had so few occasions to enjoy sharing her talents in a public setting.[192] We can easily grasp why the family wanted Felix to inherit Zelter's directorship, and we ponder why he lost in the competition. Felix's close friend Eduard Devrient was privy to the internal debates, and later revealed that many in the Choral Society were convinced that it was "a Christian institution occupying itself almost exclusively with sacred music, and therefore it would be quite unthinkable that one would propose a Jew-boy as a director."[193] Researchers seeking to illuminate the truth of what happened are now stymied, because the records of the Society meetings were destroyed during World War II.

Several months after Felix's trauma in Berlin, another *Wunderkind* was also humiliated, and this one did not survive. On March 22, 1833, Michael Beer died in the arms of his mother Amalie in Munich, five days after he had become ill with a brain inflammation.[194] When he died, Michael Beer was only 33. That spring, while living in Munich, he had been invited to participate in the opening ceremonies at a ball at the palace. The plan was to have all participants march in couples. But because he was Jewish and also looked Jewish, none of the noble ladies was willing to grace Beer's arm. To save his feelings, it was decided that he was to march alone, waving a golden baton. But later the king himself canceled this plan, leaving Beer devastated. To hide his exclusion, he pretended to be ill, and thus unable to attend the ball in any case. But then his pretend illness became reality, and five days later he was dead, from causes not at all clear to us now.[195] It was a bitter fate for a 33-year-old man to die in the arms of his mother after a humiliating rejection from court society.

It was also in March of that year that our heroine Rahel died. Her last years had been productive and contented. She and Karl became enthusiasts for the new philosophy of Claude-Henri de Saint-Simon, a utopian socialist and feminist. They prepared her writings for publication, and their salon flourished, especially as the harsh political repression lifted. But sadnesses multiplied after 1830. Her brother Ludwig died in the cholera epidemic that year, and her health began to deteriorate. During the winter of 1833 she could not leave her bed for days at a time. Her intimates in these painful months included her old friend Bettina von Arnim, her brother Moritz, and her sister-in-law Ernestine. When she died on March 17, Karl was on hand to record her last words. According to his later recollection, what she said was "What a history! A fugitive from Egypt and Palestine, here I am and find help, love, fostering in you people. With real rapture I think of these origins of mine and this whole nexus of destiny, through which the oldest memories of the human race stand side by side with the latest developments. The greatest distances in time and space are bridged. The thing which all my life seemed to me the greatest shame, which was the misery and misfortune of my life — having been born a Jewess — this I should on no account now wish to have missed." Those who read only this quote are justified in concluding that in the end she was a prodigal Jew, at least in spirit. Certainly that was Hannah Arendt's oft-cited interpretation, which is why she began her biography of Rahel with this citation.[196]

But Arendt skipped over the rest of Rahel's discussion that fateful day of her death. For she went on to tell Karl that "I have thought of Jesus and cried over his passion; I have felt — for the first time so felt it — that he is my brother. And Mary, how did *she* suffer! She saw her beloved son suffer but did not succumb; *she stood* at the cross![197] The contrast between these two quotes is her real double legacy for us. She died grateful for her Jewish destiny, yet at the very same moment she was deeply engaged in her new Christian beliefs. Rahel's deathbed utterances reveal her uneven, fragmented, brittle identity. The prodigal Jew is there, and so is the believing Christian. That those inspired by her life during the troubled twentieth century would be able to perceive only one side of that vexed double identity is entirely consonant with Jewish fate in our era. Descendants of converts likewise were forced to choose between a Jewish and a German identity.

Our investigations have uncovered the harsh reality of how the converts were seen by contemporaries who were altogether hostile toward Judaism, emancipation, and assimilation. Yet at the same time we can in some ways empathize with their decisions to solve very real problems in their lives by baptism. They wanted distinguished careers, loving marriages, a bountiful social life, and an inner identity as Germans. They could not wait for history to bring them authentic emancipation. Who among us in our century can argue that they should have forgone what they bought so dearly with a baptism? One of the ironies of the conversion story is that as we have moved forward in time, the spiritual upheavals have become fainter and rarer as motives. But even if motives were pragmatic, we must beware of rashly condemning the converts for lack of honor. History gave them few chances to be both principled and successful, unless they were born to enormous wealth.

Even if their baptisms brought them everything they wanted and everything they deserved, the loss of the best and the brightest to Judaism in this very difficult time is troubling. In the decades after we depart Berlin in 1833, the family crisis further ebbed, and the proportion choosing conversion fell. But the legacy of this era is telling. Our converts set a model for a truly craven style of assimilation, and the self-hatred among the ambitious can be seen among Jewish Germans long after Rahel died in 1833. So many of the life stories that we have explored suggest that the manner in which they separated from kin and faith made it difficult for many converts to feel and express solidarity with other converts. We have good reason to suspect that their often public animosity to those similar to themselves sparked antisemitism among unsympathetic observers. Many of us who hear their stories find ourselves divided and ambivalent as we watch how they sought to find serenity in their harsh times. One can, at times, feel pity for their struggles and admire how much some converts achieved. On the other hand we see the difficult consequences for their families and for the future of Jewry in Germany and beyond. We leave them with pity, sometimes with outrage at them and at their malicious enemies, often with sorrow for the always vanishing space for them to realize their dreams without experiencing painful, sometimes humiliating compromises. One meager solace now, at the close of this journey, is to understand how truly rare it is for individuals to find personal happiness and also do the right thing by their family, their religion, and their people.

Epilogue

I have been living with the converts who appear in this book for over fifteen years. Indeed some of those who converted during the old regime epoch have been with me for much longer, literally for most of my adult life. So often I have pondered their lives, empathized with their dilemmas, and judged their choices. I imagine them turning over the decision in their minds, then contacting a preacher, studying the new faith, dressing for the occasion, reciting what was asked of them, and exiting from the ceremony as Lutherans. To whom did they confide their new identity, and from whom did they keep it a secret? As the years passed, who was sorry, and who was at peace with their new identity?

When I began the project, my stance toward the converts was sympathetic, and without that instinct I surely would not have embarked on the book in the first place. But as the research progressed, I sometimes lost my sympathy and became disappointed with episodes of apparent hypocrisy, self-hatred, and crass self-promotion. A wide and disturbing gap appeared between my negative judgments of the converts and the enthusiasm many contemporary academics feel for ethnic mixing. For in recent years, many postmodern intellectuals have celebrated hybrid composite identities. Meanwhile I find myself vexed about the personal price of radical assimilation.

But readers of the book will surely all bring their own values and instincts to their encounter with these converts. Whatever our personal judgments, this book has illuminated several trends about Jewish conversion in modern Germany. The central challenge has been to show why the rates of baptism were so high early in nineteenth-century Berlin, and why they fell later. Rather than looking to either hostile antisemitism or its absence, our best way to account for the conversion wave was the complex mix of opportunity and discrimination during those years. The large supply of Jews who contemplated conversion shows how much opportunity Berlin provided then. That so many chose that step shows how limited their options were while still Jewish. Romance and career remained powerful incentives even after the 1812 Edict. After 1812, the struggle for civic and religious equality was stymied, and so baptism became *the only* road away from a forced membership in the still quite despised Jewish caste. Then there were those who already enjoyed wealth, education, and social connections *as Jews,* but converted so as to feel German on the inside, to feel entitled to their place in the dominant society. However passionately we might today blame the Prussian state for forcing ambitious Jews to "crawl to the cross," baptism was a way for individuals to functionally achieve emancipation. Martin Walser used the right words, but greatly misinterpreted the situation. To say that conversion was a functional, makeshift, problematic substitute for emancipation is certainly not the same as arguing that conversion *was* emancipation.

This detailed history of conversion in one city illuminates wider problems in the past. Because Germany became the classic land of radical assimilation, the history of conversion is vastly informative about Jewish and German experiences. Conversion rates tell us how fragile Judaism was in particular eras, and simultaneously reveal how permeable Christian society was. As time moved forward, the choices did become more nuanced. Whereas in the seventeenth century one could be either a Christian or a Jew, precisely in the years we have explored here a new version of Jewish practice appeared. From that moment forward, Jews faced three fundamental alternatives. They could remain traditional, commit to the harmonious modernization of Judaism, or try to escape Judaism altogether. Just what it meant to choose one of these three paths and how many and which Jews went in different directions shifted over time and across cities and countries. But the choices which emerged in this era set the terms for the centuries since.

The biographical portraits included in these pages show that it is unfair to the realities of that time to attribute opportunist motives to the converts and loyalist motives to those who remained Jewish. Just as departure involved a complex texture of feelings, ambitions, and desires, so too did loyalty. The story of the Beers and the Rothschilds illustrates that those who remained Jewish may well have found that identity very much in their self-interest. The secular converts, who were forced to make their way in a society still organized by all-too-strict borders between the faiths, pose a special problem, and we must consider the possibility that secular motives could be honorable. Certainly it was not their fault that the government made authentic emancipation so vexed, forcing ambitious Jews to convert in order to marry Christians or find fulfillment in work.

Learning the motives of individual converts and larger groups of converts helps refine our judgments. By bringing the story back to the seventeenth century, I have been able to explore the lives of those Jews chiefly motivated by spiritual and theological experiences. Precisely because they rarely improved their material circumstances after baptism, I often empathized with them. I felt for a Joseph Guggenheim, driven mad by his religious conflicts, or a Gottfried Selig, born to a prominent family who ended his days tramping through Germany trying to find subscribers to his religious publications. August Neander was certainly a poignant figure. Gazing at his modest face next to the proud self-possession of Hegel and Humboldt, I was moved by the distance he traveled, born the son of a Göttingen moneylender and in the end a professor of theology at the University of Berlin. The cost of baptism for these religious converts was often estrangement from their families and poverty. But just because the ritual of conversion expressed their own convictions, they had a chance for serenity once they were Christians.

As we moved into the nineteenth century, the emotional consequences of pragmatic baptisms were often distressing, and Lea Mendelssohn's 1799 reference to "all this hypocrisy" was often in my mind. Take for example Rahel Levin Varnhagen herself, the hero or perhaps the anti-hero of this book. She may have become a believing Christian after her conversion, but marriage determined the timing of her baptism in September 1814. But because Rahel's romantic life was so pained, and romance meant so much to a woman determined to escape her birth destiny, I empathized with her at the moment when she finally married Karl. Still, I was often distraught when her behavior seemed unbalanced and self-hating, as when she mocked her still religious Breslau relatives, or when she fawned over those who would never invite her in return to their homes. This public behavior must have damaged her self-respect. I continue to wonder whether her craven social climbing was truly necessary to achieve even a minimal fulfillment as a brainy and ambitious Jewish woman. More and more I contrasted her to the business wife Glückel of Hameln, who had lived only a century before. Because Glückel was so serene, so confident, so industrious, so communitarian, and so beloved, I increasingly see her as an alternative role model for contemporary women. Much was lost for Jewish women between Glückel's life and Rahel's life, to be weighed against what was gained.

The conversions of the circle of famous men who were a generation younger than Rahel aroused powerful conflicts for me as well, over other issues entirely. Heine, Börne, Gans, Koreff, and Saphir all shared essentially careerist motives for their choice of baptism, and Lea and Abraham Mendelssohn's decision to convert their children was also motivated by plans for later professional roles. I could certainly empathize with their ambitions or those of their parents, and lament the price they were asked to pay to become public intellectuals or artists. But I found myself celebrating the quiet courage of a man such as Leopold Zunz, who chose to remain Jewish and forgo a university career. Moritz Itzig's campaign to defend his aunt's honor in a duel made him a hero for me. When I viewed the gifted men who converted from the perspective of Jewish reform, the loss to Judaism seemed huge. When Heine turned on Börne in print even though their fates were so similar, I cringed with embarrassment at how his self-hatred looked to unsympathetic observers. So too when Ludwig Robert attacked Saphir in his play, I wondered how contemporaries viewed this lack of solidarity among those former Jews. My immersion in nineteenth-century interpretations of the career converts irritated me too. Heinrich Graetz, writing at the close of the century, forgave these men their baptisms because, he argued, they could defend the Jewish cause only *as* converts. Not only did I question whether he was historically correct; I was outraged at his utter lack of sympathy toward the women who chose baptism.

When I judged the converts critically, for their behavior either to other Jews or toward their Christian friends and enemies, I stood firmly within the Jewish world, lamenting the departure of a member of the tribe. But when I sympathized with a convert, I stood as a modern cosmopolitan, celebrating self-definition and the audacity to shape one's own identity. Again and again I returned to the radical disjuncture between individual choices and group destinies, as pressing a problem for many ethnic tribes today as it was for Jews in Germany. Each individual convert may have decided correctly *as an individual,* but if enough individuals chose baptism, the Jewish future would obviously suffer. Moreover, when one assimilated Jew attacked another in public, hostile critics would find fuel for their anti-Jewish hostility. This too was an often hidden cost to the community of extensive assimilation. The community also suffered when those leaving Judaism were wealthy and smart and well connected, because their resources were very much needed by Jewish philanthropies and political struggles.

We could well see this conflict as a case of what philosophers call the "free rider problem." It is plausible to assume that many of those who chose conversion did not wish Judaism to disappear altogether. Rather, they sought a solution to what they saw as a personal problem. Hypothetically, if every Jew were to convert, the entire people would disappear, even if no single convert willed that outcome. Does that mean that individual Jews should have changed their personal decision because of its possible consequences for the wider community? I am not sure. Many familiar with the great achievements of Jews in modern Germany will no doubt point out that the tensions between assimilation and tradition sparked the creativity of many Jewish novelists, poets, scholars, and composers. This may be true. But any assimilated Jew who expects to enjoy the pleasures of living alongside a vibrant Jewish tradition is acting as a free rider on the dedication of more traditional Jews.[1]

Even when I narrowed my gaze to the entirely personal consequences of conversion, I often wondered whether conversion was a good path. Isaiah Berlin once described the sort of comfort in the world that eluded many converts. He wrote that "when men complain of loneliness, what they mean is that nobody understands what they are saying. To be understood is to share a common past, common feelings and language, common assumptions, the possibility of intimate communication — in short, to share common forms of life. This is an essential human need: to deny this is a dangerous fallacy."[2] From this perspective, even at the individual level conversion was a mistake. In our age personal happiness is widely valued, and so among all the various judgments against conversion, this one weighs heavily with me, as it may with my readers.

The compulsion to judge converts and the entire conversion trend may well be a legacy of the Holocaust. The narrative of this book began in 1645 and ended in 1833, yet the tragic genocide has always been with us in our visits to earlier times. The question of historical continuity has been an incessant drumbeat for me. So *what did it matter*, the conversion wave, the departure of some of the best and the brightest? We know Gershom Scholem's harsh condemnation of even the loyalist Jews of the Napoleonic era. I have argued in these pages that Scholem was too harsh and unhistorical in his expectation that leaders and reformers would preserve traditional autonomy when emancipation became an option beginning in 1812. As I was finishing the book, I came upon another Zionist attack on German Jewry, in the words of Avraham Burg, a Labor Party member of the Knesset in Jerusalem. Burg wrote that "the Jews of Germany, barricaded against reality, self-satisfied, gifted, went to their deaths, with the fury they aroused in the Germans imposing a death sentence on Jews everywhere."[3]

I still shiver as I read Burg's denunciation of the behaviors I have unearthed in my research. To put my mind at rest I went through his claims one by one. First, were these converts prototypical of *all* Jewish Germans in the modern era? No, but they were particularly visible at a turning point in the modern era, and they set a pattern which continued even when the proportion choosing conversion fell later in the century. Were they barricaded against reality?

Perhaps, but such blindness might have been necessary to take on the personal risks they chose. Were they gifted? Yes, we have already met many brilliant converts, and this only for one city over just short of two centuries. In these years in Berlin certainly there is a case to be made that the most gifted often chose baptism. Did their successful assimilation arouse fury in the Christian Germans? It seems to be a good bet that this did occur; Achim von Arnim and Wilhelm Grattenauer stand as superb examples. Does that fury help explain the extermination? Here I think Burg has gone too far. He is blaming the victims, and moreover he has conflated hatred for assimilated Jews and hatred for traditional Jews. But in spite of the exaggerated simplicity of his denunciation, Burg threw down the gauntlet to the whole trend of assimilation the converts epitomized. His challenge stings even after I have tried my best to defend the converts and the entire Jewish legacy in Germany.

I send this book to the wider world now. You, my readers, can continue to unravel the puzzles and paradoxes of Jewish assimilation. I offer you these lives across the generations in Berlin as cameo dramas which reveal the tension between the particular and the universal, the bound and the free, the ethnic and the cosmopolitan, the traditional and the modern. Exploring these past lives must help us who live now to make good choices about nations, faith, and family, fully alive to the difficulty of finding happiness in a world of harsh constraints.

Appendix

The source for all data in the graphs below are the Judenkartei, Evangelisches Zentralarchiv, Berlin, Germany.

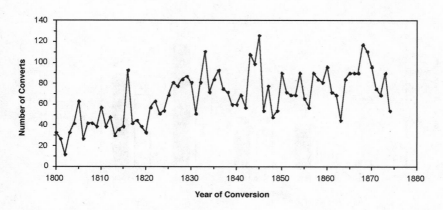

Graph One. Converts in Berlin, 1800–1874 (number of cases: 4,635)

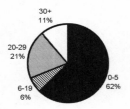

Graph Two. Ages of Converts, 1800–1874 (number of cases: 4,635)

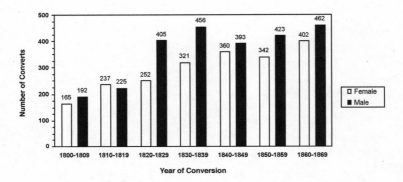

Graph Three. Female and Male Conversion Rates (number of cases: 4,635)

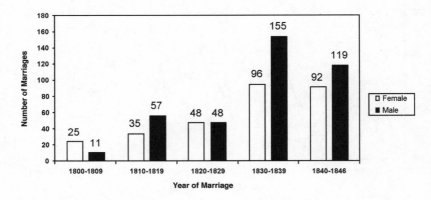

Graph Four. Berlin Converts Who Married Christians (number of cases: 686)

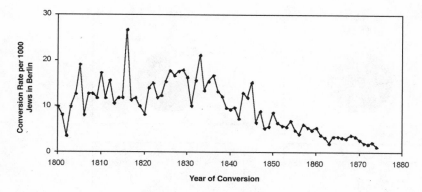

Graph Five. Proportion of Berlin Jews Converting (number of cases: 4,635). Additional data for this graph comes from Herbert Seeliger, "Origin and Growth of the Berlin Jewish Community," *Leo Baeck Institute Year Book* 3 (1958): 159–68.

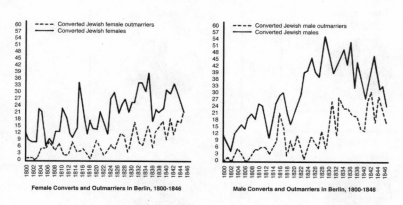

Graph Six. Comparative Rates of Conversion and Intermarriage

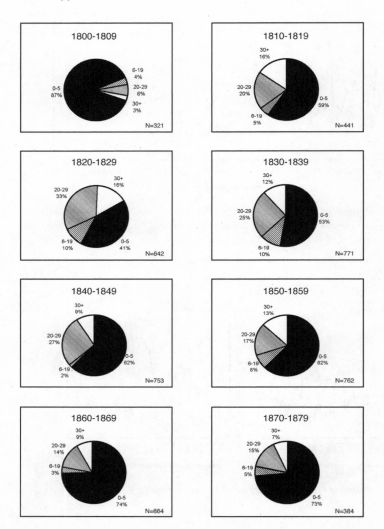

Graph Seven. Ages of Converts by Decade

Notes

Abbreviations

BAK	Bundesarchiv, Koblenz
CAJP	Central Archives of the Jewish People, Jerusalem
GJN-B	*Gross Jüdische National-Biographie* (Cernauji, 1928)
GSA	Gesamtarchiv der deutsche Juden
LBIYB	*Leo Baeck Institute Year Book*
MGJD	*Monatschrift für die Geschichte der Juden in Deutschland*
Rahel-Bibliothek	*Rahel-Bibliothek, Rahel Varnhagen: Gesammelte Werke,* edited by Konrad Feilchenfeldt, Uwe Schweikert, and Rachel Steiner, 10 vols. (Munich, 1983)
RSA	Reichssippenamt, the Kinship Research Office
ZGJD	*Zeitschrift für die Geschichte der Juden in Deutschland*

Chapter One: The Black Notebooks

1. An important inspiration for my quantitative inquiries on this era was an article by A. Menes, "The Conversion Movement in Prussia during the First Half of the Nineteenth Century," which appeared in the original Yiddish in *YIVO Historishe shriftn* i (1929). The English version appeared in *YIVO Annual of Jewish Social Science* 6 (1951), 187–203. Menes was convinced that there were no primary source records before the year 1816, and it was his skepticism that challenged me to look for eighteenth-century sources.

2. Many parishes once held special collections called the *Judenregister,* which con-

tained details on individual conversions. Few if any of these *Judenregistern* survived the war. Personal communication from Dr. Hans Steinberg, the Evangelische Kirche von Westphalen Archiv in Bielefeld, November 9, 1984.

3. Throughout this book when I use the term *Aryan* or "race" I do so historically, without in any way suggesting that the Nazi terms had or have any scientific or moral validity.

4. I am grateful to Nancy Reagin, of the Department of History at Pace University, for stressing this point at a meeting of the German Women's History Study Group in New York City in October 1999.

5. Catholic baptisms, which were included in the Berlin municipal archive volumes, are not included in any of the primary parish registers used to produce either the card indexes or the black notebooks in the Jebenstrasse archive, because from the outset the project was organized by the Protestant churches.

6. Pastor Themel described his method for carding the contents of the parish registers in a small booklet sold by the RSA: *Wie verkarte ich Kirchenbücher?* (Berlin, 1936). For background, see W. Gerlach, *And the Witnesses Were Silent: The Confessing Church and the Persecution of the Jews* (Lincoln, Nebr., 2000).

7. A short description of the name changes of the RSA can be found in the listing *Reichssippenamt* of Hans Branig et al., eds., *Übersicht über die Bestände des Geheimen Staatsarchivs in Berlin-Dahlem*, Part Two (Cologne and Berlin, 1967), 136–37. The RSA files that were once held in the Dahlem archive are now in the Bundesarchiv.

8. An example of the ambitious research plans on this theme can be seen in Wilhelm Grau, "Die historische Statistik der Judentaufen und Mischehen in Deutschland," *Blätter für deutsche Landesgeschichte* 83, Heft 3 (1937), 1–5. The *Forschungsabteilung Judenfrage* had a specific project titled "Historische Statistik der Judentaufen und Mischehen in Deutschland." Research compiled by the National Institute for the History of the New Germany can be found at the Hessische Hauptstaatsarchiv in Wiesbaden [Abteilung 211, no. 3829].

9. For more details, see my article "The Genealogy Bureaucracy in the Third Reich," *Jewish History* 11 (Fall, 1997), 53–78. On the work of the Kaiser Wilhelm Institute scholars, see Benno Müller-Hill, *Murderous Science: Elimination by Scientific Selection of Jews, Gypsies, and Others, Germany, 1933–45* (London, 1988). See also Paul Weindling, *Health, Race, and German Politics between National Unification and Nazism, 1870–1945* (Cambridge, England, 1989), and Horst Seidler and Andreas Rett, *Das Reichssippenamt entscheidet: Rassenbiologie im Nationalsozialismus* (Vienna, 1982).

10. These details can be found in "Erblinien weisen deutschen Blutstrom nach," *Preußische Zeitung Königsberg* (May 18, 1938). The estimate on the number of individual entries and the total cost is found in the notes from a meeting between RSA officials and William Stuckart from the Ministry of the Interior on May 10, 1938 (file 575, RP 39, Bundesarchiv, Koblenz; henceforth BAK).

11. See Arthur Czellitzer, *Mein Stammbaum* (Berlin, 1934), 3.

12. For the early history of the GSA, see Karl Jakob Ball-Kaduri, *Vor der Katastrophe: Juden in Deutschland 1934–39* (Tel Aviv, 1967), 52–53. See also Reinhard Rürup, "Das Ende der Emanzipation," and Herbert Strauss, "Jüdische Selbstverwaltung innerhalb der Schranken nationalsozialistischer Politik," both in Arnold Paucker, ed., *The Jews in Nazi Germany* (Tübingen, 1986), 97–114 and 125–52.

13. For a short summary of Jacobson's life and a selection from his memoir, see "Jacob Jacobson," in Monika Richarz, ed., *Jüdisches Leben in Deutschland: Selbstzeugnisse zur Sozialgeschichte 1918–1945,* vol. 3 (Stuttgart, 1982), 401–12. The entire memoir is at the Archive of the Leo Baeck Institute at the Center for Jewish History in New York City. Jacobson belonged to the Verband nationaldeutscher Juden. On the Verband see Carl Rheims, "The Verband nationaldeutscher Juden," *Leo Baeck Institute Year Book* (henceforth *LBIYB*) 25 (1980), 243–68.

14. I have relied here on Jacobson's "Bericht über die Tätigkeit des Gesamtarchivs der deutschen Juden 1932–35," now located at the Central Archives of the Jewish People in Jerusalem (henceforth CAJP), A142/90/7a. There is a parallel report for 1936 in the same file. The reference to the card indexing project can be found on page 4 of Jacobson's 1932–35 report.

15. See the section of his memoir included in Richarz, *Jüdisches Leben,* 408.

16. See Brian Rigg, *Hitler's Jewish Soldiers* (Lawrence, Kans., 2004).

17. A memorandum sent by a Herr Kayser of the RSA to the Minister of the Interior in March 1939 shows that the SS and the Gestapo were involved in the decision to move the RSA into the former GSA archive. Their rationale was that the Jewish records taken by the SS and Gestapo during Crystal Night belonged with the records already in the former GSA archive. The memorandum is found in BAK, R39, vol. 39.

18. On the fate of the Jacobson family in 1938 and 1939, see Richarz, *Jüdisches Leben,* 401. Jacobson's own indispensable publications on early Berlin Jewish history are: *Jüdische Trauungen in Berlin, 1773–1859* (Berlin, 1968) and *Die Judenbürgerbücher der Stadt Berlin 1800–1851* (Berlin, 1962).

19. There are many possible translations of the term *Mischlinge*. Many professional historians do not translate the term at all in their texts. At the United States Holocaust Museum in Washington, D.C., the translation is "cross breeds." See Jeremy Noakes, "The Development of Nazi Policy towards the German-Jewish 'Mischlinge,' 1933–1945," *LBIYB* 34 (1989), 291, n. 2.

20. See ibid., 341–43.

21. See Martin Gilbert, *The Holocaust: A History of the Jews of Europe during the Second World War* (New York, 1985), 280, regarding Chelmno.

22. See Peter Honigmann, *Die Austritte aus der Jüdischen Gemeinde Berlin 1873–1941: Statistische Auswertung und historische Interpretation* (Frankfurt am Main, 1988). I am grateful to Peter Honigmann for his continuing interest in this project.

23. I am grateful to my brother Frederick Hertz for his suggestions on these issues.

24. See Kurt Nowak, "Das Stigma der Rasse. Nationalsozialistische Judenpolitik und die christlichen Nichtarier," in Jochen-Christoph Kaiser and Martin Greschat, eds., *Der Holocaust und die Protestanten* (Frankfurt, 1988), 73–99, and Ursula Büttner, "The Persecution of Christian-Jewish Families in the Third Reich," *LBIYB* 34 (1989), 267–90.

25. Victor Klemperer, *I Will Bear Witness: A Diary of the Nazi Years, 1933–1941* (New York, 1998), 291.

26. I am grateful to Rebecca Bohling (University of Maryland), who commented on an earlier version of this point at an October 1999 session of the German Women's History Study Group of New York City.

27. Laslett refers to the volunteer work which has contributed to his research material in his *The World We Have Lost Further Explored* (New York, 1984), 289.

28. Marion Kaplan notes this pronouncement in her *Between Dignity and Despair: Jewish Life in Nazi Germany* (New York and Oxford, 1998), 232.

29. Hannah Arendt, *Rahel Varnhagen: The Life of a Jewess* (London, 1957), xii.

30. See Shulamit Volkov, "The Dynamics of Dissimilation: *Ostjuden* and German Jews," in Jehuda Reinharz and Walter Schatzberg, eds., *The Jewish Response to German Culture* (Hanover, N.H., and London, 1985), 195–211.

31. Baeck's quote is noted in Enzo Traverso, *The Jews and Germany: From the Judeo-German Symbiosis to the Memory of Auschwitz* (Lincoln, Nebr., and London, 1995), 8.

32. S. Y. Agnon, *Shira* (New York, 1989), 356.

33. A clear presentation of this view can be found in Brigitte Kallmann, "Narratives of Jewish Conversion in Germany Around 1800" (diss., University of Michigan, 1999), 1. I am grateful to Todd Endelman for bringing this excellent dissertation to my attention.

34. The first quote comes from Theodor Mommsen, who is cited in H. H. Ben Sasson, ed., *A History of the Jewish People* (Cambridge, Mass., 1976), 826. The second is from Paul Johnson, *A History of the Jews* (New York, 1987), 312.

35. For a condensed version of Walser's speech, see Martin Walser, "Wir werden Goethe retten," *Der Spiegel* (December 25, 1995), 140–46. The first volume of the diary in English is noted in n. 25 above. The second volume is: *I Will Bear Witness: A Diary of the Nazi Years, 1942–1945* (New York, 1999).

36. See Sander Gilman, *Freud, Race, and Gender* (Princeton, 1995), 109–10.

37. The full title of the book is *Der Untergang der deutschen Juden: Eine volkswirt-schaftliche Studie* (Munich, 1911). See also John Efron, *Defenders of the Race: Jewish Doctors in Fin-de-siècle Europe* (New Haven and London, 1994), 141–153. I am grateful to John Efron for discussion of Felix Theilhaber's fate in the 1930s.

38. See two essays by Scholem, both published in his *On Jews and Judaism in Crisis: Selected Essays* (New York, 1976): "Against the Myth of the German-Jewish Dialogue," 61–64, and "Jews and Germans," 71–92. For background, see David Biale, *Kabbalah and Counter-History* (Cambridge, Mass., 1979).

39. Enzo Traverso makes an important distinction between the reality of symbiosis and the myth of symbiosis, suggesting that we must investigate particular cases, rather than making global arguments on this point. See Traverso, *Jews and Germany*, 8.

40. An entire book written with this perspective is John Weiss, *Ideology of Death: Why the Holocaust Happened in Germany* (Chicago, 1996). The words "abusive marriage" are those of John Dippel, *Bound Upon a Wheel of Fire: Why So Many German Jews Made the Tragic Decision to Remain in Nazi Germany* (New York, 1996), xix.

41. Emphasis here is mine. The book is Michael Blumenthal, *The Invisible Wall: Germans and Jews: A Personal Exploration* (Washington, D.C., 1998), and these words appear on the book jacket copy.

42. Daniel Jonah Goldhagen, *Hitler's Willing Executioners: Ordinary Germans and the Holocaust* (New York, 1996).

43. For an introduction to the critiques of Goldhagen's book, see Norman Finkelstein and Bettina Birn, *Nation on Trial: The Goldhagen Thesis and Historical Truth* (New York, 1998).

44. To see how scholars use the term currently, see Sander Gilman's *Jewish Self-Hatred: Anti-Semitism and the Hidden Language of the Jews* (Baltimore and London, 1986).

Chapter Two: The Era of Religious Conversion, 1645–1770

1. See Reinhold August Dorwart, *The Prussian Welfare State before 1740* (Cambridge, Mass., 1971), 120.

2. On Lippold, see the entry on him in the German-language *Encyclopedia Judaica* 10 (Berlin, 1934), 995–96. See also Ruth Gay, *The Jews of Germany: A Historical Portrait* (New Haven and London, 1992), 84–88; Selma Stern, *The Court Jew* (Philadelphia, 1950), 47; and the article on Lippold in the English-language *Encyclopedia Judaica* 11 (Jerusalem, 1971), 287. For more detailed background, see W. Heise, *Die Juden in der Mark Brandenburg zum Jahre 1571* (Berlin, 1932; rpt. Vaduz, 1965), chap. 18, and Eugen Wolbe, *Geschichte der Juden in Berlin and in der Mark Brandenburg* (Berlin, 1937), 21.

3. This quote can be found in Heinrich Schnee, *Die Hoffinanz und der moderne Staat,* 4 vols. (Berlin, 1953), 1:48–49. Many of Schnee's interpretations are antisemitic but some of his factual material is reliable. For more information on Aaron's wife Esther (later Esther Liebmann), see my article, "The Despised Queen of Berlin Jewry, or the Life and Times of Esther Liebmann," in Vivian Mann and Richard Cohen, eds., *From Court Jews to the Rothschilds: Art, Patronage, and Power, 1600–1800* (Munich and New York, 1996), 67–77. See also O. Lassally, "Israel Aaron, Hoffaktor des Grossen Kurfürsten und Begründer der Berliner Gemeinde," *Monatsschrift für Geschichte und Wissenschaft des Judentums* 79 n.s. 43 (1935), 20–31, henceforth *MGWJ*.

4. This description of the Viennese Jews' material possessions comes from Bernt Engelmann, *Berlin. Eine Stadt wie keine Andere* (Berlin, 1986), 30. For background see A. Bruer, *Geschichte der Juden in Preussen 1750–1820* (Frankfurt and New York, 1991), chap. 1, and Ludwig Geiger, *Die Geschichte der Juden in Berlin* (Berlin, 1871; rpt. Berlin 1987), 1:1–10.

5. These descriptions of Berlin in the 1670s come from Alexandra Richie, *Faust's Metropolis: A History of Berlin* (New York, 1998), 52, and Ronald Taylor, *Berlin and Its Culture: A Historical Portrait* (New Haven and London, 1997), 34–35.

6. See Richie, *Metropolis,* 54, and Taylor, *Berlin,* 34.

7. Citing Richie, *Metropolis,* 55.

8. See Taylor, *Berlin,* 35. See also Stefi Jersch-Wenzel, *Juden und "Franzosen" in der Wirtschaft des Raumes Berlin/Brandenburg zur Zeit des Merkantilismus* (Berlin, 1978).

9. This is noted by Engelmann, *Berlin,* 31.

10. Ibid., 32.

11. Citing Richie, *Metropolis,* 56.

12. The quotation is from Stern, *Court Jew,* 47.

13. The comment regarding Aaron as a Judas figure is noted in Stern, *Court Jew,* 184. The citations from the mock will are cited in Schnee, *Die Hoffinanz,* 1:54.

14. On the demographic trends in Berlin Jewish history, see Herbert Seeliger, "Origin and Growth of the Berlin Jewish Community," *LBIYB* 3 (1958), 159–68.

15. This lament is noted in Stern, *Court Jew,* 150. See also some newer research on Liebmann by Gerda Hoffer, in her *Zeit der Heldinnen: Lebensbilder außergewöhnlicher jüdischer Frauen* (Munich, 1999), 90–108.

16. For a lively account of Jewish life in Berlin during this era, see W. Michael Blu-

menthal, *The Invisible Wall: Germans and Jews: A Personal Exploration* (Washington, D.C., 1998), chap. 3. On the government's decision to support the building of the new public synagogue, see Geiger, *Geschichte*, 1:19–23, and 2:46–47. See also the fascinating discussion of the Berlin synagogue in Richard Cohen, *Jewish Icons: Art and Society in Modern Europe* (Berkeley, Calif., 1998), 76–78.

17. See Mordechai Breuer, Part One of *German-Jewish History in Modern Times,* vol. 1, *Tradition and Enlightenment 1600–1780,* ed. Michael Meyer (New York, 1996), especially chaps. 4, 7, and 8.

18. On this point see ibid., 239.

19. This description of Eulenspiegel's satire is cited from Elisheva Carlebach, *Divided Souls: Converts from Judaism in Germany, 1550–1750* (New Haven, 2001), 70; Eulenspiegel's words can be found in Oskar Frankl, *Der Jude in den deutschen Dichtungen des 15. 16. und 17. Jahrhundertes* (Mähr-Ostrau, 1905), 66, as cited in Carlebach, *Divided Souls,* 70.

20. The volume edited by Monika Richarz, *Die Hamburger Kauffrau Glikl. Jüdische Existenz in der Frühen Neuzeit* (Hamburg, 2001) contains the most recent scholarship on this important woman. Her memoir in English is: *The Memoirs of Glückel of Hameln* (New York, 1977).

21. Glückel, now called Glikl bat Judah Lev, is using a phrase here in the Hebrew from Exodus 15:20. Her reference to the Feast of Water-Drawing is to a festive celebration in ancient Jerusalem on the last day of the fall holiday Succoth. See Hameln, *Memoirs,* 46 and 283. See Natalie Davis's essay on Glikl in her book *Women on the Margins: Three Seventeenth-Century Lives* (Cambridge, Mass., 1995).

22. Breuer, *German-Jewish History,* 1:232.

23. A sophisticated discussion of these Shabbatean converts in Germany can be found in Carlebach, *Divided Souls,* 82–85.

24. See Jacob Katz, *Out of the Ghetto: The Social Background of Jewish Emancipation, 1770–1870* (New York, 1978), 24. On Anton, see Heinrich Graetz, *History of the Jews* (Philadelphia, 1895), 5:270.

25. Carlebach, *Divided Souls,* 86.

26. Discussion of converts in Germany inspired by Shabbateanism can be found in J. F. A. de la Roi, *Die evangelische Christenheit und die Juden unter dem Gesichtspunkte der Mission* (Karlsruhe and Leipzig, 1884), 1:134, and in Gershom Scholem, *Sabbatai Sevi: The Mystical Messiah, 1626–1676* (Princeton, 1973), 668 and 768.

27. A useful summary, on which I have relied here, is provided by Norman Davies, *God's Playground: A History of Poland,* 2 vols. (New York, 1982), 1:194–95.

28. See ibid., 196.

29. See the extensive article on Frank in the *Jüdisches Lexikon* (Berlin, 1928), 2:711–23, as well as the article on him in the *Encyclopedia Judaica* (Berlin, 1930), 6:1071–79.

30. For comparison to Amsterdam, see Miriam Bodian, *Hebrews of the Portuguese Nation: Conversos and Community in Early Modern Amsterdam* (Bloomington, Ind., 1997).

31. Alexander Altmann, *Moses Mendelssohn* (University, Ala., 1973), 96.

32. For my summary of illegal Jews in Prussia I have relied on Christopher Clark, *The Politics of Conversion: Missionary Protestantism and the Jews in Prussia, 1728–1941* (Oxford, 1995), 46 and 47, and chap. 2 throughout.

33. See Rudolf Glanz, *Geschichte des niederen jüdischen Volkes in Deutschland* (New York, 1968).

34. See Adam Sutcliffe, *Judaism and the Enlightenment* (Cambridge, England, 2003), chap. 1.

35. Schudt is quoted by Clark, *Conversion*, 15. Schudt's book was *Jüdische Merckwürdigkeiten* (Frankfurt am Main, 1714), and the quote is from his foreword to Part II of the book.

36. Spener's *Letzte theologische Bedencken* (Halle, 1711), vol. 1, pt. 1, 286, cited in Clark, *Conversion*, 15.

37. Clark, *Conversion*, 59.

38. See Elisheva Carlebach, "Converts and Their Narratives in Early Modern Germany: The Case of Friedrich Albrecht Christiani," *LBIYB* 40 (1995), 73.

39. See Clark, *Conversion*, 20–22, and Martin Friedrich, *Zwischen Abwehr und Bekehrung: Die Stellung der deutschen evangelischen Theologie zum Judentum im 17. Jahrhundert* (Tübingen, 1988), 57.

40. Callenberg, *Sechste Fortsetzung* (Halle, 1734), 101, cited in Clark, *Conversion*, 65.

41. Clark, *Conversion*, 65.

42. Ibid., 76, and also 47–57. See also Paul Gerhard Aring, *Christen und Juden heute — und die Judenmission* (Frankfurt am Main, 1987).

43. See Clark, *Conversion*, 53.

44. For brief discussion of Guggenheim's life, see Carlebach, *Divided Souls*, 102, 117, 151, and 168. The quotes are on pp. 128 and 129.

45. Clark, *Conversion*, 75.

46. See ibid., 73.

47. Ibid., 51.

48. The original cite is from J. H. Callenberg, *Christliche Bereisung der Judenörter* iii (Halle, 1757), 365, quoted in ibid., 58.

49. See Carlebach, "Converts and Their Narratives," 69. Ezriel Schochat concluded that there were 300 converts in that era, in his *Beginnings of the Haskalah among German Jewry in the First Half of the Eighteenth Century* (Hebrew) (Jerusalem, 1960), 174–97. Schochat's claims were challenged by Benjamin Kedar in his "Continuity and Change in Jewish Conversion to Christianity in Eighteenth-Century Germany" (Hebrew), in E. Etkes and Y. Salmon, eds., *Studies in the History of Jewish Society in the Middle Ages and in the Modern Period* (Jerusalem, 1980), 154–70. For a summary in English of the Schochat thesis, see Katz, *Out of the Ghetto*, 34–35.

50. Clark, *Conversion*, 63.

51. Ibid.

52. On Magdalena August Navrazky, see de la Roi, *Die evangelische Christenheit*, 370.

53. On Heynemann's story, see A. Fürst, *Christen und Juden: Licht- und Schattenbilder aus Kirche und Synagoge* (Strassburg, 1892), 120–33, and Kedar, "Continuity and Change," 11–12. Heynemann's autobiography is also of interest: Johann Friedrich Heinrich Selig, *Johann Friedrich Heinrich Seligs, eines Bekehrten aus dem Judentume, eigne Lebensbeschreibung* (Leipzig, 1783).

54. See Fritz Redlich, "Jewish Enterprise and Prussian Coinage," *Explorations in Entrepreneurial History, 3, no. 3* (1951).

55. See Dolf Michaelis: "The Ephraim Family," *LBIYB* 21 (1976), 207.

56. For details on the lives of these three families, I have relied on Steven Lowenstein, *The Berlin Jewish Community: Enlightenment, Family, and Crisis, 1770–1830* (New York, 1994), 26, as well as two articles by Michaelis, "The Ephraim Family," and "The Ephraim Family and Their Descendants (II)," *LBIYB* 24 (1979), 225–46.

57. See Rolf-Herbert Krüger, *Das Ephraim Palais in Berlin* (Berlin, 1989).

58. His salary is noted in Altmann, *Mendelssohn,* 201. Here Altmann is citing a diary entry by Johann Caspar Lavater from 1763, housed in the Robert von Mendelssohn Collection in the Staatsbibliothek Stiftung Preußischer Kulturbesitz in Berlin, C ii, no. 24.

59. The letter is cited by Altmann, *Mendelssohn,* 97. The original can be found in the *Moses Mendelssohn Gesammelte Schriften Jubiläumsausgabe* (Berlin, 1929–38; rpt. Stuttgart, 1971 ff.), vol. 16, letter 62, p. 78 in the Berlin edition, and vol. 11, letter 179, p. 296 in the Stuttgart edition.

60. This analysis derives from Barbara Hahn, *The Jewess Pallas Athena: This Too a Theory of Modernity* (Princeton and Oxford, 2005), 18 and 19.

61. I am indebted for details about Mendelssohn's life in these years to Altmann, *Mendelssohn,* chaps. 2 and 3.

62. See Michael Graetz, "The Jewish Enlightenment," in *German-Jewish History,* vol. 1. On the Lavater controversy, see that volume at 336–37.

63. This claim about the real historical figure used by Lessing was made by Sara Meyer von Grotthuß, the daughter of Aaron Meyer, in a letter to Johann Goethe of May 25, 1814, cited in Hahn, *The Jewess Pallas Athena,* 25.

64. The letter was to Aaron Gumpertz, in June 1754. It is cited by Graetz, "Enlightenment," in *German-Jewish History,* 1:336. The original letter can be found in Mendelssohn's *Gesammelte Schriften* (Stuttgart, 1971), 11:10.

65. Quotation from a letter from Friedrich Lüdke to Lavater of January 23, 1770, cited in Mendelssohn's *Gesammelte Schriften* (Stuttgart, 1971), 7:306, and by Altmann, *Mendelssohn,* 224.

66. The novel is summarized in Brigitte Kallmann, "Narratives of Jewish Conversion in Germany Around 1800" (diss., University of Michigan, 1999), 117–41. The novel is: Johann Balthasar Kölbele, *Die Begebenheiten der Jungfer Meyern, eines jüdischen Frauenzimmers, von ihr selbst beschrieben,* 2 vols. (Frankfurt, 1765).

67. These are citations from Kallmann, "Narratives," 130.

Chapter Three: The Coming of Age of Rahel Levin, 1771–1810

1. See Heidi Thomann Tewarson, *Rahel Levin Varnhagen: The Life and Work of a German Jewish Intellectual* (Lincoln, Nebr., and London, 1998), 17. Tewarson is relying on Friedhelm Kemp, *Rahel Varnhagen: Briefwechsel,* 4 vols. (Munich, 1983), 4:365. There is by now a vast bibliography on various aspects of Rahel Varnhagen's life. The standard biography from an earlier era is Otto Berdrow, *Rahel Varnhagen: Ein Lebens- und Zeitbild* (Stuttgart, 1900).

2. This is noted by Henriette Herz in her memoir: Rainer Schmitz, ed., *Henriette Herz in Erinnerungen, Briefen und Zeugnissen* (Frankfurt, 1984), 42.

3. The letter is cited by Ursula Isselstein, *"Der Text aus meinem beleidigten Herzen": Studien zu Rahel Levin Varnhagen* (Turin, 1993), 30.

4. The portrait is by Daniel Chodowiecki; on this important painter, see Ronald Taylor, *Berlin and Its Culture: A Historical Portrait* (New Haven, 1997), 86–87.

5. Schmitz, *Henriette Herz*, 42.

6. Martin L. Davies, *Identity or History: Marcus Herz and the End of the Enlightenment* (Detroit, 1995), 165.

7. For an excellent survey of the regulations and practices of name changes, see Dietz Bering, *The Stigma of Names: Antisemitism in German Daily Life, 1812–1933* (Cambridge, England, 1992).

8. The salon women have attracted increasing attention over the years. For a summary of the newer research by literary historians, see Barbara Hahn and Ursula Isselstein, eds., *Rahel Levin Varnhagen: Die Wiederentdeckung einer Schriftstellerin* (Göttingen, 1987). See also Steven Lowenstein, *The Berlin Jewish Community: Enlightenment, Family, and Crisis, 1770–1830* (New York, 1994), chap. 9, and a collection, edited by Norbert Altenhofer and Renate Heuer, *Jüdinnen zwischen Tradition und Emanzipation* (Bad Soden, 1990).

9. For the details of the episode, see Dolf Michaelis, "The Ephraim Family and Their Descendants (II)," *LBIYB* 24 (1979), 230.

10. Davies, *Marcus Herz*, 177.

11. The quotation from Sara's letter of March 20, 1797, appears in Barbara Hahn, *The Jewess Pallas Athena* (Princeton, 2005), 24. The letter was published in the *Goethe-Jahrbuch* 14 (1893), 46.

12. Quote from the 1797 letter in Hahn, *Jewess Pallas Athena*, 24. The incident is summarized in Alexander Altmann, *Moses Mendelssohn: A Biographical Study* (University, Ala., 1973), 298.

13. Schmitz edition of Herz's memoir, 78.

14. Carola Stern, *"Ich möchte mir Flügel wünschen": Das Leben der Dorothea Schlegel* (Reinbeck bei Hamburg, 1990), 53; my translations.

15. The earliest edition of her memoir is Joseph Fürst, ed., *Henriette Herz. Ihr Leben und ihre Erinnerungen* (Berlin, 1858). See Liliane Weissberg, "Weibliche Körpersprachen: Bild und Wort bei Henriette Herz," in Jutta Dick and Barbara Hahn, eds., *Von einer Welt in die andere: Jüdinnen im 19. und 20. Jahrhundert* (Vienna, 1993), 71–91. See also Peter Seibert, "Henriette Herz: Erinnerungen. Zur Rekonstruktion einer frühen Frauenautobiographie," in *Der Deutschunterricht* 41 (1989), 37–50. An earlier essay on Herz can be found in F. Gustav Kühne, *Deutsche Männer und Frauen: Eine Galerie von Charakteren* (Leipzig, 1851), 215–43. In English, see Hilde Spiel, *Fanny von Arnstein: A Daughter of the Enlightenment, 1758–1818* (New York and Oxford, 1991), 120–25.

16. See Davies, *Markus Herz,* to understand Herz's place in the intellectual life of the period. See also Altmann, *Mendelssohn,* 267.

17. Steven Lowenstein, *The Berlin Jewish Community: Enlightenment, Family, and Crisis, 1770–1830* (New York, 1994), 36.

18. Altmann, *Mendelssohn,* 98.

19. See Schmitz, *Henriette Herz,* 53. For an interesting discussion of the social patterns of the early Jewish enlightenment, see Michael Graetz, "A New Sociability," in Mordechai Breuer and Michael Graetz, eds., *German-Jewish History in Modern Times* (New York, 1996), 1:271–282.

20. See Altmann, *Mendelssohn,* 98 and 724.

21. See Stern, *Dorothea Schlegel,* 36.

22. See Altmann, *Mendelssohn,* 724.

23. I discuss some of the problems with this interpretation in my *Jewish High Society in Old Regime Berlin* (New Haven and London, 1988), 188–89.

24. See Altmann, *Mendelssohn,* 350–52. See also Immanuel Heinrich Ritter, *Geschichte der jüdischen Reformation, David Friedländer, sein Leben und sein Wirken* (Berlin, 1861).

25. On the school see Ludwig Geiger, *Geschichte der Juden in Berlin* (Berlin, 1871; rpt. Berlin, 1987), 1:84 ff., and notes to vol. 1:136–37.

26. Lowenstein, *Berlin Jewish Community,* 34.

27. See Altmann, *Mendelssohn,* 738–41.

28. Ibid., 741. The original published source for Herz's comment is Johann Engel's Preface to *Moses Mendelssohn an die Freunde Lessings,* xiii–xxii. See also Davies, *Markus Herz,* 199.

29. See for example Harry Abt, "Dorothea Schlegel bis zu ihrer Vereinigung mit der Romantik" (diss., Frankfurt, 1925).

30. See Altmann, *Mendelssohn,* 264.

31. For a summary of recent research on King Frederick, see Theodor Schieder, *Frederick the Great* (London and New York, 2000).

32. Mirabeau, as cited in Taylor, *Berlin,* 59.

33. The letter appears in Konrad Feilchenfeldt, Uwe Schweikert, and Rachel Steiner, eds., *Rahel-Bibliothek, Rahel Varnhagen: Gesammelte Werke,* 10 vols. (Munich, 1983), 4/1: 235. This work hereafter cited as *Rahel-Bibliothek.* The translation is that provided by Tewarson, *Rahel Levin Varnhagen,* 93.

34. The memoir is cited in Spiel, *Fanny von Arnstein,* 115.

35. Hannah Arendt, *The Origins of Totalitarianism* (New York, 1951), 56.

36. On the Society, see Ludwig Lesser, *Chronik der Gesellschaft der Freunde in Berlin* (Berlin, 1842), and Hermann Baschwitz, *Rückblick auf die hundertjährige Geschichte der Gesellschaft der Freunde zu Berlin* (Berlin, 1892). See Lowenstein, *Berlin Jewish Community,* 131, regarding the Society's rules on conversion.

37. Lowenstein, *Berlin Jewish Community,* 41, citing Lesser, *Chronik,* 46.

38. For a summary of Brinkmann's life and his role in the salons, see my *Jewish High Society,* 123–24 and 255–56. See also Spiel, *Fanny von Arnstein,* 176–90, for an excellent summary of the correspondence between Brinkmann and Gentz about Rahel Levin.

39. Rahel's letter to her brother Markus of August 18, 1794, rpt. in Ursula Isselstein, "Rahel Levin. Bericht von einer Reise nach Schlesien," in Ernst-Peter Wieckenberg, ed., *Einladung ins 18. Jahrhundert* (Munich, 1988), 62–75. See also a letter of August 8 written to her siblings, cited in Hahn, *Jewess Pallas Athena,* 184.

40. Letter of August 8, 1794, in Hahn, *Jewess Pallas Athena,* 28–29 and 184, n. 35.

41. Even the author of a recent book admits that researchers do not understand quite why she never entered a marriage with a Jewish man. See Tewarson, *Rahel Levin Varnhagen,* 77. See also Günter de Bruyn, ed., *Rahels erste Liebe: Rahel Levin und Karl Graf von Finckenstein in ihren Briefen* (Berlin, 1985).

42. For instance Fanny von Arnstein's dowry was 70,000 thalers. See Spiel, *Fanny von*

Arnstein, 131. For the dowry amounts of some of Levin's friends, see my *Jewish High Society,* 202.

43. I am indebted for a summary of their relationship to Tewarson, *Rahel Levin Varnhagen,* 73–76. See also Hannah Arendt, *Rahel Varnhagen: The Life of a Jewess,* trans. Richard and Clara Winston, ed. Liliane Weissberg (Baltimore, 1997), 153–58, 188–90, and 303–5.

44. See Clark, *Conversion,* 53.

45. My account of the biographical events in the lives of the sisters is indebted to Hahn, *Jewess Pallas Athena,* 20–26. See also Lowenstein, *Berlin Jewish Community,* 167 and 246.

46. Sara's letter to the king of April 28, 1798, is cited in Hahn, *Jewess Pallas Athena,* 21–22.

47. Note the hostile tone in which Henriette Herz tells the story, in the Schmitz edition of her memoir, 79.

48. See Lowenstein, *Berlin Jewish Community,* 167. See also Arendt, *Rahel Varnhagen,* ed. Weissberg, 108, 126, and 299. Just what Sara Meyer's motives were for the 1788 conversion is not clear. For a useful discussion of rituals for returning converts in the seventeenth and early eighteenth centuries, see Elisheva Carlebach, *Divided Souls: Converts from Judaism in Germany, 1500–1750* (New Haven and London, 2001), 28–29.

49. These estimates can be found in my *Jewish High Society,* 58, n. 18.

50. For a summary of the case, see Eugen Wolbe, *Geschichte der Juden in Berlin und in der Mark Brandenburg* (Berlin, 1937), 211–13.

51. For a sample of contemporary opinion, see Stern, *Dorothea Schlegel,* 32–33. Steven Lowenstein suggested to me in personal communication in September 1999 that it was Fromet Mendelssohn's absence from Berlin that was decisive in the conversions of four of her children.

52. For details about the Veit sons, see Jacob Jacobson, ed., *Die Judenbürgerbücher der Stadt Berlin* (Berlin, 1962), 69.

53. See Stern, *Dorothea Schlegel,* 97–99.

54. These details can be found in ibid., 99.

55. See Ilse Kammerlander, *Johanna Fichte: Ein Frauenschicksal der deutschen Klassik* (Stuttgart, 1969), at 87.

56. For a brief biographical sketch in English, see Radoslav Tsanoff's article "Fichte" in *The Encyclopedia of Philosophy,* vols. 3 and 4 (New York, 1967), 192–96. For a longer view in German, see Fritz Medicus, *Fichtes Leben* (Leipzig, 1914).

57. Tsanoff, "Fichte," 193.

58. See Spiel, *Fanny von Arnstein,* 159.

59. Elias is cited in ibid., 162; see also Jacob Jacobson, ed. *Jüdische Trauungen in Berlin, 1773–1859* (Berlin, 1968), 240.

60. See Ellen Littmann, "David Friedländers Sendschreiben an Probst Teller und sein Echo," *Zeitschrift für die Geschichte der Juden in Deutschland* (hereafter ZGJD) 6 (1935), 92–112.

61. Cited in Michael Blumenthal, *The Invisible Wall: Germans and Jews, A Personal Exploration* (Washington, D.C., 1998), 141.

62. Cited in Gustav Friedrich Manz, "Michael Beer's Jugend" (diss., University of Freiburg, 1891), 12.

63. Berndt Wessling, *Meyerbeer: Wagners Beute — Heines Geisel* (Düsseldorf, 1984), 41.

64. On the Academy of Art in this era, see *Berlin zwischen 1789 und 1848: Facetten einer Epoche* (Berlin, 1988), an exhibition catalogue published by the Berlin Academy of Art.

65. Grattenauer's original pamphlet, *Wider die Juden* (Berlin, 1803), was published along with various responses and Grattenauer's answer to the responses. This quote appeared in pamphlet 3, p. 8. For a summary of the reactions of contemporary intellectuals to Grattenauer's pamphlets, see Spiel, *Fanny von Arnstein*, 183–85.

66. See Arendt, *Rahel Varnhagen*, ed. Weissberg, 150–60, and Tewarson, *Rahel Levin Varnhagen*, 76–77.

67. See Stern, *Dorothea Schlegel*, 18. Philippine's father had two names: Moses Zülz and Moses Bernhard. For details on the family, see Jacobson, *Trauungen*, 362–63.

68. Lowenstein, *Berlin Jewish Community*, 246–47, n. 22.

69. See Heidi Thomann Tewarson, "German-Jewish Identity in the Correspondence between Rahel Levin Varnhagen and Her Brother, Ludwig Robert: Hopes and Realities of Emancipation 1780–1830," *LBIYB* 39 (1994), 3–29.

70. For more details on Koreff, see Friedrich von Oppeln-Bronikowski, *David Ferdinand Koreff* (Berlin, 1928), and Karl August Varnhagen von Ense, *Biographische Portraits* (Leipzig, 1871), 1–45. I discuss Koreff in my article, "Why Did the Christian Gentleman Assault the *jüdischer Elegant*? Four Conversion Stories from Berlin, 1816–1825," *LBIYB* 40 (1995), 85–106.

71. See Jacobson, *Trauungen*, 241, n. 384.

72. There are several editions of his memoirs. The original edition is *Denkwürdigkeiten und vermischte Schriften*, Five Volumes (Leipzig, 1843). Abridged editions include Joachim Kühn, ed., K. A. Varnhagen von Ense, *Denkwürdigkeiten des eignen Lebens* (Berlin, 1925); Karl Leutener, ed., Karl August Varnhagen von Ense, *Denkwürdigkeiten des eignen Lebens* (Berlin, 1954), and Konrad Feilchenfeldt, ed., Karl August Varnhagen von Ense, *Denkwürdigkeiten des eignen Lebens* (Frankfurt am Main, 1987).

73. See Lowenstein, *Berlin Jewish Community*, 93.

74. Some historians have claimed that it was Rahel's friend Marianne Saaling who found Karl the post in the Hertz family, but a recent article corrects this error. See Hans Hertz, "Wilhelm Ludwig Hertz: Ein Sohn des Dichters Adelbert von Chamisso," *Archiv für die Geschichte des Buchwesens* (1970), 274. Karl's connection to the Hertz family, Hermann Eberty, was born Veitel Heymann Ephraim in 1776, became Victor Ebers in 1816, and converted in 1828. See Jacobson, *Trauungen*, 370–71.

75. See Varnhagen, *Denkwürdigkeiten und vermischte Schriften* (Leipzig, 1843), 5:159–69.

76. Ibid., 5:170.

77. On Johann and his wife Sophie, whose father Benjamin Ephraim was arrested as a spy for the French in 1806, see Lowenstein, *Berlin Jewish Community*, 92. On the Stieglitz family, see Bodo Freiherr von Maydell, *Die Stieglitz aus Arolsen. Ihre Vorfahren und Nachkommen* (Neustadt, 1956).

78. On Stieglitz's relationship to Humboldt, see Wilhelm Grau, *Wilhelm von Humboldt und das Problem des Juden* (Hamburg, 1935), 30–31. On Stieglitz's family background, see Jacobson, *Trauungen*, 349, and the article on Stieglitz in the *Grosse Jüdische National-Biographie* (Cernauji, 1928), 6:35–36, henceforth *GJN-B*.

79. Cited in Ludwig Schulze, *August Neander. Ein Gedenkblatt für Israel und die Kirche* (Leipzig, 1890), 28.

80. See Marshall Dill, *Germany: A Modern History* (Ann Arbor, 1970), 73.

81. See Thomas Stamm-Kuhlmann, *König in Preussens grosser Zeit: Friedrich Wilhelm III. Der Melancholiker auf dem Thron* (Berlin, 1992). In English, see Constance Wright, *Louise, Queen of Prussia: A Biography* (London, 1969).

82. H. W. Koch, *A History of Prussia* (London and New York, 1978), 159.

83. Ibid.

84. See Carl Atzenbeck, *Pauline Wiesel: Die Geliebte des Prinzen Louis Ferdinand* (Leipzig, 1925). For newer work, see Nina Hess, *Der Schwan: Das Leben der Pauline Wiesel 1778–1848* (Berlin, 1994); Barbara Hahn and Birgit Bosold, eds., *Rahel Levin Varnhagen. Briefwechsel mit Pauline Wiesel* (Munich, 1998); and Barbara Hahn, Birgit Bosold, and Ursula Isselstein, eds., *Pauline Wiesels Liebesgeschichten. Briefwechsel mit K. G. von Brinckmann, Prinz Louis Ferdinand von Preußen, Friedrich Gentz und anderen* (Munich, 1998).

85. On the Hufeland gathering, see Ilse Kammerlander, *Johanna Fichte: Ein Frauenschicksal der deutschen Klassik* (Stuttgart, 1969), 69.

86. Wright, *Louise*, 133.

87. Heinrich von Treitschke, *History of Germany*, 6 vols. (New York, 1915–19), 3:5. See also Peter Viereck, *Metapolitics: From the Romantics to Hitler* (New York, 1941), 63–64.

88. Koch, *History of Prussia*, 160.

89. Wright, *Louise*, 134.

90. A useful summary in English is Jerry F. Dawson, *Friedrich Schleiermacher: The Evolution of a Nationalist* (Austin and London, 1966).

91. Terry Pickett, *The Unseasonable Democrat: Karl Varnhagen von Ense, 1785–1858* (Bonn, 1985), 18.

92. See Robert Bigler, *The Politics of German Protestantism: The Rise of the Protestant Church Elite in Prussia, 1815–48* (Berkeley, 1972).

93. Friedrich Meinecke, *The Age of German Liberation, 1795–1815* (Berkeley, 1977), 28.

94. Wright, *Louise*, 140. The original quotation comes from Paul Bailleu, *Königin Luise* (Berlin, 1908), 215.

95. See Derek Wilson, *Rothschild: A Story of Wealth and Power* (London, 1988), 17–35, as well as the newer work by Niall Ferguson, *The House of Rothschild: Money's Prophets, 1798–1848* (New York, 1998).

96. Wright, *Louise*, 155–56.

97. Ibid., 154.

98. Christopher Clark, *The Politics of Conversion: Missionary Protestantism and the Jews in Prussia, 1728–1941* (Oxford, 1995), 87.

99. Ibid., 85–86.

100. Kammerlander, *Johanna Fichte,* 113.

101. Wright, *Louise,* 195.

102. Medicus, *Fichte,* 170.

103. For this summary I have relied on Helmuth Engelbrecht, *Johann Gottlieb Fichte* (New York, 1968).

104. See the older but still useful volume by J. G. Legge, *Rhyme and Revolution in Germany: A Study in German History, Life, Literature and Character, 1813–1850* (London, 1918; rpt. New York, 1970). For some scholars, Fichte's turn to nationalism was a huge mistake. See for instance Viereck, *Metapolitics,* chap. 9.

105. This quote can be found in Arendt, *Rahel Varnhagen,* ed. Weissberg, 180.

106. See Johann Gottlieb Fichte, "Beitrag zur Berichtigung der Urtheile des Publicums über die französische Revolution (1793)," in *Fichtes sämtliche Werke,* 8 vols. (Berlin, 1845–46), 6:149–50. For fascinating discussion of Jewish reception of Fichte later in the century, see Erik Lindner, "Deutsche Juden und die bürgerlich-nationale Festkultur: Die Schiller- und Fichtefeiern von 1859 und 1862," in A. Gotzmann, R. Liedtke, and T. van Rahden, eds., *Juden, Bürger, Deutsche: Zur Geschichte von Vielfalt und Differenz 1800–1933* (Tübingen, 2001), 182–90. See also Peter Hacks, ed., *Ascher gegen Jahn,* 4 vols. (Berlin, 1991).

107. Cited in Tewarson, *Rahel Levin Varnhagen,* 92. The original can be found in *Rahel-Bibliothek,* 1:328.

108. See the volume of correspondence I edited: *Briefe an eine Freundin. Rahel Varnhagen an Rebecca Friedländer* (Cologne, 1988).

109. See Petra Wilhelmy, *Der Berliner Salon im 19. Jahrhundert* (Berlin and New York, 1989), as well as Wilhelmy's newer volume, *Die Berliner Salons* (Berlin and New York, 2000). Also useful is Barbara Hahn, "The Myth of the Salon," a chapter in *The Jewess Pallas Athena,* 42–55.

110. This quote can be found in Thomas Nipperdey, *Germany from Napoleon to Bismarck, 1800–1866* (Princeton, 1996), 50.

111. Arndt's quote can be found in Luise Schorn-Schütte, *Königin Luise: Leben und Legende* (Munich, 2003), 79.

112. See Charles McClelland, *State, Society, and University in Germany, 1700–1914* (Cambridge, England, 1980), chap. 4. See also Woodruff Smith, *Politics and the Sciences of Culture in Germany, 1840–1920* (New York and Oxford, 1991).

113. See Nipperdey, *Germany,* 50.

114. Helpful here is the pioneering work of Monika Richarz, *Der Eintritt der Juden in die Akademischen Berufe: Jüdische Studenten und Akademiker in Deutschland 1678–1848* (Tübingen, 1974), 99–100.

115. The letter is found in the *Rahel-Bibliothek,* 4/2:101–2. This translation is provided by Tewarson, *Rahel Levin Varnhagen,* 125.

Chapter Four: Emancipation and War, 1811–1813

1. On this relationship see Heidi Thomann Tewarson, *Rahel Levin Varnhagen: The Life and Work of a German Jewish Intellectual* (Lincoln, Nebr., and London, 1988), 99–104, and the collection of letters I edited: *Briefe an eine Freundin: Rahel Varnhagen an Rebecca Friedländer* (Cologne, 1988).

2. See Fritz Böttger, *Bettina von Arnim: Ihr Leben, ihre Begegnungen, ihre Zeit* (Berlin, 1990), and Konstanze Bäumer and Hartwig Schultz, *Bettina von Arnim* (Stuttgart and Weimar, 1995). For interesting insights on Bettina's parents' marriage, see Ute Frevert, *Women in German History: From Bourgeois Emancipation to Sexual Liberation* (Oxford and Providence, 1988), 38–39.

3. See Ingeborg Drewitz, *Bettine von Arnim: Romantik, Revolution, Utopie* (Düsseldorf, 1969), 36.

4. For useful analysis, see Helmut Hirsch, "Jüdische Aspekte im Leben und Werk Bettine von Arnims," *Internationales Jahrbuch der Bettina-von-Arnim-Gesellschaft* 1 (1987), 61–73, as well as Rolf Spinner, *Clemens Brentano, oder Die Schwierigkeit, naiv zu sein* (Frankfurt, 1990).

5. Goethe's praise is noted in Nicholas Saul's chapter "Aesthetic Humanism," in Helen Watanabe-O'Kelly, ed., *The Cambridge History of German Literature* (Cambridge, 1997), 247.

6. Herbert Liedke, in his *Literary Criticism and Romantic Theory in the Work of Achim von Arnim* (New York, 1966), 138, argues for the first claim, and attributes the second to Reinhold Steig, *Heinrich von Kleists Berliner Kämpfe* (Berlin and Stuttgart, 1901), 3.

7. See Philipp Eberhard, *Die politischen Anschauungen der christlich-deutschen Tischgesellschaft* (Erlangen, 1937). For a summary of more recent research, see Charlene Lea, "The Christlich-Deutsch Tischgesellschaft: Napoleonic Hegemony Engenders Political Antisemitism," in Hans Schulte and David Richards, eds., *Crisis and Culture in Post-Enlightenment Germany* (Lanham, Md., 1993), 89–112.

8. See Karen Hagemann, *"Mannlicher Muth und Teutsche Ehre": Nation, Militär und Geschlecht zur Zeit der Antinapoleonischen Kriege Preußens* (Paderborn, 2002), 177.

9. Frevert, *Women,* 59, citing H. Schröder, *Die Rechtlosigkeit der Frau im Rechtsstaat* (Frankfurt, 1979).

10. See J. Kühn, ed., Karl Varnhagen von Ense, *Denkwürdigkeiten des eignen Lebens* (Berlin, 1922–23), 2:353, cited in Paul Sweet, *Wilhelm von Humboldt: A Biography* (Columbus, Ohio, 1980), 2:210–11.

11. Amos Elon, *The Pity of It All: A History of Jews in Germany, 1743–1933* (New York, 2002), 99. For a recent attempt to defend the exclusionary clauses of the Tischgesellschaft, see Jürgen Knaack, *Achim von Arnim: Nicht nur Poet* (Darmstadt, 1976).

12. For some details on Hitzig, see Jacob Jacobson, ed., *Jüdische Trauungen in Berlin 1759–1813* (Berlin, 1968), 241, n. 384. For more contemporary summaries of his life, see Eugen Grafen Breza, ed., *Galerie der ausgezeichnetsten Israeliten* (Stuttgart, 1834), 11–20; the article on Hitzig in a volume he himself edited, *Gelehrtes Berlin im Jahre 1825* (Berlin, 1825), 19–20; and the entry on him in Anon., *Jüdisches Athenaeum: Galerie berühmter Männer jüdischer Abstammung und jüdischen Glaubens* (Leipzig, 1851), 96–98.

13. For these details see Anthony Read and David Fisher, *Berlin: The Biography of a City* (London, 1994), 59–60.

14. The best source on these conflicts is Reinhold Steig, *Achim von Arnim und die ihm nahe standen,* 3 vols. (Stuttgart and Berlin, 1904), 3:431.

15. See Ursula Isselstein, *Der Text aus meinem beleidigten Herzen: Studien zu Rahel Levin Varnhagen* (Turin, 1993), 76–107.

16. Ibid., 77, quoting a letter of August 22, 1811, in *Rahel-Bibliothek,* 9:121.

17. For a brief summary of Marwitz's circumstances at that time, see Tewarson, *Rahel Levin Varnhagen,* 110–21, and Hannah Arendt, *Rahel Varnhagen: The Life of a Jewess,* ed. Liliane Weissberg (Baltimore and London, 1997), 226.

18. Quoted in Terry Pickett, *The Unseasonable Democrat: K. A. Varnhagen von Ense* (Bonn, 1985), 33. The original is in Karl August Varnhagen von Ense, *Biographische Portraits* (Leipzig, 1871; rpt. Leipzig, 1971), 63.

19. Pickett, *Unseasonable Democrat,* 64.

20. Isselstein, "Freundschaftsversuch," 77.

21. The text is available in Eric Werner, *Mendelssohn: Leben und Werk in neuer Sicht* (Zürich, 1980), 597–99, as *Anhang I.* A copy of Varnhagen's original text is now in the Leo Baeck Institute New York, and a copy was kindly provided me by Benjamin Maria Baader. See also Karl August Varnhagen von Ense, *Ausgewählte Schriften* (Leipzig, 1875), 18:112–18. Charlene Lea ("Tischgesellschaft," 97) notes that the court records on the case passed from Julius Eduard Hitzig to Ludwig Robert to Karl, but that the documents eventually disappeared.

22. See Werner Bollert, *Sing-Akademie zu Berlin* (Berlin, 1966), and Werner, *Mendelssohn,* 12–13. See also Peter Wollny, "Sara Levy and the Making of Musical Taste in Berlin," *Musical Quarterly* 77 (1993), 651–88, and Steven Mayer, "Moses Mendelssohn and the Bach Tradition," *Fidelio* 8, no. 2 (1999), 4. Levy's and Itzig's papers are located in the Familienarchiv Cauer.

23. See George Marek, *Gentle Genius: The Story of Felix Mendelssohn* (New York, 1972), 110.

24. This detail is noted by Petra Wilhelmy, *Der Berliner Salon im 19. Jahrhundert* (Berlin and New York, 1989), 97. On Arnim's previous relationship to Sara Levy, see Steig, *Kleists Berliner Kämpfe,* 633, n. 5.

25. See Lea, "Tischgesellschaft," 96.

26. All quotes from Varnhagen's document are my translation from the abridged version published by Werner in *Mendelssohn,* 597–99.

27. The details here are from Hilde Spiel, *Fanny von Arnstein: Daughter of the Enlightenment* (Providence and Oxford, 1991), 109–10. For brief mention of Moritz Itzig, see Jacob Jacobson, ed., *Die Judenbürgerbücher der Stadt Berlin* (Berlin, 1962), 51, n. 2.

28. See Heinrich Schnee, *Die Hoffinanz und der moderne Staat* (Berlin, 1953), 1:121 ff. and 169–76.

29. See Varnhagen's summary as published in Werner, *Mendelssohn,* 597. See also Peter-Philipp Riedl, " . . . das ist ein ewig Schacheren und Zänken . . . Achim von Arnims Haltung zu den Juden in den *Majorats-Herren* und anderen Schriften," *Aurora* 54 (1994), 72–105.

30. Quoted in Heidi Thomann Tewarson, "German-Jewish Identity in the Correspondence between Rahel Levin Varnhagen and Her Brother, Ludwig Robert," *LBIYB* 39 (1994), 26.

31. See Victor Kiernan, *The Duel in European History: Honour and the Reign of Aristocracy* (Oxford, 1988), 316.

32. See Ute Frevert, *Men of Honor: A Social and Cultural History of the Duel* (Cambridge, Mass., 1995), 86.

33. A useful survey is provided by Theodore Ziolkowski, *German Romanticism and Its Institutions* (Princeton, 1990), 306. For Wilhelm von Humboldt's participation in quelling a possible duel in 1826, see Terry Pinkard, *Hegel: A Biography* (Cambridge, England, 2000), 533–34.

34. I have relied here on Edward Schaub's "J. G. Fichte and Anti-Semitism," *Philosophical Review* 49 (1940), 37–52.

35. F. Nippold, ed., Hermann von Boyen, *Erinnerungen aus dem Leben des General-Feldmarschalls Hermann von Boyen*, 3 vols. (Leipzig, 1889–1890), 3:35, quoted in Peter Paret, *Yorck and the Era of Prussian Reform, 1807–1815* (Princeton, 1966), 219. Emphasis is mine.

36. Staegemann's quip is noted by Varnhagen in his summary of the Itzig incident, reprinted in Werner, *Mendelssohn*, 599.

37. See Spiel, *Fanny von Arnstein*, 109.

38. This is the formulation suggested by Brendan Simms, *The Struggle for Mastery in Germany, 1779–1850* (Houndmills, England, 1998), 79–80.

39. Thomas Nipperdey, *Germany from Napoleon to Bismarck, 1800–1866* (Princeton, 1996), 53. It is interesting to note that Rahel was close with two brothers of those arrested by Hardenberg in 1811.

40. These figures are cited in Jacob Toury, "Der Eintritt der Juden ins Deutsche Bürgertum," in Hans Liebeschütz and Arnold Paucker, eds., *Das Judentum in der deutschen Umwelt 1800–1850* (Tübingen, 1977), 162–63. Toury's statistics are confirmed by more recent research. A parallel estimate of 30 of the top 52 banking firms in 1807 being owned by Jews is cited in Ilja Mieck, "Von der Reformzeit zur Revolution," in Eberhard Bohm et al., eds., *Geschichte Berlins: Von der Frühgeschichte bis zur Gegenwart* (Munich, 1987), 1:492.

41. See Horst Fischer, *Judentum, Staat und Heer in Preußen im frühen 19. Jahrhundert* (Tübingen, 1968), 24.

42. On this stage in Dorothea's life, see Heike Frank, ". . . *Die Disharmonie, die mit mir geboren ward, und mich nie verlassen wird . . .*": Das Leben der Brendel/Dorothea Mendelssohn-Veit-Schlegel* (Frankfurt/Main–Bern, 1988); Margareta Hiemenz, *Dorothea v. Schlegel* (Freiburg, 1911); G. Schäfer, "Zur Konversion von Friedrich und Dorothea Schlegel," *Begegnung. Zeitschrift für Kultur und Geistesleben* (Heft 2, 1947), and Carola Stern, "*Ich möchte mir Flügel wünschen.*" Das Leben der Dorothea Schlegel* (Reinbeck bei Hamburg, 1990).

43. I have relied here on Sebastian Hensel, *Die Familie Mendelssohn 1729–1847* (Leipzig, 1924), 1:89 ff. See also the short article on Henriette Mendelssohn in *GJN-B* 4:338–39, and Jutta Dick's entry on Dorothea Mendelssohn in Jutta Dick and Marina Sassenberg, eds., *Jüdische Frauen im 19. und 20. Jahrhundert* (Hamburg, 1993), 278–79.

44. Zelter quoted without primary reference by Heinz Knobloch, *Herr Moses in Berlin: Auf den Spuren eines Menschenfreunds* (Berlin, 1998), 319.

45. On Lea's education and personality, see Eka Donner, *Felix Mendelssohn Bartholdy* (Düsseldorf, 1992), 14–15. The claim that Abraham and Lea met before Abraham left Berlin is made by Werner, *Mendelssohn*, 26.

46. See Jacobson, *Jüdische Trauungen*, 227, n. 359.

47. See Heinrich Eduard Jacob, *Felix Mendelssohn and His Times* (Englewood Cliffs,

N.J., 1963), 28. The classic survey is by C. Mönckeberg, *Hamburg unter dem Drucke der Franzosen 1806–1814* (Hamburg, 1864).

48. The newest work on this central family is by Niall Ferguson, *The House of Rothschild: Money's Prophets, 1789–1848* (New York, 1998).

49. Frederic Morton, *The Rothschilds: A Family Portrait* (London, 1962), 47; see also Amos Elon, *The Founder: A Portrait of the First Rothschild and His Time* (New York, 1996).

50. Jacob, *Mendelssohn*, 29.

51. Read and Fisher, *Berlin*, 60.

52. George Mosse, *Nationalism and Sexuality: Respectability and Abnormal Sexuality in Modern Europe* (New York, 1985), 78, dates this book from 1817. Other sources suggest it was published in 1810; see Günther Jahn, *Friedrich Ludwig Jahn: Volkserzieher und Vorkämpfer für Deutschlands Einigung* (Göttingen, 1992), 30.

53. See George Mosse, *Nationalization of the Masses* (New York, 1975), 129.

54. Read and Fisher, *Berlin*, 60.

55. Cited without a primary source reference in John Mander, *Berlin: The Eagle and the Bear* (London, 1959), 49.

56. Mosse, *Nationalization*, 129.

57. Cited in ibid., 128. Mosse cites Friedrich Ludwig Jahn and Ernst Eiselen, *Die Deutsche Turnkunst* (Berlin, 1916), 253. The emphasis is mine.

58. Mosse, *Nationalism and Sexuality*, 80.

59. Ibid., 78. Mosse cites Carl Euler, *Friedrich Ludwig Jahn* (Stuttgart, 1881), 122.

60. See Liah Greenfeld, *Nationalism: Five Roads to Modernity* (Cambridge, Mass., 1992), 368.

61. Ibid., 369. See Hagemann, *Nation, Militär und Geschlecht* for the most recent summary of new research on this theme.

62. This is the view taken by Euler, *Friedrich Ludwig Jahn*, 32. For a fascinating text edition published in the last years of the German Democratic Republic, see Peter Hacks, ed., *Ascher gegen Jahn*, 3 vols. (Berlin and Weimar, 1991).

63. See Read and Fisher, *Berlin*, 59.

64. These details can be found in Günter Blöcker, *Heinrich von Kleist oder Das Absolute Ich* (Berlin, 1960), 99.

65. Eda Sagarra, *Germany in the Nineteenth Century: History and Literature* (New York, 2001), 12.

66. Ibid., 100.

67. Cited in Hans Karl Krüger, *Berliner Romantik und Berliner Judentum* (Bonn, 1939), 73–74. The original letter can be found in Georg Minde-Pouet, ed., *Kleists Werke* (Leipzig, 1936/37), 1:213.

68. Pinkard, *Hegel*, 419.

69. Read and Fisher, *Berlin*, 61.

70. The letter of 1808 is included in the *Rahel-Bibliothek*, 1:380, as cited in Tewarson, *Rahel Levin Varnhagen*, 129.

71. For background, see Fischer, *Judentum*, 36–41.

72. See Stefi Jersch-Wenzel, "Legal Status and Emancipation," *German-Jewish History*, 2:25.

73. Steven Lowenstein notes Friedländer's economic position in his article "The Jew-

ishness of David Friedländer and the Crisis of Berlin Jewry," *Braun Lectures in the History of the Jews in Prussia* (Bar Ilan, Israel, 1993), 8. Lowenstein bases his calculation on Joseph Meisl, ed., *Pinkas Kehilat Berlin. Protokollbuch der jüdischen Gemeinde Berlin* (Berlin, 1962), 282, 301, 322.

74. See Sweet, *Wilhelm von Humboldt,* 1:236–237, and 2:74–75.

75. Hannah Arendt raised the issue of elites opposed to emancipation in *The Origins of Totalitarianism* (Cleveland, 1958), 18. Arendt here was disputing the dominant interpretation that the Court Jews played a positive role in the emancipation process, as argued by many historians, including Heinrich Schnee and Jacob Katz. That Schnee and Katz would agree is remarkable, considering that the two disagreed about so much. See Katz's *Out of the Ghetto: The Social Background of Jewish Emancipation, 1770–1870* (Cambridge, Mass., 1973), 29.

76. See Raphael Mahler, *A History of Modern Jewry* (London, 1971), 208.

77. Lowenstein, "David Friedländer," 11.

78. Ibid., 10.

79. See Heinrich Graetz, *History of the Jews* (Philadelphia, 1895; rpt. 1956), 505.

80. See Ismar Freund, *Emanzipation der Juden in Preußen,* 2 vols. (Berlin, 1912), 1:165–66. Freund was convinced that Hardenberg's commitment to emancipation was principled rather than personal.

81. Ibid., 221.

82. Lowenstein, *Berlin Jewish Community,* 84.

83. About his estate, see Michael Brenner, chap. 7, *German-Jewish History* 2:264. I have also relied on Jacob Marcus, *Israel Jacobson: The Founder of the Reform Movement in Judaism* (Cincinnati, 1972), 107. For older sources, see the articles on Jacobson in *Jüdisches Athenaeum,* 238–39; *Jüdischer Plutarch* (Vienna, 1848), 1:191–201, and *GJN-B,* 3:238–39.

84. These details from Friedländer's letter are cited in Freund, *Emanzipation,* 1:214. The letter itself can be found at 2:407–10.

85. Ibid., 1:219–20.

86. Ibid., 1:132.

87. See Reiner Zimmermann, *Giacomo Meyerbeer: Eine Biographie nach Dokumenten* (Berlin, 1991), 15, regarding Beer's role as Elder. See also Wilhelmy, *Der Berliner Salon* (1989), 605–9. Her name is sometimes spelled Amalia and sometimes Amalie.

88. Berndt Wessling, *Meyerbeer: Wagners Beute — Heines Geißel* (Düsseldorf, 1984), 26, discusses name changes in the family. See also Dietz Bering, *The Stigma of Names: Antisemitism in German Daily Life, 1812–1933* (Cambridge, England, 1992), 36, on the Beer family name changes.

89. There is a discussion of Giacomo's reasons for choosing Meyerbeer as his family name in Egon Jacobsohn and Leo Hirsch, *Jüdische Mütter* (Berlin, 1936), 71.

90. Wessling discusses this question in *Meyerbeer,* 39, using the verb *jiddelte.* For background, see Sander Gilman, *Jewish Self-Hatred: Antisemitism and the Hidden Language of the Jews* (Baltimore and London, 1986).

91. See Zimmermann, *Meyerbeer,* 18.

92. See Heinz Becker, "Introduction," *Giacomo Meyerbeer: Briefwechsel und Tagebücher,* 4 vols. (Berlin, 1960), 1:45.

93. See Michael Meyer, *The Origins of the Modern Jew: Jewish Identity and European Culture in Germany, 1749–1824* (Detroit, 1967), 208, n. 16.

94. Reference to the will can be found in Lowenstein, *Berlin Jewish Community,* 91.

95. Fischer, *Judentum,* 28–29. Fischer cites Ludwig Geiger, *Geschichte der Juden in Berlin,* 2 vols. (Berlin, 1871), 1:144ff.

96. The term "denizens" is used by Bering, *Stigma of Names,* 31.

97. This famous maxim was first uttered in a speech at the French National Assembly by Count Stanislas de Clermont-Tonnerre in 1789. See Paul Mendes Flohr and Jehuda Reinharz, eds., *The Jew in the Modern World* (New York, 1980), 104.

98. See Bering, *Stigma of Names,* 33.

99. See Freund, *Emanzipation,* 1:208.

100. The phrase appears in a letter that Raumer sent to Burkhard Wilhelm Pfeiffer on January 14, 1811. Cited in Freund, *Emanzipation,* 1:224. See also Kirstin Meiring, *Die Christlich-Jüdische Mischehe in Deutschland 1840–1933* (Hamburg, 1998).

101. For a clear summary, see Werner Mosse, "From *Schutzjuden* to *Deutsche Staatsbürger jüdischen Glaubens,*" in Pierre Birnbaum and Ira Katznelson, eds., *Paths of Emancipation: Jews, States, and Citizenship* (Princeton, 1995), 73. For more extensive statistical analysis see Fischer, *Judentum,* 48, nn. 67 and 69.

102. Unfortunately, Bering's discussion of this point in *Stigma of Names* (36) is most confusing on the difference between "independent households" and families. Considering that the Jewish population of Berlin in 1812 was certainly not higher than 3,300, it seems impossible that this population was distributed in 1,200 households, with less than three persons per household. All other estimates of the number of families in the community at the time suggest that the maximum was around 600. Nevertheless, Bering's conclusions about the proportion of families who made certain decisions is important, even if his raw numbers are in error.

103. On this point, see Fischer, *Judentum,* 28.

104. It is important to note here that four women were actually made citizens in 1812, among them Amalie Beer. See Jacob Jacobson, "Some Observations on the Jewish Citizens' Books of the City of Berlin," *LBIYB* 1 (1955), 388.

105. See Isabel Hull, *Sexuality, State, and Civil Society in Germany, 1700–1815* (Ithaca, N.Y., 1995).

106. See Pickett, *Unseasonable Democrat,* 34; the quotation is from Friedhelm Kemp, ed., *Rahel Varnhagen, Briefwechsel mit August Varnhagen von Ense,* 4 vols. (Munich, 1967), 2:122.

107. The journal was the *Morgenblatt für gebildete Stände.* My source is Carola Stern, *Der Text meines Herzens: Das Leben der Rahel Varnhagen* (Reinbeck bei Hamburg, 1994), 168.

108. All citations from the dream are from the summary provided by Tewarson, *Rahel Levin Varnhagen,* 120–21. Her claim about "disgrace being Jewishness" is on 121.

109. Eric Dorn Brose, *German History, 1789–1871* (Oxford and Providence, 1977), 72.

110. Thomas Nipperdey, *Germany from Napoleon to Bismarck* (Princeton, 1996), 67.

111. This is the analysis of James Sheehan, *German History, 1770–1866* (Oxford, 1989), 313.

112. Read and Fisher, *Berlin*, 61.

113. See Paret, *Yorck*, 191–95.

114. Peter Paret, *Clausewitz and the State* (New York and London, 1976), 331.

115. See Gordon Craig, *The Politics of the Prussian Army, 1640–1945* (New York, 1964), 59.

116. Brose, *German History*, 70.

117. Mieck, "Reformzeit," in *Geschichte Berlins*, 461, n. 19, citing Wilhelm Oncken, *Österreich und Preußen im Befreiungskriege*, 2 vols. (Berlin, 1876/79), 1:179.

118. See Mieck, "Reformzeit," 463, nn. 30 and 31.

119. Read and Fisher, *Berlin*, 62.

120. The king quoted in Ernst Rudolf Huber, *Dokumente zur deutschen Verfassungsgeschichte*, 3 vols. (Stuttgart, 1956–57), 1:49. Also noted in Sheehan, *History*, 315.

121. See Craig, *Politics*, 60–61.

122. For a painting from the time which shows this scene, see Wolfgang Schneider, *Berlin: Eine Kulturgeschichte in Bildern und Dokumenten* (Hanau, 1980).

123. Read and Fisher, *Berlin*, 63.

124. Cited in W. Michael Blumenthal, *The Invisible Wall: Germans and Jews* (Washington, D.C., 1998), 150, without a primary source reference.

125. Eugen Wolbe, *Geschichte der Juden in Berlin und in der Mark Brandenburg* (Berlin, 1937), 238.

126. See Fischer, *Judentum*, 29 and 33.

127. See Ursula Breymayer, Bernd Ulrich, and Karen Wieland, eds., *Willenmenschen: Über deutsche Offiziere* (Frankfurt am Main, 1999), 68.

128. This estimate is from Read and Fisher, *Berlin*, 62.

129. Ibid.

130. See Norman Kneeblatt, "Departures and Returns: Sources and Contexts for Moritz Oppenheim's Masterpiece *The Return of the Volunteer*," in Georg Heuberger and Anton Merks, eds., *Moritz Daniel Oppenheim: Die Entdeckung des jüdischen Selbstbewußtseins in der Kunst* (Frankfurt am Main, 2000), 113–30.

131. For discussion, see Fischer, *Judentum*, 39.

132. Assing's role in the war is discussed in Wolbe, *Geschichte*, 240.

133. Burg's memoir, *Geschichte meines Dienstlebens* (Leipzig, 1916), cited in Ruth Gay, *The Jews of Germany: A Historical Portrait* (New Haven, 1992), 133.

134. My sources for this paragraph include Pickett, *Unseasonable Democrat*, 35, and Otto Berdrow, *Rahel Varnhagen: Ein Lebens- und Zeitbild* (Stuttgart, 1902), 195–96.

135. Quoted by Stern, *Der Text*, 173, without primary source reference.

136. For brief mention of this love affair, see Arendt, *Rahel Varnhagen*, ed. Weissberg, 294.

137. Berdrow, *Rahel*, 196–206.

138. Stern, *Der Text*, 172, without a primary source for the quotation.

139. For details see Tewarson, *Rahel Levin Varnhagen*, 128.

140. Cited in Spiel, *Fanny von Arnstein*, 276.

141. Ibid., 129; the original is given in *Rahel-Bibliothek*, 5/3:170.

142. It is very likely that the organization she was invited to join was the Frauen-Verein zum Wohl des Vaterlandes, the "Women's Association for the Benefit of the Fatherland,"

noted in Jean Quataert's *Staging Philanthropy: Patriotic Women and the National Imagination in Dynastic Germany, 1813–1916* (Ann Arbor, 2001), 30.

143. See Blumenthal, *Invisible Wall,* 164.

144. *Sulamith* 2, Jahrgang 4 (January 3, 1816), 288. For commentary see Geiger, *Geschichte,* "Anmerkungen zum Ersten bis Vierten Buche," 190.

145. On the founding of the Luisenstift in Berlin, see Quataert, *Philanthropy,* 39.

146. Spiel, *Fanny von Arnstein,* 249. The remaining anecdotes noted in this paragraph are from ibid., 276.

147. Max Freudenthal, *Aus der Heimat Mendelssohns* (Berlin, 1900), contains the relevant eulogies.

148. For a short summary of her life, see Gerda Hoffer, *Zeit der Heldinnen: Lebensbilder außergewöhnlicher jüdischer Frauen* (Munich, 1999), 126–44. Hoffer relies on the volume by Moritz Stern, *Aus der Zeit der deutschen Befreiungskriege* (Berlin, 1914).

149. See Tewarson, "German-Jewish Identity," *LBIYB,* 17.

150. Robert's letter to Rahel of April 18, 1815, is cited in ibid.

151. The details can be found in Gustav Friedrich Manz, "Michael Beers Jugend" (diss., University of Freiburg, 1891), 15.

152. The letter is from July 10, 1815, and can be found in Becker, *Meyerbeer Briefwechsel,* 1:278.

153. Cited in Spiel, *Fanny von Arnstein,* 277.

Chapter Five: High Culture Families and Public Satire, 1814–1819

1. See Terry Pickett, *The Unseasonable Democrat: K. A. Varnhagen von Ense, 1785–1858* (Bonn, 1985), 38. See also Konrad Feilchenfeldt, *Varnhagen von Ense als Historiker* (Amsterdam, 1970), and Werner Greiling, *Varnhagen von Ense: Lebensweg eines Liberalen* (Cologne, 1973).

2. Accounts in the scholarship vary as to who took on the name when. The version here follows Heidi Tewarson, *Rahel Levin Varnhagen: The Life and Work of a German Jewish Intellectual* (Lincoln, Nebr., and London, 1998), 139.

3. See Hermann Patsch, "Als ob Spinoza wollte taufen lassen: Biographisches und Rechtsgeschichtliches zu Taufe und Trauung Rahel Levins," *Jahrbuch des Freien Deutschen Hochstifts* (Tübingen, 1991), 149–78, n. 56. According to Patsch, Marcus converted in 1818, Ludwig in 1819, and the date of Moritz's conversion is not known to him.

4. See ibid., 158–59.

5. See Françoise Tillard, *Fanny Mendelssohn* (Portland, Ore.), 42.

6. Quoted in ibid, 163. This translation is that of Tewarson, *Rahel Levin Varnhagen,* 140. The original letter can be found in *Rahel-Bibliothek,* 5/4:54.

7. This is the translation of Tewarson, *Rahel Levin Varnhagen,* 219; the original can be found in *Rahel-Bibliothek,* 2:536–37.

8. The letter appeared in Anna von Sydow, *Wilhelm und Karoline von Humboldt in ihren Briefen* (Berlin, 1906–1916), 4:395.

9. Quoted by Carola Stern, *"Ich möchte mir Flügel wünschen": Das Leben der Dorothea Schlegel* (Reinbeck bei Hamburg, 1990), 258, without a primary source reference. The emphasis is in the original, and the translation is mine.

10. This is a point made by Hannah Arendt in her *Rahel Varnhagen: The Life of a Jewess*, ed. Liliane Weissberg (Baltimore and London, 1997), 239.

11. Ursula Isselstein, "Rahels Schriften I. Karl August Varnhagens editorische Tätigkeit nach Dokumenten seines Archivs," *Rahel Levin Varnhagen: Die Wiederentdeckung einer Schriftstellerin,* ed. Barbara Hahn und Ursula Isselstein (Göttingen, 1987), 20.

12. See Stern, *Dorothea Schlegel,* 210. A new edition of the novel has been published; see Liliane Weissberg, ed., Dorothea Schlegel, *Florentin. Roman. Fragmente* (Frankfurt/ Berlin, 1987). See also Heike Frank, " . . . *die Disharmonie, die mit mir geboren ward, und mich nie verlassen wird . . .* ": *Das Leben der Brendel/Dorothea Mendelssohn-Veit-Schlegel* (Frankfurt and New York, 1988).

13. Here I am indebted to the analysis in Tewarson, *Rahel Levin Varnhagen,* 140.

14. Ibid., 245.

15. The word "intolerable" is Arendt's. The second quotation is from Rahel herself from a letter to Pauline Wiesel of February 4, 1820, unpublished. The passage is quoted by Ursula Isselstein, *"Der Text aus meinem beleidigten Herzen": Studien zu Rahel Levin Varnhagen* (Turin, 1993), 131, as cited in Arendt, *Rahel Varnhagen,* ed. Weissberg, 245.

16. Cited in Arendt, *Rahel Varnhagen,* ed. Weissberg, 248 and 363; the original is in a letter to her brother Moritz of January 29, 1816, published in Karl August Varnhagen von Ense, ed., *Rahel: Ein Buch des Andenkens für ihre Freunde,* 3 vols. (Berlin, 1834), 2:375.

17. This phrase is from a letter of February 19, 1809, and appears in the *Rahel-Bibliothek,* 1:400.

18. This list is provided by Hilde Spiel, *Fanny von Arnstein: A Daughter of the Enlightenment, 1758–1818* (New York, 1991), 278.

19. Quoted in Sydow, *Wilhelm und Karoline,* 4:458.

20. Attributed to the Prince von Ligne by Tewarson, *Rahel Levin Varnhagen,* 141.

21. See my "Album Amicorum of Rebecca Itzig," *Major Intersections,* exhibition catalogue, Yeshiva University Museum (New York, 2000), 46–49.

22. This is the suggestion made by Spiel, *Fanny von Arnstein,* 191.

23. Ibid., 286.

24. Ibid.

25. This is a quote from Spiel, *Fanny von Arnstein,* 166.

26. See ibid., 195.

27. In this paragraph I am indebted to Stern, *Dorothea Schlegel,* 255–69.

28. Ibid., 252.

29. For background, see Stefi Jersch-Wenzl, chap. 1 of Michael Meyer, ed., *German-Jewish History in Modern Times* (New York, 1997), 2:27–32.

30. Spiel, *Fanny von Arnstein,* 286.

31. These are the words of Arendt, *Rahel Varnhagen,* ed. Weissberg, 246.

32. For this detail see Tewarson, *Rahel Levin Varnhagen,* 143. Also useful is Julius Bab, *Goethe und die Juden* (Berlin, 1926).

33. This letter about Goethe's visit can be found in the *Rahel-Bibliothek* 5/4:325–28.

34. See Jacob Marcus, *Israel Jacobson: The Founder of the Reform Movement in Judaism* (Cincinnati, 1972), 107.

35. Cited in Nathan Samter, *Judentaufen im neunzehnten Jahrhundert* (Berlin, 1906), 61.

36. See Ismar Elbogen, *Geschichte der Juden in Deutschland* (Berlin, 1935), 200, on the community's readiness to give up its religious autonomy.

37. See Steven Lowenstein, *The Berlin Jewish Community: Enlightenment, Family, and Crisis, 1770–1830* (New York, 1994), 65.

38. See ibid., 27, regarding the Itzig home and 137 regarding Jacobson's first services.

39. The letter can be found in the *Rahel-Bibliothek,* 2:224.

40. Cited in Spiel, *Fanny von Arnstein,* 164.

41. See Caesar Seligmann, *Geschichte der jüdischen Reformbewegung von Mendelssohn bis zur Gegenwart* (Frankfurt am Main, 1922), 70. The quotes here are from Marcus, *Jacobson,* 108.

42. See Marcus, *Jacobson,* 109.

43. Ibid., 110.

44. On Heinemann, see the article devoted to him in the *GJN-B,* 3:39; see also Benjamin Maria Baader's discussion of Heinemann in *Inventing Bourgeois Judaism: Jewish Culture, Gender, and Religion in Germany, 1800–1870* (Bloomington, 2004), 51–52 and 148. On the "Religions-Fest," see *Jedidja* 1 (1817), 167–77; 2 (1818–19), 1–2 and 207–16.

45. Leopold Zunz, as noted in Nahum Glatzer, "On an Unpublished Letter of Isaak Markus Jost," *LBIYB* 22 (1977), 130.

46. See Michael Meyer, "Jewish Communities in Transition," in Meyer, ed., *German-Jewish History,* 2:125.

47. The list of the 972 Berlin Jews who attended the services is housed at the *CAJP,* file K Ge 2/83 and file P17-454.

48. This estimate is from Meyer, ed., *German-Jewish History,* 2:125. It seems fair to assume that the 1,000 participants would not include children, whereas the total population figure would include children.

49. Ibid.

50. These details about the service can be found in Glatzer, "Jost," *LBIYB,* where Jost reports on his 1815 visit to Jacobson's services.

51. Ibid., 30.

52. See Steven Meyer, "Moses Mendelssohn and the Bach Tradition," *Fidelio* 8 (1990), 4.

53. See Michael Meyer, "Christian Influence on Early German Reform Judaism," *Studies in Jewish Bibliography, History, and Literature in Honor of Edward Kiev* (New York, 1971), 289–303.

54. Martin Davies, *Identity or History: Markus Herz and the End of the Enlightenment* (Detroit, 1995), 157–58.

55. For the quote about the Beer home, see Heinz Becker, "Einleitung," to *Giacomo Meyerbeer: Briefwechsel und Tagebücher,* 4 vols. (Berlin, 1960), 1:36.

56. Letter of February 28, 1814, in *Meyerbeer Briefwechsel,* 1:274–75. The translation is mine.

57. See Becker, "Einleitung," in *Meyerbeer Briefwechsel,* 45. Petra Wilhelmy, in *Der Berliner Salon im 19. Jahrhundert* (Berlin, 1989), 608, lists von Montalban as a friend and social secretary.

58. See the short entry on Eberty in the *Jüdisches Lexikon* (Berlin, 1928), 4:227.

59. From Felix Eberty's *Jugenderinnerungen,* as noted in Becker, "Einleitung," in *Meyerbeer Briefwechsel,* 37. Eberty's memoirs were published as *Jugenderinnerungen eines alten Berliners* (Berlin, 1878; rpt. Berlin, 1925).

60. Reiner Zimmermann, *Giacomo Meyerbeer: Eine Biographie nach Dokumenten* (Berlin, 1991), 12.

61. Ludwig Geiger notes the book in his *Geschichte der Juden in Berlin* (Berlin, 1871; rpt. Berlin, 1988), vol. 2, *Anmerkungen, Ausführungen und urkundliche Beilagen,* 222. The author of the songbook was Jeremias Heinemann.

62. See Riv-Ellen Prell, "The Vision of Woman in Classical Reform Judaism," *Journal of the American Academy of Religion* 50, no. 4 (1982).

63. I am grateful to Benjamin Maria Baader for sharing her copies of the journal with me and for many discussions of these themes. The full title of the journal is *Sulamith, eine Zeitschrift zur Beförderung der Kultur und Humanität unter der jüdischen Nation.*

64. See G. Salomon, "Erziehungs- und Schulwesen," in *Sulamith* (1810), 183–201. For a later period, see Abraham Geiger, "Die Stellung des weiblichen Geschlechtes in dem Judenthume unserer Zeit," *Wissenschaftliche Zeitschrift für jüdischen Theologie* 3 (1837), 1–14.

65. See Meyer, ed., *German-Jewish History,* 2:125.

66. On Zunz's activities in these years, see ibid., 132–35.

67. For some useful generalizations about these trends, see Daniel Boyarin, *Unheroic Conduct: The Rise of Heterosexuality and the Invention of the Jewish Man* (Berkeley, 1997), 68.

68. Noted in David Biale, *Eros and the Jews: From Biblical Israel to Contemporary America* (Berkeley, 1997), 161. The original citation is A. M. Dik, *Masekhet Aniyut* (Vilna, 1878), 26.

69. See Leonore Davidoff and Catherine Hall, *Family Fortunes: Men and Women of the English Middle Class, 1780–1850* (Chicago, 1987).

70. Quoted in Gustav Friedrich Manz, "Michael Beer's Jugend" (diss., University of Freiburg, 1891), 46.

71. *Meyerbeer Briefwechsel,* 1:29. This is the analysis provided by Ritchie Robertson, *The "Jewish Question" in German Literature, 1749–1939: Emancipation and Its Discontents* (Oxford, 1999), 206–8 and 317.

72. For my summary of the play and its reception, I am indebted to Jeffrey Grossman, *The Discourse on Yiddish in Germany, from the Enlightenment to the Second Empire* (Rochester, N.Y., 2000), 147–52. See also Hans-Joachim Neubauer, "Auf Begehr: Unser Verkehr. Über eine judenfeindliche Theaterposse im Jahre 1815," in Rainer Erb and Michael Schmidt, eds., *Antisemitismus und jüdische Geschichte. Studien zu Ehren von Herbert A. Strauss* (Berlin, 1987), 315–37.

73. See Grossman, *Discourse,* 149.

74. Original and translation in ibid., 148, citing K. A. B. Sessa, *Unser Verkehr* (Leipzig, 1816), 18–20.

75. See Neubauer, "Auf Begehr," on this point. There seems to have been quite a market among Jews for illustrated anti-Jewish humor in subsequent years. See Peter Gay, *Freud, Jews, and Other Germans: Masters and Victims in Modernist Culture* (New York, 1978), 209–13.

76. Wurms's home entertainments are noted by Grossman, *Discourse,* 151.

77. See my article "The Lives, Loves and Novels of August and Fanny Lewald, the Converted Cousins from Königsberg," *LBIYB* 46 (2001), 95–112.

78. Some of the drawings of the characters in *Unser Verkehr* are reproduced in Peter

Dittmar, *Die Darstellung der Juden in der populären Kunst zur Zeit der Emancipation* (Munich and London, 1992), 199–217, and in Jefferson Chase, *Inciting Laughter: The Development of Jewish Humor in Nineteenth-Century German Culture* (Berlin and New York, 2000).

79. The Schuckmann proposal was never carried out. See Dietz Bering, *The Stigma of Names: Antisemitism in German Daily Life, 1812–1933* (Cambridge, England, 1992), 44–47. The Ministry of Finance announcement is cited in Françoise Tillard, *Fanny Mendelssohn* (Portland, Ore., 1996), 46.

80. Cited in Jacob Katz, *From Prejudice to Destruction: Anti-Semitism, 1700–1933* (Cambridge, Mass., 1980), 94–95.

81. For a brief summary of Rühs's career, see the article on him in *Deutsche Biographische Enzyklopädie* (Munich, 1998), 8:452.

82. Friedrich Rühs, *Über die Ansprüche der Juden an das deutsche Bürgerrecht* (Berlin, 1816), cited (without page reference) by Michael Meyer, *The Origins of the Modern Jew* (Detroit, 1967), 140.

83. Quoted in Marvin Lowenthal, *The Jews of Germany: A Story of Sixteen Centuries* (Philadelphia, 1936), 231, without page reference to the Rühs book.

84. In a recent article criticizing traditional views of antisemitism, Zygmunt Bauman argues that Rühs can also be read as a kind of relativist pluralist. See Bauman's "Allosemitism: Premodern, Modern," in Bryan Cheyette and Laura Marcus, eds., *Modernity, Culture and "The Jew"* (Cambridge, England, 1998), 145.

85. For a sophisticated interpretation of this issue, see Berdring, *Antisemitismus*, 48–49. Other scholars blame the entire nationalist movement for hostility to liberal values. See Peter Pulzer, *The Rise of Political Anti-Semitism in Germany and Austria* (Cambridge, Mass., 1988), 31.

86. On the theme of baptism making Jews "more German," see Paul Lawrence Rose, *Revolutionary Antisemitism from Kant to Wagner* (Princeton, 1990), 128, and Katz, *From Prejudice to Destruction*, 197.

87. On this detail see Günter Steiger, *Aufbruch, Urburschenschaft und Wartburgsfest* (Leipzig and Berlin, 1967), 78. Discussion of the work being read at taverns can be found in Meyer, *Origins,* 140. Meyer has relied on Sigmund Zimmern, *Versuch einer Würdigung der Angriffe des Herrn Professor Fries auf die Juden* (Heidelberg, 1816). For background on Fries's philosophical contributions, see the article on him in the *Neue Deutsche Biographie* (Berlin, 1960), 5:608–9. Scholars who discuss Fries's attitudes toward Jews rarely take him seriously as a thinker on other issues. For a useful summary, see George Williamson, "What Killed August von Kotzebue? The Temptations of Virtue and the Political Theology of German Nationalism," *Journal of Modern History* 72 (2000), 890–943.

88. See Pinkard, *Hegel,* 114–15.

89. Ibid., 221 and 352.

90. Lea's letter can be found in Sebastian Hensel, *Die Familie Mendelssohn* (Berlin, 1879), 104; translated as *The Mendelssohn Family, 1729–1847* (New York, 1968). The letter is also cited in Tillard, *Mendelssohn,* 44.

91. Deborah Hertz, "Why Did the Christian Gentleman Assault the *jüdische Elegant?* Four Conversion Stories from Berlin 1816–1825," *LBIYB* 40 (1995), 94.

92. See Larry R. Todd, *Mendelssohn: A Life in Music* (New York, 2003), 18.

93. Ibid., 31. On Bella Salomon's home, see "Von der 'wuesten Stelle' zur Top-Adresse," www.stadt.plan.mitte (June 9, 2003), 1. It is fascinating to see that although she opposed baptism, Bella took the family name of Bartholdy in 1812 when she became a citizen, as noted in Jacob Jacobson, ed., *Die Judenbürgerbücher der Stadt Berlin 1809–1851* (Berlin, 1962), case 283.

94. See Todd, *Mendelssohn,* 136.

95. On Koreff see Friedrich von Oppeln-Bronikowski, *David Ferdinand Koreff. Serapionsbruder, Magnetiseur, Geheimrat und Dichter* (Berlin, 1928).

96. Ibid., 61.

97. For a summary of recent research on her life, see Peter Seibert, "Henriette Herz: Erinnerungen. Zur Rekonstruktion einer frühen Frauenautobiographie," *Der Deutschunterricht: Beiträge zu seiner Praxis und wissenschaftlichen Grundlegung* 41 (1989), 37–50, as well as Liliane Weissberg, "Weibliche Körpersprachen: Bild und Wort bei Henriette Herz," in Jutta Dick and Barbara Hahn, eds., *Von einer Welt in die andere: Jüdinnen im 19. und 20. Jahrhundert* (Vienna, 1993), 71–91. See also Amos Elon, *The Pity of It All: A History of the Jews of Germany, 1743–1933* (New York, 2002), 75.

98. See Todd, *Mendelssohn,* 15.

99. See F. Gustav Kühne, *Deutsche Männer und Frauen: Eine Galerie von Charakteren* (Leipzig, 1851), 226.

100. Geiger, *Geschichte,* 2:189.

101. See Glatzer, "Jost," 131.

102. See Jeffrey Dawson, *Friedrich Schleiermacher: The Evolution of a Nationalist* (Austin, Tex., 1966), 135.

103. For these details see Ernst Carl Jarck, *C. L. Sand und sein an Kotzebue verübter Mord* (Berlin, 1831), 88. This summary is provided by F. Gunther Eyck, "The Political Theories and Activities of the German Academic Youth between 1815 and 1819," *Journal of Modern History* 27 (1955), 31–34.

104. For these details I am indebted to the article "Wartburgfest 1817," in *Lexikon der Deutschen Geschichte* (Stuttgart, 1977), 1261.

105. Alexandra Richie, *Faust's Metropolis: A History of Berlin* (New York, 1998), 115.

106. A useful summary can be found in George Mosse, *The Nationalization of the Masses: Political Symbolism and Mass Movements in Germany from the Napoleonic Wars through the Third Reich* (New York, 1975), 129. See also Willi Schröder, *Burschenschaftsturner in Kampf um Einheit und Freiheit* (Berlin, 1967), 183–85.

107. See Mosse, *Nationalization,* 77. For Jahn's own formulations, see Friedrich Ludwig Jahn, "Deutsches Volkstum," in Carl Euler, ed., *Friedrich Ludwig Jahns Werke* (Hof, 1884), 1:321.

108. Friedrich Münch, "Jugend-Erinnerungen," in *Deutsch-amerikanische Monatshefte* 1 (May 1864), 388, cited by Eyck, "The Political Theories," 31, n. 13.

109. For a good short description of the festival, see Williamson, "What Killed August von Kotzebue?" 922. On Saul Ascher, see Ellen Littmann, "Saul Ascher: First Theorist of Progressive Judaism," *LBIYB* 5 (1960), 107–21.

110. Rudolf Frank, ed., Heinrich Heine, *Reisebilder (Die Harzreise),* in Heine's *Sämt-*

liche Werke (Munich, 1923), 4:36–37. This translation is provided by Littmann, "Ascher," 110.

111. This translation of these sentences from Ascher's *Germanomania* is provided by Shmuel Almog, *Nationalism and Antisemitism in Modern Europe, 1815–1945* (Oxford, 1990), 11–13.

112. The student who penned these sentences is not identified in my source, Uriel Tal, "Young German Intellectuals on Romanticism and Judaism — Spiritual Turbulence in the Early Nineteenth Century," in *Salo Wittmayer Baron Jubilee Volume* (Jerusalem, 1974), 920.

113. On Börne's intellectual experiences in his Berlin period, see Orlando Figes, "Ludwig Börne and the Formation of a Radical Critique of Judaism," *LBIYB* 29 (1984), 361.

114. See Norbert Altenhofer, "Henriette Herz und Louis Baruch — Jeanette Wohl und Ludwig Börne," in the catalogue *Ludwig Börne 1786–1837*, ed. Alfred Estermann (Frankfurt, 1986), 211–21.

115. Figes, "Börne's Critique," *LBIYB*, 360. See also Martin Schneider, *Die kranke schöne Seele der Revolution. Heine, Börne, das "Junge Deutschland," Marx und Hegel* (Frankfurt, 1980).

116. Here I follow the account provided by Willi Jasper, *Keinem Vaterland geboren: Ludwig Börne, eine Biographie* (Hamburg, 1989), 66.

117. Ibid. On the theme of name changes, see Bering, *Stigma of Names*, 36–43.

118. According to Chase, "his readers were aware that Börne himself came from a Jewish background." See Chase's *Inciting Laughter*, 77.

119. See ibid., 94, for additional details.

120. These two events are noted in ibid., 95. What is not clear from any of the accounts of this episode is why his conversion became known because of the arrest.

121. Figes, "Börne's Critique," *LBIYB*, 360.

122. See Helmut Bock, *Ludwig Börne: Vom Ghettojuden zum Nationalschriftsteller* (Berlin, 1962), 153.

123. For a short reference to this episode, see Michael Holzmann, *Ludwig Börne: Sein Leben und sein Wirken* (Berlin, 1888), 95.

124. On this point see Georg Heuberger, "Ludwig Börne — Juif de Francfort," in Estermann, *Ludwig Börne*, 250.

125. See Jacob Toury, *Die politischen Orientierungen der Juden in Deutschland* (Tübingen, 1966), 14.

126. On this point see Ludwig Marcuse, *Ludwig Börne: Aus der Frühzeit der deutschen Demokratie* (Zurich, 1977), 100.

127. See Holzmann, *Börne*, 102.

128. Chase, *Inciting Laughter*, 71. See also Walter Hinderer, "Die Frankfurter *Judengasse* und das Ghetto Europas: Der praktische Hintergrund von Ludwig Börnes emanzipativem Patriotismus," *Germanisch-Romanische Monatschrift* 24 (1974).

129. Friedrich Meinecke, *Erlebtes 1862–1901* (Leipzig, 1941), 208, quoted in Gordon Craig, *The Politics of the Prussian Army, 1640–1945* (New York, 1964), 77.

130. Carl Ludwig Sand, "Zum Achtzehnten des Herbstmonats im Jahr nach Christo achtzehnhundert und siebenzehn auf der Wartburg," in *Carl Ludwig Sand, dargestellt durch seine Tagebücher und Briefe von einigen seiner Freunde* (Altenburg, 1821), 127. I am using the translation of Williamson, "What Killed August von Kotzebue?" 922.

131. The literature on Follen is large. For an introduction in English, see Edmund Spevack, *Charles Follen's Search for Nationality and Freedom: Germany and America, 1796–1840* (Cambridge, Mass., 1997).

132. Lewis Feuer, *The Conflict of Generations: The Character and Significance of Student Movements* (New York, 1969), 63.

133. Williamson, "What Killed August von Kotzebue?" 891.

134. Ascher's book is *Die Wartburgs-Feier: Mit Hinsicht auf Deutschlands religiöse und politische Stimmung* (Berlin, 1818).

135. Williamson, "What Killed August von Kotzebue?" 909 and 911.

136. Ibid., 918.

137. Ibid., 890.

138. Lewis Feuer cites Humboldt in *Conflict*, 64, n. 32.

139. Williamson, "What Killed August von Kotzebue?" 940.

140. See Helmut Reinicke, *Gaunerwirtschaft. Die erstaunlichen Abenteuer hebräischer Spitzbuben in Deutschland* (Berlin, 1983), 60.

141. Eleonore Sterling, "Anti-Jewish Riots in Germany in 1819: A Displacement of Social Protest," *Historia Judaica* 12 (1950), 119.

142. Feuer, *Conflict*, 64.

143. Ibid., 121, n. 7.

144. An older work is C. Krollmann, *Warum gab es im Jahre 1819 eine "Judenhetze"?* (Berlin, 1899). The most recent and comprehensive analysis is Jacob Katz, *Die Hep-Hep-Verfolgungen des Jahres 1819* (Berlin, 1994).

145. Sterling, "Anti-Jewish Riots," 131.

146. See ibid., 122, n. 10.

147. Eric Werner, *Mendelssohn: A New Image of the Composer and His Age* (London and New York, 1963), 28.

148. Franz Rühl, ed., F. A. von Staegemann, *Briefe und Aktenstücke zur Geschichte Preußens unter Friedrich Wilhelm III* (Leipzig, 1902), 3:7; cited by Sterling, "Anti-Jewish Riots," 133.

149. Sterling, "Anti-Jewish Riots," 138.

150. *Sulamith* 6, 1, Heft 1 (1819), 34, quoted in ibid., 138, n. 82.

151. For a fascinating analysis of his reaction to these riots, see Sander Gilman, *Jewish Self-Hatred: Antisemitism and the Hidden Language of the Jews* (Baltimore, 1986), 163–64. The review can be found in Börne's *Sämtliche Schriften* (Düsseldorf, 1964–68), 1:415–21. I have relied on the translation published in Chase, *Inciting Laughter*, 249–53.

152. "Extermination" is the word used by Chase, *Inciting Laughter*, 130.

153. Katz, *From Prejudice to Destruction*, 100.

154. Sterling, "Anti-Jewish Riots," 131.

155. For a survey of his life story, see Gerhard Masur, *Friedrich Julius Stahl. Geschichte seines Lebens. Aufstieg und Entfaltung 1802–1840* (Berlin, 1930), as well as Robert Kann, "Friedrich Julius Stahl: A Re-Examination of his Conservatism," *LBIYB* 12 (1967), 55–74.

156. Masur, *Stahl*, 42–43.

Chapter Six: The Entrance Ticket to European Civilization, 1820–1833

1. For excellent background on the politics of Baden in this era, see Dagmar Herzog, *Intimacy and Exclusion: Religious Politics in Pre-Revolutionary Baden* (Princeton, 1966).

2. The letter appears in *Rahel-Bibliothek,* 2:609–10, and is cited by Heidi Tewarson, *Rahel Levin Varnhagen: The Life and Work of a German Jewish Intellectual* (Lincoln, Nebr., and London, 1998), 180.

3. See Ronald Taylor, *Berlin and Its Culture* (New Haven, 1997), 120. On the emergence of the term *Biedermeier,* see Terry Pinkard, *Hegel: A Biography* (Cambridge, England, 2000), 433 and 733, n. 29.

4. See Alice Hanson, *Musical Life in Biedermeier Vienna* (Cambridge, England, 1985).

5. Ibid., 109 ("commonplace events") and 117.

6. Georg Hermann, *Das Biedermeier* (Hamburg, 1965), cited in George Marek, *Gentle Genius: The Story of Felix Mendelssohn* (New York, 1972), 97.

7. See Ulrike Weckel, "A Lost Paradise of a Female Culture? Some Critical Questions Regarding the Scholarship on Late Eighteenth- and Early Nineteenth-Century German Salons," in *German History* 18 (2000), 310–36, and Barbara Hahn, *The Jewess Pallas Athena: This Too a Theory of Modernity* (Princeton, 2005), especially the chapter "The Myth of the Salon." I respond to Hahn's critiques of my work in the Preface to the new edition of *Jewish High Society in Old Regime Berlin* (Syracuse, N.Y., 2005).

See also the collection of primary sources gathered by Rolf Strube, ed., *Sie saßen und tranken am Teetisch: Anfänge und Blütezeit der Berliner Salons 1789–1871* (Munich and Zurich, 1991), Roberto Simanowski et al., eds., *Europa: ein Salon? Beiträge zur Internationalität des literarischen Salons* (Göttingen, 1999), and Peter Seibert, *Der literarische Salon: Literatur und Geselligkeit zwischen Aufklärung und Vormärz* (Stuttgart, 1993).

8. The most recent edition of Lewald's autobiography is Ulrike Helmer, ed., Fanny Lewald, *Meine Lebensgeschichte,* 3 vols. (Frankfurt am Main, 1988). For a short English version, see Hanna Lewis, trans., *The Education of Fanny Lewald: An Autobiography* (Albany, 1992). See my two articles on Lewald: "Work, Love, and Jewishness in the Life of Fanny Lewald," in Frances Malino and David Sorkin, eds., *Profiles in Diversity: Jews in a Changing Europe* (Detroit, 1991), 202–22, and "The Lives, Loves and Novels of August and Fanny Lewald, the Converted Cousins from Königsberg," *LBIYB* 46 (2001), 95–112.

9. The novel was entitled *Prinz Louis Ferdinand: Ein Zeitbild* (Berlin, 1859). See also Marieluise Steinhauer, *Fanny Lewald, die deutsche George Sand* (Berlin, 1937), and the more recent studies: Gudrun Marci-Boehncke, *Fanny Lewald: Jüdin, Preußin, Schriftstellerin* (Stuttgart, 1998); Gabriele Schneider, *Fanny Lewald* (Reinbeck, 1996); and Brigitta van Rheinberg, *Fanny Lewald. Geschichte einer Emanzipation* (Frankfurt and New York, 1990).

10. This was the situation I describe in my *Jewish High Society in Old Regime Berlin* (New Haven and London, 1988), 158–59.

11. Petra Wilhelmy-Dollinger, *Die Berliner Salons* (Berlin and New York, 2000), 128, lists the names of 12 noble salon women.

12. My description of the Staegemann salon is indebted to ibid., 105–7 and 114–15, and the same author's earlier volume with a similar title: Petra Wilhelmy-Dollinger, *Der Berliner Salon im 19. Jahrhundert* (Berlin, 1989), 848–60. See F. Gustav Kühne's chapter on Elisabeth in his *Deutsche Männer und Frauen* (Leipzig, 1851), 184–213, and also Margarete von Olfers, *Elisabeth von Staegemann: Lebensbild einer deutschen Frau 1761–1835* (Leipzig, 1937).

13. For a summary of von Crayen's salon, see Wilhelmy-Dollinger, *Die Berliner Salons* (2000), 124–25.

14. On Elise von Hohenhausen, see ibid., 136–38, and also Wilhelmy-Dollinger, *Der Berliner Salon* (1989), 687–89.

15. The Konditorei Stehely was a favorite spot for dissidents in Berlin then. See Julius Schoeps, *Bürgerliche Aufklärung und liberales Freiheitsdenken: Aaron Bernstein in seiner Zeit* (Stuttgart and Bonn, 1992), 43, n. 101.

16. Of interest here is Bernd Wegener, "Über den ästhetischen Thee," *Neue deutsche Hefte* 30 (1983), 284–97.

17. See Martin Davies, *Identity or History? Marcus Herz and the End of the Enlightenment* (Detroit, 1995), 162. Fanny Lewald's memories of her visit to Herz can be found in "Fanny Lewald bei Henriette Herz: 'Ich habe alle Menschen gekannt,'" in Strube, *Sie saßen,* 300–312.

18. This is the analysis suggested by Davies, *Marcus Herz,* 157.

19. See the articles on each of the sisters by Barbara Hahn, in Jutta Dick and Marina Sassenberg, eds., *Jüdische Frauen im 19. und 20. Jahrhundert: Lexikon zu Leben und Werk* (Reinbeck, 1993), 112 and 154–55. An article on Sara can be found in Wilhelmy-Dollinger, *Der Berliner Salon* (1989), 651–53. The sisters are noted in Jacob Jacobson, ed., *Jüdische Trauungen in Berlin, 1773–1859* (Berlin, 1968), 251, n. 408, as well as in Ludwig Geiger, "Vor 100 Jahren," in *ZGJD* 3 (Braunschweig 1889), 225–26. See also Karl August Varnhagen, "Frau von Grotthuß und Frau von Eybenberg," in his *Gesammelte Schriften,* ed. Ludmilla Assing (Leipzig, 1874), 18:75–81.

20. I have relied here on Cécile Lowenthal-Hensel, ed., *Preußische Bildnisse des 19. Jahrhunderts: Zeichnungen von Wilhelm Hensel* (Berlin, 1981), 78–79.

21. This letter is discussed in Jacob Jacobson, ed., *Die Judenbürgerbücher der Stadt Berlin 1800–1851* (Berlin, 1962), 79.

22. On Henriette Mendelssohn, see Dick and Sassenberg, *Frauen,* 278–79.

23. For information on the Cohen family, see Jacobson, *Jüdische Trauungen,* 362–63. Jacobson notes that the Cohen children were converted in England before their parents were baptized in Berlin. One Cohen son later received the new name van Baren, and he married a Christian woman from the Hindenburg family. Two of the Cohen sons died in the War of Liberation. See Wilhelmy-Dollinger, *Die Berliner Salons* (2000), 80, and also Wilhelmy-Dollinger, *Der Berliner Salon* (1989), 623–25.

24. On Solmar, see Wilhelmy-Dollinger, *Die Berliner Salons* (2000), 156, and Wilhelmy-Dollinger, *Der Berliner Salon* (1989), 840–41. Fanny Lewald's memories of Solmar's salon from the 1840s have been published in Strube, *Sie saßen,* 222–27.

25. Heinrich Heine, who was a friend of Moritz Veit's future brother-in-law Joseph Lehmann, was brought by Lehmann to the Veits' Thursday gatherings. Joseph Lehmann was a bookkeeper, later editor of a literary journal, and director of a railroad. In 1831 he

married Philipp Veit's daughter Therese. See Jacobson, *Judenbürgerbücher*, 66 and 275. It was at the Veit home that Heine met Gans, Moser, Zunz, and others for the first time. See Hans Reissner, *Eduard Gans: Ein Leben im Vormärz* (Tübingen, 1965), 93.

26. For a discussion of the Tiergarten villa from a somewhat later era, see Frederic Bedoire, *The Jewish Contribution to Modern Architecture, 1830–1930* (Jersey City, 2004), 220–34.

27. See Reiner Zimmermann, *Giacomo Meyerbeer: Eine Biographie nach Dokumenten* (Berlin, 1991), 13. Michael's remark about his father is cited in Berndt Wessling, *Meyerbeer: Wagners Beute—Heines Geißel* (Düsseldorf, 1936), 25.

28. Zimmermann, *Meyerbeer*, 13. The list of guests at the Beers can be found in Wilhelmy-Dollinger, *Der Berliner Salon* (1989), 605–9. See also the description of the Beer salon in Wilhelmy-Dollinger, *Die Berliner Salons* (2000), 149–51.

29. See Wilhelmy-Dollinger, *Der Berliner Salon* (1989), 850.

30. This quote is cited in Gustav Friedrich Manz, "Michael Beer's Jugend" (diss., University of Freiburg, 1891), 12. Manz is citing a letter of Rahel's published in Ludmilla Assing, ed., *Briefwechsel zwischen Varnhagen und Rahel*, 6 vols. (Leipzig, 1874–75), 6:43.

31. These incidents are from Rahel's diary entries of December 29 and 30, 1819. The sentences are quoted in Hannah Arendt, *Rahel Varnhagen: The Life of a Jewess*, ed. Liliane Weissberg (Baltimore and London, 1997), 241 and 358. This episode calls into question Amos Elon's claim that after she returned to Berlin, "much had changed" for Rahel, and that now "her friends returned her invitations." See Elon's *The Pity of It All: A History of Jews in Germany, 1743–1933* (New York, 2002), 109.

32. See the useful discussion on this point in Wilhelmy-Dollinger, *Die Berliner Salons* (2000), 131.

33. Unpublished diary entry of December 29, 1819, cited in Arendt's *Rahel Varnhagen*, ed. Weissberg, 241. The later quotes in the paragraph are from Weissberg's note on 358.

34. On this point, see Reissner, *Gans*, 160. For a collection of contemporary essays, see Douglas Moggach, ed., *The New Hegelians: Politics and Philosophy in the Historical School* (New York, 2006).

35. Elon, *Pity*, 111.

36. Reissner, *Gans*, 98.

37. See Hans Berglar-Schröer, *Wilhelm von Humboldt* (Reinbeck, 1970), 119.

38. Reissner, *Gans*, 28.

39. See John Toews, *Hegelianism: The Path toward Dialectical Humanism, 1805–1841* (Cambridge, England, 1980), 108. Toews's 2004 book, *Becoming Historical: Cultural Reformation and Public Memory in Early Nineteenth-Century Berlin* (Cambridge, England, 2004), came to my attention too late to be fully utilized here.

40. Both these quotes appear in Toews, *Hegelianism*, 104.

41. Elon, *Pity*, 112.

42. This is a selection from the remarkable document "Outline of Matters in Need of Improvement among Jews," reproduced in Elon, *Pity*, 113–14, citing from an unnumbered file from the Zunz Collection at the National and University Library, Jerusalem.

43. See Friedrich Schleiermacher, *On Religion: Speeches to Its Cultural Despisers*, trans. John Oman (New York, 1958), 238.

44. This is a quotation from Michael Meyer, chap. 7, in *German-Jewish History,* 2:132.

45. Ibid., 105. Meyer is citing N. N. Glatzer, ed., *Leopold Zunz. Jude-Deutscher-Europäer* (Tübingen, 1964), 103.

46. I am indebted for many of these details to the meticulous list of Verein participants included in Reissner, *Gans,* 174–89.

47. On Jost, see Ismar Schorsch, "From Wolfenbüttel to Wissenschaft: The Divergent Paths of Isaak Markus Jost and Leopold Zunz," *LBIYB* 22 (1977), 109–28.

48. See Reissner, *Gans,* 83.

49. For background on this time in Heine's life, see Jeffrey Sammons, *Heinrich Heine: A Modern Biography* (Princeton, 1979), chap. 8. See also Reissner, *Gans,* 93, and Norbert Waszek, "Aufklärung, Hegelianismus und Judentum im Licht der Freundschaft von Heine und Gans," in Joseph Kruse et al., eds., *Aufklärung und Skepsis* (Stuttgart and Weimar, 1999), 226–41.

50. Sammons, *Heine,* 109.

51. For discussion of his living arrangements see Hugo Bieber, ed., *Heinrich Heine: Confessio Judaica. Eine Auswahl aus seinen Dichtungen, Schriften und Briefen* (Berlin, 1925), 13. The women's auxiliary that Heine worked with is noted in Philip Kossoff, *Valiant Heart: A Biography of Heinrich Heine* (New York and London, 1983), 64.

52. See Bieber, *Heine,* 13. Unfortunately the date is confusing, for Zunz quit his post as preacher for the Beer temple in 1822.

53. Heine's *Briefe aus Berlin* is published in a collection entitled *Reisebilder* (Leipzig, 1981).

54. Both these quotes can be found in the *Heinrich Heine Säkularausgabe* (Berlin and Paris, 1970–), 20:71–72, cited in Sammons, *Heine,* 91.

55. Sammons, *Heine,* 49.

56. Ibid., 129.

57. Heinrich Heine, *Historisch-kritische Gesamtausgabe* ed. Manfred Windfuhr et al. (Hamburg, 1973–), 6:192, noted in Sammons, *Heine,* 75.

58. Sammons, *Heine,* 82.

59. See Wessling, *Meyerbeer,* 35.

60. See Daniel Purdy, *The Tyranny of Elegance: Consumer Cosmopolitanism in the Era of Goethe* (Baltimore, 1998), chap. 7. Heine notes the kinds of clothes which expressed one's hostility to Philistine values in his *Briefe aus Berlin,* 594.

61. This description is from Elon, *Pity,* 117, without a primary source reference.

62. See Wessling, *Meyerbeer,* 35.

63. Heine, *Briefe aus Berlin,* 590.

64. The phrase "heathens in the Fatherland" was used by Anton von Stolberg, as cited by Christopher Clark, *The Politics of Conversion: Missionary Protestantism and the Jews in Prussia, 1728–1941* (Oxford, 1995), 89. Clark cites a dissertation by J. Althausen, "Kirchliche Gesellschaften in Berlin, 1810–1830" (Halle-Wittenberg, 1965), 21. Many of my points in the pages which follow were first suggested in chap. 4 of Clark's volume.

65. Clark, *Politics,* 131.

66. Ibid., 136.

67. Ibid., 144.

68. For useful background, see Todd Endelman, *Radical Assimilation in English Jewish History, 1656–1945* (Bloomington, 1990), 148–49.

69. See Clark, *Politics,* 137. Two other books are of interest here: W. T. Gidney, *A History of the London Society for the Promotion of Christianity Among the Jews* (London, 1908), and Stephen Neill, *A History of Christian Missions* (Harmondsworth, England, 1986).

70. On Julius Eduard, see J. F. A. de la Roi, *Die evangelische Christenheit und die Juden,* 2 vols. (Berlin, 1891), 1:191–92.

71. On Frey, see the article "Apostasie," in *Encyclopedia Judaica* (Berlin, 1930), 6:1211, and Endelman, *Radical Assimilation,* 147–48.

72. Rose's address is printed in full in *Neueste Nachrichten* 6 (1822), 65–70, as cited in Clark, *Politics,* 133.

73. This account of Tholuck is based on de la Roi, *Christenheit,* 1:128–130.

74. Ibid., 130. No first name for Sontheim appears in the source.

75. Ibid.

76. Jost's words come from a letter of 1822 to Meyer Ehrenberg, as cited in Schorsch, "Wolfenbüttel," 116. The original text can be found in Nahum Glatzer, ed., *Leopold and Adelheid Zunz: An Account in Letters, 1815–1885* (London, 1958), 34–35.

77. On the conflicts between Schleiermacher and Hegel, see Toews, *Hegelianism,* 61.

78. For the first quote, see Reiner Zimmermann, *Giacomo Meyerbeer: Eine Biographie nach Dokumenten* (Berlin, 1991), 14; the second is from Heinrich Heine, cited in Gustav Karpeles, *Heinrich Heine's Memoirs: From His Works, Letters, and Conversations,* 2 vols. (London, 1910), 1:113.

79. These statistics are provided by Konrad Jarausch, "The Sources of German Student Unrest, 1815–1848," in Lawrence Stone, ed., *The University in Society* (Princeton, 1974), 2:557.

80. A good summary of these problems can be found in Toews, *Hegelianism,* 25.

81. See Jarausch, "Unrest," 534, n. 14.

82. I rely here on Monika Richarz, *Der Eintritt der Juden in die Akademischen Berufe* (Tübingen, 1974), 99.

83. See R. Larry Todd, *Mendelssohn: A Life in Music* (New York, 2003), 102.

84. Ibid., 98, citing Sebastian Hensel, *The Mendelssohn Family from Letters and Journals* (New York, 1881), 1:115.

85. See de la Roi, *Christenheit,* 2:184–85.

86. Hensel, *The Mendelssohn Family,* 1:75.

87. On Zelter, see Dietrich Fischer-Dieskau, *Carl Friedrich Zelter und das Berliner Musikleben seiner Zeit* (Berlin, 1997).

88. Quoted, without a primary source reference, in Peter Mercer-Taylor, *The Life of Mendelssohn* (Cambridge, England, 2000), 44.

89. This is a letter of October 21, 1821, cited in Marek, *Gentle Genius,* 114, without a primary source reference.

90. Marek's summary of the letter of July 8, 1829, cited in ibid., 86.

91. Direct quotation from the same letter, in ibid., 87.

92. Quoted from the article on Zunz in the *Encyclopedia Judaica* (Jerusalem, 1972), 12:701. Hannah Arendt has an analysis of the class conflict within Prussian Jewry that is

very relevant to Zunz's attack on the Beer temple. See her *The Origins of Totalitarianism* (Cleveland, 1958), 64. See also Luitpold Wallach, *Liberty and Letters: The Thoughts of Leopold Zunz* (London, 1959), and Peter Wagner, *Wir werden frei sein: Leopold Zunz, 1794–1886* (Detmold, 1994).

93. Schorsch, "Wolfenbüttel," *LBIYB*, 109.

94. Cited without a primary source reference in Michael Meyer, *Response to Modernity: A History of the Reform Movement in Judaism* (New York, 1968), 52.

95. For additional information, see ibid., chaps 1 and 2; Meyer's "The Orthodox and the Enlightened: An Unpublished Contemporary Analysis of Berlin Jewry's Spiritual Condition in the Early Nineteenth Century," *LBIYB* 25 (1980), 101–330; and also his article "The Religious Reform Controversy in the Berlin Jewish Community, 1814–1823," *LBIYB* 24 (1979), 139–55.

96. Meyer, *Response*, 57.

97. See Michael Meyer, " 'Ganz nach dem altern Herkommen?' The Spiritual Life of Berlin Jewry Following the Edict of 1823," in Marianne Awerbuch and Stefi Jersch-Wenzel, eds., *Bild und Selbstbild der Juden Berlins zwischen Aufklärung und Romantik* (Berlin, 1992), 236.

98. See Harold Hammer-Schenk, *Synagogen in Deutschland. Geschichte einer Baugattung im 19 und 20 Jahrhundert* (Hamburg, 1981), 1:162–63.

99. See Andreas Braemer, *Judentum und religiöse Reform: Der Hamburger Tempel 1817–1938* (Hamburg, 2000), as well as his "The Dialectics of Religious Reform: The Hamburger Israelitische Tempel in Its Local Context," *LBIYB* 48 (2003), 25–37.

100. This point has been suggested by David Biale, in his *Eros and the Jews* (New York, 1992), 229.

101. Information on Albertine is sparse. See Lowenthal-Hensel, *Preußische Bildnisse*, 73–74, and Todd, *Mendelssohn*, 289.

102. In addition to Clark's *Politics*, 37, 132, and 153, see also Clark, "The Limits of the Confessional State: Conversions to Judaism in Prussia, 1814–1843," *Past and Present* 147 (1995), 159–79, and his "Jewish Conversion in Context: A Case Study from Nineteenth-Century Prussia," *German History* 14 (1996), 281–97.

103. For an excellent discussion of this circle, see Lothar Kahn, "Heine's Jewish Writer Friends: Dilemmas of a Generation, 1817–1833," in Jehuda Reinharz and Walter Schatzberg, eds., *The Jewish Response to German Culture: From the Enlightenment to the Second World War* (Hanover and London, 1985), 120–36.

104. We learn of this from a letter written by I. M. Jost on September 28, 1822, cited in Glatzer, *Leopold and Adelheid Zunz*, 16. It is impossible to tell from this source exactly when Zunz considered conversion.

105. Ibid., 126.

106. This argument draws on themes which I have discussed with Todd Endelman of the University of Michigan for many years.

107. Reissner, *Gans*, 113.

108. Adeleid's attitude to Rahel is discussed in ibid., 18, and her Christian women friends are noted at 22.

109. The novel can be found in August Lewald, *Gesammelte Schriften* (Leipzig, 1846), 12:125–388.

110. I am indebted here to Kahn, "Heine's Jewish Writer Friends," 129–31. See also Reissner, *Gans,* 188–89, and the short entry on Lessmann in Julius Eduard Hitzig, ed., *Gelehrtes Berlin im Jahre 1825* (Berlin, 1826), 150. Another source is Hans Reissner, "Daniel Lessmann in Vienna and Verona," *LBIYB* 14 (1969), 203–14.

111. This interpretation is noted in Kahn, "Heine's Jewish Writer Friends," 130, n. 27.

112. See Albert Friedländer, "The Wohlwill-Moser Correspondence," *LBIYB* 11 (1966), 272, and Reissner, "Daniel Lessmann."

113. Details can be found in Sammons, *Heine,* 96–110.

114. Toews, *Hegelianism,* 129.

115. See Reissner, *Gans,* 108–9.

116. Cited without primary source reference in Elon, *Pity,* 123.

117. Heine's letter to Moser of September 17, 1823, in H. Bieber, *Confessio Judaica* (Berlin, 1925), 90.

118. Quoted in Elon, *Pity,* 124–25, without primary source reference. Todd, *Mendelssohn,* 126, notes that a leftist intellectual named Hermann Franck was with him at the baptism.

119. Ernst Elster, ed., *Heines sämtliche Werke,* 7 vols. (Leipzig and Vienna, 1887–90), 7:407, as cited in Sammons, *Heine,* 109.

120. *Heinrich Heine Säkularausgabe* (Paris, 1970–), 20:113, in a letter of December 14, 1825, as cited in Sammons, *Heine,* 108.

121. Reissner, *Gans,* 113.

122. Ibid., 95, from a January 9, 1826, letter to Moser, as cited by Sammons, *Heine,* 109. See also Sander Gilman's *Jewish Self-Hatred: Antisemitism and the Secret Language of the Jews* (Baltimore, 1987), 177.

123. Quoted in Elon, *Pity,* 132, without a primary source reference.

124. Quoted in ibid., 110, citing *Säkularausgabe* 21:120.

125. Ibid., 36.

126. Ibid., 126.

127. Ibid., citing a letter of April 23, 1826, published in Bieber, *Confessio Judaica,* 64.

128. Pinkard, *Hegel,* 541.

129. Johann Braun, "Die 'Lex Gans' — Ein Kapitel aus der Geschichte der Judenemanzipation in Preußen," *Zeitschrift der Savigny-Stiftung für Rechtgeschichte* 102 (985), 94, n. 119. The translation is mine.

130. Quoted in Glatzer, *Leopold and Adelheid Zunz,* 16, without a primary source reference.

131. See Reissner, *Gans,* 119.

132. Lowenthal-Hensel, *Preußische Bildnisse,* 89.

133. See Tewarson, *Rahel Levin Varnhagen,* 220.

134. See Heidi Tewarson, "German-Jewish Identity in the Correspondence between Rahel Levin Varnhagen and Her Brother, Ludwig Robert: Hopes and Realities of Emancipation, 1780–1830," *LBIYB* 34 (1994), 25–26.

135. On Robert's play, see Jefferson Chase, *Inciting Laughter: The Development of Jewish Humor in Nineteenth-Century German Culture* (Berlin and New York, 2000), 37, n. 50. I also rely here on Kahn, "Heine's Jewish Writer Friends," 131–36.

136. See Pinkard, *Hegel,* 542.

137. On Saphir, see the brief entry in Anon., *Gelehrtes Berlin im Jahre 1825* (Berlin, 1826), 235; Paul Friedrich, ed., *Bilder aus Romantik und Biedermeier* (Berlin, 1922); Kahn, "Heine's Jewish Writer Friends," 131–34; as well as his own writings, including *Meine Memoiren und anderes* (Leipzig, 1887) and *Ausgewählte Schriften* (Brünn, n.d.).

138. Cited in Kahn, "Heine's Jewish Writer Friends," 133, without a primary source reference.

139. Ibid., 133, citing Saphir himself in Part III, vol. 10, of his *Ausgewählte Schriften*, 22.

140. Pinkard, *Hegel*, 544.

141. Kahn, "Heine's Jewish Writer Friends," 134.

142. See Willi Jasper, *Keinem Vaterland geboren: Ludwig Börne, eine Biographie* (Hamburg, 1989), 98, citing the edition of Ludwig Börne's *Berliner Briefe* edited by Jasper (Berlin, 2000), 238.

143. This and the previous quotation come from Sammons, *Heine*, 134.

144. See Jasper, *Börne*, 97.

145. Ibid., 99, citing a letter of Börne's included in Jasper's edition of Börne's *Berliner Briefe*, 248.

146. Jasper, *Börne*, 86, citing Jasper's edition of Börne, *Berliner Briefe*, 244. See also Martin Davies, *Marcus Herz*, 162.

147. These details are from Tewarson, *Rahel Levin Varnhagen*, 182.

148. See the older edition of Börne's letters edited by Ludwig Geiger: *Ludwig Börne, Berliner Briefe 1828* (Berlin, 1905), 25.

149. Jasper's edition of *Berliner Briefe*, 222, 224, and 223, as cited in Jasper, *Börne*, 86.

150. Elon, *Pity*, 136, citing the original letter in *Rahel-Bibliothek*, 9:679–82.

151. The letter is cited without primary source reference in Peter Mercer-Taylor, *The Life of Mendelssohn* (Cambridge, England, 2000), 51–52.

152. For discussion on this point, see Lowenthal-Hensel, *Preußische Bildnisse*, 68.

153. See ibid., 28–29.

154. See R. Larry Todd, *Mendelssohn: A Life in Music* (New York, 2003), 75–78.

155. Ibid., 120.

156. For additional details on Felix's career, see Celia Applegate, *Bach in Berlin: Nature and Culture in Mendelssohn's Revival of the St. Matthew Passion* (Ithaca and London, 2005).

157. Cited in Mercer-Taylor, *Mendelssohn*, 66.

158. Ibid.

159. Cited in Eric Werner, *Mendelssohn: A New Image of the Composer and His Age* (London, 1963), 75.

160. Todd, *Mendelssohn*, 188.

161. Cited in ibid., 187, in a letter Fanny sent to Karl Klingemann on December 23, 1827, in Hensel, *Mendelssohn Family*, 1:151.

162. On Marx, see Applegate, *Bach in Berlin*, 36–37. The quote about Marx's influence in the Mendelssohn household is cited in Todd, *Mendelssohn*, 128; the original reference is Eduard Devrient, *My Recollections of Felix Mendelssohn Bartholdy and His Letters to Me* (London, 1869; rpt. New York, 1972), 35.

163. Cited in Heinrich Dorn, "Recollections of Felix Mendelssohn and His Friends," *Temple Bar* (February 1872), 401.

164. Todd, *Mendelssohn*, 128, citing Christina Siegfried, "'Der interessanteste und problematischste seiner Freunde'—Adolph Bernhard Marx," in Bernd Heyder and Christoph Spering, eds., *Blickpunkt Felix Mendelssohn Bartholdy* (Cologne, 1994), 35–44.

165. Cited in Todd, *Mendelssohn*, 587, n. 100, from a letter from Zelter of May 25, 1826.

166. For details, see Lowenthal-Hensel, *Preußische Bildnisse*, 98–99.

167. Cited in Marek, *Gentle Genius*, 141.

168. Ibid.

169. See Applegate, *Bach in Berlin*, 30.

170. Mercer-Taylor, *Mendelssohn*, 75.

171. Ibid.

172. Cited in Pinkard, *Hegel*, 620, quoting Günther Nicolin, ed., *Hegel in Berichten seiner Zeitgenossen* (Hamburg, 1970), 393–94.

173. See Christhard Hoffmann, "Constructing Jewish Modernity: Mendelssohn Jubilee Celebrations within German Jewry, 1829–1929," in Rainer Liedtke and David Rechter, eds., *Towards Normality: Acculturation and Modern German Jewry* (Tübingen, 2003), 40–41.

174. Heine's letter was written in 1846. Lassalle, unlike Heine himself, never was baptized; see Elon, *Pity*, 145.

175. I have relied here on the account provided by Mercer-Taylor, *Mendelssohn*, 89.

176. W. Michael Blumenthal, *The Invisible Wall: Germans and Jews* (Washington, D.C., 1998), 172.

177. See Todd, *Mendelssohn*, 18.

178. Heinz Becker, "Introduction," *Giacomo Meyerbeer: Briefwechsel und Tagebücher*, 4 vols. (Berlin, 1960), 1:37 and 38.

179. See the chapter on Amalie Beer in Egon Jacobsohn and Leo Hirsch, eds., *Jüdische Mütter* (Berlin, 1936), 69.

180. The dowry documents can be found in the Beer-Meyerbeer Collection, Leo Baeck Institute, New York City, AR 3185. The dowry for the marriage was 50,000 thalers.

181. Heinrich Laube's comments are cited in Marek, *Gentle Genius*, 149.

182. Blumenthal, *Invisible Wall*, 174–175.

183. See Jaspers, *Börne*, 153.

184. Cited without primary source reference in Elon, *Pity*, 138.

185. See Blumenthal, *Invisible Wall*, 177.

186. Elon, *Pity*, cites this quote on 140.

187. From a letter Heine wrote to Ferdinand Hiller, October 24, 1832, in the *Heinrich Heine Säkularausgabe*, 21:40.

188. Cited in Marek, *Gentle Genius*, 197.

189. Ibid.

190. A useful discussion of Heine and Meyerbeer's relationship at this juncture can be found in Sammons, *Heine*, 222, where this quote is cited.

191. Ibid., 245–46.

192. My summary here is indebted to Marek, *Gentle Genius*, 200–205.

193. Quoted in ibid., 205, without primary source reference.

194. This account derives from the article on Beer in Anon., *Jüdisches Athenaeum: Galerie berühmter Männer jüdischer Abstammung und jüdischen Glaubens* (Leipzig, 1851), 7–13.

195. See August Friedrich Graf von Schack in *Ein halbes Jahrhundert* (Stuttgart, 1888), 341.

196. See Arendt, *Rahel Varnhagen,* ed. Weissberg, 15.

197. As cited in Tewarson, *Rahel Levin Varnhagen,* 222–23, quoting the original letter, appearing in *Rahel-Bibliothek,* 1:43–44.

Epilogue

1. I am grateful to Martin Bunzl for discussion on this theme in philosophy.

2. Isaiah Berlin, "Epilogue: The Three Strands in My Life," *Personal Impressions* (London, 1998), 258–59.

3. Burg was reviewing Ruvik Rosenthal, *Rehov Haprachim* 22 (Hebrew) (Tel Aviv, 2003), in *Haaretz* (June 13, 2003).

Index

Haskalah (Jewish Enlightenment), 48,
49, 52, 104, 134, 197
Hassidism, 30
Hedemann, August von, 80, 130
Hedemann, Elisabeth von, 130
Hegel, Georg Wilhelm, *183;* and dislike
of Johann Ancillon, 180; enthusiasm
for French rule, 69; friendship with
Karl Zelter, 83; honors Karl Gutzkow,
212; professional activities of, 145,
179, 185, 186, 200; rationalism of,
185; relationship with Jews, 185, 198,
200, 203, 209–10; rivalry with Friedrich von Savigny, 184
Heidereutergasse Synagogue, 24–26,
137, 190
Heine, Albertine, 193, *194*
Heine, Heinrich (Harry Heine): admiration of for *Sephardim,* 30; appearance
of, 179; background of, 177–78; conversion of, 155, 197, 198–200, 201,
220; criticizes Felix Mendelssohn, 210;
criticizes Jewish reform, 177; hatred of
toward Rothschilds, 161; lifestyle of,
204; marriage of, 193; is mocked by
Moritz Saphir, 203; in Paris, 212–14;
at reform services, 171, 177; relationship with Saul Ascher, 152; in the
Verein, 176–77
Heine, Salomon, 177–78, 191, 212, 214
Heine, Samson, 177
Heinemann, Jeremias, 135
Hensel, Wilhelm, 193, 206–7
Hep hep riots, 160–62, *163,* 173, 202
Hertz, Fanny, 64, 73
Hertz, Jacob, 64
Herz, Henriette (née de Lemos): back-
ground of, 46; conversion of, 147–48;
friendship with Rahel Levin, 45; hos-
tility of toward reform services, 136;
isolation of, 169; marriage of, 46, 54;
relationship with Ludwig Börne, 153,
204–5; in Rome, 126; salon of, 47; in
Vienna, 130–31
Herz, Leopold von, 100

Herz, Markus, 46, 65, 131, 153
Heynemann, Philipp (Gottfried Selig),
37, 219
Heyse, Julie, 207
Heyse, Karl, 187, 207
Heyse, Paul, 207
Hirsch, Solomon, 160
Hitzig, Elias Daniel (Elias Daniel Itzig),
58, 62
Hitzig, Julius Eduard (Isaac Itzig): and
Arnim-Itzig duel, 84; conversion of,
62, 146; facilitates Rahel Levin's bap-
tism, 125; under French surveillance,
110; professional activities of, 80; at
Staegemann's salon, 168
Hitzig, Mirjam (Mirjam Itzig), 58, 62
Hoffmann, E. T. A., 208
Hohenhausen, Elise von, 168–69, 179
Hohenhausen, Leopold, 169
Hufeland, Christian Wilhelm, 67, *183*
Huguenots, 21, 32, 50
Humboldt, Alexander von, 89, 99, 168,
182, *183,* 208
Humboldt, Caroline von, 65, 80, 119,
132, 147, 172
Humboldt, Wilhelm von, *183;* and dis-
like of Johann Ancillon, 180; and dis-
like of Tischgesellschaft, 79–80; and
dueling, 85; early relationship with
Jews, 65, 89; helps plan University of
Berlin, 74; on Jews, 126, 128; reaction
of to August von Kotzebue's murder,
158; as representative of the Diet of
the German Confederation, 175; at
Staegemann's salon, 168; supports
equal rights for Jews, 108, 128, 131; at
Vienna Congress, 127; visits Jewish
salons, 172, 208

Iffland, August Wilhelm, 96
Infant conversion, 61, 194–95
Institutum Judaicum, 33
Intermarriage: assimilation through, 176;
degree of success of, 10; discussion of,
53; Edict of *1812* on, 124; as explana-

Mendelssohn, Henriette, 56, 88–89, 146, 170, 206
Mendelssohn, Hinni, 206
Mendelssohn, Joseph, 90, 92, 137, 159, 186, 206
Mendelssohn, Lea (née Salomon), *90;* at the Beer salon, 172; and children's baptism, 146–48, 186, 219–20; as competitive mother, 211; conversion of, 186–87; courtship and marriage of, 89, 90–93; funds Society for Scientific Criticism, 201; and home at Leipzigerstrasse, 206; and patronage of high culture, 207–8; philanthropy of, 119; relationship with Henriette Mendelssohn, 170, 206; twenty-fifth wedding anniversary, 210; wealth, 93
Mendelssohn, Moses, 36, background of, 39–40, 60; centennial of, 210; death of, 47, 48–49; marriage of, 40; patriotism of, 40, 50; and pressure to convert, 36, 40–41, 42, 137; wins essay contest, 50
Mendelssohn, Nathan, 146
Mendelssohn, Paul, 193, 207
Mendelssohn, Rebekka, 91, 207
Mendelssohn, Recha, 45, 137, 206, 211
Merkel, Garlieb Helwig, 143–44
Metternich, Klemens von, 100, 127–28, 131, 157, 168
Meyer, Aron, 55
Meyer, Ester, 41–42
Meyer, Marianne. *See* Eybenberg, Marianne von
Meyer, Sara. *See* Grotthuß, Sophie von
Meyerbeer, Giacomo, *107;* decides against conversion, 105–6, 146; disliked by Felix Mendelssohn, 213; health problems of, 211; *The Huguenots,* 202; name change of, 103; in Paris, 122, 136–37, 146; performs at Beer salon, 172; reaction of to *Unser Verkehr,* 141; relationship with Heinrich Heine, 178, 214; successes of, 59, 146, 211; during War of Liberation, 122

Michaelis, Johann David, 40
Mirat, Crescene, 193
Missionaries. *See* Pietists
Montalban, Antoinette von, 138
Moscheles, Isaac, 172
Moser, Moses, 176, 197, 199–200
Moses, Meyer, 55
Mosson, Minna, 211

Navrazky, Magdalena, 36, 193
Nazi genealogy project. *See* Judenkartei
Neander, August (David Mendel), 64–65, 182, *183,* 219
Neumann, Wilhelm, 62, 64, 68
Nicolovius, Georg, 180
Noah, Mordechai Manuel, 176
North Star Club (Nordstar Bund), 62, 65, 147

Olfers, Ignaz von, 168
Oppenheim, Moritz Daniel, 199

Paulus, Heinrich, 143
Peddlers, 26, 31
Pereira, Heinrich von, 130
Pereira, Henriette von, 130
Philanthropy, patriotic, 119–20, 134, 170, 175
Pietist, 26, 31–36, 71, 180–81
Pogroms, 27
Prochazka, Leonora, 120
Protected Jew (*Schutzjude*), 23, 98

Ranke, Leopold, 208
Reform rabbis, *192*
Reform services (Berlin): Beer temple and, 105, 136–40, 171, 177, 189, 195–96; closing of, 189–90; conversion rates and, 191; elitism of, 149; innovative nature of, 139, 189, 190; Israel Jacobson's role in, 135–36, 176; at the Leipzig fair, 190; as response to religious crisis, 133–40; women and reform, 139–40
Revolution of *1830,* 212